Governing Sound

Governing
Sound

The Cultural Politics of Trinidad's Carnival Musics

Jocelyne Guilbault

The University of Chicago Press
Chicago & London

Jocelyne Guilbault is professor in the Department of Music at the University of California, Berkeley. She is the author of *Zouk: World Music in the West Indies.*

The University of Chicago Press, Chicago 60637
The University of Chicago Press, Ltd., London
© 2007 by The University of Chicago
All rights reserved. Published 2007
Printed in the United States of America

16 15 14 13 12 11 10 09 08 07   1 2 3 4 5

ISBN-13: 978-0-226-31059-6 (cloth)
ISBN-13: 978-0-226-31060-2 (paper)
ISBN-10: 0-226-31059-0 (cloth)
ISBN-10: 0-226-31060-4 (paper)

Library of Congress Cataloging-in-Publication Data

Guilbault, Jocelyne.
    Governing sound : the cultural politics of Trinidad's Carnival musics /
Jocelyne Guilbault.
        p. cm. — (Chicago studies in ethnomusicology)
    Includes bibliographical references (p.), discography (p.), and index.
    ISBN-13: 978-0-226-31059-6 (cloth : alk. paper)
    ISBN-10: 0-226-31059-0 (cloth : alk. paper)
    ISBN-13: 978-0-226-31060-2 (pbk. : alk. paper)
    ISBN-10: 0-226-31060-4 (pbk. : alk. paper)
    1. Calypso (Music)—Trinidad and Tobago—Trinidad—History and
criticism.   2. Carnival—Trinidad and Tobago—Trinidad—History.   3. Calypso
(Music)—Social aspects—Trinidad and Tobago—Trinidad.   4. Calypso (Music)—
Political aspects—Trinidad and Tobago—Trinidad.   I. Title.
    ML3486.T7G85 2007
    781.64—dc22

                                                              2006035030

♾ The paper used in this publication meets the minimum requirements of the American National Standard for Information Sciences—Permanence of Paper for Printed Library Materials, ANSI Z39.48-1992.

CONTENTS

CD TRACK LIST

1. Sam Manning: "Lieutenant Julian" (1929), oratorical calypso (also called "Sans Humanité")
2. Unknown singers: "We Goin' to Cut the Wood" (1956), lavway at funeral wakes (bongo)
3. Machel Montano and Xtatik: "Daddy Axe" (1998), ragga soca
4. Brother Resistance: "Cyar Take Dat" (1996 version), rapso
5. Machel Montano and Xtatik: "You" (2005), soca
6. Machel Montano and Xtatik: "On the Road" (Brancker Version), Peter C. Lewis featuring Machel Montano (2003), soca
7. Rikki Jai: "Sting She" (2001), chutney soca
8. Rikki Jai: "Hamareh Galeeyah" (2001), chutney version
9. Rikki Jai: "Hamareh Galeeyah" (2001), chutney soca version

ACKNOWLEDGMENTS

Governing Sound would not have been possible without the generous support of distinct institutions, communities, and individuals. I am grateful to the Social Sciences and Humanities Research Council of Canada, the University of Ottawa, and the University of California, Berkeley, for sponsoring my multisited research in the Caribbean, in Canada, and in the United States over many years. I am also indebted to Allison Demas and Teresa Lee-Fook of the Copyright Organization of Trinidad and Tobago, Daniel Sheehy, Atesh Sonneborne, and Cathy Carapella of Smithsonian Folkways Recordings, Liz Montano of Masuso Publishing Company, and Alvin Daniell for helping me obtain the appropriate rights for the musical examples included in the CD. I also want to thank the *Guardian* newspaper in Trinidad, Calypso Rose, Crazy, Frankie Francis, and Daphne McIntosh, as well as Liz Montano, manager of Machel Montano and Xtatik, for granting me permission to reproduce photographs from their collections. My archival research greatly benefited from the generous support of the newspapers—in Trinidad, the *Mirror* and *Trinidad Express;* in Barbados, the *Nation* and *Voice of Barbados;* and in Antigua, the *Outlet*—and of the National Archives of Antigua. Each newspaper allowed me to photocopy numerous articles it published on the calypso music scene. I also want to acknowledge the Trinbago Unified Calypsonians Organization (TUCO) and the National Carnival Commission (NCC) for their continued support throughout this research by facilitating my meetings with many calypsonians. In Toronto, my participation in Caribana was greatly facilitated by the generous help of the Caribbean Cultural Committee and Cadmus Relations and also by the warm hospitality of Selwyn Charles, Jai Ojah-Maharaj, Beverley Diamond, and Brigido Galvan; and in Barbados at the Crop Over Festivals, by the Carnival Committee.

My most sincere thanks go to the publishers who kindly granted me permission to use excerpts of their songs on the CD: Black Stalin, Brother Resistance, Calypso Rose, Crazy, Denyse Plummer, Winsford Devine for De Mighty Trini's song, Valerie Roberts for the late Lord Kitchener's song, Lord Superior, Liz Montano for Machel Montano and Xtatik, Shadow, and Rikki Jai. I especially appreciate these artists' willingness to meet with me and to grant me written and verbal consent to include audio excerpts of their work in *Governing Sound*. It is for this reason that I especially regret that I cannot include specific excerpts related to chapters 2, 4, and 5 that have disputed rights.

My greatest debt is to the many members of the calypso music community whose knowledge, guidance, and critical insights have informed every page of this study. To mention all the names of those who helped me and to give thanks to everyone is impossible here. But I want to single out Junior and Ruth Telfer, Black Stalin, Roy Cape, Ella Andall, Alvin Daniell, Brother Resistance, Lambert Philip, Michael and Joycelyn Germain, and Monty Dolly for their warm hospitality and for sharing with me their invaluable knowledge of the calypso music scene and soundings (the ongoing physical and emotional reverberations sounds produce). Their critical understanding of the sociopolitical, economic, and cultural dynamics that animate the production, circulation, and reception of Trinidad's Carnival musics in the islands and abroad have profoundly oriented my analysis. Their remarkable patience, continued support, and close friendship have moved me deeply.

In Barbados, I owe a special debt of gratitude to Gabby, Eddy Grant, Red Plastic Bag, Edwin Yearwood, Adonijah, Sach Moore, Bunny Best, Elizabeth Watson, Curwen Best, Elton "Elombe" Mottley, Keith Ellis, Trevor George Marshall, Poonka, and the Admiral. In Antigua, I am most indebted to Conrad Luke, Short Shirt, King Obstinate, Swallow, Scorpion, Edwards "Onyan" Toriana, Singing Althea, Calypso Jo, King Progress, Mighty Bottle, Ed Mack, Jagga Junior Martin, Dorbrene O'Marde, Prince Ramsey, Tim Hector, Kenny Nibbs, Marius Christopher, Ted Isaac, and Jerome Blau. Their deep understanding of the soundings and dynamics of the local calypso scenes in Barbados and Antigua, and the entire region, has illuminated how I wrote about not only the music but also the cultural politics that animate these scenes. I want to thank them for generously sharing their knowledge and supporting this project.

I am most grateful also to the community of Trinidadian scholars, whose work has been an inestimable source of inspiration to me. In particular, I want to thank Gordon Rohlehr, Rawle Gibbons, Keith Nurse, Rhoda Reddock, Patrica Mohammed, Hollis Liverpool, and Louis Regis, with whom I had stimulating, generative exchanges and whose friendship I truly cherish. I also want to thank warmly Mungal Patasar for his insights into distinct East Indian musical practices crucial to my study. In the United States, I want to acknowledge the generous help and support of both Shannon Dudley and Stephen Stuempfle, whose work on steelbands has been for me transformative. My exchanges with Peter Manuel and readings of his publications on East Indian music in the West Indies have also been enlightening. I want to thank journalists Peter Blood, Terry Joseph, and Debbie Jacobs for feeding me daily with insightful commentaries on the Trinidadian calypso music scene, and also Michael Goodwin for his richly detailed profiles of key figures in Carnival musics. I am also grateful to photographer and journalist Gary Cardinez for giving me much support in my photography ventures during the course of this project.

I am indebted to the many musicians and arrangers who have patiently guided my analysis of different historical moments in Trinidad's Carnival musics, in particular, Lambert Philip, Enrique Moore, Pehlam Goddard, Leston Paul, the late Clive Bradley, Earl Ince, Earl Rodney, Fortuna Ruiz, Kenny Philips, Wayne Bruno, Carl "Beaver" Henderson, Sylvon Sylvester, and the late Frankie Francis in Trinidad; Franky McIntosh in New York; and Nicholas Brancker in Barbados. Many thanks also to deejay Christopher Edmunds in the Bay Area (San Francisco) for tuning me to the latest soundings of Caribbean Carnival musics in and outside the islands.

I also owe much to the kindness and generosity of several record collectors, without whom I could not have done this research: Ray Funk (Fairbanks, Alaska), Shawn Randoo (Trinidad), George Maharaj, John White, Richard Fitzroy, and Tony Boissière (Toronto, Canada), and David McBurney and Daniel Bittker (San Francisco). My understanding of the Carnival music business has been greatly enhanced by Liz Montano (Machel Montano and Xtatik's manager), Robert Amar (owner of the Caribbean Sound Basin recording studio), Frank Martineau (co-owner of Spektakula Promotions International), Ellis Chow-Lin On (Charlie's Roots' music manager) in Trinidad, Isaac McLeod (a cultural promoter) in New York, and Anne-Marie Stephens (a cultural promoter) in Oakland.

Many thanks also go to my research assistants, who helped transcribe interviews and musical excerpts, create a database, produce computerized musical notation, and format my manuscript: in Ottawa, Ellen McIsaac, Rachel Beausoleil-Morrison, and Brigido Galvan; and in Berkeley, Carla Brunet and Francesca Rivera. I am indebted to Julie Humphrey for transcribing interviews in record time and also to Joan and Candace Hintzen for helping me transcribe lyrics. I also want to thank Beth E. Levy and John Lynch for their able editorial assistance. I am grateful to Jim Coates, Kathleen Karn, and especially Glen L. Robertson, from the University of California, Berkeley, for their providential help in preparing the digital material for the photographs, and to Serge Locat, from Montreal, for lending his expertise in producing the CD accompanying this book.

Many people have read various incarnations of chapters or the entirety of what follows and have greatly helped refine my arguments. I want first to give a special note of appreciation to my editor at the University of Chicago Press, T. David Brent, for his unfailing support and critical input in this project and to Elizabeth Branch Dyson for so caringly guiding the manuscript through the various production stages. I am also grateful to Erik Carlson, manuscript editor at the University of Chicago Press, for his remarkable, transformative editorial eye. I also thank the anonymous readers for helping me greatly sharpen my arguments. I must give particular thanks also to David Theo Goldberg, director of the Humanities Research Institute at the University of California, Irvine, and to all the members of the collaborative research group organized by Josh Kun, for the stimulating sessions and valuable debates carried out in the spring of 2002, which are without doubt embedded here. For their wonderful friendship, insightful critiques, and remarkable sensibilities in commenting on my manuscript, I also want to thank Veit Erlmann, Charles Hirschkind, Thomas Turino, Conrad Luke, Rhoda Reddock, Ray Funk, Line Grenier, and Val Morrison. I am greatly indebted to Richard Crawford for his sustaining support and generous help in crafting my text. The sustained support and wonderful team spirit of my colleagues at the University of California, Berkeley—especially Bonnie Wade, Ben Brinner, and Olly Wilson—and of my colleagues at the Department of African American Studies have also in myriad ways helped me complete this work. I am particularly grateful to my dear friends, Percy and Joan Hintzen, with whom I have shared intellectual engagement, political affinities, enduring affection, and some of the greatest food and parties over the past ten years. Finally, my heartfelt thanks go to my family for always being there, and to Donald Moore, who in the midst of great physical pain has cared, critiqued, prompted, and inspired me to go further.

INTRODUCTION

In 2002, a Trinidadian daily newspaper's article announced that the homes of two legendary calypsonian figures, Lord Kitchener and Roaring Lion, would be turned into museums. In the midst of listing Roaring Lion's many accomplishments, the article pointed out, it is "Lion who . . . is the person who gave Trinidad and Tobago its sobriquet 'the Land of Calypso' when asked by US President Roosevelt 'where are you from?' after a command performance."[1] This stunning reply shows how the artist used calypso not only to identify himself in relation to a specific territory and national belonging, but also to indicate how the music of calypso defines the land where he comes from. It further suggests that, even though calypso is composed and performed in all the English-speaking islands, in the artist's mind, Trinidad and Tobago is incontestably where calypso mainly resides and thrives.

This anecdote exemplifies how, early in the twentieth century, calypso had been implicated in the articulation of the nation-state, national belonging, politics of representation, and power relations. Calypso is of course not the only music to have played such a role. Several studies in postcolonial countries have documented how specific musical genres have been enlisted to further nationalist projects to the extent that many nation-states today can hardly be imagined without them (or the other way around)—as, for example, Brazil and samba, the Dominican Republic and

1

merengue, and Argentina and tango, to name only the most obvious cases in the Americas.[2] After years in and out the Caribbean studying the rich musical repertoire of several islands, I wanted to know how it is that only one music became emblematic of nation and identity in a Caribbean country as culturally complex as Trinidad.

This book emerged from a series of basic questions: What conditions of possibility and political technologies (e.g., bans and competitions) have allowed calypso, and not another music, to become the expression of national belonging in Trinidad?[3] No music can ever speak for everybody or create unanimity even in one community—let alone in a whole nation-state. So whom does calypso represent, and whom does it exclude? Calypso historically has been performed and heard mostly during the Carnival season. And until recently, it has been given little attention in the media and has been infrequently featured in shows during the rest of the year. What strategies or forces have thus supported its valorization and circulation and made it possible for calypso to keep its high profile for Trinidadians at home and abroad? In other words, how has it competed with the many other musics that have been part of the local soundscape?

Calypso has a history dating back to the mid-nineteenth century and has taken different forms and been played with different arrangements and instrumentations. So given calypso's long history, has it always enjoyed the pride of place that Roaring Lion in the 1940s was alluding to? And what version of calypso has been implicitly or explicitly described as emblematic of true "kaiso"—a term used locally to refer to "authentic" calypso—in the Caribbean popular imagination today?

Ironically, just as I began this project in 1993, I was taken aback by hearing many calypso artists, musicians, and aficionados speak about the imminent death of calypso after complaining about what seemed to them a takeover by soca during Carnival. As it turned out, the growing popularity of soca and of several other musical offshoots of calypso, most particularly, chutney soca and ragga soca—often grouped together under the generic name "party music" because of their high-tempo, light lyrics and focus on dance and pleasure[4]—throughout the 1990s and to this day did not lead to the fulfillment of the gloomy prediction of calypso's death made earlier by some observers.[5] But it became abundantly clear that these musics were being discussed in relation to each other, and that the commercial success and growing prominence of so-called party music was at once translated as evidence that it had displaced calypso from its hegemonic position as *the* sole music synonymous with Carnival. According to most observers, since the 1990s soca has unquestionably been the main music heard on radio and television and the main music played at parties during Carnival, whereas calypso has been heard and performed almost exclusively in calypso tents and yearly competitions (calypso tents are sitting-audience types of performing venues). Whereas the number of soca recordings has been steadily increasing, comparatively few calypso CDs have been released during the same period.

In this study, I focus on what has actually been displaced through this shift. So-called traditional calypso has often been defined by its musical form (three or four verses alternating with a refrain) and its focus on sociopolitical commentary. Has calypso's form or its lyrics' focus been modified in the process? Calypsonians were typically black, male, and lower class.[6] Have the new musical offshoots changed the kinds of racialized, classed, and gendered bodies historically associated with calypso? In turn, I focus on the performers and audiences of these new musics. How might they unsettle Roaring Lion's claim made in the 1940s that calypso is the emblematic expression of Trinidad's national belonging? My overarching question remains, What is it that the new Carnival musics perform that calypso does not?

Research Problematic

This book provides a critical genealogy of calypso, focusing on how it became emblematic of Trinidadian national identity.[7] It examines the conditions that enabled this distinctive musical practice to be valorized, contested, and targeted as a field of cultural politics. It shows how calypso has been both a site of empowerment and a target of competing powers during both the colonial regime and independence. It elaborates how it has been inextricably linked to socioeconomic projects and political technologies to govern, manage, and improve the conduct of racialized subjects.

I focus on the cultural politics of calypso in order to foreground how musical practices are constitutive of subjectivities that are positioned in relations of power. Musical practices contribute to this positioning—and are also positioned by an articulation of institutions, individuals, and collectivities. Under colonial rule, musical performances on slave plantations represented for colonial officials and plantation owners an expression of cultural inferiority understood as "racial difference" and a threat to normative morality. In contrast, for slaves these performances enunciated at times explicit critiques of the colonial social order. At a later historical moment, nationalists spoke through calypso to valorize formerly subjugated identities, voice emancipatory political projects, and articulate national identity. In these instances, culture has been a terrain of contentious struggles entangled with social, political, and economic inequalities. As *Governing Sound* will elaborate, such struggles further reveal questions of morality, aesthetics, and sensibilities that not only reflect but also inflect hierarchies of race, class, and gender.[8]

Most publications on calypso have tended to address projects of governing primarily in relation to state politics, more specifically, during the colonial regime with the white British administration and after independence with the political party in power.[9] While I also acknowledge how state agencies have deeply influenced calypso's orientations and central positioning on the island, I move away from viewing governing as isomorphic with the state. Instead, I point out the myriad of micropractices in which calypso has been interpolated, ranging from calypso tents to music tours, writings in newspapers, recording sessions, radio broadcasts, and performances for foreign audiences. I emphasize how various powers, including not only those of the state (institutions, laws, elected officials), but also others that are distinct from the state (record industries, intellectuals, artists), have informed calypso. In so doing, I stress how, at times conflicting with one another, at other times reinforcing each other, these various powers have at once marked calypso's expression, valorization, and circulation. Together, I show, they have been constitutive of the ways in which calypso became an emblem of national belonging.

In this study, I found Michel Foucault's notion of governmentality particularly useful, as it encouraged me to view music as a "field of social management." It has required me not only to pay attention to musical institutions and music making, but also to examine the micropractices of power that are effected through music in ways that avoid at least two misconceptions: that these micropractices of power effected through music are necessarily bounded by a common cause or objective—as some "resistance music" studies have often proposed; and that they are derivative of an overdetermining source of power—as the colonial administration or the state have often been assumed to be in several popular music studies. As Tony Bennett remarks, rather than "view[ing] the activities of all branches of the state and . . . of civil society too as contributing to the reproduction of that power," Foucault's notion of governmentality or governmental power "has no such anchorage, authorization or function. . . . [It] does not rest on some unifying principle of central power (the sovereign, the state)."[10] Rather, it recognizes the simultaneous diversity of projects and technologies that are specific to different agencies (say, the church, calypso tent managers, calypsonians) and their differentiated fields of management. Furthermore, it acknowledges how not only one, but several regimes of values might be competing within the same historical context. Within this perspective, what the analytic of governmentality and its focus on distinct "arts of governing" has prompted me to examine is how calypso has been simultaneously the target of several competing powers and the terrain through which the production of national subjects has been instantiated and intensely debated.[11] For example, when in the 1950s Calypso Rose began performing as a calypsonian, the church community to which she belonged criticized her moral values and explicit sexuality as a dangerous product of performing this music. Yet for her, calypso became the platform from which she voiced to a wide audience feminist positions in a highly patriarchal milieu. In this example, the arts of governing that converged on music as conduct include gender, class, and church.

In the 1990s, after hearing repeatedly from several musicians, calypsonians, calypso aficionados, and calypso scholars how soca (and, by extension, all the musics derived from it, including ragga soca and chutney soca) had become commercialized, trivial, devoid of inspiration, and repetitive, this much was clear to me: their attack on soca could not be seen as being soca's own fault, as it were, or stemming from supposed "defects," such as that it was the product of commoditization and therefore unavoidably lacking aesthetic value. By positing party music as a trivial and interchangeable commodity, this approach reproduced the same kind of critiques addressed to global pop. As Line Grenier cogently remarks, it not only ignores the artistic investment and the positioning of its makers, but also neglects the aesthetic discrimination and value judgments of its consumers. It also overlooks the ways in which its success—its ability to communicate, to sell, and to last as a genre—is not based on simply producing familiarity, but rather on cultivating difference.[12]

The harsh critiques of soca obviously did not have to do with soca alone, but also with the much larger socioeconomic, political domain of calypso from which it emerged and to which it was compared. As Trinidadian novelist Earl Lovelace put it in reference to the fight steelbands had to wage to be granted musical legitimacy, to understand what is said about the aesthetic, one has to address the political, that is, the various practices that are actively engaged not only in establishing a regime of values, but also in contesting the one that prevails.[13]

In the attempt to assess soca's sociopolitical, musical, and other values, the goal is not to refute the critiques made by many calypso advocates. My preoccupation is a different one. In looking at calypso, I am interested in examining the discursive formations sustaining the "regime of values"—involving not only aesthetics, but also morality and conduct—that has conferred on calypso its canonical status and against which soca is judged.[14] I am also interested in investigating the constellation of historically constituted demands (e.g., emerging from Emancipation from slavery in 1834 or the change of Trinidad's political status in 1962) that have oriented calypso's dynamics and orientations and contributed to its centrality during the colonial regime and the nation-building project of Trinidad and Tobago. Similar to Line Grenier's enquiries about global pop, my analysis of soca seeks to illuminate the complex web of industrial strategies, cultural activities, technologies, institutions, and discourses that have contributed not only to how much soca and its stars have circulated, but also to the ways in which both have come to matter in specific ways for a great number of people from the late 1970s but, most particularly, from the 1990s onward.[15]

In this light, I see the terms "tradition" and "artform" commonly used in Trinidadian parlance, in the media, and in the literature to refer to calypso, as evocative not only of the particular ways Trinidadians usually think (or have been encouraged to think) about calypso. I understand these terms also as evocative of the distinctive practices, modalities, and regulations from which the use of these terms has emerged. In my view, "tradition" is not an essentially timeless cultural practice or a univocal monolith. Rather, I examine calypso as a tradition along the lines of Alasdair MacIntyre's reflections on moral-political discourses, "as an historically extended, socially embodied argument which . . . is at least in part about what constitutes the goods that give point and purpose to that tradition."[16] In that sense, what is named "tradition" is always, in Raymond Williams's words, a "*selective tradition:* an intentionally selective version of a shaping past and a pre-shaped present, which is then powerfully operative in the process of social and cultural definition and identification."[17] The same can be said about "artform": what is termed "artform" always emerges in tandem with particular rationalities, discursive practices, and sites that selectively elevate a particular musical practice above others—in the case of calypso, above all other local musics. Throughout the book, I analyze the political, social, cultural, and economic implications that these hegemonic ways of constructing calypso as "tradition" and "artform" have had for different groups, including calypsonians, on the island. For the moment they began their careers, calypsonians unavoidably become entangled with the cultural politics of that tradition—at once to contest it and to reinforce it.

While the analytic of governmentality proves useful to study the cultural politics of calypso both as a genre and as a music scene, I do not use it to explain everything. Its emphasis on linking power to the deployment of strategies leaves unexplained the tangible effects produced by several activities and practices that have more to do with improvised celebration or unanticipated situations than with calculated effects.[18] It would be reductive to speak of certain musical gestures or dance moves only in relation to rationalities or political projects. For that reason, in this study I also highlight the unplanned circumstances that come into play in the articulation of contingent processes that produce significant outcomes. The key term here is "articulation." In accordance with the work of Stuart Hall, the notion of articulation recognizes that, while particular circumstances assemble a number of distinct processes whose interaction is "not necessary, determined, absolute and essential for all time,"[19] in their combination—in their articulation—these processes can have consequential effects. I am thinking about how, for example, the U.S. sailors stationed in Trinidad, calypso, and censorship in the early 1940s *in their articulation* produced a particular lyrical tendency in calypso during that particular historical period. Furthermore, "by adopting this concept of articulation along with a non-essentialist approach to identity," as Keith Negus suggests, I am able to raise critical questions about the ways in which the particular cultural practices of calypso and of its musical offshoots (rapso, soca, chutney soca, and ragga soca) have become connected with specific political projects and social identities—importantly, without assuming a necessary link between the artists' and audience's social labels (black, male, young, or working class) and those particular types of music.[20]

Some critics have charged governmentality with representing society as "a network of omnipresent relations of subjugating power" to the point that, in their views, "it precludes the possibility of meaningful individual freedom."[21] To avoid this danger, I emphasize agency within my analytic of governmentality.[22] In this study, agency refers to *what* has generated tangible outcomes in Trinidad's calypso music scene. The "what" here includes various entities, such as demographics (the size of Trinidad's population compared to that of other islands), activities (competitions), and migration (from the small islands to Trinidad)—all of which have played a role in the shaping and valorization of Trinidad's music scene. It also includes, of course, human subjects, on whom I focus more specifically in relation to musical entrepreneurship.[23] By "musical entrepreneurship," I mean projects that deal with music as commodity in capitalist markets and aim to make profits. I refer to individuals who are self-disciplined, in charge of their own projects, and accountable for both the success and failure of their ventures. So in addition to showing how, say, various state organizations, private corporations, or religious institutions have effected, in Foucault's famous expression, the "conduct of conduct" in calypso, soca, and chutney soca musical practices, I also show how artists and other individuals have initiated projects of their own with tangible transformations: in the best circumstances, in their own lives, by attaining a certain state of well-being, spiritually, socially, or financially; at other times, in their own community or throughout their nation-state, by contributing to the revisiting, displacing, or transforming of the dominant political, economic, institutional regime of values. Conduct is thus both a target that the self works on—exerting agency—and also a terrain of so-called external interventions.

In this book I emphasize entrepreneurship as a distinctive target of governing as well as a mode of self-conduct. While many people conceive entrepreneurship as a chief characteristic of neoliberalism, I trace its long history through Trinidadian calypso from the end of the nineteenth century with the emergence of the calypso tents to the 1990s onward with the creation of numerous new ventures dealing with musical rights, record sales on the Internet, and show management—highlighting the distinctive features cultural entrepreneurship has taken on at different moments during that history.

In tandem with my focus on agency, I examine the conditions that have enabled certain individuals to effect change. Inspired by Bennett's insights, I focus on the ways diverse projects, technologies, and rationalities enacted through competing arts of governing position various individuals (e.g., calypsonians of different race, gender, class, and musical background) in distinct power relations. In so doing, I examine how some individuals thus become able to deploy significant influence over consequential practices (e.g., politics of inclusion or exclusion, production of new audible entanglements, and musical redefinition of what should stand as emblematic of Trinidad and Tobago in nationalist discourses).[24] Accordingly, throughout the book, I provide biographies not only to avoid homogenizing experience, but also to show in relation to what and in which forms individual agency has been deployed in calypso and the calypso music scene.

Here a clarification of the terms I am using is in order. Drawing on the work of Thomas Turino, I use the expression "nationalist discourse" to refer to discourses that are explicitly part of "a political movement or ideology that bases the idea of legitimate sovereignty on a coterminous relationship between a 'nation' and a state."[25] By extension, I refer to the music constructed as "emblematic of the nation-state" in relation to the array of discursive practices that have been explicitly part of nationalist political movements and programs. On the basis of these definitions and as has been described above, the space and the music most associated with the nationalist project in Trinidad and Tobago have been Carnival and calypso.[26]

In this book, I use the expression "calypso music scene" to refer not only to calypso, but also to the new Carnival musics and the numerous practices that have emerged in tandem with them since the mid-1970s. This is not because there was no musical scene before that time. If scene is defined as a geographic location in which many musical practices coexist,[27] then calypso (before it produced any musical offshoot) was definitely part of a scene—as any music necessarily is. In the 1960s, besides calypso during Carnival, Latin music such as bolero, cha-cha, and mambo and African-American soul constituted the main repertoire in dancehalls during the weekends. In contrast with this definition of scene, used to map a particular territory and the coexistence of musical practices within it, I speak of the "calypso music scene" first as a means to distinguish the ensemble formed by all Carnival musics—their interrelationships and particular dynamics—from calypso as "tradition" and "artform." I also use the term "scene" to highlight how this set of musical practices formed by calypso and its musical offshoots share sonic characteristics, form a cluster of musical activities, are connected through the Carnival period and other times of festivities, and are not bound only to a place. In addition, I refer to "scene" both to emphasize the flexible cosmopolitan character of these musics and to draw attention to their distinct diasporic movements and trajectories.[28] Three years after arriving from Jamaica in England on a boat, M.V. Windrush, Lord Kitchener—whose sobriquet evokes imperial circuits traveled by the famous British colonial officer in India and Egypt—sang "London Is the Place for Me" (1951). Two years later, he wrote "Africa My Home." After opening his own club in Manchester, touring the United States for six months, and staying in England for a few more years, he returned to Trinidad in 1963. Like musical scenes, as I later elaborate, diasporas are not fixed but rather are historically variable by being radically shaped by power relations and constantly defined or redefined to mark boundaries of exclusion.[29]

Historically, I link the "calypso music scene" with what I call the "era of neoliberalism," during which calypso musical offshoots became prominent. For the purpose of this study, I focus on the 1990s onward, the period during which, particularly in relation to culture (and thus Carnival and its related musical activities), the state redefined its responsibilities and priorities; the private sector became a key to boosting the GNP; and cultural entrepreneurship played a vital role in organizing national musical activities, and in reinforcing and creating new partnerships among and across discrepant diasporas. In so doing, I establish a temporal distinction from the other historical moments, colonialism and independence, that I discuss exclusively in relation to calypso. Furthermore, I emphasize how the distinct socioeconomic and political dynamics of the neoliberal era have provided the conditions that have enabled the new Carnival musics to challenge calypso not only musically and commercially, but also politically, by destabilizing its historical and hegemonic role in performing and authenticating Trinidadian national subjects and subjectivities.

Fieldwork

Multisited Fieldwork

As both calypso and the new Carnival musics have been transnational from the moment of their emergence, so too, I thought, should my fieldwork be. My study of the Trinidadian Carnival music industry had to explore not only its "roots" on the island, but also the various routes along which its musics circulate and thrive. In an attempt to examine the cultural politics of the Trinidadian Carnival musics' networks and the musics and musicians that they privilege, my project embraced several sites where Trinidadian calypso and soca-related musics have been promoted, produced and reproduced, and consumed. Since 1993, I have been commuting back and forth to Trinidad, spending at times two months, at other times only two weeks, and exceptionally five months, during my sabbatical in 1997. Between 1997 and 1999, I also did fieldwork in Barbados and Antigua, two other major centers of calypso and soca that historically have had much contact with Trinidad.[30] Given that both celebrations simultaneously take place during the first weekend of August, I attended part of both festivals each year and spent several weeks on each island before and after the celebrations were held. In addition, in 1995, 1996, and 2001, I did fieldwork in Toronto, Canada, where Caribana, one of the largest Trinidadian-style Carnivals in North America is celebrated—incidentally, as in Antigua and Barbados, also during the first weekend of August. Between 1995 and 1998, I also attended Carnival in Ottawa and Montreal—which is celebrated at different times during the summer chosen not to conflict with each other. In spite of their small size, the Caribbean diasporic groups living in these two cities have regularly played mas and held Carnival shows and parties during the two or three days preceding the Carnival day parade.[31]

This multisited project was not meant to provide an equally thorough examination of the Carnival music industry in all these places. Neither was it meant to compare the various Carnival organizations or the Carnival musics in each locale, as these various sites are not comparable in terms of population size, ethnic and racial group composition, economic resources, cultural politics, musical sensibilities, and migration patterns and networks. The goal in examining the various Carnival diasporic groups and sites, furthermore, was not to create one Carnival archetype that would speak for all the groups and sites concerned.[32] Rather, I used this multisited ethnography to help me trace the musical influences and networks of Trinidad-style Carnival and Trinidadian artists around the islands and in diaspora. Most important, this fieldwork approach served to chart what Shalini Puri terms "marginal migrations," that is, the intraregional movements, the points of contact and exchange among calypso and soca artists, and the sources of tensions that exist among them—the cultural politics that have informed islanders' interrelations, which, Puri remarks, are often overlooked in the field of contemporary Caribbean and diaspora studies and research on the Caribbean global capitalist economy.[33] It enabled me to gauge the different types of exchanges, flow of information, and material access that the various Carnival sites—in and outside the islands—have provided for Trinidadian artists. Put another way, it has allowed me to assess the relative importance that the Trinidadian calypso and soca music industry has had historically and has currently in relation not only to other calypso and soca centers in the English-speaking islands, but also in several Caribbean diasporic Carnival sites in Canada.

The benefits of having been able to conduct this research project over several years have been manifold. First, it has allowed me to observe the many socioeconomic and political challenges calypsonians and soca artists face at different moments during the year, in many of the different locales where they produce and perform their music. Second, it has enabled me to record how Trinidadian musical experiments in soca, chutney soca, ragga soca, and rapso have been promoted and enjoyed and simultaneously critiqued and contested locally by various groups and individuals embracing contrasting cultural politics and regimes of values. Third, by visiting the calypso tents and attending the calypso and soca competitions in Trinidad over several years, I was able to appreciate how much the pleasure and excitement in calypso and soca come from understanding the skillful references and witty responses to previous songs, themes, expressions, musical riffs, and dance movements associated with particular artists, key historical moments, or events. Over time I could map better how calypso and soca typically embrace many voices and sounds, joys, and concerns from the past into the present.

Constituting an Archive

My study draws on many different types of sources. Over the years, I used interviews as main points of entry to learn about the politics and poetics of calypso music making and the calypso industry. I interviewed calypso, soca, chutney soca, and rapso artists, arrangers, studio musicians, band musical directors and musicians, competition judges, recording studio and record shop owners, sound engineers, journalists, private cultural entrepreneurs, promoters, producers, record collectors, journalists, television program hosts, cultural critics, Caribbean-based academics, dancers, emcees, Orisha priests and priestesses, Baptist practitioners, fans and detractors, and key members of both the calypso associations and the Carnival committees in Trinidad and in the other sites where I did fieldwork—all of whom had something to do directly or indirectly with the production, valorization, and circulation of Trinidadian calypsonians and soca artists locally, regionally, and internationally. Some of these interviews were taped; others were recorded in field notes.

Along with the interviews, I focused on newspaper articles published in Trinidad, Barbados, and Antigua since the 1960s to examine the ways in which calypso and, later on, soca have been conceived, valued, and discussed in relation to other discursive practices—religious, political, economic, musical, feminist, and diasporic. In constituting such an archive, I was able to trace how the artistic personae of calypsonians and soca artists were construed, according to which criteria major hits were identified, and what counted as major feats in the calypso and soca music industry. In addition to the local popular press, I consulted academic publications, student dissertations, and magazine articles to examine the many issues through which the calypso music scene has been constructed at different times, by different people with varying interests.

The commercial recordings I collected include some compilations from the 1930s, 1940s, and 1950s, but mainly releases from the late 1960s onward. In the islands, the search for commercial recordings released more than ten years ago—actually, more than five years ago would be more accurate—represents a difficult task. Record shops in general do not keep in store old recordings, and it is not part of the habit for most people in the islands to build record collections.[34] The most important calypso record collectors, significantly, live outside the islands.[35] Thanks to the help of several of these collectors, I was able to gather some of the key songs and sounds that have marked the different calypso and soca musical eras since the 1960s.

Commercial videos of showcases, competitions, calypso tents, and interviews—along with my regular attendance at many of these events—have greatly enhanced my understanding of the important role that dress, bodily expression, dance movements, lighting, and space play in the effectivity of calypso and soca performances.[36] My dancing at numerous events has also provided me with insights about calypso and soca that would not have been otherwise accessible.

As an active participant within multiple audiences of the calypso music scene, I am well aware of how individual and collective agencies are entangled with musical performances. From this perspective, I focused on the crucial role audiences have played in enacting the cultural politics of Trinidad's Carnival musics. In this study, "audience" has both conceptual and empirical import. I conceive audience in relation to the three crucial terms of my analytic: governmentality, articulation, and agency. First, as targets of power, audiences are sites of regulation and discipline. For example, in the nineteenth century, freed slaves were prohibited from playing drums at Carnival because officials feared that such rhythms might lead a collective mass toward an uprising. Later, white upper-class parents prohibited their children from mingling with black audiences in calypso tents and other Carnival spaces. Last year, while Machel Montano blasted sounds at the Jean-Pierre complex to an almost exclusively Afro-Trinidadian audience, in San Fernando, the chutney soca competition gathered an almost exclusively East Indian crowd. (The expression "East Indian" is used in Trinidad to refer to the descendants of the indentured laborers that came from India to work on the plantations after Emancipation; it is also used to distinguish persons of Indian descent born in Trinidad from Indians born in India and from the first nations or Native Americans—the Arawak, the Carib, and the Taino—who were the first inhabitants of the island.) Audiences can mark distinct boundaries of inclusion and exclusion. There are inflected by the actual and imagined composition of their membership.[37]

When I refer to audience, I mean not solely a collection of embodied listeners assembled to witness and hear a particular musical performance at a distinct place and time. I also refer to audience as a group of listeners to a type of music who are not necessarily physically present at a live show. In the 1920s, ethnic record labels emerged to target a new market of Caribbean migrants living in New York City. Such targeted listening audiences combined with well-organized channels of distribution actually reached some white Americans, extending calypso consumers beyond the boundaries of its intended targets. By focusing on articulation, I highlight how distinct combinations (e.g., ethnic recording labels, Caribbean migration, and white Americans' interest in new, exotic sounds) provided conditions of possibility for new calypso audiences to be created, expanded, and nurtured.

Audiences in my view can exert agency. They can enunciate aesthetic judgments that influence performers' selection of songs as well as jury's decisions in competitions. They can inform communities of affinity and reinforce social and political exclusions. As consumers, they contribute to both the form and the marketing of distinct commodities. They can also confer commercial value on particular artists and the latters' products. In 1974 a crowd's anger at the judges' decision to deny Shadow the Calypso King crown became channeled into popular sentiment that encouraged revelers to demand that the bands performing on trucks circulating through the city on Carnival Tuesday play his song, "Bassman." Juries that tabulated the popularity of Shadow's song emanating from these trucks declared this artist the Road March winner. In turn, Shadow's winning this award became crucial in enabling him to procure contracts for live performances that year. Such instances that convey the agency of audiences— in some of which I was an active participant—foreground those that I later highlight in distinct times and places.

My multiple identities informed the varied activities in which I took part during the course of this research. As an audience member of calypso tents, soca parties, and chutney soca competitions and as a purchaser of CDs, I actively joined an array of overlapping audiences. As a musician, I talked "shop," that is, used technical musical language with calypso and soca arrangers, musicians, and artists to learn about what has characterized the sound of calypso and soca in different historical periods. As a collector of both newspapers and recordings, I focused far more on aspects dealing with historical issues, and on what was documented and what was not. As an interviewer, I often assumed the role of a journalist, to which the main calypso and soca artists are very accustomed. Only at times were the roles reversed: the interviewees were asking the questions, aiming to learn more about where I was coming from than I had initially explained. One of the most unique, but also most important moments where the exchange was truly bidirectional was with Gordon Rohlehr, one of the most respected public intellectuals and researchers of popular culture in the Caribbean, who, from the first minute we met, placed his own tape recorder next to mine. At a most practical level, this should really not be that unusual a situation, since the information provided to me could be used for many other purposes by the very person providing the information. Politically, and specifically in terms of power relations, it should be in fact a common practice that the local "informant" be equally in control of the interview situation instead of being controlled by it. The challenge of a postcolonial research ethic is precisely to forge creatively relations in which both interviewer and interviewee mutually benefit from the exchange. Such an ethic is then not only about taking seriously informants' concerns and desires surrounding the politics of knowledge, but also about the ways their concerns and desires radically shape my research practices.

From the time I began doing research in the Caribbean in the late 1970s, I have been acutely aware of my position as a foreign researcher and the opportunities my education, the institutional and financial support I have received, and my white skin have granted me. I have also been aware that such a position, as any other position, never stands still and does not really sum up my experience in the islands.[38] In Trinidad, for example, while at times I have been called "culture vulture" by some half-joking friends, at other times, I have been treated and made to feel as a sister, a longtime friend, and an "auntie." While on some occasions I have been perceived as a threatening white woman, on other occasions the labels of "musician," "researcher," and "teacher" affixed to me have displaced the issues of race and sexuality. My point is that the different types of exchange and levels of sharing I have experienced and the various ways in which I have been perceived cannot be neatly compartmentalized in the misleading binary divide of foreigner versus nonforeigner, with the ensuing series of associations each of these terms carries. As has been widely acknowledged, multiple relations of power complicate how we are positioned and position ourselves, and how we position others. I emphasize class, gender, and nationality as salient dimensions of social difference as well as race, culture, and diaspora. Positions and positionings also include the geographical locations where one grew up, where one resides, and the translocal routes that articulate with one's own situated practices.[39] In "commuting" back and forth between North America and Trinidad and several other Caribbean islands over a long period of time, not only have I developed long-term relationships, but I have also become involved in the transnational circuit of many calypso and soca artists and Carnival revelers, show promoters, and academics focusing on the Caribbean.[40] In so doing, I have not become West Indian, or, put another way, my experience as a commuter has not changed my national identity and identification as a French Canadian from Quebec. What this commuting has led me to develop is a series of affinities and a special connection with particular circuits of the transnational Caribbean space.[41] The statements I make and the questions I raise in this study should thus be read in relation to both the limits and possibilities my particular experience has produced.

Inspired by several publications in ethnomusicology and anthropology over the past two decades, I have used in this study several biographical narratives to grapple with the issues of multiple subjectivities and transnational networks. I found biographies useful, as cultural critic George Lipsitz explains, not to provide an archetype or the model of an heroic figure, but rather to show how people position themselves and are positioned socially in the space they live.[42] Biographies can show not only how subjectivities are informed by a complex web of relations, but also how such a web of relations can prove at times to be limiting, at other times enabling the subject positions these individuals can adopt.

The choice of biographies is thus not accidental. In his studies, Lipsitz chooses biographies that are inspiring, that promote a politics of hope—without falling into the naive emancipatory narratives that dismiss how the travails of life are negotiated on a daily basis.[43] What is important to him is to avoid taking what may appear as eccentricities as simply that—eccentricities. Instead, he argues, these eccentricities often mark the emergence of "new subjects."[44] In this study, I also chose to focus on biographies that promote a politics of hope, but with slightly different goals in mind: to show how the resistances or new possibilities offered by these biographies have been not only elaborated into more oppositional or emancipatory discourses, but also at times recontained in ways that have secured rather than disrupted the status quo.[45] I have also incorporated biographical narratives that have been conceived locally as contributing to the articulation of new cultural formations, and as embracing new notions of ethics and aesthetics in response to current historical conditions.

Aperçu of *Governing Sound*

This book is in two parts. Part 1 concentrates on how, from the time of its emergence, calypso was deeply entangled in the deployment of colonialism and anticolonialism, and in the articulation of the nation-building project. The first three chapters focus on the connections between the broad-scale dynamics of colonial and postcolonial regimes and the musical practice of calypso as a disciplinary site and site of authentication of the newly independent nation-state's subjects. I pursue these connections for at least two reasons: as Ann Laura Stoler attempted to do in her study of the colonial regime in Indonesia, "to identify what Foucault might have called the microphysics of colonial [and postcolonial] rule[s]," [46] and, as importantly, to illuminate the diverse forms of agency and change that calypso enabled at different moments in its history. In these three chapters, I show how, through calypso, cultural racism, Christian morality, gendered distinctions, and class hierarchies intersected with local and global capitalist economies. I also show how, from the outset, these colonial and postcolonial legacies have informed the configuration and dynamics of the calypso music industry.

Focusing on the contrasting biographical narratives of five calypsonians, chapter 4 examines how calypso provided the terrain on which the construction of the national subject between the 1960s and 1980s was simultaneously defined and contested in terms of race, gender, and class. Chapter 5 analyzes how, in the aftermath of independence, certain calypso sounds privileged by key arrangers and calypsonians during the 1960s and 1970s became not only hegemonic, but also emblematic of the nation's musical sensibility.

In part 2 of the book, I focus on the new Carnival musical practices—soca, rapso, chutney soca, and ragga soca—and the ways in which they have contributed to the redefinition of Trinidadian cultural politics in the neoliberal era. I examine the new rationalities, contingencies, desires, and musical experiments that have animated these new musics and enabled them to gradually displace calypso from its centrality as national expression. Chapter 6 probes the origin stories of each of new Carnival musics and the diverse subjectivities they bring forward. It investigates how these new musics incite discourses about musical authenticity, sexuality, and permissible pleasures on and off the national stage of Carnival and within and across Trinidad's discrepant diasporas. It highlights how, each in its own way, they reconfigure the highly debated issues of race and ethnic relations, body politics, and national identity. Foregrounding their audible entanglements with multiple diasporas, it explores how they help articulate not only various senses of belonging but also, I argue, new cultural formations. [47] To understand how these new ways of thinking are enunciated musically and materially, chapter 7 focuses on the musical practices of two leading figures in the Carnival music scene. Based on interviews and musical analyses, it investigates how they express their respective imaginings of nation and of diasporic subject in terms of both locations and translocal relations. It examines not only how they view their own contributions, musically, socially, and politically, but also their own position, financially. Chapter 8 addresses how, along with such new ways of thinking, a number of musical entrepreneurships that are distinct to this neoliberal era have reorganized the functioning of the Carnival musical scene. From the National Carnival Commission's new mandate to the creation of new musical enterprises and the emergence of new fields of expertise dealing with musical rights, this chapter shows how the Carnival music scene is articulated and disciplined according to new ethics and a new sense of accountability. The coda elaborates the critical import of *sound work* and my analytic of governing sound. Using these critical tools as a prism to analyze calypso and its musical offshoots in the context of proliferation, I stress calypso's generative transformations. I focus on the historical conditions of possibility that enabled the emergence of these distinct musical practices and what these formations have produced.

PART 1

Calypso

Calypso's Historical Entanglements

This chapter situates calypso within the transnational and trans-cultural circuits of Trinidadian colonial history. It introduces the place and people involved in the production of calypso and the circumstances that made it simultaneously a target of disciplinary power, a source of empowerment, and a means to generate revenues.

In the first section of this chapter, rather than assume the equation of Trinidad and calypso, I examine the historical conditions of possibility and the political technologies that have fused those cultural imaginaries together. In both popular and academic discourses, invocations of Trinidad's organic relation to calypso are often taken as self-evident truths. Instead, I show how Trinidad became historically entangled with calypso. To do so, I explore the material conditions that have enabled Trinidad, as opposed to another country, to be constructed as *the* defining territory of calypso.

In the second section, I focus on the sociopolitical and economic conditions in which calypso emerged. I highlight the complex configuration of forces converging in Trinidad that produced a society difficult to rule: the competing colonial powers, slavery, the nonhomogeneous migration cultures, and the United States' imperialist influence.[1] I show how in this highly heterogeneous population—divided as much by its diverse languages as by its religious values and political desires—Carnival and its musical expression, calypso, came to be viewed as central to the colonial project.

In the last section, I trace calypso's transcultural and transnational histories to demonstrate how, from the outset, calypso's sounds have been hybrid products enmeshed in colonial cultural politics, and yet not dictated by them. From this perspective, I point out how musical tours, recordings, migration, new instrumental technologies, and audiences from and outside Trinidad have also spurred the continual transformation of calypso. The complex and contentious cultural politics that informed calypso's emergence, as the following chapters will illustrate, have become reworked in subsequent historical moments, shaping distinct articulations of Trinidadian identities, notions of nation, and diasporas.

Trinidad as the Land of Calypso

Trinidad is not the only Caribbean island where calypso has been performed. Historians from Barbados, for example, have claimed in recent years that calypso was widely practiced on their island as early as the seventeenth century.[2] Today, nearly all English-speaking islands offer calypso competitions every year. However, Trinidad's material conditions combined with its unique sociopolitical history have given Trinidad a privileged position over the other English-speaking islands of the Caribbean region in claiming calypso as emblematic of its land.

The large size of the island (4,828 sq km), its great natural resources,[3] and the critical mass of its population (1.3 million inhabitants) in comparison to that of the Eastern Caribbean islands (the populations of the English-speaking islands vary from 1,400 in Barbuda to 278,300 inhabitants in Barbados) led to a greater volume of cultural and economic activity in Trinidad.[4] Early in Caribbean history, intraregional migration constituted one of the first and most important means of how Trinidadian calypso established its influence in the English-speaking region. Subject to limited opportunities in their own lands, West Indians migrated to larger and more prosperous adjacent territories in search of work. The unique position of Trinidad in terms of natural resources and commercial opportunities drew migrants from all over the region from the early nineteenth century.[5] As a result, Trinidad became (and continues to be) a training ground for many musicians. For example, Lionel Belasco was born in Barbados or, as some people argue, in Caracas, Venezuela, spent his preteen years in both Venezuela and Trinidad, and subsequently became one of the most important calypso entrepreneurs in the first half of the twentieth century. In the same way, well-known trumpet player Dave

Wilkins, born in Barbados, joined Trinidadian orchestras and bands in the 1930s and was introduced to calypso for the first time. By the 1950s, he was recording in England with two calypsonians from Trinidad who became legendary figures, Lord Kitchener (Aldwyn Roberts) and Lord Beginner (Egbert Moore).[6] By then, several other musicians from various islands were attending Trinidad's Carnival and calypso competitions yearly in order to improve their musical skills and chances of winning the competitions held in their own islands.

Musicians' migrations to Trinidad benefited not only the migrants but Trinidadians as well. Indeed, many tunes from the neighboring West Indian islands—brought to Trinidad by migrants, visiting boat crews, and individual traders—have contributed to the richness and variety of Trinidadian calypso.[7] From the time of colonization, many other islands were also producing songs similar, if not identifcal, to calypso. Up to the 1950s, for example, the musics called mento from Jamaica and biguine from Guadeloupe embodied melodies, formal structures (strophic or verse-refrain), and rhetorical strategies (such as double entendre) strikingly similar to those of calypso. Calypsonian Atilla the Hun (Raymond Quevedo) underscored this connection when he published several calypsos (some dating from around 1900) that he attributed to other islands, including Martinique, Dominica, Guadeloupe, Jamaica, St. Vincent, St. Lucia, the Bahamas, and the Grenadines.[8]

By the 1950s, Trinidadian calypso was disseminated to other islands through performance and instruction. In personal interviews, several musicians from Dominica and St. Lucia recounted, for example, how their first police band directors were trained musicians from Trinidad who would often write down calypso arrangements in order to make them part of the standard repertoire. (In Trinidad, calypso musical arrangements began to be written down in the late 1940s).[9] Given that until recently most brass band musicians playing calypso have come from police bands—one of the few institutions in the islands that provides instruction in playing, reading, and writing music—the influence of the Trinidadian police band directors around the West Indies was significant.[10]

The relatively few calypsonians in the other islands could not compete with Trinidad's numerous calypsonians, nor could they achieve similar exposure, since they lacked the infrastructure to develop or promote their songs that their Trinidadian counterparts had. By 1939 the colonial administration and the bourgeoisie in Trinidad were dedicated to holding calypso tent competitions to elect the Calypso King of the Season— which, after countless battles, finally took place in 1953 as the first true national competition.[11] In contrast, even though the first official Calypso

King competitions in most English-speaking islands of the Eastern Caribbean began in the second half of the 1950s, few achieved national significance until the 1970s.[12] Together with their early exposure through commercial recordings (described below), the great number of Trinidadian calypsonians on tour in and outside the region over the past century has ensured Trinidad's central position in the calypso music scene.

Competing Powers

Competition among and within Colonial Regimes

The uniqueness of Trinidad's colonial history has contributed greatly to the transcontinental and transcultural formations of Carnival and of calypso, as well as to the importance they have both acquired locally.[13] Competing colonial regimes long vied for political control in Trinidad; consequently, as was the case in most other islands the colonial white elite was never united. Spain claimed Trinidad as a colony as early as 1498 but did not get serious about colonizing the island until the late eighteenth century. To encourage immigration to Trinidad, the Spanish king Charles III issued a royal proclamation, or *Cedula,* in 1783 offering free lots of land to citizens friendly to Spain, provided they were Roman Catholics.[14] After the French Revolution and the abolition of aristocratic and bourgeois privilege, French planters and free coloreds from Martinique, Guadeloupe, St. Lucia, Dominica, St. Vincent, and Grenada flocked to Trinidad, bringing with them as many black slaves as possible, since for each slave the owner was given a parcel of land. (The term "coloreds" during this historical era referred to children of mixed black and white couples, many of whom were enfranchised. The term "black" was understood to designate a person of unmixed African descent, or predominantly African descent.) By the 1790s, the new settlers were joined "by a number of Saint Domingue royalists who had offered their services to the British forces during their ultimately abortive campaign to undermine the Haitian Revolution and wrest Haiti from both the Black Jacobins and the French."[15] Within a short period, then, Trinidad became essentially a French-speaking island. As the saying goes, "Spain reigned, but France ruled."

The situation became further complicated after Trinidad was ceded to Britain in 1802. For nearly the first forty years of British rule, the island remained Spanish in its bureaucracy. Only in 1840 were the illustrious *cabildo* and judiciary replaced by a town council and English criminal laws. Throughout its colonial period, Trinidad represented contested terrain among the colonial powers: the Spanish ruling the island had regarded the French-speaking planters and free coloreds as a threat, the British governors had despised the Spanish administration, and the Church of England had created tension with the Catholic Church by taking over the latter's place as the state church under British rule—this even though a large majority of the population was Catholic. The colonial process of Trinidad thus resulted in a history of confrontations, not only between the white colonial elite and the enslaved Africans, but also within and among the white colonial powers. Such confusion and discord among the elite produced decades of inefficient and inconsistent administration, conflicting interests among various population groups, and fights over power. In this context, cultural formation became contested terrain among the colonial regimes, by being conceived as coterminous with the formation of the colony each aimed to establish.[16]

The problem for the British colonial administration was to keep under control the heterogeneous cultures of the many populations living on the island. Trinidad in the nineteenth century was a migration culture, with one of the most diverse populations of the entire Caribbean region. In addition to the Spanish, the French, the British, and the slaves of French planters, some twelve thousand free blacks and free coloreds from the French and British plantations also lived in Trinidad. As Bridget Brereton indicates, "They ranged from prosperous and educated planters, slave-owners, and professionals to illiterate peons and free black artisans and hucksters." Importantly, she notes, "The size and economic importance of this group [the free coloreds and free blacks] were to be significant in forming the island's social structure."[17]

In 1834, when the abolition of slavery in Britain was proclaimed, Trinidad freed over twenty thousand enslaved people, according to Rosanne Marion Adderley, "almost all identified as black rather than of mixed race" and born mostly in the Caribbean.[18] In addition, in the following years, Trinidad experienced major waves of immigration. Between 1810 and 1860, Trinidad received almost one thousand black immigrants from the British West India Regiment; eight thousand Africans rescued by the British navy from illegal slave ships; and a small number of people of "'Spanish-African-Amerindian' descent from Venezuela, popularly called 'peons.'"[19] Seeking to replace the manpower lost during Emancipation, Trinidad also received large groups of Indians, who were employed as contract laborers on the island from 1845. Brereton reports that "in 1871 they accounted for 25.1 per cent of the total population; 143,939 people arrived from India during the period 1845–1917."[20] Finally, groups of immigrants, including Portuguese, coloreds from Venezuela, Chinese,

Corsicans, Scots, Swiss, Germans, and Italians also came to Trinidad throughout the nineteenth century. Peter van Koningsbruggen describes the diversity of this ethnic mix as "exceptional, even by contemporary Caribbean standards."[21]

Social Hierarchy and Legacies of Colonial Racism and Morality

From the outset, colonial racism produced a rigid hierarchy of social strata that revolved around assertions of cultural difference understood to be rooted in biology, descent, and purported group essences. Writing in 1953, Lloyd Brathwaithe explains, "The existence of a large variety of ethnic groups has led, not to the development of an eclectic cosmopolitanism, but to a certain separateness of the groups and a ranking of them in terms of superiority and inferiority, as groups."[22]

Under the British colonial regime during the nineteenth century, the upper class composed exclusively of whites, as Peter van Koningsbruggen puts it, functioned more like a caste than like a class, making it virtually impossible for nonwhites and people of mixed ancestry to penetrate their ranks.[23] At the opposite end of the spectrum, the lower class consisted primarily of blacks. The middle class, composed mainly of coloreds and freed black slaves, emerged as a new social category—"the Creoles"—that over time came to embody several meanings. In the late nineteenth century, according to Brereton, the term "Creole" usually meant a person born in Trinidad of European and African descent. It could be used without or with specifications, as in "white Creole" or "Afro-Creole."[24] A French Creole in turn was understood to be a person of European descent, usually French, but possibly also from other European countries, born on the island, who identified herself with, or was associated with, the French Creole group. To further complicate its definition, the category "Creole" referred not only to country of birth and race, but also to class and culture, involving primarily the interactions between whites, blacks, and coloreds—people of European, African, and mixed descent.[25] Within this social order, the middle-class groups found themselves in the ambivalent and difficult position of trying simultaneously to be accepted by the whites and to distance themselves from the blacks. Significantly, by defining "Creole" as exclusively positioned between black and white, those claiming this relational identity explicitly excluded those not considered part of this spectrum—namely, the East Indians.

The indentured Indians and their descendants were isolated from anyone else not only because of their late arrival, but also by being placed under a particular government department and a number of restrictions

and kept on the estates as indentured laborers. The colonial social stratifi-
cation based on ethnic affiliation and purity further impelled groups to
cling to their ethnic identity as tightly as they could.[26] Not surprisingly,
then, the Indians also isolated themselves from the rest of the society
by emphasizing their own cultural, social, and religious values. In addition, for both the white colonial administration and the former slaves, as
Brereton indicates, the East Indians' languages, physical appearances, religions, and culture were so strikingly different that "[they] were regarded
as an exotic group, marginal to Trinidad society, insufficiently integrated
to be considered a part of it."[27]

During the second half of the nineteenth century, occupation inter-
related to the deeply divisive racialized colonial regime served as an instrument to reinforce the social hierarchy on the island. Hence, nonwhite
migrant groups, plus those who were conceived as "not quite white," were
placed on the lowest ranks of society and were labeled on the basis of
their work: the East Indians "were referred to as coolies, meaning slavish
laborers or imbeciles"; the Portuguese, as "dirty shopkeepers who spoke
'rash-potash' instead of English"; and the Syrians, as "door-to-door ven-
dors of manufactures" or as money lenders, a socioeconomic position
resented by the other groups.[28]

During the colonial regime, moral regulation also normalized a particular form of social order.[29] From the start, the colony was essentially
patriarchal. The dominating perspective and personnel construction of
male, white, Protestant, English colonial administration structured the
society along deeply unequal gendered lines. Following the particular
conceptions of "the English way of life," women were supposed to belong
within the household and to have a domestic identity. Their purpose was
to embody well-ordered families, and thus to reflect as well as to uphold
a well-ordered society. In such a vision, "they could not therefore be
thought as having a public existence."[30] Women's activities in Carnival
were thus especially targeted and disciplined as a major means through
which the male English administration legitimated its rule.

This rigid social hierarchy of Trinidad's society became part of the
colonial legacy that continues to animate social relations to this day—in
spite of the gradually more open class system resulting from greater access
to education, increased association between members of the three groups,
and, in a few cases, miscegenation. While independence in 1962 brought
a drastic shift in Trinidad's politics, it did not erase the divisive racialized
tensions among groups.

The Afro-Creoles and the East Indians continue to bear the divisive legacy of the colonial regime and to function as two separate groups. Hence,

in 1956, after the decisive creation of the People's National Movement (PNM)—the first party government of the country, which, headed by an Afro-Creole Oxford-trained scholar, Dr. Eric Williams, was to lead the British colonies of Trinidad and Tobago toward national independence in 1962—the struggle over power, politically and culturally, now unfolded between the poles of a two-party system: the PNM and the opposition, the Democratic Labor Party, which consisted of a variety of groups with a clear East Indian preponderance, including the People's Democratic Party (PDP)—the main opponent to the PNM in the 1956 elections.[31] With a two-party system in place, the ethnic demarcation between the blocs proved an ominous sign for the future. While the new political structure celebrated a culturally hybrid Trinidad, it also consolidated racialized voting blocs, leading to "the development of opposed bourgeois nationalist Afro-Creole and [East] Indian political parties" and, hence, an "us and them" mentality.[32]

After the 1956 elections, the local white elite lost its political power. Though small in demographic size, it maintained economic power, thanks to its accumulation of capital throughout the colonial period.[33] The severe erosion of whites' ability to influence how "culture," including music, would be legislated and valorized within Trinidad represented a devastating loss precisely because whites' hegemony over what constituted legitimate culture was crucial to colonial rule.

Throughout the colonial regime in Trinidad, culture served not only as one of the prime instruments through which the colonial administration governed, but also as a privileged terrain to rally the competing colonial powers. Even though a tradition imported to Trinidad by the French plantocracy, "Carnival seemed to be one of the few institutions that served to bring all the Whites together."[34] Even though the English disliked the French because the French planters formed the white majority at the beginning of the nineteenth century and thus represented a threat to English rule, they viewed the festival as an occasion to form a coalition with them "because they saw the necessity of a united white front against ambitious Free Coloreds and Blacks."[35] Together, the colonial elite saw Carnival and its expressive culture—especially singing, playing musical instruments, and dancing—as a means to inculcate Christian morality and reinforce colonial order. As David Scott would put it, Carnival thus became a target of power and one of the most important terrains where power could be not only exercised, but also "displayed." The problem was that the targeted Carnival was transnational and transcultural from the outset and continually transformed, forever elusive, and impossible to control.

Transnational and Transcultural Histories

Calypso's Emergence from a Migratory Circuit

From its inception, calypso emerged through a migratory circuit of peoples and commodities and a radical asymmetry of power. This complex traffic allowed musical knowledges and practices to mingle, fuse, and transform each other. As a crucible of unequal power and transcultural encounter, this "contact zone," to use Mary-Louise Pratt's expression, produced the conditions of possibility for calypso's emergence as a constitutively hybrid product.[36] African musical practices on colonial plantations such as calypso drew from and creatively combined an array of musical traditions, blending a variety of influences from Africa, Europe, and the Americas.

While some statistics exist about the number of Africans brought to Trinidad, little is known about the traditions of words and music that they knew and shared. However, even a brief account of the enslaved population groups brought to the island gives important clues about the complex milieu in which the new local musical practices were forged. As Rohlehr indicates, census statistics from 1813 indicate that the enslaved people brought to the island that year were captured from six areas of West Africa, Central Africa, and Mozambique. Those born in the New World were drawn from other British, French, and Spanish colonies, including Barbados, Martinique, Saint Domingue, and Venezuela.[37]

Out of this multinational population of nineteenth-century Trinidad emerged a vast repertoire of musical genres and dances. Among the best known are the calinda (also spelled "kalinda" or "kalenda"), the jhouba, the bèlè (bel Air), and the bamboula. The little information that exists on these song-dances was culled from various diaries written by white chroniclers, who described them by evoking different musical traditions. Consider, for example, the following excerpt, cited as one of the most complete descriptions of calinda, the song-dance allegedly most influential in calypso's formation: "The tune Calinda was bad enough. In Louisiana, at least, its song was always a grossly personal satirical ballad, and it was the favourite dance all the way from there to Trinidad. . . . The Calinda was a dance of the multitude, a sort of vehement cotillon. The contortions of the encircling crowd were strange and terrible, the din was hideous. One Calinda is still familiar to all Creole ears, it has long been a vehicle for the white Creole's satire; for generations the man of municipal politics was fortunate who escaped entirely a lampooning set to its air."[38] Usually accompanied by the banjo and tambour (African instruments), the calinda was portrayed by white reporters as featuring musical elements they associated with both Europe (ballad and cotillon) and Africa (bodily contortions and din)—descriptions that could be telling not only of the writers' condescension toward calinda's African sensibilities, but also of the fusion process already underway.

According to Andrew Pearse, the word "calinda" in the New World was applied to many dances, but in Trinidad—and this is important to the later historical construction of calypso—the dance incorporated some of the eccentric and violent movements of stickfighting, was performed by a man or a woman, and embodied the dramatic duel between the drummer and the dancer in counterpoint.[39] Significantly, it is these characteristics of the calinda—song of satire and derision, embodiment of a dramatic duel, and accompaniment to stickfighting—that were later selected by nationalist writers to identify the calinda as the ancestor of calypso.

The origins of calypso, however, remain a contentious issue. One form of bèlè song-dance described as featuring "songs of praise and satire" that were "plaintive and melancholic" has also been said to be at the origin of calypso.[40] However, given the conflicting documentation on bèlè and on most other songs and dances before Emancipation, Hollis Liverpool's conclusion is that "the calypso was not the descendant of any one particular form of song, but owed its origin to the numerous songs, rhythms, and dance traditions present in Trinidad during the time of African enslavement."[41] In fact, it could even be argued that what is today called calypso may have combined, as it often still does, different song forms, musical instruments, and musical values commonly associated with several musics performed during that period—some derived from African influences, and others not.[42]

What follows is an account of some of the elements that have been involved in calypso's continual transformations. With the many efforts to anglicize the island through education, calypso songs began to be sung partly in French Creole, partly in English, and the first calypso to be sung entirely in English appeared in the early 1890s.[43] With the many competitions organized to "improve" the repetitive form of the calinda songs and to promote the English language, a new form, called the oratorical, or "sans humanité," calypso, then emerged.[44] This new form, highly hybrid, retained some aspects of the calinda songs: the use of minor keys;[45] the vindictive tone, reflected in the words "sans humanité" (without pity) ending the last line of each stanza; the context in which calinda used to be performed, requiring two or more singers to improvise insults against each other for the approval of the audience; and the improvisatory style characteristic of what was known as the picong era (from around the first decade of the twentieth century to the 1920s), which, as Rohlehr explained, converted "the traditional rivalry and violent confrontation into a struggle for verbal mastery in the backyard tents of Port of Spain."[46] While the oratorical calypso may have borrowed from "the litanic chanting of the Catholic Church," it reportedly borrowed equally from many other delivery styles from Carnival characters, such as those of "the batonnier, Pierrot and Carnival Robber," enacted in masquerade long before.[47] (♪ CD track 1, "Lieutenant Julian," by Sam Manning.)

At the same time, the "sans humanité" calypso contrasted in several ways with the earlier form. It featured more lines in each stanza—eight lines as opposed to four in the calinda songs—and also, instead of the parsimonious use of a few French Creole words per line, it used sophisticated and often "invented" English-sounding words in longer lines of text.[48] As the legendary calypsonian Roaring Lion recalled, "At that time, singers went to the library . . . before they began to compose," so much did they want to impress their audience and win the competitions.[49] The humor displayed in word games permeating these songs—including making fun of jargon-type language—was the former slaves' response to those pressuring them to use English instead of French Creole lyrics. Together with humor, the oratorical calypso effectively "retained the derisiveness, the topicality and the picong noted in the kalenda" and continued its "relentless attacks on the upper classes and dominant elites."[50]

While the oratorical calypso became popular during this period, older song forms did not disappear. After 1900, several younger singers opted to sing in the previous form—the four-line form, called "single tone"—supposedly, according to a middle-class calypsonian, to focus on the glorification of sexual symbolism, itself a remnant of the jamet Carnival.[51] (The jamet Carnival, discussed at length in the next chapter, refers to provocative gestures performed during Carnival as a form of protest against the colonial administration's repressive measures during the 1860s and 1870s.) From the 1890s to the 1920s, two quite different tendencies thus existed side by side, "one requiring fine speech and relating to the ethos of an educated elite, and one of abuse based on the common man's mother-wit and total command of French Creole [which] could and did often meet in the same calypsonian."[52]

The selection of instruments used to accompany calypso singers varied tremendously according to the constraints and opportunities Afro-Trinidadian musicians faced at different historical moments. By the 1840s, in addition to the drum and banjo, many musicians among the former slaves had mastered European instruments, such as the guitar, flute, violin, and cornet, while playing for the plantation owners' and the white colonial elite's favorite ballroom dances—including waltzes, jigs, the white elite version of Bel Air, and also the quadrille, which, after having been viewed as the most popular ballroom dance in the 1820s, was still performed up to the 1920s.[53] By the 1890s, the "string band" from Venezuela brought to Trinidad by the immigrant peons during the nineteenth century was adopted, not only by the Creole upper and middle class, but also by the lower-class Afro-Creole calypsonians in their concert performances, Carnival practice sessions, and the Carnival itself.[54] Venezuelan-type string bands consisted of guitar, cuatro (a small, four-string, guitar-shaped instrument), mandolin, banjo, and chakchak (shakers, also spelled shac shac or chac-chac), to which in Trinidad were often added flute and violin. In addition to accompanying calypso, the string band players during this period also often played two Venezuelan dances, the paseo (a promenade) and the Castilian (a fast waltz).[55] Significantly, string bands included members who were often of mixed background. While Afro-Creoles formed the majority, there were also a few musicians of mixed descent (black and white) and, in some cases, individuals of Chinese ancestry.[56]

From the late nineteenth century, Trinidadians were regularly exposed to African-American musical practices. The newly revived Tennessee Jubilee Singers, on their second tour in Trinidad in 1891, stayed over a month and a half—and may have passed on some of their repertoire to avid Trinidadian music learners.[57] By the 1880s some African-American musics were incorporated into local performances. The local whites were "performing in blackface using repertoire published by North American songsters," while the African revelers, also imitating the American minstrels, "instead of blackening [their] faces, whiten[ened] theirs over a black charcoal base, plac[ing] red spots on their cheeks and w[earing] the 'Uncle Sam costume of scissor-tailed coat, tight striped trousers, white gloves, and tall beaver hat.'"[58] The sparse publications of calypso lyrics and melodies performed during that period make it difficult to assess how these practices influenced calypsonians during that period. By the 1920s, however, some of the African-American musics were part of many calypsonians' and their accompanying bands' repertoires.

Several singers performed as much as vaudevillians as they performed as calypsonians.[59] In 1922, Afro-Creole musicians performing for the Carnival of the middle and upper classes were playing jazz in both a full string band and a brass band formation.[60] In 1924 they were playing swing in the dancehalls on Carnival Sunday and for masqueraders in the streets on the following day.[61] From at least 1927 until 1935, there were yearly Carnival jazz band competitions, and in 1935 an intercolonial jazz band competition was even organized.[62] The list of winners on Dimanche Gras at the Queen's Park Savannah indicates that in 1925 yankee singing bands (bands singing American songs) were still performing and entering competitions, as was also the case until the early 1930s for the minstrel bands and tamboo-bamboo bands. By the 1940s, it was standard practice for black musicians and singers to learn the latest American tunes through the scores sent along with movie reels.[63] By the 1950s, steelbands during Carnival were playing the Charleston, "popularly called the marico"— which was apparently then sweeping the country—while the performers and masqueraders were waiting for the bands in front of them to move forward.[64] Some calypso arrangers of the time were incorporating musical features such as chord progressions, solos, and instrumentation inspired by New Orleans jazz and swing, as can be heard in Rupert Nurse's arrangements of Lord Kitchener's and the Mighty Terror's tunes recorded in England.[65]

If black musicians and singers during this period expanded their musical knowledge, they—the singers, most particularly—still earned their reputation mainly, if not exclusively, through performing calypso. Such a predilection for calypso was hardly surprising. After having been the target of power of both the white colonial administration and the middle class for nearly a century, calypso had not only acquired more prominence and symbolic importance than any other music in the country. It had also by then become the music most commercially valuable by being linked to Carnival and its overseas circuits.

On the Move with Recordings

The impact of calypso recordings was profound, both culturally and economically. The first recordings of Trinidadian music were made with two American recording companies, Columbia Records and the Victor recording firm, in New York in 1912, at the time when West Indian immigration to the United States began to represent a sizable population and when American recording companies were launching "ethnic music" to attract a new market from among the many immigrants in the United States. The 1912 recordings featured exclusively instrumental music performed by "Lovey's band, then the most respected string band in Trinidad, [which] came to New York to make phonograph records." It included not only calypsos but also paseos with titles in Spanish such as "Manuelita," "Cavel Blanco," and "666 Trinidad Paseo."[66] The second recording session of Trinidadian music, with Victor, was made in Trinidad in 1914. It featured Julian Whiterose recording for the first time a vocal calypso, Jules Sims singing calindas, Lionel Belasco performing piano solos, and also East Indian music.[67]

Whereas until 1927 recordings of Trinidadian music were almost exclusively instrumental, by the 1930s they featured mainly sung calindas and calypsos. This may have been because calypso was judged to be the only "authentic" and most original music of Trinidad, or because it enacted some of the North American musical standards and aesthetics, or because after the turn of the century it was usually sung in English. Or it could have been because Trinidadian record dealers, such as Eduardo Sa Gomes, made it their mission to promote calypso.[68] In any event, recordings enabled Trinidadian calypso to reach out to new audiences, not only in the English-speaking West Indies, but also "Americans with no connection to the West Indies . . . The English and the Africans in British colonies (the Gold Coast, Nigeria, South Africa, and so forth),"[69] and, in so doing, to become the primary music, if not the only music, associated with Trinidad and Tobago. Furthermore, by being featured on commercial recordings abroad, calypso acquired an even greater prominence at home.[70] The recordings from 1912 onward of Trinidadian music bands, the first radio broadcast from the United States to Trinidad in 1934 by calypsonians, and the record sales among a wide range of audiences all acted as "important symbolic gesture[s] in legitimizing calypso outside Trinidad in the eyes of Trinidadians themselves."[71]

In the attempt to reach a wide market, calypsonians (or perhaps the record companies) labeled their songs under various terms besides the locally well-known term "single tone calinda," including as wide a variety as the following: calypso swing, calypso fox trot, Trinidad Carnival paseo, Grenada paseo, Tobago paseo, and Creole calypso.[72] While recordings may have provided incentives for calypsonians to expand calypso's musical boundaries, some recording companies in 1937 were in turn hunting for something else: "old Trinidad folk songs . . . calypsos, and specialized tunes belonging only to Trinidad, so that the records can be sold in America and all over the world, to give Trinidad greater publicity, and to preserve the music of the generations gone by—music which is now in danger of becoming extinct."[73] In spite of the many attempts by the white administration and middle class to deafricanize Carnival music, such a call from the American record companies for old calypsos may have contributed to the revival and use, for instance, of the lavway, a short refrain in call-and-response style. (♪ CD track 2, "We Goin' to Cut the Wood" by unknown singers.) Such lavways became frequently used in combination with the ballad form in the new calypsos composed from the late 1930s to this day (e.g., Christopher "Tambu" Herbert's 1990 song "No, No, We Ain't Goin' Home," whose refrain is based on a call and response).

However, calypso sounds never stayed still. In the aftermath of independence, in spite of the competition regulations designed to promote "truly one nation" and to feature the cultural patrimony "strictly" from the land of Trinidad, calypso competitions nevertheless featured audible entanglements that crossed the borders of Trinidad's territory. To give just a few examples: by the 1970s, electric instruments, including the Hammond B-3 keyboard, prominently featured in several American musical genres, became a standard part of the calypso band. Latin American and American jazz big band styles of arrangement, already influential in the 1950s and 1960s, were still incorporated in well-known calypsos, such as "Margie," by Lord Kitchener, arranged by Clive Bradley (1970), and "Man Is Boo" with Black Stalin, arranged by Boogsie Sharpe (1982). By the late 1970s, rhythmic patterns on the high hat, musical riffs on the keyboard, and bass lines from African-American disco were fused in calypso by some of the most prominent musical arrangers of the time, such as Pelham Goddard and Ed Watson. In 1970s and 1980s, calypsonians as well as calypso arrangers continued to be immersed in listening to and, in some cases, practicing many "foreign" musics, including soul, twist, boogaloo, funk, reggae, disco, and break dance. This trend is well illustrated by the Mighty Sparrow, who during that period composed, among others, "Boogaloo Calypso" and "Calypso Twist."

Within the newly independent state of Trinidad and Tobago, other musical explorations were taking place. In the early 1970s, calypso—then performed in official functions as the music emblematic of the nation-state, even though it starred Afro-Creole performers almost exclusively—was fused with East Indian musical elements as a means to bind and represent musically the two historically divided Trinidadian communities. Even though by the late 1970s this new musical fusion, called soca, made serious forays in transforming musical tastes,[74] soca songs continued to be seen as detractors of "traditional" calypso. As a result, they were not seriously considered in calypso competitions and were featured only as pieces of entertainment subordinate to the main show. (Part 2 of the book will discuss at length the emergence of soca and the new issues it raised.)

Yet, paradoxically, calypso incorporated several sounds and musical technologies from the African-American diaspora (e.g., disco rhythmic patterns on the high hat and Hammond B-3 keyboard)—revealing musically that for calypsonians these particular musical elements held a special status. They conceived these sound bites not only as embodying their own entanglements with the American scene, but also as necessary both to access the North American market and to compete locally with contemporary North American musics: in other words, to reach out to both international and local audiences.

Articulation of Diverse Audiences and Locations

While many of the calypsonians' creative processes and activities were informed by, as well as responded to, the many restrictive measures put in place by both the white administration and the Creole middle class, they were not confined to them. They evolved through commercial opportunities and incentives that at times bypassed entirely and at other times only remotely overlapped with the deployments of political and moralistic control by the colonial administration, the church, or the middle class. I am referring here in particular to the articulation of five main processes which, drawn together between 1919 and 1956, had tangible effects on calypsonians' creativity and activities. These include tourism, recordings, touring, the establishment of the U.S. military and naval bases in Trinidad during World War II, and radio broadcasts. Not only did each of these provide sources of employment for calypsonians, but each called for a different type of entertainment and catered to a different audience— thereby giving calypsonians much room to explore and experiment with both tunes and lyrics.

From early in the twentieth century, tourism constituted a major element of Carnival. In 1932, Anthony writes, a great number of people were taking the train from different parts of the country districts to attend Carnival in Port of Spain, arriving in town the night before to head straight for the dancehalls. In addition, "there were a number of visitors from the other West Indian islands . . . and a great many tourists from the Orient liner S.S. Otranto" whose stop in Trinidad was organized to coincide with Carnival.[75] As tourists grew in number from that point on, the bandleader known as the chantwèl turned into a calypsonian and a solo artist during Carnival and began to assume the role of entertainer. By then, the calypsonian had adopted a new persona: through the use of verbal self-inflation, calypsonians were now projecting themselves not only as the "sweet man," or alternatively as the macho man in "control" of several women, but also as one living in the barrack yard, positioned to learn about scandals and bacchanals—as a man both to be feared and to be admired.[76]

With tourists gathering in calypso tents—one of the main venues where calypso was performed—calypsonians now had new incentives to use English instead of French Creole (also called patois, or patwa) in their lyrics.[77] With the calypso tents as their main performing venues and this new clientele, they also had to widen the scope of their lyrics. As Liverpool notes, "They now had to study international affairs, read newspapers, follow the scandals of the middle and upper classes, and turn rumors and whispers into calypsos for the benefit of patrons." [78] Besides using the rebellious calinda song and its constant alternation between song leader and chorus, calypsonians used the strophic oratorical verses "that stressed picong and 'war,' and the ballad in which the events of the day were narrated." [79] Hence, by the 1930s, the language, forms, and style of calypso were modified not just because of the pressure exercised by the white colonial regime and the local middle class, but also for commercial reasons.

Thanks to the tourists and the recordings that helped promote calypso, touring became a major source of employment for calypsonians. Its impact was manifold: from the early 1920s it created a new pan-Caribbean artistic culture by bringing together musicians from various islands to play in the same band or various bands from different islands in the same show. As a result, it exposed Trinidadian musicians to various musical genres from the region. Conversely, by playing with other musicians, calypsonians on tours helped calypso spread among musicians and singers from the region.

In its turn, the presence of American sailors and other military personnel stationed at the U.S. base set up in Trinidad during World War II had a profound impact on the production and circulation of calypso as well as on the livelihood of calypsonians themselves. Replacing the absent tourists during the war, the Americans inadvertently helped boost the entertainment sector in the country, provided in particular by calypso, by becoming regulars at calypso shows and any other venues where calypso was performed.

According to Rohlehr, singing for the Americans profoundly influenced calypsonians in several regards: it "led to a partial abandonment of coded language by some singers, whose treatment of sexual themes became correspondingly more direct. Double-entendre, however, remained as a highly admired device, and would in later years flower alongside the more direct methods of the wartime breed of calypsonians." [80] Donald Hill refers to the depiction of calypso during this era as filled with risqué songs; Liverpool uses the local expression "smut songs" to refer to these songs "built around the sex act"—which, he explains, still required "satirical skill and creativity, for the singers had to produce masks and double entendres to make their calypsos seemingly clean in the face of the laws and unwritten morals of the society." [81] According to several authors, the effect of singing for the entertainment of American marines "had been to shift the emphasis from social relevance to diversion," to produce "innocuous" and even "silly" songs on fantastic themes and humorous situations, but also to produce songs with a new musical energy and a change in melodic pattern.[82] While the American presence may have contributed to the renewed importance of up-tempo calypsos and "light" lyrics, it simultaneously helped calypso gain locally and internationally not only greater recognition, but also greater commercial value. Socially and politically, by the end of the war the United States had "virtually replaced Britain in the Trinidadian mind as de facto center of imperial power"—a feat that a few years later would greatly help nationalists to push forward their project of independence.[83]

If the impact of tourism, recordings, touring, and the American presence on calypso was profound musically, it was equally remarkable for the calypsonians themselves. They were now embarked on an individualist journey, looking not only for prestige within their own communities, but also for individual success based on recognized talent and commercial gains. "Individual idiosyncrasy in style" combined with "the drive towards self-fulfillment" was now redefining calypsonians' vocation.[84]

The historical entanglements with calypso's emergence that I have chronicled in this chapter should not be consigned to a bygone era. Rather, in the chapters that follow, I elaborate how the legacies of colonial racism and morality as well as the transnational and transcultural circuits that have informed calypso since its inception continue to influence contemporary articulations of Trinidadian identities and power relations. In the next chapter, I detail the governing technologies that have targeted calypso and the competing political, economic, and cultural projects pursued through this musical practice. I show how colonial administrators, slaves and their descendants, middle-class Creoles, and Afro-Trinidadian nationalists and calypsonians themselves all enunciated distinct political aspirations through calypso.

Governing the Conduct of Carnival and Calypso

Calypso since its inception has been enmeshed with distinctive notions of race and freedom, progress and morality. Its contours have been charted through verbal duels on slave plantations, calinda songs performed in the streets of Port of Spain on Carnival Tuesday following Emancipation, cunning double entendre composed for American sailors stationed in Chaguaramas during World War II, and sociopolitical commentaries electronically amplified inside Lord Kitchener's tent in a newly independent nation-state. In this chapter, I probe how calypso came to be constructed as the terrain on which power hierarchies and politics of exclusion were enacted. I show how calypso's cultural practices and their enduring historical sediments have fused Enlightenment legacies of progress fostered by colonial administrators, Christian missionaries, and their religious converts with the histories of struggle and memories of community shared by enslaved Africans.[1] By tracing calypso's cultural practices through distinct historical moments and in specific sites, I show how calypso has contributed to the configuration of a national subject in the "authenticating" space of Carnival.

Since Emancipation, Carnival has served as a privileged arena to police and contest the boundaries of permissible cultural expression. Both colonial administrators and freed-slave participants elaborated through Carnival a sociopolitical formation. In such deployments, authenticating assertions of belonging to distinct communities simultaneously entailed exclusions from others. As Carnival became understood as the exclusive domain of enslaved Africans, and hence of the black political subject, it marginalized the histories of other diasporas, notably South Asian, entangled with the nation-state of Trinidad. Thus understood as a political technology, Carnival since its inception has articulated the cultural politics of race, nation, and diaspora. The politics of authenticity I examine pivot on how the selective tradition of calypso came historically to dominate the cultural contours of Carnival and became emblematic of the nation-state. In my vision, tradition is not a passive cultural inheritance, but rather an operative force shaping the past, present, and future. Seen in this light, selective traditions are saturated by hegemonic processes, at once the objects and the arena of contentious cultural politics.[2]

This chapter uses a genealogical approach to highlight how colonial and postcolonial technologies of power have construed culture, and calypso in particular, as a problem-space. I use the term "problem-space" in reference to a demarcated terrain where the conduct of subjects is specifically targeted.[3] My genealogical approach demonstrates how calypso provided a privileged space for the enslaved Africans and their descendants, the white colonial administration, and the Creole intellectuals and merchants to foresound their sociopolitical aspirations, desires, and values.[4] In each case, my focus is less on subjects' intentions than on the technologies and practices deployed to produce consequential effects. I show how calypso from the outset has been deeply entangled with questions of rule and governing as well as with popular struggles over the cultural conduct of racialized subjects. As a problem-space, calypso gathers the disciplining of Christian morality, patriarchal gender relations, and normative body politics. At the same time, calypso legitimates distinct musical sounds, styles, and subjectivities. In this chapter, I show how, despite its transcultural and transnational histories, calypso has been constructed as emblematic of blackness and as a target of the colonial regimes and, in the wake of independence, as emblematic of the nation-state of Trinidad and Tobago.

Repressive Measures

After Emancipation on 1 August 1834, freed slaves celebrated their freedom by reenacting the Canboulay (Cannes Brûlées) together with the "blowing of horns, shells, cracking of whips and recreating scenes of enslavement," and performing stickfighting all over the country.[5] Nearly a decade later, perhaps to reappropriate the history of their enslaved living conditions parodied earlier by the white elite,[6] both Canboulay masquerade and stickfighting bands accompanied by calinda songs, percussion instruments, and dances took their place as main features of Carnival.

By the 1850s the Carnival space was radically reconfigured. The white European upper class and the middle-class Creoles had receded from the streets during Carnival. They refused to associate themselves with the freed slaves and to be confronted by the song leaders of the stickbands, called chantwèls, whose songs not only provided support to the stickfighters boasting the merits of their champion in song, but also "showed their hatred of bondage and of the dominance of the Whites."[7] They entertained themselves by visiting each other and holding their own parties, thus reinforcing their tightly knit circle. The white colonial administration, which would have preferred to ban Carnival altogether, could not do so for at least two reasons: it feared a genuine revolt by the former slaves, and it wanted to avoid the open hostility of members of the colored middle class who would see such a state intervention in Carnival as blatantly excessive. In addition, says Koningsbruggen, "the Carnival season was an important opportunity for all kinds of festivities for them too."[8] After Emancipation, the colonial administration fought to uphold its position of power by deploying a myriad of measures to keep the former slaves at bay.

The values and morality of racialized subjects as well as their economic productivity and political governability became explicit targets of colonial rule. The social hierarchy and the colonial division by race, class, religion, and nationality informed not only the ways the different population groups interacted with each other, but also the ways in which the cultural values embraced by each group were assessed. In a nutshell, the white European elite viewed European traditions—Victorian sexual mores, religion, social behavior from clothing styles to modes of interaction, its construction of gendered relations, and artistic expressions including music—as the pinnacle of civilization, and everything else as unworthy of respect. Placed in this frame, the traditions associated with blacks were judged barbarous, demonic, dangerous, or, at best, silly, irresponsible, uncontrolled, and unimaginative. In artistic terms, their music was described as noise—chaotic, disorganized, and disturbing—and their dances as lascivious and offensive. In short, traditions associated with the former slaves were viewed as in need of eradication or, at the very least, control. Yet, as will be shown below, many of these traditions aroused curiosity and interest among members of the white European elite and the Creole middle and upper class. This was all the more reason why the colonial administration attempted to show discipline and to discipline the former slaves: on the one hand, to avoid blurring the line between masters and slaves and, on the other hand, to avoid the slaves' use of dance assemblies to plot insurrections. In such a context, musical practices and dances often served the purpose of social control.[9]

Only rarely did the white colonial administration regard the East Indians as a direct threat. In fact, given this group's isolation from them and the other groups, the administration did not use their music as a target of power as they did with the former slaves. For their part, most former slaves shared the colonial prejudices vis-à-vis East Indian music, while also despising the East Indians for having taken the menial plantation work they themselves had left behind. The East Indians actually tended to regard the Afro-Creoles [referring here to all former slaves and any children from black and white couples] as deculturated, as people who early in the colonial period had sacrificed their culture for that of their masters, and who furthermore "disdained hard work, and squandered their earnings on rum, clothes, and fêtes."[10] Even though at the everyday level East Indians and freed slaves and their descendants developed social relations over time and profited mutually from some musical exchanges, in several domains the two cultures remained quite separate. The other population groups, small in number and lacking political power, never became the targets musically of those holding power in Trinidadian history.

Using Carnival and its music as the terrain on which to exercise authority, the white administration launched a series of repressive measures to regulate the former slaves' activities. It issued ordinances and bans restricting the practices and the times during which the former slaves could perform them. In 1849, ordinance 6, passed to restrict Carnival to two days, incensed the black population and set in motion a tug-of-war between the two groups.[11] Renewed attempts by the governor in 1858, and even by the archbishop of Port of Spain in 1862, were made to ban the wearing of masks.[12] In 1868, a desperate effort was made to stop African practices by passing laws banning "the playing or dancing to any drum, gong, tambour, banjee, or chac-chac between the hours of ten in the evening and six o'clock the next day . . . obscene songs and dances, the blowing of horns, and the carrying of lighted torches."[13]

Despite these measures, fear that "festivals were thin smoke screens for the imminent rebellion of peasants, workers and the urban unemployed" persisted.[14] With the coming of the infamous Captain Baker as inspector-commandant of the police force in 1877, this fear turned into paranoia. His repeated attempts to stop Carnival worsened the conflicts between the different population groups, which reached their apex in 1881 with "the Canboulay riots" in which several people on each side were wounded. From the same impulse, even though "the [East] Indians had been perceived as a 'docile, manageable' labor force," the Hosay celebration (also referred to as the Shia Muslim celebration of Muharram) that had become a festival of national proportions involving not only Muslims, but also Hindus and Afro-Creoles, was violently suppressed in 1884.[15]

One of the peculiarities of the British colonial regime was that from the late nineteenth century the Creole middle class showed a high degree of involvement in the exercise of governing. Caught in between their desire to promote their social standing and their denied access to the whites' privileges, their affinities with some of the slaves' customs and yet their conscious estrangement from them, the coloreds developed their own space and ways to exercise agency. By disengaging themselves publicly from anything "African," the Creoles legitimated their position through association with the white colonial elite. Repeatedly, some members of the Creole middle class used the newspapers to pressure the governor and his cabinet to purge Carnival of its so-called unsavory elements. Yet, privately, "many middle class persons patronized the barrack yard not only to gain the favors of prostitutes and indulge in the more open sexual atmosphere of the lower class, but also to participate in the Africans' form of Carnival festivity."[16] By adopting publicly a prudish and moralistic approach, the middle class could hope to avoid scandals and the risk of losing their position on the social ladder. Hence, it is not surprising to read how in 1890 the *Port of Spain Gazette* expressed its support of law enforcement and, as a means to highlight its own "high" moral standards, made disparaging remarks on the so-called immoral activities of the black lower class: "The authorities, particularly the police, will soon have to make the usual preparations for ensuring peace and order during the coming Carnival. And it is hoped that this year they will strip it of the second main feature that disgraced the old Carnivals, namely the obscene songs and attendant orgies in which immorality among the young acquires new impetus every year. The other main feature, the fighting and rioting, has happily almost altogether disappeared, but in evil consequences it cannot be considered worse than its companion evil, with which our streets reek as with a moral pestilence."[17] During the colonial regime, morality was an important instrument that simultaneously helped the white, male, Protestant, English administration to legitimate its position and the Creoles to distance themselves from the lower-class masses that were socially, politically, and economically subordinated.[18] A great majority of Creoles agreed with the white colonial administration that the calinda and calypso songs accompanied by so-called indecent dance movements and gestures typical of the jamet Carnival had to be removed. (According to

Brereton, the term "jamet" referred to "a lower-class person whose life centers around fighting, singing, dancing, drumming and Carnival. The word is derived from the French 'diamêtre' or underworld type.")[19] In the mid-1870s, newspapers articles condemned the jamet Carnival as "an increasingly wild, noisy and violent Canboulay."[20]

Most writings of the time chastised women especially for their provocative behavior, for "startling bystanders by opening their bodices and exposing their breasts . . . openly solicit[ing] men (particularly of the middle class), w[earing] sexually revealing clothing and danc[ing] indecently on the streets."[21] According to Jacob Elder, the jamet women sang sexual "cariso" songs before these songs were appropriated by men—a remark that makes them responsible for the upsurge of immoral songs and dancing in the jamet Carnival.[22] In all cases, by being contrasted with those of the ideal Victorian woman, the gestures and rebellious attitude of the jamet women spurred the strongest reactions and condemnations among the middle class and white colonial elite. Significantly, notes John Cowley, in the late nineteenth century, "there was a high increase in female and juvenile convictions for crime." A report written in 1884 confirms that many of the women taken to jail were female singers, "singing at the top of their voices, as if in defiance of the law and of all decency."[23] Combined with these repressive measures, the fierce struggle of male Afro-Trinidadian chantwèls to assume leadership not only in the workplace, but also in Carnival allegedly led to the near disappearance of female chantwèls at the turn of the twentieth century.[24]

Improvement Technologies

In the aftermath of the Canboulay and the Hosay riots, the white colonial administration changed its governing technologies and, instead of using physical force, began to guide conduct through education. To control the content of the calinda and calypso songs, it had to get rid of French Creole, still in 1866 the language most people spoke, though most could also understand and speak some English."[25] Since the 1840s there had been attempts to anglicize the island. Interdenominational schools had been set up by the Mico charity, "an English organization with its board of trustees in London, that received major sums of money to educate the children of the freedmen."[26] However, only half the population, and hardly any African children, were instructed. A special commission was created to examine the problem, and renewed efforts were deployed to improve education. By 1886 literacy in English had increased, though at the expense of both French and French Creole.[27]

This change of disciplinary approach by the white colonial administration was not the result of sovereign decisions. In fact, it was mitigated by the growing involvement of the Creole middle class in sociopolitical and economic affairs. Growing significantly in number during the 1880s and 1890s, Creole professionals and business people "articulated the need for a more representative government" and "sought the modification of Crown Colony Government."[28] One way they gained a political voice was to take sides with the lower-class masses and to intervene relentlessly against any decision made by the white colonial administration and the clergy that could be deemed elitist and antiproletarian, and that could endanger Carnival.

For most members of the Creole middle class, the objective was thus not to abolish Carnival, but to improve it. In the 1890s business firms organized competitions "in which chantwèls were offered prizes for singing the best songs in promotion of the merchandise of sponsoring firms"—a practice "continued in the tents well into the 1940s."[29] Even though the tamboo bamboo (bamboo stems cut in three different sizes used as stamping tubes and tapped on the ground) that had replaced the banned drums after 1884 were never outlawed and continued to accompany singing during Carnival well into the 1930s, the organizers of singing competitions in 1919 "excluded all bamboo and bottle musicians."[30]

With these efforts deployed to "improve" Carnival masquerade and music, and with the jamet Carnival coming to an end by the 1890s, the white- and Afro-Creole middle and upper classes gradually returned to the streets to celebrate Carnival once again.[31] Their return was marked by an effort to lift Carnival above its "ugly" features. For example, a 1912 article in the newspaper *Argos* encouraged people to replace the jamet's "monstrous" costumes with "figures of continental peasants, Spanish toreadors, milkmaids."[32] Musically, individuals from the middle and even upper class attempted, according to Jacob Elder, "to improve the calypso in literary style, introducing more complex musical forms while using the litany forms of the calinda songs as the basic melodic framework."[33] Others tried to improve calypso by encouraging calypsonians to use string bands, as opposed to African instruments, for musical accompaniment. What is striking is that all these strategies aiming to "upgrade" calypso and masquerade were put to work in competitions, using the very practice of the jamets and stickfighting bands to turn it into a "respectable" European type of contest.[34]

From the 1900s to the mid-1950s, the Creole middle class grew in size and was now composed of two main groups: businessmen and intellectuals. Businessmen during this period continued their attempts to improve Carnival to make Carnival a tourist attraction for a wide range of audiences. In addition to the use of newspapers, they waged their campaign through sponsored competitions to purge Carnival of its unsavory features—in their view, its erotic elements, violence, and vulgarity—with the hope of replacing what was called the "Ole Mas" (African-derived elements) with the "Pretty Mas" (European-derived elements). Along these lines, not only were the "wining" dance movement typical of many African traditional styles based on gyrations of the waist and calypso lyrics with double meaning disparaged by the bourgeoisie and by religious groups, such as the Faithful Brothers of the Souls in Purgatory Friendship Society, in newspapers articles and other public sites, but those who performed them were also discouraged from entering any competitions.[35] Some Creole middle-class writers began sending their own lyrics to calypsonians as a means to help them improve their craft, while generally keeping themselves unknown to the public. Others tried to improve calypso melodies by proposing to use English or American melodies such as vaudeville tunes instead, and to change the words to suit the selected themes—hoping that calypso would gradually adapt itself to these so-called more aesthetically (or ideologically) pleasing sources.[36]

In 1938, under the initiative of the Port of Spain City Council, a Permanent Carnival Improvement Committee was formed to oversee the improvement of calypsos that required all calypsonians to submit their songs for scrutiny before they could be sung in tents.[37] Competitions in each tent were organized, and prizes were awarded to the winner known as the "Calypso King of the season."[38] These competitions, however, were meant to devalue calypsos based on double entendre and to elevate those considered to have serious lyrics. In 1949, the Carnival Improvement Committee made its first attempt to centralize all competitions in order to gain even more control over all Carnival performance practices and spaces. However, only in 1953 could the Committee claim to have reached its goal—a historical moment that will be discussed at length in the next chapter.

While many of the Creole middle class's efforts were devoted to "improving" calypso's music and lyrics, other efforts were still aiming at devaluing the African-derived contributions to Carnival. At the expense of all other activities in Carnival, the Carnival Queen competition from 1946 to the early 1960s was promoted as the symbol of attractiveness and as the highlight of the Dimanche Gras show. Big budgets were allocated to make this event the climax of Carnival, not only to displace the calypso competitions—the central item in Carnival competitions—but also to promote whiteness as the enduring racial reference for beauty and superiority. (Not until 1971, after much lobbying from the lower class, black nationalists, and calypsonians, did a black woman win the Carnival Queen competition.)[39] Such an impulse from the Carnival Improvement Committee reveals how its white- and Afro-Creole middle-class members were deeply marked by their ambivalent position: on the one hand, seeking to please the white colonial administration and to adopt its standards and, on the other hand, participating in African-derived traditions while simultaneously aiming to "tame" them.

From the 1900s to the mid-1950s, the white colonial administration created new laws to control calypso songs to deal with its worst fears, including a perpetual fear of scandal and also of the increasing popularity of both Marxist and black nationalist ideologies (Garveyism or any other form of militant black or proletarian ideology) among the middle and lower classes.[40] "As popular political awareness increased," Rohlehr remarks, "methods of control needed to be updated."[41] In 1920 a sedition bill was passed, and calypso tents were placed under plainclothes police surveillance. During the 1930s heavy censorship of literature, films, and songs dealing with communism or anti-imperialism was deployed to protect the colonial administration's and middle class's positions. In this context, explains Rohlehr, "the link between calypso and politics, calypsonian and politician became stronger."[42] Any song that projected a positive image of Africa or blackness or of a "Negro Worker" (and thus evoking the combination of "le rouge and le noir, being Red and being Black")[43] might be deemed threatening by the authorities. Under the Theatres and Dance Halls Ordinance in 1934 and regulations passed in 1935, calypso tents and singers were targeted: for any dancing or singing to take place in public, the organizers were required to obtain a license; any songs or ballads considered by the authorities to be "profane, indecent or obscene" were banned; calypsonians could be arrested for bringing public ridicule or contempt on any individual or section of the community.[44] In short, by resorting to the law, the white colonial administration attempted to stop calypso and Carnival from disseminating any propaganda or highlighting scandals that could destabilize its position of power. It feared that audiences would endorse any proposal to bring about change. However, these efforts proved unsuccessful: the nationalist movement held sway among the middle and lower classes and achieved independence in 1962.

Nationalist Technologies

Soon after taking office, the newly elected, predominantly Afro-Creole party in power (the PNM) sought to confirm its independence from the colonial powers culturally as well as politically. Many technologies were thus deployed to build a national culture. Several new national institutions were created, including the national library and national folkore archive.[45] Nationwide activities, such as the Prime Minister Best Village competitions, were sponsored to help develop local pride in the cultural heritage and to build a national culture.[46] Despite these efforts, the cultural expressions of the various ethnic groups remained unevenly represented. In pursuit of its own identity and economic and political interests during the colonial period, the Creole middle class had come not only to take part in Carnival, but also to regard calypso as its own cultural heritage and the popular symbol of the new nation-state.[47]

As the first prime minister of the new state government, Eric Williams proceeded to "nationalize" Carnival by announcing several important structural changes: instead of the private sector (notably, the Guardian's Neediest Cases Fund), the state would now run the Carnival. In place of the existing locally organized Carnival Improvement Committee, composed of prominent people from the private sector, the state government set up the Carnival Development Committee (CDC), appointed the committee members—usually people who "were also members of, or [had] some other close relation to the ruling political party"[48]—and promised financial help with prizes. It nationalized the calypso competitions, as well as all the other competitions held during Carnival, and placed them under the direction of the CDC, renamed in the late 1980s the National Carnival Commission (NCC).

Following these new measures, calypso, in Louis Regis's words, "was declared national music."[49] For the grand independence celebrations in 1962, a Calypso King competition was organized to mark the beginning of this new era in Trinidad's history. For Afro-Creole middle-class intellectuals and PNM politicians, calypso was the artistic expression that best presented Trinidad's worldview—even though it embodied nearly exclusively a male Afro-Trinidadian perspective. Speaking about Sparrow as the great calypsonian, the author and seminal figure in black politics C. L. R. James writes, "[His] use of the language over and over again makes memorable lines of ordinary Trinidad speech. He represents, makes known what the people really think, what they really are and how they speak."[50] For James, as well as other prominent social activists and intellectuals, calypso's emphasis on language was thought to have the power to bring change. As calypsonian Black Stalin (Leroy Calliste) later put it, "Ah mean, we get licks to learn English. So we speech is resistance language."[51] He continues: "It is important to see us through our language. . . . Of course, the music is for the world but, again, through our eyes. As we know, kaiso is more than a music. It's a way of life. Kaiso is everything: It is how we eat, how we walk. Kaiso is the anthem that things run on. That's we rhythm, we everything!"[52] It is this vision of calypso, articulated by Trinidadian nationalists, that inspired most English-speaking islands in the 1970s, then on the eve of becoming independent nation-states, to give national significance to calypso.[53] After great attempts to "improve" calypso during the colonial period, the Creole middle class, now at the head of the state, associated calypso with the processes of cultural identification and political emancipation—at least, it should be stressed, for members of the Afro-Trinidadian diaspora and of the Creole middle class then forming the leading social activists and political leaders of the country.

Many initiatives by Creole nationalist supporters helped promote calypso as national music. In the aftermath of independence, several Afro-Trinidadian scholars and journalists produced studies and articles, expanding the documentation on calypso already published during the colonial regime. As Rohlehr points out, by the 1940s, with the growing popularity of calypso in the United States, the endless controversies calypso raised on the island, and the wave of nationalism that began to rise after the "Butler riots" of 1937 (a labor union strike led by Tubal Uriah Butler that ended in a riot in 1937), Creole middle-class intellectuals began to show an interest in theorizing about the origin of calypso.[54] Although no consensus was ever reached, calypso was now considered an artform. Already in 1943, a journalist in the *Trinidad Guardian* "regarded Calypso as 'the national music of the people of Trinidad.'"[55]

To the near exclusion of all the other musics performed on the island, from the 1940s nationalists and aficionados began collecting calypso lyrics and melodies.[56] Small books focused on the origin and development of Trinidad's folk songs, claiming Trinidad as the land of calypso.[57] Short articles addressed change in calypso;[58] others focused on the calypsonians.[59] From the midsixties, detailed analyses of calypso lyrics and music began to appear in doctoral dissertations, monographs, and articles from popular and academic presses.[60] In 1966, one of the first doctoral dissertations entirely devoted to the study of calypso focused on the evolution of the "traditional" calypso and an analysis of song change.[61] A few studies focused on calypso's linguistic affinities with Yoruba traditions and African-derived religious practices such as the Shango cult still practiced in Trinidad.[62] In the 1970s, other publications examined the development of calypso, its contribution to contemporary society, and its relation to politics.[63]

In their turn, Trinidad's ministries and other state agencies promoted local calypso through education, national competitions, and regulations. In both elementary and high schools, calypso competitions were organized to encourage students to develop the rhetorical and musical skills privileged in the calypso tradition. Through national state-sponsored competitions held during Carnival, calypso as a genre thus became normalized. It became embedded in the historical imaginary of the PNM-led nationalist project, articulating the tensions between the nation-state and other Caribbean diasporas, within and among local discrepant diasporas, and within the nation-state.

Before independence, calypsonians from other countries—usually, like most Trinidadian calypsonians, from the Afro-Caribbean diaspora—could and did participate in competitions. As Rohlehr recalls, "Since the thirties, musical bands would come across from Guyana to play in Trinidad Carnival. Up until Independence Guyanese calypsonians participated. In fact, in 1957 King Fighter and Lord Coffee were both finalists in the calypsonian competition." But, he adds, "When Trinidad became this thing called a nation, immediately people kept saying, you know, you cannot have these people participating in a *national* competition."[64] As a result, even when a calypso from a foreigner was clearly the favorite in the Road March competition—as was the case with "Tourist Leggo," by Short Shirt from Antigua in 1977—the winning prize nevertheless went to the next most appreciated song by a Trinidadian composer.[65] After 1978, no Trinidadian calypsonian living abroad could be admitted to participate in the national calypso competitions—a prohibition that continues to this day.[66]

Along the same lines, songs with too many obvious "outside" influences—including those from other islands—would not be selected in the semifinals. Artists who included in their compositions musical aspects from other genres—even from the Caribbean diaspora—would be told that they were going astray. And such statements would not be uttered only by the CDC, but also by their peers, who had developed, in tandem and in tension with the calypso competitions, a specific idea of what calypso should and should not be. In an interview with Winthrop R. Holder published in 2001, Black Stalin said,

> Kaiso is always kaiso watchdog. . . . Kaisonians always watch their art for themselves. . . . Because within the last few years you notice you hear about five or six kaisos dealing with too much waving. Kaisonians coming out and looking over their own thing and saying, "There's too much waving in kaiso." So we decide for we own self to clean up the waving. We don't wait for the radio

station or anybody else to tell we that there's too much waving in calypso. . . .
When there were too many calypsongs, and people were going too song-wise
and moving away from the authentic calypso progression, Kitch sang,

> Too much calypsong
> Too much calypsong
> Bring back the old time re-minor
> Too much calypsong

That was on his '67 album he did with Ron Berridge accompaniment,
Kaisonians always try to straighten out the art and take care of the art. So
Kaiso is kaiso own watchdog![67]

By preventing migrant artists from entering competitions, excluding songs
with too many "outside" influences from being selected in the semifinals,
and admonishing artists for going "astray" with their diasporic sensibilities, these formal and informal disciplinary measures sought to produce
a musical scene articulating an isomorphism between people, place, and
culture—what Liisa Malkki refers to as "sedentarist metaphysics."[68] These
measures effectively worked to reinforce borders, identify citizens as those
rooted in the land, and construct culture as emerging only from within
the nation-state. Ironically, even though they featured nearly exclusively
the African diaspora and its diasporic experience, calypso competitions
enabled the nationalist projection of a sedentary population and a stable
artform emerging from the land.

Concomitantly, this mapping of the nation-state, its people, and culture
helped reinforce at least three disavowals:[69] that the local population of
Trinidad and Tobago was itself constituted through transnational migration; that the nation-state encompassed many different types of subjects in
terms of race, ethnicity, religion, sexual orientation, gendered roles, and so
on, and not all people rooted in the land enjoyed equal rights as citizens;
and that the cultural phenomenon celebrated—calypso—also proceeded
from transnational fusion. Put another way, the threats that the inclusion
of Afro-Trinidadian migrants, other Afro-Caribbeans, and "foreign" aesthetics in calypso competitions visibly and audibly posed seem resonant
with Barnor Hesse's study of the multicultural politics of England. First,
considering the Caribbean diaspora as transnational process would have
"deeply unsettle[d] the idea of self-contained, culturally inward-looking
national identity."[70] Second, the acknowledgment of "cultural entanglements" in sound, sight, and values would have also disrupted the idea that
national and social forms are unitary and singular.

These disavowals may help explain why a calypso such as "Split Me in Two" (1961), by the Mighty Dougla, even though highly relevant to Trinidad's society and granted a high profile the year it earned the Calypso King Song award, was soon to be forgotten.[71] "Split me in Two" describes the traumatic isolation of a child of mixed race, the dougla (the offspring of an East Indian and an Afro-Trinidadian couple), in a society marked by political division between blacks and East Indians. As Shalini Puri writes, "In the postcolonial context of racial competition, the dougla disrupts what Daniel Segal has called the system of 'racial accounting.'"[72] Its disavowal in dominant discourses of race in Trinidad has been traced by Bridget Brereton and Rhoda Reddock to "the highly vexed sex ratios within the Indian population during the period of indentureship, as well as to Hindu notions of caste endogamy. It is in this context that the pejorative term 'dougla' or bastard was initially applied to people of mixed Indian and African descent and its identity disallowed."[73] From independence to the late 1980s, the nationalization of Carnival and calypso competitions and the establishment of competition regulations deployed as political technologies to build a unitary national culture did little to address the historical erasure of either the dougla or the non-Afro-Trinidadian ethnic groups.[74] Their absence from the official sphere of the national calypso competitions served to confirm that in postcolonial Trinidad, to use M. Jacqui Alexander's insightful 1994 article title, "Not Just (Any) *Body* Can Be a Citizen."[75]

The historical prominence of calypso during the colonial regime, the nationalist movement, and the nation-building project had other tangible consequences. It diverted writers from documenting other musical practices performed by Afro-Trinidadians and any other ethnic groups. Written material about Indo-Trinidadian musical practices and sound recordings of those traditions remained scarce until the late 1970s.[76] Apart from these few efforts to promote Indo-Trinidadian music, hardly any publications or audio-visual documents exist on the musics produced and performed by the other ethnic and racial groups—the Chinese, Syrians, Lebanese, and the local whites.[77] A few studies of the "Spanish," also called "payoles" or "cocoa-pañoles" (descendants of peons from Venezuela and new immigrants) were appearing by the 1970s and focused nearly exclusively on parang, the music performed during the Christmas period.[78]

Both nationalist constructions of calypso and publications on that subject carried the sediments of the colonial past. As a result, they perpetuated the tensions between the local diasporas and socially gendered roles. Calypso continued to be marked as Afro-Trinidadian, male, and lower class. In that context, Chinese singers such as Chiang-Kai-Shiek, Rex

West, and Dr. Soca fulfilled the role of the joker by keeping the audience in stitches with practically the same acts every year.[79] As Koningsbruggen notes, they deliberately performed in a clumsy comic style, exaggerating the body movements, vocal inflexions, and mannerisms of a calypsonian so as "to confirm the firmly held conviction on the part of sectors of the public and of calypsonians themselves that this style of singing is a prerogative of the blacks." The author adds, "It is acceptable to make fun of the 'peculiarities' of the Chinese in that very area where Indians and Creoles are extremely wary of one another in public in order to avoid racial tensions. The Chinese aspirations to take part in the calypso circus are realized in buffoonery, while Indian calypsonians, such as Drupatee in the late 1980s, are eager for their calypso interpretations to be taken seriously."[80]

Artists from other groups, even though usually invisible in competitions, regularly appeared in calypso tents. Like the Chinese artists, they were usually presented as curiosities, or to produce a good laugh from the audience. A white artist who could "wine" would be featured as a curiosity (most whites are assumed not to be able to perform "wining" moves), or as a sensation (that is, as a truly unusual talent for a member of that group).[81] In the nineties, that practice continued. In two consecutive Carnivals, a couple from Germany was hired to perform in Spektakula, one of the leading calypso tents in the country. While the husband sang his calypso, the wife skillfully wined onstage in ways that produced sheer amazement from the crowd—the exception proving the rule that whites usually can't dance. Another year, an American male singer performed a calypso accompanying himself with a bagpipe—an instrument seen as incongruous as himself, a white American, in a calypso tent in Trinidad.

White performers from Trinidad rarely appeared on a calypso stage. The few exceptions over the years—including Raymond Quevedo (Atilla the Hun), Denyse Plummer, and Robert Elias (De Mighty Trini)—have more often been Portuguese (Quevedo) or Lebanese in descent, or Creole (one black parent, the other white), than French or British (descendants of the white colonial elite). While these artists from minority groups on the island have had access to the calypso tents and, in some cases, to calypso competitions, they have often been looked upon with suspicion, in tandem with their middle-class socioeconomic background (Denyse Plummer's career, exceptional in many ways, along with that of De Mighty Trini, will be discussed at length in chap. 4). Their performances might be greatly appreciated, but their talents as "true" calypsonians are often questioned. Because they often do not compose their own calypsos, but instead—thanks to their financial resources—hire some of the best calypso composers in Trinidad to provide them with songs, they are placed in a particular category in the calypso scene: included but, according to many, not fully accepted.

From independence until the mideighties, female calypsonians of any ethnicity, class, or race remained scarce in calypso competitions, following the severe earlier propaganda against their participation. In spite of disparaging remarks from family members and male calypsonians, however, some notable exceptions emerged, mainly, if not exclusively, from the black community. In 1972, Singing Francine performed as a finalist in the Dimanche Gras calypso competitions—which, in and of itself, is seen as a major achievement by any standard for aficionados of the calypso music scene. She won national recognition with her song "Carnival Fever." During the 1970s and 1980s, she performed regularly in calypso tents and in major festivals and concerts in and outside the islands.[82] Calypso Rose, in her turn, surpassed all prevailing expectations about women calypsonians by becoming in 1978 the first woman to win the calypso competition title. However, it took more than twenty years for a female calypsonian to win the title again (women's contributions to calypso will be discussed at greater length in chap. 4).

If in the aftermath of independence the PNM government initiated many activities to promote national culture, it made little use of the media.[83] Its procrastination in changing the infrastructure set up by the British colonial administration was consequential: local music continued to be marginal in daily programming. As Roger Wallis and Krister Malm report, "In the early 1980s, Trinidad had [still only] two radio companies each broadcasting a program on AM: the National Broadcasting Service (NBS), owned by the government, and Radio Trinidad, formerly owned by Rediffusion International which was part of the Lord Thomson media empire."[84] These stations opened up only FM channels—thus providing Trinidad with four domestic radio channels in all—in the mideighties. And until 1986, there was only one TV station, provided by the government-owned Trinidad and Tobago Television (TT&T). No official media policy was formulated, nor were any new licenses for radio or TV companies granted, during the thirty years of uninterrupted PNM rule.[85] Instead, ad hoc decisions and informal rulings were applied to deal with particular cases. As Robin Balliger has pointed out, "While there was an expansion of print media during Trinidad's oil boom of 1974–82, as late as 1990 there were only four radio stations and one TV station (Skinner 1990)."[86]

That the state continued centralized control of electronic media established under colonialism may be seen as not surprising, but rather in line with its desire to nationalize the sectors of activities controlled earlier by the colonial administration. More surprising, however, is that the new state hardly changed the programming.[87] For the most part, Radio Trinidad, created in 1947, continued to feature the programs selected under the British colonial regime: "BBC news eight times a day, as well as BBC soaps and a small amount of local cultural programming."[88]

This fact reflects the continuing cultural ambivalence of the Creole middle and upper class at the head of the PNM government. While it valued Carnival, calypso, and steelbands "as the major symbols of the national culture of Trinidad," it nonetheless still showed "its penchant for foreign, quasi-colonial values," according to Koningsbruggen.[89] Put another way, their decision not to change the radio programming suggests that they still saw European values as the standard of respectability and as the cultural capital synonymous with social success. Thus, calypsos received little airplay after Carnival Tuesday until, after years of heated debate in the newspapers, the official policy of Trinidad radio stations was changed in 1967. Even then, only a few calypsos were played during Lent or at any other time of the year.

The dilemma experienced by calypsonians in their dealings with broadcasters is captured eloquently by Lord Superior's "Cultural Assassination," performed in one of the calypso tents at the 1980 Carnival.[90] In his song, Lord Superior complains that, despite his arduous struggle to establish his own radio station, he has been unable to procure state permission for his venture. He musically laments that state control of radio serves to perpetuate a colonial disavowal of nonwhite Trinidadian culture. His criticism of state silencing of what he calls "local culture" is that it amounts, in his words, to cultural assassination. Significantly, in his song Lord Superior conceives of East Indian and African diasporic musics as being constitutively entangled with indigeneity grounded in locality and land.[91] The scant airplay of local music, including calypso, together with the refusal to grant licenses, signaled the burden of the colonial legacy on the elected party's members and the detrimental impact their cultural ambivalence about European and African-derived values had on the national media policy, making it rife with contradictory impulses.

Such contradictory impulses were deeply felt in the calypso music industry in relation to not only national media, but also customs duty policy. Even though the state nationalized calypso competitions, it provided hardly any economic support for calypso recordings or incentives to invest in calypso as a commodity. Similarly, even though the Afro-Creole middle-class businessmen reaped substantial benefits from tourism generated by Carnival and thus calypso, they provided little, if any, funding for the owners of recording studios producing nearly exclusively calypso.

In the 1970s "Trinidad could boast two record pressing plants and some ten recording studios." However, the owners were usually able to conduct their operations and ensure continuity only for a short time (often no more than three years), partly because of "the oil price boom producing better financial conditions for the music-makers"—which meant that calypsonians could afford to go to New York to make their recordings in state-of-the-art studios[92]—and also for the lack of governmental support. In 1981, a local record producer explained the difficulties as follows:

> In all the years we couldn't get concessions out of the government. There was no way we could afford to pay the customs duty and purchase tax required. It was something like 96 per cent. Total madness. . . . We find that the industry has had no encouragement whatsoever from the local media, from the local retail outlets and from the administration. We get absolutely no support. So it is extremely difficult to hold it together. Our industry is active three months of the year. It is this period, Christmas and Carnival. I am very happy that the papers now have given this some exposure. Later on after the Carnival, when the industry collapses, when the people become aware of that there is no such thing as a local industry, maybe I will be able to use this as support.[93]

By the end of 1982, the local record producer's gloomy prediction that the local music industry would collapse was confirmed. By then, not only had the two record-pressing plants closed down, but also only a few recording studios were still functioning. It was only after this collapse that in 1983 the Trinidad and Tobago cabinet removed the levies on local recordings coming into the country to help strengthen the local recording industry—effectively marking the beginning of a new era.[94]

Self-Governing Technologies

Caught between a white colonial administration that worked toward their complete assimilation of European values and behaviors and a Creole middle and upper class that oscillated between an aspiration to climb the ladder of social nobility and a political ambition to lead the masses, the freed slaves and their descendants depended on their own skills to survive and fight for their own welfare. By the 1860s, a vast majority of former slaves in Port of Spain had no money and no employment. Most of them lived in the worst conditions, in the back streets in wooden barracks, "divided up into rooms accommodating whole families," all competing for such basic social amenities as water and the use of a toilet.[95] With little possibility of privacy, life went on in the yard, inevitably with clashes and conflicts leading people to learn independent ways. As Koningsbruggen writes, "They needed a quick tongue to stand up to and deliver criticism. This atmosphere of constant competition led to a hierarchy of rivals, between whom a degree of relaxation of tension sometimes arose during the traditional pastime of dance, song and stickfighting." [96]

The freed slaves' anger about their wretched living conditions and rebellion against the repressive laws of the white colonial administration, the untrustworthy behavior of the Creole middle class, and the condemning church were most publicly demonstrated in Carnival. The more they were subjected to restrictions, the more they retaliated and displayed their resentment and hostility through songs of derision and other performances aimed at disturbing and shocking the upper class. Their fierce attitude increasingly permeated the annual festival to such an extent that by the 1870s, "the critics were calling the festival 'jamet Carnival'" because of the low character and social level of the street participants." [97] One of the most vivid descriptions of the jamet Carnival is provided by Brereton and is reproduced here:

> The festival was almost entirely taken over by the jamets, who had created in the backyards of Port of Spain their own sub-culture. . . . Yard 'bands' were formed. . . . The big Carnival bands were a combination of several yards bands. The jamets, who were the band members, were the singers, drummers, dancers, stickmen, prostitutes, pimps, and "bad johns" in general. They boasted their skill and bravery, verbal wit, talent in song, dance and drumming, their indifference to the law, their sexual prowess, their familiarity with jail, and sometimes their contempt for the Church.
>
> Probably the most objectionable feature of the diametre Carnival was its obscenity. Bands of prostitutes roamed the streets making indecent gestures and singing 'lewd' songs. There were also traditional masks, with explicit sexual themes. . . .
>
> Bands . . . used the days of Carnival to pay off old grudges or to increase their prestige at the expense of other bands. . . . Such affrays were, of course, illegal and numerous arrests were made each Carnival. Yet the street fights continued until the early 1880s. [98]

Following the Canboulay riots in 1881, the poorest and most marginalized population living in Port of Spain transformed the yards where they were confined into performing spaces and spaces of sociopolitical creative expression. These yards became not only the main location for rehearsals of Carnival songs of the bands, but also the refuge for stickfighting. In this context, the duels of many stickfighters were transferred into song duels,

or calypso wars, in which each opponent tried to outwit the other—
a tradition that to this day is continued by some calypsonians through
their skill at incorporating all the classical ingredients of picong.[99] The
precursors of the bamboo and coconut branch (cocyea) "tents" of the
early twentieth century,[100] the yards provided a space for calypsonians to
use more daring expressions and biting critiques that often ran counter
to the tastes and norms of those who felt more at ease in a middle-class
setting. Here the members of the disenfranchised masses dominated the
audience, and their reception of the songs not only influenced the popularity of the artists, but also exerted strong pressure on the competition
judges during their visits to the tents.[101]

To avoid the severe censorship marking this era, calypsonians developed
new subversive technologies. They now created fictions from observed
domestic situations, current events in the newspapers, and rumors.[102] They
also resorted to new forms to express their views: by the 1920s, calypso
ballads had become "the vehicle for narratives about the everyday lives
of ordinary Trinidadians"; [103] by the 1930s, calypso duets and calypso dra-
mas served to enact fictive roles to humor or ridicule particular people
or situations; [104] by the 1940s, fantasy and bizarre comedy provided an
escape from the harsh conditions of daily life; and throughout the period,
double entendre evolved as the standard technique used in songs to refer
to sex—a rhetorical technique that became an art in and of itself—and
pompous, unnatural high style similar to that used in oratorical calypso
served as a favorite tool to imbue lyrics with satire.

By the second half of the 1930s, with the recession, the growing labor
unions' unrest, the strikes, the Butler riots, and the worsening conditions
of poverty and hunger, calypsos became, in Rohlehr's words, "the major
forum for the expression of working-class dissent and satire of real or
rumoured middle-class misdemeanours." [105] Along with the wave of nationalism, calypsonians began recording their songs in vernacular English
instead of the British English imposed in Trinidad by the colonial powers. In so doing, they at once challenged the dictates of the white colonial
administration and reinforced local pride among members of the lower
class and those living in diaspora. They seem also to have promoted local
language through their songs as a way of distinguishing themselves further in the emerging regional and international recording markets.

Throughout the colonial period, members of the black lower class
fought for their rights not only through the words in their calypsos,
but also through the musical instruments they used to accompany their
songs. From the time of slavery, they met the banning of drums with
defiance and resourceful alternatives. First, the response by former slave

musicians was "to beat old boxes and bits of metal, but by the 1890s . . .
to experiment with bamboo" and develop what became known as the
tamboo bamboo.[106] Following the 1937 interdiction of using these instruments to accompany calypso songs in competitions, the playing of
tamboo bamboo almost disappeared from Port of Spain and moved to
the countryside.

During the same period, in the mid-1930s, the steel pan emerged
and quickly became a most popular instrument in poor Afro-Trinidadian
neighborhoods.[107] At first created out of an oil drum, the steel pan began
as a multipitched percussion instrument and was gradually transformed
into a mellow-sounding one with an impressive range of percussive and
melodic possibilities. Transformed into an instrument with twelve pitch
tones, it became suitable for Western classical compositions as well as
Caribbean music.

Calypso and steel pan were quickly associated with each other because
they shared similar backgrounds, political affiliations, and performance
contexts. Both were connected to Afro-Trinidadians from the most de-
prived socioeconomic areas; both were also targets of, and responses to,
the colonial regime. Even though several musical practices and people
from different ethnic groups contributed to the continual transformation of calypso and steel pan over the years, social activists and nationalists constructed both calypso and pan as essentially Afro-Trinidadian.[108]
As groups of players formed steelbands all over the country, they saw the
pan as politically signaling an Afro-Trinidadian grassroots involvement in
Carnival.

If social activists and nationalists viewed calypso as embodying "the
voice of the people," they saw the steel pan as being literally "the people's
instrument." Their partnership was both ideological and musical: ideological, because the cultural politics of both calypso and pan did not historically include all "the people," but rather enacted a particular version
of Trinidadianness; musical, because calypsonians were the first and, for a
long period, the only custodians and historians of the steel pan, recording the technical progress of the instrument in song.[109] (Lord Kitchener's
contributions to pan music will be described in chap. 5.) The result of
this partnership was mutual reinforcement. By featuring calypsos almost
exclusively during the Carnival season and in "Panorama" (the yearly
steelband competitions which started in 1963),[110] the steel pan proved
effectively "instrumental" in promoting calypso. Officially declared the
national musical instrument of Trinidad and Tobago and a national trea-
sure in September 1992, the steel pan extended its recognition to calypso
by making it its music of choice.

The fights waged by the black lower class to improve its living conditions and socioeconomic status during the colonial regime did not end with independence in 1962. In its aftermath, the psychological and institutional legacies of colonialism still loomed large. As Zeno Obi Constance reports, racism, corruption, and economic inequality were rampant. Anyone with dark skin found it impossible to obtain employment in banks and white-owned businesses. Institutions of secondary education favored the admission of whites and the fair colored whether they had ability or not. The school curricula, European oriented from the colonial days, continued to inculcate disgust and distrust of anything African or Indian. Negative attitudes toward African and African-influenced religions such as Orisha and Spiritual Baptists caused them to be ridiculed or, at best, barely tolerated. " 'Black and ugly,' 'Black and stupid,' or 'pickey head' were common insults of the day."[111] Combined with the influences of the worldwide rebellion of youth and, more important, the Civil Rights and Black Power movements in the United States, the local conditions were ripe for rebellion and revolution. Strikes, marches, political arrests, killings, and, on two occasions, states of emergency marked the 1970s in Trinidad and Tobago.

Inspired at the time by the Black Power movement, many social activists, intellectuals, and politicians formed new coalitions in response to the state's failure to address the plight of the lower-class blacks. Along these lines, the National Joint Action Committee (NJAC) was born. Formed by students protesting the discrimination allegedly suffered by Caribbean students at the University of Sir George Williams in Canada in 1969 and by members of a radical trade union movement, the political party NJAC was created that year with one main mission: to raise black consciousness and to fight for black rights.[112]

Like the white colonial administration, the Creole middle class, and the nationalists, the NJAC focused on the arts as a means to form a new society—in this case, one in which racial equality and social justice for blacks would prevail. And as in the previous historical cases, the NJAC focused on calypso as both the site and the instrument through which to change mentalities, and on competitions as its main technology to mobilize Afro-Trinidadian participants and audiences.[113] Soon after its formation in 1969, the NJAC organized its first Festival of Black Traditions in Art, and the party ran it during the 1970s and 1980s to encourage the participation of not only the young and the old, but, importantly, also women, before merging such events with yearly national calypso competitions. These competitions—including "the Young Kings, the Calypso Queen, the Calypso Pioneers (for singers between the ages of four and eight) and the Calypso Jewels (for those above the age of eight)"—continue to be held to this day and, in Regis's words, "have gone a long way towards rewarding and inspiring the artists and enriching the calypso scene."[114]

Even though the CDC (a state-sponsored agency) and the political party NJAC granted calypso institutional support and national recognition, the technologies they used to do so, competitions, brought only limited income to the artists. As had been the case since the beginning of the twentieth century, calypsonians after independence relied on their own entrepreneurial skills to survive as full-time artists. Self-employed, they competed in the marketplace for job opportunities. They managed their own careers and were responsible for disciplining themselves to produce at least two tunes to audition in the calypso tents and enter in competitions. They recorded tunes and participated in the commoditization of culture by distributing and selling their own records at local shops or directly to people. In order to be full-time calypsonians, to improve themselves as artists, and to bolster their socioeconomic conditions, they sought every opportunity to perform and to earn an income—however little it might be. Hence, while the governing technologies deployed by the state and the Creole middle class to guide calypsonians' conduct unquestionably generated particular performance conditions, they did not determine calypsonians' practices. Rather, the great number of restrictions on calypsonians produced sometimes conditions of possibility that the artists explored to the best of their abilities—making their music forever changing and thus impossible to fully control.

In Trinidad, control over sound and dance was at the core of defining colonial and postcolonial powers and boundaries. In this context, calypso figured prominently in colonial and postcolonial interventions. As a field of social management regulated by laws and policed by public morality, calypso offered the conditions of possibility to target a wide range of concerns: race and sexuality, gender and class, language and religion, as well as social order through spatial and temporal allocations. Central in the articulation of Trinidad cultural politics for more than a century, calypso constituted the terrain on which to address issues of identity and senses of (be)longing.

Over its long history, calypso has not been the object of unitary politics. Rather, an array of different constituencies competed over calypso's cultural and tangible effects. Claimants included not only the white colonial administration, nationalists, the clergy, and the Afro-Creole middle and lower class, the East Indian diaspora and other ethnic groups. They also included recording companies and cultural entrepreneurs from Trinidad and various diasporic locations. Like sexuality as described by Foucault, calypso was "useful for a great number of maneuvers and capable of serving as a point of support, as a linchpin, for the most varied strategies."[115] It foresounded contradictory political projects, positions, and practices, and was part of social formations that were highly unstable.

Calypso's definitions as much as its soundings thus greatly varied by being grounded in a multitude of heterogeneous micropractices.[116] Early in the nineteenth century, calypso emerged from the mix of African-derived songs performed on slave plantations. From the mid-nineteenth century onwards, it became the vehicle for disciplinary technologies and the selected musical expression on the island through which the white colonial administration and the Afro-Creole middle class exercised their powers. Through force, through prizes, as well as through the creative initiatives of its exponents, calypso became the recipient of an amalgamation of African, European, Latin American, and American musics and instruments—giving way simultaneously to a wide range of musical expressions. Writers on calypso in the 1920s nonetheless began to speak of calypso as a "tradition." Such invocations conjured up a long-followed practice rooted in the land and were used to attract tourists in Trinidad and to foster a foreign audience to purchase recordings. By the 1940s, both nationalists and social activists had begun to refer to calypso as an "artform," as a musical expression that demonstrates artistic skill and labor as well as musical knowledge and experience. By the 1950s, calypso had been propelled to the select platform of nationally held competitions and at the same time reached its greatest height in the North American recording music industry. By the 1960s, the calypso "artform" was confirmed as the authentic national expression of Trinidad and Tobago, in ways that disavowed its multitude of musical transformations and cultural, ethnic, racial, class, and gender exclusions.

In this chapter, attending to calypso as the target of different regimes and technologies of power helped explain not only how calypso came into view and became of public interest, but also how its characteristics emerged from competing interests and sensibilities. It showed how calypso from the outset was enmeshed in struggles over the racialization of subjects, over economic capital, and over configurations of power within and beyond Trinidad. Identifying who deployed strategies to control calypso and what sustained the discourses on calypso in turn showed that it was neither the state nor any other agency alone, but different regimes of power (linked with the state, the church, the Creole middle class, and the black lower class) that were involved. Similarly, it showed that it was not one technique alone (e.g., legal sanctions), but different types of techniques (e.g., the teaching of English and prizes) that were at work. Overall, what distinguishes the second half of the nineteenth and the twentieth century in Trinidad is the wide range of devices that were created to monitor, transform, promote, and protect calypso.

In the next chapter, I focus on calypso competitions not only because they embody many different and divergent interests and thus exemplify a nonunitary politics concerning calypso. I focus on calypso competitions also because they have been arguably one of the most highly generative technologies of power, one that has given rise to, oriented, and transformed many other practices—political, social, cultural, artistic, legal, and economic. Moreover, calypso competitions from the early 1900s have informed in crucial ways how, then and to this day, the calypso music scene and calypso music industry have been constituted.

3

Power, Practice, and Competitions

> Every Calypsonian's dream is to reach the pinnacle: the monarchy.
> Sugar Aloes, quoted by Liza Hassanali, *T&T Mirror,* 2002

This chapter concentrates on how the disciplinary technologies embodied in calypso competitions have had tangible effects on calypsonians' lives and the calypso music industry. It shows how, through their conditions of possibility and restriction, these competitions have encouraged particular musical products and markets, as well as the construction of specific social and political alliances. It also shows that, while the disciplinary technologies deployed through calypso competitions have transformed the calypso scene, they have not determined its course. Rather, their influence on the cultural politics of identity, nation, diaspora, citizenship, and national musical "tradition" through competitions has operated only relative to, or in tandem with, many other forces informing the calypso scene.

This chapter, then, focuses on the social relations, aesthetics, and material conditions that, together with the disciplinary technologies, have informed calypso competitions' audible entanglements. It also examines how calypso competitions have not only emerged from, but also constituted distinct social, economic, political, aesthetic, and physical conditions of possibility for individual and collective expressions, not to mention financial incomes in Trinidad.

In this vein, the chapter shows how the entanglements made audible and visible through calypso competitions foreground a multitude of social relations: between calypso competition judges and performers; between performers and their audiences; between the consumers and organizers or producers; and among performers. It also shows why the competitions cannot be heard in isolation. Like any musical practices, they are never "merely musical," but invariably positioned in relation to other practices—social, political, and economic.[1] While focusing on competitions, this chapter also focuses on practices that are part of the calypso music scene and cannot be separated from the dynamics that inform the competitions, including calypso tents, Road March competitions, fetes, and touring. It examines both the formal and informal networks that calypso competitions have helped to create within this musical scene. In addition, it shows how calypso competitions have been valued and positioned in relation to other musical practices (re)produced, performed, and consumed in Trinidad (e.g., soca and reggae).

Above, I refer advisedly to "aesthetics" along with the social, economic, political and physical conditions informing calypso competitions. By aesthetics, I mean not only musical sensibilities, tastes, and notions of who qualifies as a "true, true" calypsonian, but also deportment onstage, hairdo, outfits, musical training, the use and preference of particular musical instruments, and the hiring of specific arrangers. By aesthetics, then, I do not mean something "outside" material conditions, nor do I mean that analytically they can be reduced to material conditions. Rather, I imply that to speak about aesthetics, one has to speak about their entanglements with the political and the material conditions that have contributed to their articulation. In this chapter, I thus try to focus as much on the political, socioeconomic practices as on the specific soundings that are assembled in calypso competitions, attending to their distinct forms, rhythms, tempos, and affective resonances for individuals and communities.

When calypsonians complained about not having enough rehearsal time with the band supplying the accompaniment for the competition finals, they were speaking not only about material conditions that would enhance or undermine their chances of winning the title on the night of Dimanche Gras—including the budget allocated for band rehearsals, the time each calypsonian has with the band, the number of calypsonians and the number of songs that the band will accompany, and the musical competence of the musicians and of the backup singers hired to accompany the artists. They were also speaking about an ensemble of material conditions not of their own choosing yet influencing their performance, artistic expression, and potential for financial gain.

In this chapter, then, I highlight the material conditions with which competitions have been audibly entangled. Material conditions here are analytically understood as the physical location where the competitions take place (e.g., the Savannah, a field three and one-half miles in circumference where horse races were held, was historically designated as the main location where mas band, calypso, and steelband competitions took place). They also include the venue itself, the physical measurements of the permanent stage on which the competitions unfold—which, in the Savannah, is extremely large (296 feet long by 48 feet across), making it particularly difficult for a solo artist to hold the audience's attention.[2] They also include the space reserved for the media and the distance members of the audience must cover to attend the calypso competition show held at the Savannah on Dimanche Gras in the evening.

Material conditions further involve the competition infrastructure, including the Carnival Development Committee (CDC), later renamed the National Carnival Commission (NCC), which until 1998 was responsible for the selection of the jury committee and in charge of the personnel selling the tickets, ushering the patrons to the right aisles, providing security services, and so on. They also encompass the financial capital invested and generated by the patrons, the NCC, the calypsonians, and the musicians through the competitions. Additionally, they comprise the period during which the competitions are held (the season, how many days, how many hours) as well as the media that promote and broadcast competitions. In this chapter, I view material conditions as the particular assemblages of things, people, organizations, time, and space from which calypso competitions are generated. And while I see them as incorporating some sediments from the past, remnants of colonial legacies, I also see them as the products of distinct historical moments.

Competitions are by no means the only site from which to examine the material conditions informing calypso. Other performing occasions—parties, shows, tours, and recording sessions included—embody many of the same conditions, among which are relations with media, performance time allocated to each artist, and seasonal activities.[3] However, calypso competitions have historically served not only, in Gayle Wald's expression, as the "authenticating" spaces of national culture and identity in Trinidad, but also, as this chapter will show, as critical influences on many of these other calypso activities.[4] They have displayed in unique ways how the possibilities and limitations of the disciplinary technologies and material conditions in which they have unfolded have characterized calypso as a sociomusical practice. Examined over time, the competitions show how, through their institutional establishment, they have normalized the inclusion and exclusion of specific sounds, people, and identities. They also reveal how they have enabled particular markets and products, as well as formal and informal economies. Yet the competitions have also impinged on calypsonians' artistic freedom, performing schedules, access to certain circuits, development of particular collaborations, and sources of income. As political technologies used by several groups, they stand among the best-documented musical practices since the late nineteenth century in Trinidad, and thus constitute an especially rich archive for research.

This chapter focuses on calypso competitions since the time of independence. This historical period, particularly in the 1960s and 1970s, set the standards by and through which calypso competitions are held to this day. However, I begin by highlighting aspects of the competitions held during the colonial era that, until recently, have continued both to enable and to inhibit the development of certain social relations, aesthetics, material conditions, and possibilities in calypso. My recourse to the past here, as Nikolas Rose puts it, "is more a gathering of clues than a reconstruction of events."[5]

Competitions during the Colonial Era

Calypso Competitions as Pastime

Trinidad's colonial administrators did not invent the competitions that animated many of the freed slaves' recreational activities. Historical records indicate that, from the time of Emancipation, the recently freed slaves regularly engaged in "calypso wars" in which they would try to outdo each other in contests of singing and verbal skill, and in which betting typically took place. As Rohlehr reports, the "deeply ingrained spirit of competition" among members of the black population was displayed in the calypso war in a man-to-man contest of improvisation—emulating traditional stickfighting but using only words. The goal was usually not to defend against an enemy but to raise and to safeguard one's own reputation.[6] Calypso war competition was as much about entertainment as it was about prestige. Moreover, it offered through humor a means "to remind the overreacher that his identity lay within the group, and that however high he might ascend, he could be leveled."[7] Significantly, calypso competitions first took place mainly, if not exclusively, among the black population, and more specifically, among members of the lower classes.

Calypso Tents

By the 1920s, calypso as entertainment and a paid commodity was institutionalized with the creation of calypso tents. Initially built of bamboo
with coconut palms for a roof, the tents provided shelter under which
the Carnival bands could practice, learn songs, and discuss the affairs of
the band.[8] As they became major attractions, the tents were turned into
more formal spaces in which invited guests and passersby eventually had
to pay an entrance fee for their enjoyment.[9] Here, competitions helped
to draw business for the tent. Throughout the Carnival season, songsters
would visit each other's bands and compete against one another in song.
They would also perform picongs among their own tent's group, to the
delight of the audience.[10] (Picongs are songs of provocation through humor, ridicule, or insult that were composed on the spot and meant to
"defeat" one's opponent.)

The focus on competition eventually led the tents to adopt a very particular format in their show presentation—a format that would influence
the ways in which calypso concerts and parties continue to be held to
this day. Although in 1921 the calypsonian "Chieftain" Walter Douglas
attempted to run his own tent with a one-man calypso show (featuring
only himself as the main singer), his experiment did not last long. For as
soon as finances improved, he replaced his one-man show with a team
of five or six singers. The fact is that, even if it was reserved for the end
of the show, picong, or calypso war competition, remained the tent audiences' favorite attraction, and it required the participation of several singers.[11] This may be one of the reasons that calypso tents have traditionally
featured a lineup of singers.[12] At any rate, this philosophy—"the more
artists, the better"—developed by the calypso tent entrepreneurs in the
1920s to draw audiences was adopted and promoted by members of the
Creole middle class involved in coordinating calypso competitions during Carnival. It allowed them to increase their control of both the artists'
behavior and the content of their songs.

Carnival Improvement Committees

One of the first attempts to control the performances in the calypso tents
was formalized by the governor chancellor, who, in 1919, appointed the
petitioners, people from the middle and upper classes, to enhance calypso
lyrics. The committee members would visit the tents and make sugges-
tions to the singers, composers, and bandleaders; they would also send
in their recommendations to the *Argos* newspaper.[13] In 1939, a Carnival

Improvement Committee composed of the mayor, a few city counselors, and a representative of the police force was instituted, as its name suggests, to improve and also to coordinate the calypso tent activities. The Committee proposed "to hold competitions in each of the calypso tents at which prizes will be awarded, the first and second in each qualifying for a general competition to be staged at the Prince's Building at which an attractive prize either in money or kind will be awarded."[14] The winner, Rohlehr indicates, would be known as "the Calypso King of the season."[15] In spite of these efforts, however, there was no "national" Calypso King competition in any true sense. There were several Calypso King competitions held by several organizations besides the Carnival Improvement Committee; the rivalry among them meant that any claim to the title "Calypso King of the season" would be disputed by the winners of the different competitions.[16]

In 1949 the Carnival Improvement Committee announced that it intended to control all competitions in Port of Spain. After countless battles against any attempt to regulate such major features of Carnival as the parade of bands, the Dimanche Gras Queen competition, and the selection of a Calypso King, the Carnival Committee eventually prevailed. Using the philosophy "the more, the better" developed earlier by the calypso tent entrepreneurs, the committee outdid all the other organizations in the number of artists it brought to the stage and made the Dimanche Gras a showcase for the most creative talent in the country.[17] In 1953, the first true National Calypso King competition took place, and the tradition of holding national calypso competitions yearly was established.

The Norms of Calypso Competitions since the 1950s

By 1953, most of the elements that have given calypso's national competition its unique configuration had been set forth. From that time onward, the state became its main organizer. Whereas the colonial administration had worked in concert with the bourgeoisie to temper Carnival activities, after independence the PNM took over the organization of the festivities, promoting Carnival as a symbol of Trinidad and Tobago's patrimony and culture, and as a prime tourist attraction.[18] In practical terms, the state-sponsored CDC became responsible not merely for appointing the committee overseeing the calendar of Carnival celebrations and the selection of the judges. It also financed certain necessities (e.g., the rental of spaces and of sound systems and the hiring of accompanying musical bands and of security officers) for most of the major traditional competitions held during Carnival—including that of calypso. In line with PNM rhetoric, the CDC emphasized moral principles and promoted national unity, even while identifying itself mainly with members of the Creole middle class and attracting mostly participants of the black lower class. Like previous Carnival committee organizations under the colonial regime, it also attempted to exercise control, through various forms of censorship, over the content of the songs believed to threaten morality or to attack the reputation of the ruling elite.

According to Rohlehr, "Calypsonians of the 1970s—Chalkdust and Stalin, especially—felt that the Calypso Monarch competition regularly discriminated against singers of political dissent," [19] preventing such artists from participating in the finals or from winning the competitions. That perception was still widely shared in 1998, when Sugar Aloes, a strong critic of Basteo Panday, the prime minister of the time, lost the crown and placed second with his song "Ah Ready to Go to Jail." In this calypso, Sugar Aloes first called Panday's wife a "kitchen mechanic," and in a subsequent and even more blunt attack, "he crooned that she reminded him of the song 'The Lady Is A Tramp.'" [20] A few weeks after Carnival was over and the heated debates over this picong on the prime minister's wife and other calypsos criticizing the prime minister's actions and rhetorical blunders (e.g., his reference to striking teachers as "criminals" and calypsonians as "semi-literate social deviants") had calmed down, a new clause was added to the legal code: clause 7, entitled "Offensive Behavior." Similar to pieces of legislation drafted during the colonial regime, it aimed to control both dissent and criticism. [21]

Since independence, all calypso competitions have followed the same format: they are seasonal, and typically held during Carnival, except for special occasions (e.g., the anniversary of independence); they include semifinals and finals; and the winners receive prizes in cash and in kind. For the winners, in particular, the national competitions represent a major source of income—not so much because of the prizes given on such occasions but because, as will be discussed below—they serve as a passport for regional and international tours.

Occasionally, calypsos can be heard in contexts other than competitions and tents, or outside the Carnival period. They may be performed, for instance, in dancehalls by calypsonians invited for a guest appearance, or in special shows organized for a seated audience. Outside the Carnival season, their presence in Trinidad and elsewhere in the region is marginal. (Historically, the only exception took place during World War II, when calypso constituted a main source of entertainment for the American soldiers stationed at the military base at Chaguaramas, Trinidad). In the media, calypso recordings by the most successful calypsonians may

also be heard, but most observers contend that this rarely happens outside the Carnival season. In any event, the calypsonians who are invited
to perform (regardless of the occasion) or who are sponsored to make a
recording (whether in Trinidad, Barbados, the United States, Canada, or
elsewhere) are those who have made their name and reputation in the
tents and especially in the calypso competitions.

The Politics of Aesthetics and the Articulation of Artistic and Political Practices through Competitions

The implications of the calypso competitions as the organizing principle
of the calypso music industry have been both profound and manifold.
The "competition" framework has fostered not only a particular ter-
minology and particular kinds of discourses, but also specific activities,
institutions, knowledges, alliances, histories, sensibilities, hopes, and frus-
trations. It has fostered what Foucault would call a "domain," which, in
Nikolas Rose's words, "is constituted with describable conditions and
dependencies on other discourses, practices, and strategies, but whose relations with them are governed by no simple principle and unified by no
global cause." [22] So while much attention in the rest of the chapter will be
devoted to examining the ways in which calypso competitions have been
informed by different forces and have produced a series of new possibilities, strategies, and a whole range of outcomes, an equal emphasis will be
placed on showing how the tangible effects of calypso competitions are
neither the reflections nor the representations of something else.

The Politics of Musical Aesthetics

Calypso competitions gave rise to particular ways of speaking about calypsos and calypsonians and of forming opinions about them. The musical aesthetics of calypso are usually discussed in relation to the criteria
used to judge the competitions. Since the 1950s, these criteria have usually been measured as follows: melody (30 points), lyrics (30 points), rendition (20 points), presentation (10 points), and originality (10 points).[23]
(For the criteria of other competitions held during Carnival, see app. 1.)
Without question, the ways in which both songs and artists have been
presented to the audience have been greatly influenced by these categories. Read, for example, how a well-known and respected writer from
one of the leading daily newspapers in Trinidad describes the 1998 song
"Misprint," by calypsonian Pink Panther: "Pink Panther is having yet
another bumper season at Calypso Revue. In terms of *originality, concept,*

lyrics and *melody*, 'Misprint' is an outstanding piece of work."[24] Also note how another leading writer describes the talents of calypsonians entering one of the most important calypso competitions ever, namely, the Biggest Universal Calypso King Show (BUCKS), held in 1988:[25]

> Cro-Cro is the most fearless calypsonian singing today. He is not bothered by those who disagree with his style. . . . They [the judges] might cringe at his *lyrics* but they can't disagree with his flawless *diction* or his commanding *stage performance*. Much has been said of his controversial lyrics, but hardly anyone mentions his ability to weave those lyrics together in a very tight, organized way. His compositions create a sense of anticipation.
>
> Chalkdust is always the most feared of any calypsonian in a contest. He has a highly analytical mind, vast experience on *stage* and the ability to compose a new calypso for any occasion. His *lyrics* are strong and he should be given credit for his fight to keep lyrics alive when it seemed that so many contestants in past competitions were allowing lyrics to slide for music. His *integration of music and lyrics* continue to improve. . . . He has . . . the ability to be subtle in his lyrics.[26]

It could be suggested that such ways of speaking about calypsos and calypsonians are typical only during Carnival season or when they are written in relation to a given competition. However, calypsos and calypsonians receive media attention almost exclusively during that period of the year and in relation to that kind of event. And when mention of them is made in other times or circumstances, it is usually—albeit not exclusively, as will be discussed below—on the basis of such criteria that their reputation has been built, criticized, or promoted.

To speak of calypsos and calypsonians in relation to the criteria established in calypso competitions has had the double function of not only describing but also prescribing what calypsos and calypsonians should be. Even though their exact meanings are always left to interpretation—and thus are multiple and not necessarily consensual—these criteria have nonetheless been used as political technologies to define and distinguish the exceptional calypso compositions from the ordinary ones, and the stars from the amateurs. The selection of certain criteria and not others in calypso competitions has thus played a major role in shaping the evaluation of calypsos and calypsonians in very specific ways.

For example, it is instructive to note the great number of points allocated for lyrics and the absence of points allocated specifically for intonation in calypso competitions. This can mean that, in practice, while missing one word in the performance of a calypso may compromise a contestant's chances of winning the competition, singing a few notes out of tune may not. Paradoxically, however, a song judged to go astray from "traditional" calypso, to feature too many changes (usually in terms of melody and arrangement), may prevent a calypsonian from winning the Calypso Monarch title. According to several calypso aficionados, this was allegedly the case when Sparrow sang "Rose"—a composition deemed not to sound like a calypso, because of its too slow tempo and its unusual musical structure—and lost the crown.[27] The debate that ensued raised the questions not only of what changes were acceptable in calypso, but significantly, of what *the* tradition against which these changes were judged was. As Raymond Williams aptly remarks, the traditions against which change is usually posited are in fact "selective traditions," that is, "an intentionally selective version of a shaping past and a pre-shaped present, which is then powerfully operative in the process of social and cultural definition and identification."[28] Along the same lines, as Trinidadian novelist Earl Lovelace noted in relation to the steelband's historical movement, to claim new aesthetics, one has to address the political.[29]

The Articulation of Artistic and Political Practices

In calypso competitions, as in any competitions, the selection of judges and their selection of winners are as much political acts as artistic ones. The public and the contestants are well aware that the judges' qualifications (musical training and competence, personal musical tastes, knowledge and experience of specific musical genres) cannot be totally dissociated from issues of race, class, political agenda, and propaganda. The jury, as Koningsbruggen remarks, chosen by the NCC, "is clearly middle-class by nature" and hence likely to "endorse many of the objectives of the commission."[30] For this reason—sometimes before a given competition takes place, but usually after the results are known—questions are raised about whether the judges' decisions were based on fairness or fraud, or whether political bias and censorship played a role in unanticipated defeats. However, as Koningsbruggen argues, the results of calypso competitions do not necessarily reflect consensus among the jury members.[31] Many members of the jury have earned their artistic reputation working in the calypso music scene, which helps to explain their affinities with the musical tastes of the black lower class and their sympathy for many of its controversial expressions in the calypso competitions. Moreover, even though the middle class dominates the organization, its control over the competition's content and results is limited. Several other forces, including the calypsonians, the public, and commercial markets, also exercise pressure forcing the jury to make choices not necessarily corresponding to its own interests or taste.

This is well illustrated by the Mighty Sparrow, who, bypassing the official values of decency and respectability, not only won the public's favor and the crown many times, but also helped expand calypso's range of lyrical, melodic, and physical expression. His daring personality, artistic skills and sensibility, and indomitable pride played an important role in challenging and transforming both calypso and the rules of the competition that prevailed before his entry on the scene. While Sparrow may have been influenced by the trends set by earlier calypsos focusing on sexual themes to entertain the American sailors stationed at the U.S. base in Trinidad during World War II, as Rohlehr indicates, Sparrow's risqué songs became more risqué than ever before.[32] His sociopolitical commentaries set new limits for incisive criticism of the political party in power. His songs defied the norms of "tradition" and embodied new melodic structures, blending those of love ballads and folk songs. As was most likely the case for other well-known calypsonians' calypsos, some of his songs included compositions written by ghost writers—a practice that challenged the commonly held belief that "true-true" calypsonians compose their own songs. His body movements onstage celebrated sexuality, excess, and self-assertiveness in ways that redefined physical freedom in calypso performance. Unlike his predecessors and contemporaries who, before the 1970s, gave more emphasis to facial expression and comic gestures, Sparrow placed a new emphasis on synchronizing body movements, rhythm, and dance with the lyrics. As Rohlehr indicates, from the time he entered the calypso scene in the mid-1950s, Sparrow punctuated rhythmically what he was saying in songs such as "Sir Garfield Sobers," "Carnival in 68," and "Ten to One," to name only a few.[33] According to several calypso aficionados, it was Sparrow who started to "wine" onstage in a woman's style[34]—in contrast with men's traditional way of dancing calypso (e.g., Lord Kitchener's), which tended to place less importance on such body movements.

The rhetoric of national unity articulated by the political parties in power and promoted by the NCC through calypso competitions has often been subjected to severe scrutiny and even disrupted by expressions of skepticism. In 1981, Black Stalin was chosen as second runner-up with his composition "Vampire Year." As Louis Regis indicates, in this song Stalin successfully unmasked the complicity of organized religion in the political process and the fear the ganja-smoking Rastafarians aroused among politicians. He also shattered the illusion that the political parties necessarily work for the betterment of all Trinidadian citizens. Classifying the ruling elite as "blood-suckers fastening and fattening themselves on the blood of the electorate,"[35] Stalin decried class division and exploitation. Calypsos considered divisive—for example, those addressing the issue of class, and others focusing either on the division between ethnic groups (Cro Cro's "All Yuh Look for Dat" [1996]), or on the exclusion of certain people in political rhetoric (e.g., the dougla, as in the Mighty Dougla's "Split Me in Two" 1961 and De Lamo's "Trinity Is My Name" [1994])[36]—ran counter to the NCC's goal of using competition as a means of nation building. But through the crowd's support and/or the ambivalence of the jury, they nonetheless ranked among the highest entries in the competitions.

Audience pressure has been most audible at times of controversial decisions. Until the emergence of soca and other related Carnival musics competing with calypso for the limelight during Carnival, it could often be predicted that the calypso earning the strongest public support, yet failing to win the Calypso Monarch competition, would win the Road March title that year.[37] Road March competitions are based on the number of times a calypso song is heard on Carnival Tuesday (Mardi Gras). Throughout the day, steelbands or live bands playing in the back of trucks or, alternatively since the 1970s, large hi-fi systems heading mas bands on the moving wheels of large vans blast their favorite calypsos of the season all over Port of Spain until they reach the Savannah, their final destination, where they perform one last time their selected tune. This competition is supposed to represent the people's choice. Here the judges have little say; their function is simply to keep a tally of the Road Marches played at various designated spots in the city. Crowd pressure was unmistakably exercised when in 1974 Shadow lost the crown to the Mighty Sparrow. His song "Bassman" had enthralled the crowd with its new rhythmic and melodic bass line. With this new sound, which revolutionized calypso arrangements from then on, Shadow had captured the audience in the calypso tents and parties. (Shadow's contribution to the transformation of calypso's arrangement will be discussed at length in chap. 5.) His defeat in the calypso competition was avenged by the public's selection of his song as the Road March winner that year.

As Koningsbruggen points out, the influence of calypso audiences is usually exercised not only at the end, but from the start of the judging process.[38] New calypso compositions are first introduced and evaluated in the calypso tents, whose main audience, apart from a few calypso aficionados from the higher social circles, is traditionally from a black lower-class background. By the time the NCC jury visits all the tents in the weeks before Carnival weekend to choose the candidates for the semifinal, an emotionally involved public has already loudly voiced its opinion about the candidates. The jury can hardly ignore the majority's strong support for some and charged response to others during its selection. Even though the jury's decision will be influenced by its own preference, it cannot deviate too far from the public's opinion. To do so would not only damage the jury's credibility, but might create angry outbursts that could tarnish the image of Carnival as a celebration of national unity.[39] In addition to its political weight, the public also represents a market whose musical preference must be taken into consideration, if the calypso competitions are to attract patrons and promote tourism.

With the black lower class responsible for producing calypso, on the one hand, and the Creole middle class's ambivalence about it, on the other, calypso competitions constitute a fertile terrain for diverse and contrasting political and aesthetic expressions. As cultural technologies for both the privileged Creole middle class and the black lower class, they simultaneously mediate these groups' differences and ensure the vitality of the artform. Yet as a tourist attraction they also follow the whims of consumer music markets. Hence, the success of a calypso tune can hardly be said to result from any single source—whether the state-run NCC organization, the reputation of the calypsonian, or record sales—but by all of these forces combined. Nonetheless, because competitions largely function between different camps, the selection of winners is almost invariably a controversial affair. Much is at stake in the outcome: for fans who identify themselves with a particular calypsonian, their sociopolitical stances and musical tastes are under stress. For many members of the middle class, their own sense of values is at risk and may be undermined. For groups that have been to a large extent excluded from competitions (e.g., women and East Indians), their acknowledgment matters greatly and, for many, constitutes an important corrective to their feeling of near erasure in this authenticating space of the national subject, culture, and identity. For the calypsonian participants especially, male or female, their plans for the year greatly depend on the competition's outcomes. Winning for them represents not only prestige but also, in many cases, the means to earn a livelihood through the near guarantee of several contracts at home and abroad.

On Framing Success through Competitions

Success Stories

However controversial their results, calypso competitions constitute the framework within which calypsonians establish their fame, develop networks, and are offered performance contracts. In the calypso music scene, star figures are indeed not represented in the media or in published biographies according to their positions on the charts (derived from amount of radio airplay or record sales) or through promotional material prepared by agents or managers. Rather, success in the calypso music scene has usually been equated with the number of times an artist has won competitions, either over the years or within a given year. Over the past forty years, for example, the Mighty Sparrow has acquired his reputation as the king of the kings of calypso by winning not only a series of Calypso Monarch and Road March competitions, but also by winning the Calypso King of the World competition both times it was held. Lord Kitchener has been identified as a great calypso composer by having won a record number of Road March titles, and also by having created the most tunes for Panorama competitions.[40] David Rudder has been known as a success story from the time he won all three titles in 1986: the Calypso Monarch, the Junior King, and the Road March. Calypso Rose has been acknowledged as a star pioneering figure in her own right since having been the first female singer to win the Calypso Monarch and the Road March in 1978. Denyse Plummer, in her turn, has been known as the queen of the calypso scene for having won more competitions than almost anyone else in the business. (She won the National Calypso Queen competitions organized by the National Joint Action Committee four times, and one time when it was organized by the Trinbago Unified Calypsonians Organization, the Calypso Queen of the World competitions four times and the Calypso Monarch competition in 2001.) As a female calypsonian, Singing Sandra has been celebrated for having won twice the Calypso Monarch crown (in 1999 and 2003)—a feat unmatched to this day.

The fame of such stars has also been extended to artists and musicians who have worked with them. For example, musical arrangers including Frankie Francis, Art de Coteau, Pelham Goddard, and Leston Paul have made their reputations and dominated the calypso scene at different historical periods, after they were identified as responsible for arranging songs for artists who won calypso competitions.

In the same vein, lyricists (at times, composers too) have earned their reputation in the calypso scene by having supplied "winning" material to calypsonians. For example, among the most respected songwriters in Trinidad, Winsford "the Joker" Devine, is known for having composed much material for the Mighty Sparrow; he has also written for several other artists over the years, including Machel Montano, among others; Dennis Franklyn Williams, dubbed "Merchant," has also been recognized for writing songs for some of the best-known calypsonians, including Designer, Crazy, and Baron; and over the past few years, Gregory "GB" Ballantyne has earned his reputation by providing artists such as the Mighty Prowler and Kervin Dubois with songs that led them to place in the first three positions in competitions. Such composers have been widely recognized as models for other writers, as well as being the most sought-after writers for calypsonians.

Some artists are considered important in the calypso scene, even though they may have won only one competition, or none at all. Such artists, including for example, Sugar Aloes, Cro Cro, Crazy, Colin Lucas, and the Original De Fosto, have achieved their stature by having been regularly selected as finalists or semifinalists over many years. In some cases, their position in the competition results has outraged the public, bringing even greater support for these artists. This has been especially true of Shadow, who, as the subject of controversies in the judging since his turbulent entry into calypso competitions in 1974, has enjoyed the stout support of many calypso aficionados. (For the record, he finally won the Calypso Monarch title in 2000, and in 2001, both the Soca Monarch and Road March titles.)[41] The point here is that, even though calypso competitions have typically raised heated debates between (1) jury members and calypsonians, (2) the public and the jury, (3) calypsonians themselves and (4) members of the audience, they have nonetheless set the terms—or, more appropriately, the criteria—according to which these debates have taken place.[42] And that is not all. While the competitions themselves are products of particular historical conditions, they have in turn produced distinct social, aesthetic, and material conditions that have at times enabled calypsonians to develop their musical careers and at other times limited their chance of success.

In the calypso music scene, artists are introduced and confirmed as "stars," for example, through the competition's own publicity network. This network extends worldwide through the Caribbean diasporic populations and Carnival organizations. Immediately after the competition results are announced, the names of the winners are known worldwide, either through promoters attending the competitions or reliable contacts responsible for transmitting the information. Sometimes, in fact, a few days before the competitions, when the results can be easily predicted, or just hours after the competitions are over, show contracts, agreements for overseas performances, and tours are signed.

Thus, show promoters and tent managers play a key role in reinforcing the fame of calypso artists. By inviting "confirmed" calypsonians to be part of their shows, they are helping to promote and reify these artists' reputations. In the same vein, the media personalities involved in television broadcasts, radio stations, and daily newspapers reinforce the stardom conferred on calypsonians by giving the artists they believe will win—and later the artists who *have* won the competitions—more airplay, interviews, and featured articles for weeks before and after the competitions. One notable exception to the seasonal focus of most media on calypso artists was the television program called *Calypso Showcase*, initiated by calypso archivist, lyricist, and manager Alvin Daniell, in 1991 and broadcast weekly on the national television station (TT&T) until 2000.[43] It was designed to honor the lifetime achievements of some of the most renowned calypso artists through interviews, videos, and film footage of their musical biographies.

Other rituals of valorization have been developed over the past decade outside Carnival season. For example, in Trinidad, the NCC created the Top Twenty Calypso Award ceremony in 1988 to honor, usually in late December, the composers of the twenty best songs of the year. In the United States, the Sunshine Awards ceremony was created in 1989 in the American Grammy style and has since been held in New York, usually in October, to pay tribute to the creators and performing artists involved in Caribbean artforms—including calypso—according to various music categories (songs, lyrics, arrangements, productions, and so on). For calypsonians, these rituals have served to confirm the feats achieved in competitions, but they have not created new alternatives to foster recognition.

Star and Antistar System

From the organizing principle of the calypso competitions emerges what could be described as a star system and an antistar system. In line with a star system, winning a competition guarantees a calypso artist the limelight in all the local media—even if only for a few days. Television or radio broadcasts devote much attention to the two songs that have earned the artist the title in that year's competition; a summary of the artist's musical history will typically highlight such broadcasts. Winning a competition also means that the artist will be asked to perform on special occasions locally and, in addition, to take part in international tours throughout the rest of the year.[44]

Yet, from a music business point of view, the organizing principle of calypso competitions could also be seen to foster an antistar system on several counts. While it is clear that winning a calypso competition gives pride of place to an artist, such benefits last only until the next competition. Even though the former winners enjoy respect and reputation in the calypso milieu, they receive invitations to perform outside the Carnival season only if, in that year, they have participated and again ranked high in the competitions. (The exceptions are the handful of calypso artists who have won several times and demonstrated year after year their ability to compete and rank high in the competitions. Even when these artists skip a competition, they are still part of the roster of artists touring the overseas Carnivals and other special fetes.) Furthermore, if a former winner decides not to compete in a particular year but to perform only in a calypso tent, he or she will probably receive little or no local media coverage. In marketing terms, this means that the competition helps to promote artists, but for only a limited time (the Carnival season); moreover, the kind of promotion it offers is restricted to the one or two songs selected for that year's events. Radio broadcasts during Carnival time only rarely feature the winning titles from previous years, and seldom if ever any of the other songs recorded with these winning titles.[45] From this, it could be argued that calypso competitions are less about "pushing" an artist's career than about both promoting a national culture and exercising some control over its social, political, and cultural contours.

In the same vein, calypso competitions and calypso tents could be seen as contributing to an antistar system by featuring a big lineup of artists in each presentation. Based on the philosophy "the more artists, the better," promoted under the colonial regime, calypso competition finals feature from twelve to twenty performers, and calypso shows during and outside Carnival feature as many as ten performers every night. Moreover, both competitions and calypso shows hire only one band and one group of backup vocalists to supply the musical accompaniment for all singers, and they allow each artist to perform only one or two songs per night. In such a context, the artists have little opportunity to present the various aspects of their repertoire and the full range of their skills (e.g., different music styles, lyrical focuses, and compositions). Moreover, they usually have little chance to perform at their best. Given the great number of artists performing on a given night and the great number of songs they perform as a whole, the band rarely has enough time to rehearse with each individual—with the result that the accompaniment is more "in place" for some songs than for others. In the same spirit, a calypso poster, whether it is to announce a competition or a show, hardly ever features one artist alone, but rather shows many names and many faces. Only occasionally are there bigger close-up photographs of individual calypso personalities. Since the posters usually offer no other information, only an informed public can appreciate the list of guest artists, let alone identify the more experienced and most famous ones among them. Thus, it could be argued that, as in the case of competitions (albeit for different reasons), the aim of the producers organizing calypso shows has been less to promote an artist than to sell a show.

The organization of calypso competitions and calypso shows described above has had further implications for the calypso artists' individual attempts to make further inroads into the regional and international markets. Limited to singing only one or two songs at most shows, calypso artists usually lack the financial resources to hire a manager to help them promote their careers. As a result, apart from the manager working as part of the organizing team of an entire show, there is rarely any artist manager involved in the calypso milieu. The artists themselves have to deal not only with establishing and maintaining contacts, but also with negotiating contracts with the organizers of calypso shows at home and abroad. Perhaps this fact—that calypso artists have traditionally handled the business side of their artistic activities themselves—along with their love of and commitment to maintaining the artform, has contributed to the flexibility of the calypso industry. For example, while the salary for the accompanying musicians is usually fixed in advance—without the band, there can be no show—the payroll for the calypso artists may at times vary with the profits made during each evening or the series of performances during a given period. In business terms, this has often meant that no contract is signed before a performance, for artists' pay may vary in relation to the attendance at the show.

Colonial and Postcolonial Legacies in the Economy of Competitions and Their Implications for the Calypso Music Industry

The honor and prestige gained by appearing in shows remain profoundly meaningful for performers—sufficient incentive for many of them to perform for low or uncertain pay. This may help explain why, until the late 1950s, calypsonians continued to participate in the calypso competitions in spite of the marked difference in the prizes allocated for the Carnival Queen competitions and the calypso competitions. The Carnival Queen competition, organized by a local newspaper with full sponsorship, was a beauty contest aiming to promote what its sponsors, members of the Creole culture, then regarded as the ideal beauty, that is, "the somatic type of the colored with light brown skin and Caucasoid traits." [46] Until then, the focus on the Carnival Queen competition had been based on the belief that it would help Carnival gain in attractiveness what it would lose in vulgarity. In order to make it the highlight of Carnival, a disproportionate amount of prize money was allocated for the Carnival Queen competition. To justify the meager prize money given to the winners of the Calypso competition, the organizers claimed that the prestige of winning should outweigh monetary considerations and that the participants should "think more of the honour of being acclaimed King, than of 'filthy lucre.'"[47]

In 1955, however, the total amount in cash value received by the Calypso King—including $50 and a silver cup along with a return trip to Barbados—was ridiculously small compared to that received by the winner of the queen competition: approximately $7,500 in the same year.[48] It took the Carnival boycott—staged by the Mighty Sparrow, the Calypso King of 1956, and Lord Melody (Fitzroy Alexander), one of the most popular calypsonians of the time (who both refused to appear at the Carnival Dimanche Gras show, during which the final calypso competition is held), for the Carnival Development Committee to react to the demands of calypsonians to be respected as professionals.[49] Since then the prizes for the calypso competitions have been gradually adjusted, and today they represent a substantial sum of money. For example, in 1998, the top prizes in the Calypso Monarch competition in Trinidad included a Honda Civic car, TT$100,000 cash, a trophy, and other prizes.[50]

In addition to institutionalizing competitions and making them the official prestige-making agency, the colonial and postcolonial regimes have left other legacies that continue to influence how the calypso music scene operates today. For example, calypso competitions and calypso tent shows continue to be central to the Carnival season, but also restricted to it. The church's prohibition, nearly a century old, of singing or humming calypso during the Lent season or on any Sunday of the year has undoubtedly affected the ways in which calypso has been experienced, and how its reputation has been construed as a seasonal activity.[51] In the views of most calypso fans, artists, and organizers interviewed, that legacy has made it difficult for many people in the Caribbean to overcome the perception that calypso is a seasonal phenomenon.

Competitions have not only informed the ways in which calypsos and calypsonians have been defined, valued, and positioned (artistically, politically, economically, and socially). They have also shaped several other aspects of the calypso music industry. As shown in a report on the entertainment sector of Trinidad and Tobago prepared by Ralph Henry and Keith Nurse, calypso generates most of its income from performance.[52] This is the case for several reasons. Within the framework of tents and competitions, performance has been the decisive factor for winning fame and commercial success in calypso. It should be remembered that calypso competitions are judged exclusively on the basis of the artists' performances on the night of the competition. Omitting a line of text because of a memory slip, entering on the wrong beat, or failing to make contact with the public would prevent an artist from winning—regardless of his or her success outside the event. On the one hand, performance has traditionally been highly valued among members of the black population. On the other hand, piracy, sampling, bootlegging, and counterfeiting have dramatically prevented artists and publishers from getting their fair share of royalties from recordings and, as a result, led many artists to focus on performance rather than on recordings to earn incomes. In this context, competitions have played a major role in making performance central to the economy of the calypso music industry. As indicated earlier, for all the contestants, but especially for the winners, calypso competitions have represented the springboard to local show contracts, overseas performances, and tours.

The institutionalization of calypso competitions has given a particular rhythm to the economy of the calypso music industry as a whole. This can be observed in the number and frequency of calypso shows presented before, during, and after Carnival and the competitions. All calypso shows are indeed scheduled in relation to the dates when the Carnival and competitions are held. As the Carnival and competitions grow near, calypso activities intensify. In relation to the yearly calendar, calypso artists speak of a high and a low season, determined by the times during which Carnival, calypso competitions, and related calypso shows and parties take place in Trinidad and Tobago and elsewhere around the world.[53] It should be noted, however, that for the best-known artists, the low season has become quite short, since Carnival is now celebrated in different countries at different times of the year, from the month before Lent through the month of October.[54] (See app. 2 for an illustration of the list of Carnivals and festivals published in the magazine *Carnival*.)

Most calypso shows during and outside Carnival are organized according to the tent tradition and thus, as mentioned earlier, usually include between twelve and twenty performers, each limited to singing only one or two songs a night. So though they may be well known, very few calypsonians are financially wealthy, let alone millionaires. Given that performance is the main source of income and is usually done in the company of several other calypsonians, the performance fees—even for the best-known artists—are modest compared, say, to those earned by some reggae artists. For example, while the most renowned calypsonians might earn between US$3,000 and US$15,000 for a one-night performance in Trinidad in 1998, dancehall artists of the stature of Shabba Ranks or Buju Banton earned as much as US$25,000, and the lesser known ones between US$5,000 and US$10,000.[55] Even in the case of hit songs within the local, regional, and international Carnival music scene, recordings are usually sold in relatively small quantities and earn few royalties. Between 1993 and 1998, for example, most interviewed artists who are considered calypso star figures have acknowledged selling between three and five thousand copies of their yearly recordings and rarely as many as ten thousand.[56] Success in the calypso music industry has thus usually been measured not through the amount of money artists have made. Rather it has depended on their achievement within the world of calypso competitions and their criteria.

Calypso competitions have also helped to shape the economic activities relating to calypso recordings. Even though, as mentioned earlier, the focus in the calypso scene is on performance, recordings have always been seen as important, too, and their production is tied to calypso competitions. In the past, when recordings were still expensive to produce, they came as a reward to the winners who could count on supporters and sponsorship to help defray the costs of production. Over the past two decades, since making recordings has grown much cheaper, they have become a promotional tool for artists to gain public support before competitions and a prerequisite to publicizing their songs in their next performing venues.

The yearly tradition of Carnival and calypso competitions has pressured calypso artists to release a recording every year. When they are not able to release a full album on time for the Carnival season, whether for artistic or budgetary reasons, calypso artists must at the very least now release the two songs they have prepared for the upcoming competitions—either as demo copies or as part of a CD or cassette compilation. Since the 1980s, the tacit rule has been that songs entering competitions need to be aired on radio to be part of the race. As part of a strategy to gain even greater support, artists should, if they can, make these available for public sale. As a result, in either case, local recording studios have traditionally had their most financially productive period a few months before Carnival time. Today, the situation has changed somewhat; recording studios are now busy all year long. Since Carnival over the past twenty years has begun to be celebrated around the world at different times of the year, artists from different islands and from overseas are now recording their two songs for their Carnivals and local competitions at different times of the year. In all cases, however, calypso recordings continue to be conceived, produced, and released almost exclusively in relation to calypso competitions.

The pressure on calypso artists to release a recording every year has influenced the amount of money they can allot to each production. The amount of time between recordings is usually insufficient for the artists to raise enough money to cover their expenses. As a result, most calypso recordings are produced with a low budget and in quantities ranging most often between two hundred and one thousand units; if the first series has sold rapidly, they are reproduced only up to three or five thousand units. To limit the cost of studio time, recordings are often made rapidly, resulting in low sound quality—which, one could argue, makes it harder for calypso artists to be in a position to negotiate deals with major distribution companies. Furthermore, and regardless of the sound quality, large companies do not readily cater to small music industries. As the owner of Island Records, Chris Blackwell, explained in an interview: "It's very hard in the early stages to get them interested in sending two hundred pieces of something somewhere, because they're geared up for moving hundred of thousands. You've got to take the time to get the records into those markets in the early stages yourself. . . . They can't be expected initially to get that excited about sending two hundred records somewhere." [57] In summary, calypso activities have been regulated by the Carnival season and, until recently, were organized almost exclusively from and around calypso competitions. The yearly productions of calypso recordings have suffered from low production budgets and minimal distribution. Because they are released in small quantities, the sales potential of calypso records has been further undermined by lack of access to the major distribution channels that—and this is part of the vicious circle—are designed to distribute products only in large quantities. Faced with such limitations, calypso artists and organizers have had to function "outside" the conventions of the so-called mainstream music industry, following different market rules, different economic vectors, and different sets of priorities.

Formal and Informal Economic Sectors

To this day, the calypso music industry has relied on both formal and informal sectors for its operations. In ways similar to those described by anthropologist Deborah Pacini Hernandez for the Dominican popular music *bachata*,[58] contracts in the calypso music business have often been closer to informal agreements ratified only after the fact by formal documents. As noted above, calypso performance contracts are often signed not before, but after the show and calibrated to the ticket revenues made at the door. (As will be discussed in part 2, this practice is slowly changing, particularly in tandem with soca, chutney soca, and ragga soca artists.) In its turn, the degree of "formality" recording contracts exhibit often varies in relation to both the owner of the recording studio and the producer in question—in most cases, the singer or composer him- or herself. To help an artist, owners of recording studios in Trinidad have often agreed to receive a small portion of the payment at the time of recording and to wait for full payment until the artist has been able to make some money from the product.

As in the case of *bachata*, described by Hernandez, the point of greatest intersection between formal and informal economy is at the production stage. As producers of their own recordings, calypso artists often use recording studios not only at home, but also abroad, mainly in the United States and Canada, where formal contracts constitute the rule more than the exception. Artists also require the services of pressing plants and, regardless of whether they are located in the islands or abroad, have to pay these companies cash up front to cover the cost of the supplies involved (magnetic tapes, compact discs, recording covers, etc.). After these initial stages, however, the calypso music economy remains largely dependent on extended informal practices and networks.

Distribution agreements sometimes take the form of formal contracts between a calypso producer and non-Caribbean owners of big record stores such as HMV. However, because distribution agreements are usually made between the calypso artists and producers and their friends or family members, no formal documents are signed, and only verbal deals are negotiated. A certain number of recordings is usually placed in consignment at these friends' or family members' own record shops, or left with them to be distributed by hand to specific record stores in their own cities or neighborhoods (in London, New York, Toronto, and other large cities). Most of those small calypso traders do not pay taxes or keep records. In the same way, the informal network composed of disc jockeys and special fete organizers helps promote an artist's songs by playing his or her recordings, but it is not integrated into or regulated by the formal economy of the country where these activities take place.[59] At another level, the illegal dubbing and sale of cassettes and CDs at makeshift street stalls—carried out not only throughout the Caribbean but also at the different locations where overseas Carnivals are celebrated—may also be said to constitute the informal economic activities of calypso industry. While such an informal sector formed around calypso often functions without making direct payments to the artists through copyright royalties, for example, it undoubtedly allows a wide range of people otherwise excluded from the formal music industries to participate in and to be empowered by the calypso music business. For this privilege, however, the artists pay the bill.

Domestic and International Markets

From the description above, one can begin to see how many of the practices of the calypso music industry have not produced—and are not designed to produce—substantial incomes for calypso artists. Not only are the artists themselves responsible for the production costs of their recordings, but much of the profit from their recordings ends up in the pockets of others (due to transactions or uses without copyright royalties, illegal dubbing, and so forth). Their performance wages are usually relatively low (given the big lineup of artists at calypso shows) and not guaranteed, depending on ticket revenues at the door. These economic practices of the calypso music industry have forced many calypso artists to keep a day job to make ends meet. For the more famous artists, such economic conditions have led them to seize every opportunity to perform, because performance in the calypso business remains to this day the surest way to earn a living.

Over the past three decades, the creation of a multitude of overseas Carnivals has greatly benefited the more renowned calypso artists by providing them with more venues at which to perform and new pools of audiences. The various Carnival committees' strategies to plan their Carnival celebrations at different times of the year to avoid competing with other Carnivals and to attract tourists have indeed allowed more calypso artists to have more work opportunities than ever before, all year long. Concomitantly, the spread of overseas Carnivals has also served, it could be suggested, to reinforce the ways in which calypso competitions in tandem with the nationalist project have promoted a conservative politics of representation and cultivated protectionist measures for those defined as Trinidadian citizens.

The Trinidadian calypsonians who have been made stars by the competitions depend upon Caribbean diasporic populations and organizations for their living.[60] Apart from the affective, cultural, and political ties that bind them to many members of these diasporic populations, calypsonians need to maintain their social relationships with many such people in order to continue their touring schedule. This means, for example, regular phone calls and other forms of interaction. At the same time, these artists help to perpetuate the long-standing protectionist system through which, in order to receive recognition, an artist must win (or at least participate in) a calypso competition in the home-island society—Trinidad. A migrant artist relatively successful in his or her host country, who may be appreciated for providing moral and economic support to calypsonians from Trinidad during their tours, is not extended the same opportunities to perform at home (i.e., back in Trinidad). This system is reinforced within diasporic populations, meaning that overseas Carnival organizers usually invite mainly—if not exclusively—the calypsonians who have won competitions in Trinidad to perform in their concerts.

The rules of calypso competitions allow only artists living in Trinidad to participate. Established in the aftermath of independence but still in force today, they have helped perpetuate the construction of Trinidadian citizens as sedentary and as bound to Trinidad and Tobago's territory. As a result, they have simultaneously helped maintain the hegemonic position of the nation-state of Trinidad and Tobago vis-à-vis its diasporas (Trinidadians and Tobagonians living abroad) as the point of origin where "Trinidadianness" can be defined. To put it another way, the rules of calypso competitions have served to reinforce the conflation of the two terms, "state" and "nation," and their distinct realms of politics, territorial and cultural. In contrast with the competitions featuring calypso musical offshoots that now invite artists from any place and any nation to participate, calypso competitions have thus continued to be construed as what ensures both the authenticity of calypso as a tradition and the preservation of Trinidad and Tobago's patrimony, as well as what guarantees and promotes its politics of difference.

In the next chapter, I turn to the musical biographies of five artists to examine how the disciplinary technologies, social relations, aesthetics, and material conditions informing calypso competitions have been audibly entangled in their careers as calypsonians.

4

Calypsonians Onstage

> In my view the great artist is the product of a long and deeply rooted
> national tradition. . . . But the universal artist is universal because he
> is above all national. A supreme artist exercises an influence on the
> national consciousness which is incalculable. He is created by it but he
> himself illuminates and amplifies it, bringing the past up to date and
> charting the future.
>
> C. L. R. James, "The Artist in the Caribbean"[1]

This chapter focuses on calypsonians' experiences, the challenges
they face in entering the calypso music business, and the pressures and exhilaration they feel in performing its rhythms and
rites.[2] It also explores how, through calypso and calypso competitions, artists perform the tensions within the nation, between
nation and diaspora, and within and among diasporas, which
are the central preoccupations of this book. My aim here is to
cast light on how the politics of inclusion and representation in
the official rhetoric of the nation since independence has been
negotiated on "stage."

In order to accomplish this, I examine the careers of Black
Stalin, Calypso Rose, Denyse Plummer, Crazy, and De Mighty
Trini. As calypsonians, they form a heterogeneous group within
the calypso music scene in terms of race, gender, class, ethnicity,
and musical style. One of my goals in selecting these particular

artists is to destabilize notions of calypso as a unified field, as featuring one voice, one sound, and one type of body. Precisely because, as one could easily gather from the preceding chapters, "not just (any)body can be a calypsonian,"[3] this chapter investigates the permissible differences performed on the calypso stage. My aim is not to make visible and audible personae who have been overlooked in the literature on calypso. The calypsonians I selected are prominent artists whose identities as men and women, black and white performers, and representatives of particular classes and ethnic groups are well known to calypso aficionados, journalists, and researchers. I focus on these artists because they have incited public debate about the very tensions that have figured prominently in defining the nation. They have raised questions about what and who constitutes the musical tradition standing (in practice, if not officially) as emblematic of Trinidadianness, as well as what and who defines citizenship and morality in Trinidad and Tobago. Accordingly, my narration of their musical life stories is constructed around these issues and does not pretend to be exhaustive.

My choice of these five calypsonians is also motivated by the ways Trinidadian discourses have positioned them in relation to the body politics mapping citizenship and national culture.[4] In Trinidad, "race" and "ethnicity" are deployed in distinct ways: while Afro-Trinidadians, East Indians, and Chinese are racialized categories, that is, based on what are perceived as "fixed" attributes,[5] most Trinidadians refer to them in ethnic terms. In this context, ethnicity involves cultural values and practices that are usefully considered more malleable than bodies—and thus, at least in official rhetoric, more amenable to nation building. In contrast, the racialized category of whiteness is used to refer to the imperial powers, colonial and neocolonial, to white people, whether from Europe or elsewhere, who represent (and in most cases, still are) the better-off financially.[6] (Syrians and Lebanese are also recognized as white; while small in number, they include many merchants who are seen as both prominent and affluent.) Acknowledging the historical prominence of certain bodies in terms of race, ethnicity, and gender in calypso competitions illuminates how, in the performance of the nation onstage, race and ethnicity have been gendered, and gender has been racialized and ethnicized.

Another goal in examining the careers of these five calypsonians is to address individual experiences. In doing so, my hope is to avoid producing an analysis of the calypso music scene that denies its subjects—the calypsonians—their particular stories, as would a grand narrative in which pains, joys, feats, and desires were washed over with what Carolyn Kay Steedman has called "a patina of stolid emotional sameness."[7] Another reason, related to the first, is to see how the calypsonians' telling of their stories is shaped by what they know of the social world and their place within it. It is critical to know whether a calypsonian recalling past competitions or recasting the economic struggles at the beginning of his or her career is currently earning a regular income from a regular day job or cannot earn a living at all. Similarly, it helps to situate the perspective from which a calypsonian speaks if one knows that he or she has been the object of gendered discrimination or, alternately, has been considered the ideal subject within the calypso music scene. The same holds true for journalists and other writers: knowing about their own positionings helps one understand the conclusions they reach in their writings about calypsonians. The point of this study is to see how the journey of each calypsonian is told in ways that illuminate—and, at the same time, reassess—the cultural politics (personal and institutional) of past historical moments in tandem with the present in Trinidad.

My own account of the five calypsonians' careers is oriented by the issues that interest me and by my own experience over the past decade as a musician/observer and as an ethnographer of the calypso scene. After hearing and seeing the five selected calypsonians perform several times in different venues over the years, watching the audience's reactions, speaking with them, and discussing them with other calypsonians, musicians, fans, and detractors, I have also come to form my own opinion about their feats and struggles. What follows are stories that come from many other stories, at times combining and at other times emphasizing particular versions and authors, all contributing in their own ways to both the enunciation and the critical examination of the cultural politics that is the subject of this study.

Black Stalin: Emblematic Figure of Calypso

Stalin, The Bob Marley of Calypso.

> *Sun,* 22 May 1985

I always think of Stalin as a unique calypsonian . . . different from the average calypsonian. . . . I always refer to him as a poet, a historian, and a philosopher. He is a social commentator but with a difference. His tunes always carry a melody.

> Trinidadian archivist Rocky McCollin in the TT&T documentary
> *Black Stalin: One Day at a Time,* 1982

Here is a calypsonian who, over the years, has kept his artistic integrity intact. Here is a man who has fought for everything he believes in, who has used the calypso form to rail at the injustices he perceives and who has acquired a huge following to whom he is both preacher and talisman, a man really, who is a lightning rod for discontent in the society.

Editorial, *Trinidad Express*, 3 March 1987

Stalin . . . is one of Trinidad's heaviest hitters. He's won the Monarchy five times, making him one of the most frequent winners in the history of the art form. Also one of the most beloved—and perhaps the most highly respected.

American Journalist Michael Goodwin, *OffBeat*, May 1995

In 1999 he [Black Stalin] won the title of Calypso King of the World.

http://www.nalis.gov.tt/national_icons/BlackStalin.htm

I begin with the musical story of Leroy Calliste, known under the calypsonian name of "Black Stalin." Not only one of the best-known calypsonians today, he is also one whom many local observers see as a quintessential figure of calypso. Every calypsonian's story is unique, because of the juncture of particular social, economic, and historical events, activities, relationships, and discourses at specific moments during his or her life. Nonetheless, after recording the experiences of about forty seasoned calypsonians, there appear to be particular patterns about who and what defines "national culture" through calypso. Even though, during the 1960s, he let his hair grow into dreadlocks—a choice that remains unusual for most calypsonians to the present day—Stalin's sociopolitical commentaries, musical style, race, gender, and class typify what, in the popular imagination, calypsonians are all about. Hence, in many ways, Stalin provides a reference point for aspiring calypsonians, and one to which many soca artists are compared.

Black Stalin (born in 1941 in San Fernando, Trinidad) is Afro-Trinidadian. Like most calypsonians, he grew up in a low-income family, with his parents laboring in the young oil industry. Significantly for Stalin, his father was born in Grenada; as immigrants, Grenadians, like many other nationals from small islands, were long viewed with hostility because of cultural difference and competition for jobs.[8] In addition to these tensions, his father worked alongside the union leader Tubal Uria Butler, who became one of the national heroes of Trinidad. In Stalin's words, "Once your father is Grenadian and he working in the oil [industry], your house is politics."[9] From childhood, then, Stalin found himself in the midst of struggles for better living and working conditions.

Like most calypsonians, Stalin received no formal musical training, but he was exposed to music at an early age. Importantly, part of his identity as a "true, true" calypsonian derives from having grown up with the musical traditions widely believed to be fundamental to calypso. In interviews with me and in published biographies, Stalin highlights how he learned about various Afro-Trinidadian musical practices. His Trinidadian mother was a chantwèl (song leader) who used to call the hymns at a *Shango palais* (where the Shango rituals are held) and at a Spiritual Baptist church. This is what Stalin calls "my primary music school."[10] His older brother, a pan player, provided his "secondary school" by teaching him to play pan. Through his father, who was a stickfighter, Stalin also became familiar with the rhythms typical of this tradition. Along with these musical training grounds, Stalin learned about the "African art of storytelling" through such early teachers as George Jeremiah and Roy White, who were deeply involved at the time in educating youth in the history and culture of Africa.[11]

As it did for many youths in his neighborhood, and most calypsonians of his generation, Stalin's formal education ended after primary school. He took various odd jobs, working, for example, as a tally clerk at the Pointe-a-Pierre docks. But his early dream was to become a calypsonian. He first appeared onstage as a dancer, then made his calypso debut in 1959 by singing at the Good Shepherd Hall in Ste. Madeleine, in southern Trinidad. From then on, Stalin followed in the footsteps of most established calypsonians by going through the performing rites by which one then gained, and still gains, access to the calypso music scene.

First, in line with "the tradition," he adopted a calypsonian name. Until the 1980s, calypsonians were generally known under sobriquets that formed an integral part of their image. As the prominent calypso lyricist Gregory Ballantyne explains, "The very names chosen by the early calypsonians—'Spit Fire,' 'Viking,' 'Terror,' 'Tiger,' and 'Roaring Lion'— are a clear testimony that calypso is in essence a protest artform."[12] Anointing the new member into the scene, the calypsonian Lord Blakie named Leroy Calliste "the Black Stalin" at the start of his career—a name that Stalin as a neophyte never dared to question and which the sponsor never explained. Was it to signal that Calliste would rule the calypso scene so that contestations would be impossible? Whatever the reasons, by adopting the sobriquet Blackie gave him, Stalin came to be seen as an exponent of sociopolitical commentaries in calypso.

Stalin then took the next, almost unavoidable, step—unavoidable, that is, if one wants to earn a place in the calypso music scene: he entered calypso competitions. In 1962, he captured the South Crown (the winning title of the calypso competition held in the southern part of Trinidad), and he also made the semifinals in the National Calypso Monarch competition in Port of Spain. When I asked him about the importance of these competitions for him professionally, Stalin's answer was unambiguous: "It appoints you in your career."

In a milieu where recourse to "tradition" is crucial to establishing authenticity, credibility, and aesthetic and political permissibility, credentials and influences are often emphasized. In a one-hour TT&T documentary entitled *Black Stalin: One Day at a Time* (1982), Stalin's friend and fellow calypsonian Valentino, whose work between the midseventies and nineties was "rooted like Stalin in Black Power consciousness," celebrates Stalin's calypsos for carrying on the traditions of "the old school." [13] In his words, "Stalin is very roots, very rootsiful. He is re minor. I think, this is the essence of Stalin's calypsos. The re minor, his melodies, and his topics." The "re minor" melodies (melodies written in D minor) were most popular during the 1930s and 1940s; today they are regarded as "real kaiso," or truly authentic calypso. Adding legitimacy to his pedigree, Stalin explains in this 1982 video how he developed his skills by being in close conversation with calypsonians deemed the "old masters" of the trade. In the same documentary, Stalin proudly traces his musical lineage as follows: "Most of the guys from the very olden days, I sorta related to. I had the opportunity of having, you know, a little conversation with a couple of the guys, like I had a rap with Spoiler once. . . . I remember De Coteau. . . . Beginner, my personal friend and one of the men who sorta showed me around into the calypso business. . . . I had the opportunity of havin' a rap with Pretender, I spent ten years with Kitchener, I sang with Sparrow with him onstage, you know." In an interview with me, Stalin further explained how the calypsonian known as Successor influenced how he composes melodies and delivers his lyrics with a particular style of phrasing.

Stalin's apprenticeship with many of these calypsonians developed through his performances in the tents—one of the most important training grounds, if not *the* most important, in calypso. In 1964, he was hired to perform in the Original Young Brigade (OYB), the Mighty Sparrow's tent, which dominated the calypso scene at the time along with the Revue, headed by Lord Kitchener, who had recently returned from England. From 1967 to the late 1970s, he worked in Kitchener's tent, where he developed a close relationship with the legendary figure. Speaking to Alvin Daniell on his *Calypso Showcase,* Stalin tells how the song that took him to the finals in 1969, "A Tribute to Martin Luther King"—a powerful eulogy to the Civil Rights leader, celebrating his advocacy of nonviolence and his dream of racial equality—was the result of what he learned from Kitchener during those years: "Well I must say at that point, after meeting Kitchener, I was able to really understand it [calypso]. Kitchener in terms of calypso . . . if the meter isn't right, if the words don't rhyme . . . because I spent somethin' like ten years very close to him and there I sorta learned the fine art about the pen, about penning a calypso. So in 1969 when I got into the final, I was now ripe then, you know, just under Kitchener's hand and ready to go. And my, that was a beautiful year." Competitions may be rewarding for a select few: the finalists and the winners. Yet most calypsonians view them as too restrictive for at least three reasons: they limit artists' performances to no more than two songs, the judges' results are too subjective, and the normative criteria used to judge competitions stifle creativity. Like many before him, Stalin twice attempted to break away from this yoke by not entering competitions, in 1965–66 and 1976–78. But each time, he was forced to reconsider his position and accept the competitions as the gateway to regional and international tours. As he explained to me, it is through these tours *outside* the Carnival season that calypsonians have been able to increase their performing skills and prestige while also securing their incomes for the rest of the year. As he recalled, it was in the year he won the South Crown in 1962 that he first toured the Caribbean in the company of seasoned calypsonians, including Killer, Robin, Creole, and Magic.[14] And it was after reaching the finals for the first time in the national calypso competitions in 1967 that he became a recording artist with his first 45, featuring "Beat My Tune" and "Culture First."[15] Therefore, despite the constraints and demands, and fully aware of all the implications, Stalin reentered competitions in 1979 and was a contestant every year until 2000. Through the competition frame, Stalin has earned an enviable position in the calypso scene. As of 2004, he had won the Calypso Monarch competitions five times, defeating two reigning Calypso Monarchs in 1995, had been named second runner-up three times, and had been a finalist nineteen times in the Calypso Monarch competitions. In 1999, he won the most prestigious competition in which the Calypso Monarchs from many Caribbean islands compete among themselves, which earned him the title of Calypso King of the World.

Black Stalin's international reputation as a "true, true" calypsonian, to use the Trinidadian expression, has been earned by demonstrating that he excels in the artistic skills considered fundamental to the "calypso artform." Based on the local normative conception in the calypso milieu of an artist as one who combines expressive skills not only in music but in dance, poetry, and singing, "true, true" calypsonians are expected to

produce their own material. This definition has encouraged artists to develop their talents in each of these artistic domains, as indeed has been true
for Black Stalin. It has also meant that those who engage in collaborative
work with a composer, lyricist, or songwriter risk severe damage to their
reputations as calypsonians. As a result, the work of the collaborators—
especially songwriters—has traditionally not been credited on album covers. This tacit requirement that they should be the authors of what they
sing has also meant that artists singing traditional calypsos have usually
refrained from singing cover versions.[16]

   In line with this normative definition of calypsonian, Stalin has
been recognized as a champion. He sings calypso, and he composes his
own tunes and lyrics. Over the years, Stalin has been acknowledged as
a "champion calypso tunesmith" for his uncanny ability to write biting sociopolitical commentaries (e.g., "Ism Schism," warning about the
dangers of adopting political orientations uncritically, and "Nothing Eh
Strange," a stinging attack on corrupt organizations and political "systems"). Focusing on one particular character (e.g., Gene Miles in "Nothing Eh Strange") or a particular country (e.g., Grenada in "Ism Schism"),
his calypso stories make audible disturbing experiences close to "home."
At other times, Stalin skillfully sings two stories in one by using double
entendre, not to evoke sex, as is often the case in such instances, but rather
to mix party or love stories with reflections on distressing sociopolitical
conditions (e.g., "Part-Time Lover or No Full-Time Lover," a critique
of those who claim to love calypso but play instead foreign music most of
the year). In the Caribbean, Stalin's lyrics are often hailed as examples of
the true art of storytelling with all of its characteristic rhetorical prowess.
In fact, in several interviews I conducted with calypsonians, musicians,
and fans, he was consistently compared to a West African griot, whose
singing style is believed to be at the origin of calypso.[17]

   As important as lyrics are in calypso, calypsonians must be able to perform them effectively onstage in order to win public favor. In this regard,
Stalin has been acknowledged as a master of the stage for his magnetic
contact with his audience. In the calypso tents and the calypso competitions in Trinidad as well as in shows during Caribana in Toronto, I was
struck by how Stalin establishes connection with the audience from the
moment he sets foot onstage. He acts his story, moving across the stage to
address everyone in the audience. He does a few dance steps to punctuate
key lines of his lyrics, often using them as hooks and moments of relief
in his songs. The tight collaboration he nurtures with the musicians and
with the backup vocalists creates a mood of intimacy that spills beyond
the stage. This "One Love" mood, however, is at times used to mobilize

the audience to heighten political awareness of injustice. Such was the case with Stalin's electrifying performance of "Burn Dem," which won him the crown in 1987. Joining St. Peter at the gate of heaven, Stalin makes sure that all the corrupt leaders throughout history will be punished for their evil deeds and not be allowed in. Calling the names of Drake, Raleigh, Rhodes, Victoria, Mussolini, Columbus, Thatcher, Reagan, he urges Peter "to throw them all into the fires of hell." [18] Recalling his own experience of Stalin's performance the night of the finals, anthropologist Peter van Koningsbruggen writes,

> During the performance in the final, Black Stalin was dressed in a cloak which fell in capacious folds, decorated with a pattern of hellish yellow flames against a fiery red background. His rasta locks were tucked into a gigantic beret made of the same material. Gesticulating wildly, his cloak billowing around him, he ran from one end of the stage to the other, which was fenced off by figures dressed in red with blazing torches. Rockets and fireworks were launched from different parts of the stadium, which had been darkened for the occasion, and their flares seem to underline the grim message of the calypsonian. The public went out of their minds. Thousands of people stood up and danced, cheered and chanted with their clenched fists raised "burn them!" [19]

Ever since "A Tribute to Martin Luther King," Black Stalin has been associated with black politics. Accordingly, his 1979 Calypso Monarch–winning calypso "Caribbean Man" has been interpreted by many as referring only to West Indians of African descent (thereby excluding East Indians and members from other ethnic groups). Along these lines, it has been at the center of many controversies even though, according to Hollis Liverpool, that song counts West Indians among the "all of us ... from Africa, India, Syria, Jerusalem or Portugal who have had common backgrounds of toil, travel, alienation, depersonalization, dehumanization." [20] These peoples, according to this interpretation, must unite before any regional institution such as CARIFTA or CARICOM can be created. [21]

While he has insisted in several other songs on the need to unite locally and regionally (e.g., "We Can Make It If We Try," "Look at the Bright Side," and "A Message to Sundar," a tribute to Sundar Popo, the renowned East Indian artist from Trinidad), Stalin has unquestionably been recognized for his calypsos focusing on the experience of black men and women—a focus that has led many of his fans to bestow on him the affectionate nickname "Black Man." In contrast to many calypsos picturing women as the main source of men's problems, both emotional and financial, or as the object of sexual double entendres, Stalin's compositions value women's strength. Songs such as "Stay Giving Praises" (about the black woman's ability to support her black man in times of adversity), and "Black Man Feelin' to Party" (a tribute to the black woman for holding the family together and deserving the love of her black man partner after years of sacrifice), led his wife to say in the documentary *Black Stalin: One Day at a Time* that Stalin makes her proud to be a black woman.

While Stalin has complied with many of the requirements of the calypso scene—adopting a sobriquet, entering competitions—he has attempted to change others. After having performed in the tents for more than a decade, Stalin joined calypsonians Valentino, Relator, and Astor Johnson in trying to change the tent format by challenging the seasonally limited schedule and the large lineup of artists, which prevents anyone from performing more than two songs per night.[22] In 1976, the People's Kaiso Court was formed with a program designed to promote "conscious" (politically meaningful) lyrics and to feature a smaller number of calypsonians so that each could sing three or four songs per night and enjoy a wider exposure. The Court was "in session" for two years (1976 and 1977), but financial and logistical difficulties doomed it. Immediately thereafter, Stalin performed in other tents, still the most important venue for regular performance during Carnival season. He sang in a tent called the Kingdom of the Wizards, then again in Kitchener's tent, and over the past few years in the Kaiso House tent, even though all of them followed traditional procedures.[23]

Most calypsonians have been involved in the business side of calypso, and Stalin is no exception. In addition to his work organizing the People's Kaiso Court, he became an emcee in 1968 and, later on, a member of the management committee in Kitchener's tent until 1976. Like most other leading calypsonians, however, Stalin withdrew from such activities to concentrate on his work as a performer and composer.

Following a "do-it-yourself" philosophy of career planning, Stalin has worked with no official manager. With the help of a few friends and family, he has usually handled the bookings, prepared stage outfits, and organized his own concerts. Like many of his fellow calypsonians, Stalin has also been the executive producer of most of his recordings: he himself covers all expenses related to his recording projects. In addition, he has often acted as his own musical director by supplying his arranger with many of the lines for the arrangements (thus overseeing the quality of his own recordings) and by choosing his own musicians. In this respect, Stalin has enjoyed a privileged position because he has been able to work for over twenty years with one of his closest friends, the acclaimed musician Roy Cape, and his band, dubbed the Roy Cape Kaiso All Stars.

From a music business perspective, calypsonians—especially those like Stalin with so-called serious lyrics—have faced manifold problems: the lack of radio airplay and television promotion, even during the Carnival season; the near absence of coverage in the press outside Carnival time; the insufficient sources of funding for recording projects; the chronic problem of distribution; and, for the copyright owners, the financially disastrous impact of cassette piracy. As Stalin once remarked, the fight for calypso promotion, recognition, and circulation does not stop at the local level: "We still have that international fight to make kaiso [calypso] international alongside funk and reggae—a work where we get no assistance from nobody: it's still an independent war."[24]

While he believes that calypsonians should be able to make ends meet from their art, Stalin upholds a populist philosophy. In his view, "Those who try to demand big pays or big audiences can't survive long in the business with that mindset: Kaiso is for poor people; it is from poor people. These people can't afford to pay big money to go and hear you. You have to go to them. So if there is fifty people in a place to come and see me, I am happy."[25] At the same time, Stalin adds that calypso has had a very long continuous history in the music business—from the early twentieth century to the present, an unusual feat for most mainstream popular musics. "Since 1941, Kitchener is getting a penny for singing calypso; today in 1995, he is still getting money for singing calypso. It may not be enough for building a swimming pool, but plenty enough to build a bathroom—and the bathroom is there."[26] In other words, calypso has never been about big money. Nevertheless, it has provided, if only modestly, for the lives of many artists, who, Stalin believes, should be thankful, despite the hardships.

Apart from his earnest attempts to change the format of the tents and bypass competitions, Stalin's activities as a tent performer, participant in national calypso competitions, touring artist, and the manager of his own career have unfolded in ways reinforcing the tenets of the calypso music business. As an iconic figure of calypso—whether he participates in competitions or not—he performs all year long locally, regionally, and internationally in the cities where important Caribbean diasporic groups now reside.

Notwithstanding his idiosyncrasies (e.g., wearing dreadlocks), Stalin's persona as a black man from the lower class goes hand in hand with the body politics that have historically informed the definition of the calypsonian and, by extension, of the national subject onstage featuring national culture. His artistic style cultivates what is considered locally the West African griot's tradition of storytelling and the musical forms of

older generations.[27] His lyrical focus on sociopolitical commentaries en-
capsulates an aspect that has been most privileged in the literature about
calypso. While his calypsos do not challenge the normative definitions
of gender roles, they give more respect to women than many others do.[28]
Since the 1990s, in tandem with the new political landscape, in which
East Indians play an unprecedented role, his emphasis on nation building and unity among Afro-Trinidadians and East Indians is explicit both
in his lyrics and in his collaborations with East Indian artists (including
Sundar Popo and Rikki Jai) and dancers onstage and, more recently, even
on recordings (with Rikki Jai in 2003). His focus on the Afro-Caribbean
diasporic experience, his recognition of and collaboration with Indo-
Trinidadians, and his artistic support of younger calypsonians combined
with his creative skills and victories in calypso competitions all have helped
to place Stalin among the most renowned and, as journalist Michael Goodwin put it, "as one of the most beloved in the calypso music industry."

Calypso Rose: Challenging Male Hegemony in Calypso

The Undisputed Calypso Queen of the World
The only female calypsonian to have won both the National Calypso Monarch and
Road March titles. That was in 1978 with her renditions "Her Majesty" and "Come
Leh We Jam." In fact the only other calypsonians to have accomplished this musi-
cal feat are Sparrow in 1956 and 1972, and David Rudder in 1986. This year Calypso
Rose was honoured for her outstanding contributions to the artform at the annual
Caribbean Music Awards held in New York. Earlier for Carnival 1993, she was also
paid tribute to by the National Women's Action Committee at its annual Calypso
Queen show, where she was presented with a $10,000 cheque and a plaque.
Trinidad Express, 28 July 1993

For the next hour and a half she exhibited the same bounce, stamina, and brilliant
stage savvy that made her into the Queen of Calypso who recorded back-to-back
Road March titles in 1977 and 1978.
David Coffy, *Trinidadian Guardian*, 2 August 1993

"Years gone by, the whole of the Caribbean was highly religious," said Rose. "And
in Tobago where I come from they figured (especially the women's groups and the
churches) that a woman singing calypso is no woman at all."
Sonia Thomas, *Arts and Entertainment*, n.d.

Calypso Rose's musical story helps introduce key issues in the calypso
music scene in the 1960s and 1970s: the struggles of female artists in

the calypso music scene, the force of social and artistic conventions on a female calypsonian's musical practice, and the relation of both the Christian clergy and the state with calypso. Her story also highlights how the unique conditions in which artists emerge contribute to their sensibilities, desires, and limitations. It also shows how the artists' own initiatives can at times help shape the musical scene in which they participate.

In the early 1960s, Rose was struggling. Her entry into the calypso scene transgressed received notions of women's place and behavior in society. Based on their understandings of women's roles at home as mothers and wives and of calypsonians as people engaged in scandalous lifestyles—excessive drinking and numerous sexual affairs—the women's divisions in church organizations disapproved of her for taking part in a scene they considered inappropriate for women. In 1969, her song "Pudding"—which reached the finals and created a stir since, typical of the humorous style of calypso during that period, it was based on a sexual double entendre—led to a further reprimand. A Baptist minister asked Rose to change some of the lines and, reluctantly, she made a few revisions. All these pressures combined, she said in an interview with Alvin Daniell on *Calypso Showcase,* "broke my spirit." Even though her song that year had been well received by calypso tent audiences, she did not win.

In addition to the pressure exercised by women's groups and a church minister, Calypso Rose faced sexist exclusions and rigid constructions of what constitutes "calypso tradition." After losing the 1969 competition, she asked the jury why she had placed third in the competition, and they gave her two reasons: first, a woman can never win a Road March and, second, containing only three verses as opposed to the traditional four, her song was considered too short. Such answers fueled her determination for the rest of her career to fight such attempts by judges to exclude certain people from qualifying as calypso winners and their privileging of a particular calypso form. After this incident, she said, "I came punching back year after year."[29] In 1977, she won the Road March with her song "Tempo"—the first time in the history of calypso that a woman ever won any Road March competition. The next year after, in addition to winning the Calypso Queen competition for the fifth time (1972, 1973, 1974, 1977, 1978), she won the Dimanche Gras calypso competition—significantly wearing a costume based on the colors of the flag—and also the Road March. In Calypso Rose's account, her victory forced the CDC to redesignate the title Calypso King as Calypso Monarch, thereby conceding that women as well as men could be leading figures in the national forum of calypso competitions.[30]

In most interviews I conducted with other calypsonians, musicians, and fans in and outside the islands, Calypso Rose' s remarkable achievements are usually related by highlighting first and foremost her winning of the Calypso Monarch and Road March competitions in 1978. This emphasis on these two competitions, in my view, is revealing of at least two important aspects of the calypso music scene: the authoritative power not only of the male calypso competitions in granting fame and access to large markets, but also of Trinidad's own competitions in ultimately "determining" who's who in Caribbean calypso. Even though Calypso Rose had already won the Virgin Islands Calypso King competition against eleven male calypsonians in 1963[31] and the Calypso Queen competitions in Trinidad three times before (1972, 1973, 1974), only when she won the Road March in 1977 and the Calypso Monarch competition and, for the second time in a row, the Road March in 1978 were her feats as a calypsonian widely acknowledged by the local, regional, and international audiences.[32]

A specific historical conjuncture of family and nationalist politics informed Rose's experience of, and experiments with, calypso. On the one hand, she grew up away from her father, who condemned calypso, with relatives who lived in a community where the artform was vibrant. On the other hand, she received personal encouragement to sing calypso from Dr. Eric Williams, leader of the first party government in Trinidad and Tobago, at precisely the moment when he launched his political project to include all citizens in a unified nation. Known by the sobriquet of Calypso Rose, Afro-Trinidadian Linda McArthur Sandy Lewis (née Sandy) was born in Tobago in 1940. At the age of nine, she was sent to live with her father's brother and his common-law wife in Barataria, Trinidad—bringing her physically closer and exposing her more intensely to calypso's main hub of activity. Throughout her childhood, Rose loved singing and performed at school concerts. At age fifteen, she witnessed an incident that prompted her to write her first calypso, "Glass Thief," when she saw a man stealing glasses from a lady and running through the market. One year later, in 1956, already known for her performance abilities at schools, she was asked to sing for the recently elected Dr. Williams when he came to Tobago. Impressed by her performance, he encouraged her to sing in a calypso tent—a radical departure from calypso's gendered norms. At the time calypso was a male-dominated domain and calypsonians were seen as womanizers, who indulged in "easy living off immoral earnings" and "elaborate masking and self-evasion."[33] In spite of calypso's moral condemnation by the majority of those in the middle and

upper classes, in 1957 Rose auditioned, encouraged by Williams's suggestion, and was hired in the tent called Roving Brigade. From 1958 to
1961 she performed along with the Mighty Spoiler. In 1964, she moved
to Kitchener's tent.[34]

Her performance in calypso, I would argue, was probably made easier
by living away from her strict, religious father. Her father, who was a
Spiritual Baptist preacher,[35] vehemently objected to her singing a music
he believed to be demonized: "My father used to say, 'You cannot serve
two masters at the same time; you cannot serve Christ and attempt to
serve the devil.' In the good old days, these people, they thought of calypso and steelband as the devil's work. You know, so long as you are
not in the church and singing a hymn, you are singing outside of that,
that belongs to the devil." In Rose's view, neither her father nor church
groups understood then that calypso "is an art, it is our culture from Africa."[36] They still followed the legacy of the colonial regime that debased
local culture. Interestingly, in my interview with her, Rose repeatedly described calypso as an "African" artform, always positively valorizing this
cultural legacy. In this postcolonial moment, Rose's coupling of calypso
and Africa inverted a colonial technology that debased the people racialized as African and their cultural practices. Calypso Rose felt strongly
about the social importance of calypso songs and the need to carry on the
calypso tradition of "domestical, spiritual, economical, and political commentary." Undoubtedly influenced by the nationalist movement, led by
Afro-Creole leaders, which viewed calypso as emblematic of the newly
independent nation-state as well as by the Black Power movement, which
promoted the recognition of African heritage, Rose viewed with pride
calypso as African and Trinidadian.

Such national and transnational visions of political rights and redis-
tributive justice informed Rose's insistence on women's equal participation in the valorized cultural tradition of calypso. She deeply resented
gender politics that confined men and women to assigned roles. Acting
as a feminist—though not calling herself one—she wanted to show that
"whatever a man could do, a woman can do too." For her, the calypso music scene became an arena where she could fight sexist segregation.[37] As
Maude Dikobe explains in her study of female calypsonians in Trinidad,
in order to redefine gender roles and gain access to the male-dominated
preserve of calypso, women have had to accept and at the same time ma-
nipulate some of the existing conditions of the calypso scene. In so doing,
their practices have involved what Judith Butler refers to as "simultaneous
acts of subversion and collusion."[38]

Accordingly, to be part of the calypso scene, Rose followed some of the performing rites of the trade and performed in a tent, as she explained to me, "at a time when no other women were performing at such venues." When author and calypso archivist Rudolph Ottley asked Rose how she managed "to keep your talent going and also keep your dignity as a woman amongst them [all these men]," she answered by explaining how economic pragmatism and her own conduct combined to earn her male companions' help and respect:

> I was an attraction in their calypso tent. . . . They could make money because there's a woman singing in that tent and we wanna go and see that woman. . . . They had me like a sister in there and Spoiler would show points you know. . . . Back then, was like a family and even these calypsonians today, Duke and the King, Black Stalin . . . they call me sister, tanty. . . . All these guys now they have a title for me because I maintain myself in a way to be respected at all times and I have shown them respect [meaning also that she taught them respect for women?], and that is the reason I believe I am still standing today in the calypso arena.[39]

Such description highlights how, in opposition to colonial condemnations of calypso as a decadent threat to family and social morality, Rose conceives calypso as a social milieu that is imbued with the affects of kinship and respectful conduct. This, however, contrasts with the view that some female calpysonians conveyed to me, reflecting their anger at seeing some young aspiring female singers trade sexual favors for career advantage.

Like many other calypsonians before her, she began to sing in tents as a "helper." In contrast to the "contracted singers," who had a salary, helpers received whatever remained from ticket sales. When she became a contracted singer, her salary moved from five to one hundred dollars per week. By 1967, she was making one hundred fifty dollars per week.

After performing in calypso tents, Rose took what she saw as the next required step to succeed in the calypso business: in 1967, she entered competitions. In Rose's view, competitions have not always been fair to her. On several occasions, gender and aesthetic politics worked in tandem to discriminate against her. Preconceived notions that women should not sing calypso, and furthermore that they should not engage in sexual double entendre, allegedly prevented her from winning several competitions. In her summary of Rose's struggles in competitions, journalist Glenda Cadogan echoes a popular sentiment I often heard voiced. She provocatively resorts to the rhetorical expression, "it is said that" to suggest the judges' unfairness to Rose. Citing her accomplishments during the first decade of her career, Cadogan writes:

> 1967—*It is said that* Rose won the Road March with the hit, "Fire in Meh Wire," but she is denied the title as the Road March goes to a male.
>
> 1972—*It is said that* Rose came second in the Road March but the honor is given to a male. Her hit that year, "Engagement Ring."
>
> 1975—Rose officially wins the second prize for Road March. Lord Kitchener wins by one point.
>
> 1977—Rose is awarded the Class II Silver Merit of Trinidad and Tobago, one of the nation's highest honors.
>
> 1978—*Everybody's* celebrates its first anniversary by honoring some individuals. Rose is named as its Woman of the Year.
>
> 1978—Rose becomes the first . . . woman to win the National Monarch title of Trinidad and Tobago. Her two tunes also come first and second in the Road March as she retains the Road March title.[40]

Unlike Sparrow, who continued to enter competitions after winning two titles in the same year, Rose never reentered competitions after winning the Calypso Monarch, the Road March, and the Calypso Queen titles in 1978. By then, she had moved to New York (in 1977) and was focusing on other markets, not only in North America, but also in Africa, Europe, and Central and South America. To this day, very few calypsonians—male or female—have been able to maintain a high profile in the calypso scene after moving outside the Caribbean. Rose, however, along with the Mighty Sparrow, is one of the few exceptions. She continues to perform all year round, both at home and abroad. Using the business acumen she developed over the years, in the early nineties she even dabbled in the calypso business by opening a tent in two consecutive years—a bold venture she had to abandon because of financial losses. As a result of all these activities, since the midseventies she has received more than fifty awards recognizing her contributions as a calypsonian and a "top female" artist. She has also been the guest of honor in several countries, including Liberia and Belize. She has toured in the Caribbean, Europe, Africa, North America, and Central and South America.

While Rose radically transgressed a core convention of kaiso early in her career by performing in a male-dominated milieu, she actively endorsed main tenets of a hegemonic calypso "tradition." In accordance with the usual definitions of a "true, true calypsonian," Rose composes her own tunes and lyrics. Repeating the requirement that calypsonians must compose the tunes they sing, she uses this definition to explain why

many women "have not lasted in the calypso scene. It is because they
have not written their own material." In fact, few female calpysonians
have written their own songs and even fewer play an instrument—a skill
Rose acquired and honed on a guitar and keyboards while observing men
play. Moreover, she also composes songs for other calypsonians, making
her an all the more unique figure. Despite her musical skills, however, like
many of her male counterparts, Rose gives carte blanche to her arrangers
and does not question their decisions.

Like Black Stalin, Rose established her pedigree with reference to legendary figures of her era. In so doing, she positioned the bouncy rhythms
of her songs, the lyrical strategies she uses in her compositions, and her
dancing style in line with the artists who became canonical figures in calypso. In particular, she speaks of the Mighty Spoiler and Sparrow as having greatly influenced her musical orientation. These two artists made
a profound impression on her, especially in the ways they composed
and performed both humorous songs and sociopolitical commentaries,
and Rose's early goal was to carry on this legacy throughout her career.
In this vein, she composed many sociopolitical commentaries, including "No Madam," addressing the socioeconomic plight of women. This
tune addresses the disgracefully poor salaries of women domestics, who,
after doing all the household chores, would earn only twenty dollars a
month. She also composed several sexual double-entendre songs, which
have enthralled her audiences and become hits. Among these, "Fire in
Meh Wire" quickly became a classic in her repertoire. It is an up-tempo,
party style of calypso, in which she begs her neighbor Ramsing to come
extinguish her fire. When I saw her perform this song in a show at the
Normandy "Under the Tree" (the name of the show series organized by
the hotel Normandy), her teasing smile, winks at nearby fans, and playful
"wining," made the audience "get on." Her expressive and explicit rendition of the sexual innuendo with groans, moans, and suggestive pelvic
movements in fact reminded me, as it has many other people, of Sparrow's
mesmerizing performing style.[41]

In one interview with me, Calypso Rose confirmed Sparrow's influence on how she delivers her songs. As she recounts, "I had heard Sparrow with Jean and Dinah in 1956 and I thought, oooh! That guy has talent.... I had never seen Sparrow in those times, but I just visualized him
moving. . . . He was one of my mentors. . . . His voice, very captivating.
By the voice, I knew his movements and what he was doing."

Emulating her mentor, Rose focuses on stage performance. And in
interviews today, she attributes her enduring success to her capacity to

move audiences during her performances. However, her sensual dancing has been attacked more than once. As Dikobe explains, in the 1970s, "her aggressive professional behavior, forcing her way on stage and into the calypso industry, led to rumors that she was a lesbian"—a common tactic in Trinidad for denigrating women.[42] Her refusal to conform to so-called nice and decent woman's behavior often gave rise to criticism, as when "the *Guardian* and Evening News deemed her the 'Queen of Smut.'"[43] Her unabashed play with sexual references, gestures, and props—using, for example, the microphone as a phallic symbol,[44] associated with male performers' personae and prerogatives—angered many people, including feminists, church members, and male chauvinists. I interpret such negative responses to Rose as public sentiments expressing judgments that fault her for socially reproducing oppressive gender relations, defying women's proper role as the bearer of family values, and displaying conduct deemed vulgar and immoral. In response to such attacks, Rose has asserted that certain instruments, like the drums and the bass, command her expressive response, and certain lyrics require her to mimic their meaning physically. In spite of the disparaging remarks, Rose continued to sing and perform in her expressive style, in defiance of sexist segregation and Victorian rules aiming, in her words, "to stifle the culture."[45]

Rather than lacking morality, Rose has emphasized how spirituality is crucial to her musical sensibilities and diasporic affinities. In speaking to me about those artists who made a profound impression on her, Rose mentioned Mahalia Jackson, the great African-American gospel singer. Sharing a similar Baptist religious background, she was impressed not only by Jackson's remarkable artistic abilities and achievements, but also by the ways she kept her faith and political support for the Civil Rights movement central throughout her career. In her own way, Rose explained, she attempted to do the same: while still performing calypso, in 1987 she became an ordained minister—ironically following in the footsteps of the father who disapproved of the very music through which she has explored her spirituality. Rose has repeatedly described her affinity with African-American spirituals as "the African aspect" in her calypso performances, a point echoed in most published interviews and in my meetings with her. In reaction to state laws prohibiting the practice of African and Afro-Christian-related cults until relatively recently, she often made audible the sounds of her Baptist upbringing in her compositions:[46]

If you should listen to the calypso that won the National Monarch title "I Thank Thee." I thanked the Baptist religion. There are so many people out there in this country [Trinidad and Tobago] who are Baptist or Shango-Baptist or Adventist or Pentecostal, but they are ashamed to own it. I don't know why. . . . So, if I am a calypsonian, why should I be ashamed to own my religion? Hell no! I'll tell the world, I am a true, born Spiritual Baptist. If you listen to the tune "Come Leh We Jam," that tune is a deep adaptation of Baptist and that is something that I did not really think to create. That tune was given to me while sleeping or astral traveling. That's me and you can't take it out.

Along with her adamant fight against legislation aiming to eradicate the practice of Afro-related religious practices, Calypso Rose has been a fervent advocate for women's rights. Here is how she encouraged young women to emancipate themselves from sexist understandings and practices to assert their political rights:

> Long ago, the parents have three sons and three daughters and they would spend the money to send the sons abroad to study law and doctor. And they will send the daughters to learn to sew and learn to cook because that, they figure, is the women's world. God did not tell us women must stay in the kitchen and make babies all the time and the men go and educate themselves. They are equal opportunities out there for all persons in the world. In the musical industry, long ago, there were fear within the female genders. If I go and sing in a short pants, what would they say? If I do this, what they would say? But now? They have voices, and we have voices. We stand up to be recognized. We stand up to be counted. So, women should be able to hold their role in any position, or any type, of things they want to do. Do not let this gender thing keep you down. Liberate yourself. That is what I taught myself. And I thank God for that. If I had not taught myself, I would not be Calypso Rose the way I am.

On the one hand, Rose is recognized by the great majority of female artists in calypso and soca as having greatly facilitated women's participation in the national forum of calypso. On the other hand, it could be suggested that through her own success she has further reinforced the dominance of Afro-Trinidadians in embodying the national subject in the authenticating space of Carnival. During the course of her career, she has not made racial tension or unity a central issue, but has rather assumed the central position of Afro-Trinidadians in calypso. Like Stalin, she claims a pedigree that emphasizes "African" heritage in her approach to the artform. Unlike him, however, she places spirituality at the heart of her calypso compositions and of her creative, thinking self. While Stalin has expressed his connection to the United States through black politics,

Rose has enunciated hers through a spirituality she feels links her to African-Americans.

Rose followed the normative career trajectory of calypsonians by first performing in tents and then entering competitions, but she also defied that convention in at least two ways: she moved to New York in 1977 and stopped entering competitions in 1978. In so doing, she challenged the construction that authentic culture can only emerge within that nation-state—the "sedentarist metaphysics" that establishes an isomorphic relation between nation, place, and culture.

Artistically, Rose has performed calypso, the "national culture," according to the terms set by male calypsonians. She composes her own songs, plays musical instruments, and adopts a deportment onstage similar to that of male performers. Like them, she writes songs with sexual double entendre that indulge in play while also socially reproducing gender stereotypes. Her asserted goal, however, has been to demonstrate that female calypsonians can be as strong artistically as their male counterparts. Moreover, women, she underscores, can actually "beat" men in calypso competitions—which she did in 1978—in what had become over the years their exclusive domain. For Rose, her most important achievement has been precisely that: to open doors, to "set the standards" for other generations of female calypsonians and, most important, to demonstrate that women can be "true, true" kaisonians and also among the most successful ones. Her efforts to redefine gender politics in the calypso music scene have been deployed not so much by relying on the lyrical content of her songs as by capitalizing on calypso's performative power—one she embodies through relentless touring and appearances in Carnival circuits. Through the duration and intensity of her long career, she has greatly increased women's visibility as calypsonians.[47]

Denyse Plummer: Bringing Whiteness Onstage

Denyse Plummer convincingly wins TUCO's Queen title
The former Calypso Queen of the World sealed the victory with the presentation of her second offering, the popular, patriotic "Nah Leaving." Her customary flamboyant costuming, aided by a troupe of gold-coloured moko jumbies dancing away in the auditorium added the finishing touches to the winning performance.

David Cuffy, *Newsday*, 14 February 2001

It was a class act from a lady who has endeared herself to her country by her sterling performances, jumpy calypsos and abiding patriotism.

Ken Ali, *Sunday Punch*, 17 February 1991

People want something more than hearing a song, they want to see something, hence, my costuming.

Denyse Plummer in an interview with Angela Fox, *Sunday Punch*, 16 February 1992

Denyse Plummer had much working against her when she began her career in the calypso music scene. Her white skin—which, regardless of her own social background, associated her with the middle or upper class—combined with her socially gendered position as a woman and her association with nightclub performances as a ballad singer caused many Afro-Trinidadians to resent her. However, she was able to overcome prejudice and dislike and earn the title of the Queen of the calypso scene by having won more competitions than any other woman in the business. She won the National Calypso Queen competitions organized by the National Joint Action Committee four times, and once also when it was organized by the Trinbago Unified Calypsonians Organization (TUCO). She also won the Calypso Queen of the World competitions four times, and the Calypso Monarch competition once (2001).

Plummer's musical story shows how issues of race and class have infused calypso and fomented great tension. It also highlights how calypso as a selective musical tradition has produced boundaries of exclusion. Furthermore, her story reveals how negative stereotypes about calypso among the middle and upper classes have severely restricted artists from such classes from entering the calypso musical arena. Denyse Plummer was born in 1953. Even though she is "Creole" by local definition in having a white father and a black mother, her phenotypes combined with her middle-class background cause her to be perceived as white.[48] When she was fourteen years old, Plummer had already decided to become a singer. However, because of the stigma—the smutty image—attached to women singing calypsos at that time, she chose to be a pop singer, performing a wide musical repertoire at nightclubs. She entered the calypso scene relatively late (at the age of thirty-four) after one of the most famous pan arrangers, Boogsie Sharpe, asked her to sing the song he had just composed for the Panorama competitions.

Plummer confessed that she had three limitations: "My first limitation was that I had never done calypso before; my second limitation is that I was white and all calypsonians were black—calypsonians form a black culture; and I was a pop singer."[49] However, for Sharpe, her musical abilities and experiences honed in nightclubs trumped her limitations and would enable her to compete successfully as a calypso contestant.

Combined with Sharpe's providential offer and her desire to become involved in the calypso music scene, she decided to enter competitions.

> So I went down to the semifinals, which Trinidad describes as the "cultural graveyard." Because that is a very difficult audience and even their own people, people that they like . . . if they don't particularly like the song, they usually stone you, they send missiles at you . . . a lot of people have been subjected to that.
>
> So I knew that it was going to be an initiation ceremony. I knew that they were waiting on me and that they were going to give to me, good and proper. So said so done, I got on the stage, I had two songs to compete and most people who are stoned, they leave right away and they never finished their second song or their first song and they leave crying and in a mess.
>
> Story for me before backstage that they had placards out there waiting on me and missiles and so on. . . . I prayed very hard before I went out there and I knew, I said to myself I am going to finish this, because this is silly. If it's because I was not singing good or my songs were bad, I could understand. If it's just because of the color of my skin, and I am a Trinidadian and this culture is mine, I was born and bred here. To me, I became very vindictive and I went out there very angry, not showing it in my face, but determined that they are not going to stop me from doing my culture. So I went out there, so said so done, every missile came at me, then, you know, you cut an orange and you suck it and they rub it in the ground, the dirt and they throw that at you, toilet paper, putties . . . beer bottles, everything came at me. What I did is that I sort of picked up the toilet paper and the missiles and turned them in as part of the act and made it into a choreography and the people couldn't believe what I was doing. By the end of the performance, they were applauding . . . and basically it is just a group of about thirty people who come to the front out of fifteen thousand people and they are the ones who are there to do it to you. But the other people saw the strength and the courage . . . and they sort of applauded. . . . I make it sound as though it was easy for me, but it was the most terrible experience I have ever been through, I wouldn't wish it on a dog, and it's just that God saw me through to the end and that's how I started eight years ago and I realized that I was doing it well.

Plummer rebelled against the racialization of citizenship and national culture. She challenged the implicit politics of exclusion based on race and class that animated calypso, the musical tradition understood to be emblematic of the nation-state. As she explained to me, "You know, our national anthem says, 'Every creed and race find an equal place and may God bless our Nation.' How can you have a national anthem like that and every creed and race cannot be a part of their country and their culture. I thought it was nonsense and I have always been a fighter ever since I was young." Even though a few other women were involved in the calypso music scene at that time, including the United Sisters—Singing Sandra, Lady B, Marvellous Marva, and Tigress—Twiggy, Abbi Blackman, Lady Wonder, and Lady Iere, Plummer remarked that she fought her way into the scene without their help. Here racial tensions seemingly trumped socially gendered bonding. Especially at the beginning of her career, Plummer was encouraged to learn about performing calypso by men. She worked closely with influential calypsonians and pan arrangers such as Black Stalin and Boogsie Sharpe, who, as she often acknowledges in interviews, have profoundly influenced her career. As Calypso Rose did with Spoiler, Plummer learned from Stalin how to perform in the idiomatic calypso style, including, for instance, how to phrase her lyrics and where to breathe during her song to produce powerful rhythmic delivery.

Unlike Rose's calypsos, however, Plummer's songs do not address religious issues and have little feminist content. The notable exception is "Woman Is Boss," a celebration of women's abilities in whatever they do, which in 1988 led her to great acclaim and instant recognition in the calypso music scene.[50] While some of her songs, such as "The Message," address children's experiences and education, most of her lyrics focus on Trinidad as territory and nation—leading journalist Ken Ali to refer to her "abiding patriotism." Many of her calypsos, including "La Trinity," "Together Right Here," "A Nation Forges On," and, more recently, "Nah Leaving," all refer to the beauty and riches of Trinidad and Tobago, the strength of its people and unity among them—the latter celebrating what she, as "white" and as a woman, presumably would like to see. Even though she admits to problems in Trinidad—"They say meh country so stressful, so tense . . . with race hate . . . too much violence"—her position is "Nah Leaving." As she previously explains in "Together Right Here," "My country, my Trinidad, for me to leave you, I must be mad."[51]

When I asked about her contributions to the calypso world, she answered:

> D.P. Basically, what keeps me going in this business is what I think that I do
> to make a difference: bridging the gap among races in my culture is some-
> thing that I cherish very much; the total uplifting of women in all aspects
> of life; the educating of the children to stay away from negative forces and
> showing them positive forces. And also my music is different from the

traditional calypso and soca music. If you listen to my albums, the beat and the melody lines are more modern, they are more crossover, they are more world beat, and I think that it's important if you want to reach the young children, because everything is changing, and the more you modernize your music, the more ears you get to listening to you. So, I concentrate on the youth, where I think the problems are most important. That is the reason I tend to have my melody and rhythms a little more modernized.

J.G. Can you tell me more about your views concerning the use of new music technology in calypso?

D.P. Yes, because we want to get the music to an international standard. I mean, you want calypso or soca artists at the Academy Awards, the Grammies, the whatever, in America. That is not going to happen until it is recognized internationally as a type of music. Reggae has already gotten there.

On the one hand, Plummer emphasizes how she understands her calypso practice as performing cultural work locally: promoting both national unity in multiracial Trinidad and gender equality and providing educational guidance to youth. On the other hand, she highlights how musical standards for local youth are deeply tied to international use of modern sound technology, linking local sensibilities to other musics and places. In this perspective, she views the valorization and commercial success of Trinidadian calypso as being greatly connected to the United States' recognition of the artform by its most prominent music institutions.

Plummer's conception of calypso as having both cultural and commercial value resonates with the views of Afro-Creole middle-class members during the colonial regime and political leaders during the nation-building era who conceived Carnival and calypso as both performing and reinforcing worldviews and mores and providing sources of national incomes. In the same way, her notion of calypso as doing cultural work is not antithetical to making money, particularly in relation to benefiting the country of Trinidad. As she explains, "I am of no use to my country if I can't try to open that door and get our music understood internationally and recognized. At the same time I have to sell my country and my culture to bring foreigners in for Carnival, so that U.S. money can come in to our country and our economy can flourish. The job of every calypsonian is to go out there and do something for the economy by bringing foreigners into here, spreading the news of our culture, of our Carnival, when it happens, and bring them by the thousands in February. That is our job, not just go out there and jump your kin on the stage and try to sell yourself." Drawing on this vision of the calypsonian's mission not only to promote Trinidad's national culture, but also to attract tourism to boost the GNP, Plummer sees her performance as a spectacle that caters to both sound and sight. She explains her emphasis on costumes as follows:

> Ever since I have been going to shows, I always felt cheated when I see these big stars come onstage and they look just like the persons sitting next to you or worse. You know, I feel cheated. You say, "God, I pay all that money to see this guy and he just looks so normal, so ordinary." ... And so when I entered the calypso world, it was perfect for me, because the way I look at it, when I go to see a calypso queen, this is what I see: Trinidad is Carnival, calypso, steelband; all go together; it's one package. When you visit us, come to see calypso, it is related to Carnival, which is color, which is costume, which is flamboyant, excitement. So when you present the calypso queen onstage with foreigners in the audience, they are looking to see Carnival, they are looking to see the package. They don't want to see a girl who comes out in a dress with high heels and pearls around her neck. It does nothing. It's a letdown. As soon as I entered the calypso world, I got very heavy into costume and color and I never appear onstage unless I am in full costume, lots of color, excitement, headpiece, everything. It's just as whole package that I am selling.

Plummer's focus on elaborate costume contrasts with that of most other calypsonians, both male and female. Given my interest in how race is performed on the calypso stage, I asked if her emphasis on costumes had been in any way used to de-emphasize the fact that she is white. "It has nothing to do with the racial part of it. It was just my concept of what we sell in Trinidad. If I am going to sing calypso, if I am going to take it to the world, I am taking the whole package. When they see me, they must want to come home and say, 'God, if this is how the queen looks, we are going for Carnival, I want to wear a costume like that,' you know? It sells the whole concept of what tourism is in Trinidad: Carnival." For Plummer, calypso is not only what accompanies masquerade; it is in and of itself part of the spectacle. Unlike most calypsonians, she fuses music and elaborate costumes to enact what, in her view, makes the artform unique to Trinidad and inextricably linked to Carnival. As Trinidadian archivist and author Rudolph Ottley wrote, "Who could forget the 'Minshall' like costuming of her 1991 stage character or Denyse herself dressed in 'Boxing Gear' singing 'Woman is Boss.' "[52] He adds, "Her presentation truly enhances her calypsos rather than distracts from them."[53] For others, however, "Plummer's costumes, hairdos, and stage props make her look a bit like a Vegas showgirl" compared to most other female calypsonians' unadorned presentations.[54] I understand such critiques as faulting her as much for her unique emphasis on costumes and tourism—which in this view is seen as being at the expense of the artform—as for looking "wrong" (false) for the part—not being Afro-Trinidadian and yet singing calypso. In all cases, the undeniable appeal that her costuming has had for many and the controversies it has raised for others in combination with her being the only white Trinidadian woman performing in the calypso music scene have attracted attention and placed her in the limelight.

In the calypso context, Plummer is a nonconformist. By virtue of being born in Trinidad, she claims her right to perform in the scene that has been dominated by black males from the lower class. She also takes the artistic license to perform her calypsos in a nonnormative style—playing with the excess of the Carnivalesque in costumes, colors, and number of figurants onstage with her (e.g., moko jumbies, dancers, and children). In addition, unlike most calypsonians, who have traditionally sung only calypsos, she prides herself on singing songs from genres other than calypso and soca. In so doing, she arguably challenges the widespread notion that Trinidadianess can be expressed only through calypso and soca. While she writes some of her songs, she also openly hires or works in collaboration with lyricists and composers, including Boogsie Sharpe, Reynold Howard, and Christopher Grant, to name only a few. This practice challenges the notion that calypsonians must be the authors of what they sing, confronting the myth that "true, true" kaisonians write all their songs.[55]

Along with other calypsonians of her generation, such as David Rudder, who, before singing calypso, was involved in pop and rock music—a crossover hardly ever heard before the mid 1980s—Plummer kept her own name instead of resorting to the use of a sobriquet.[56] Instead of creating a persona with a name seeking to evoke exploits or power (such as Lord Kitchener or Roaring Lion), she used her own name allegedly as part of a new cultural politics in the calypso business. As in pop and rock, such new politics in calypso transforms individuals with ordinary names into larger-than-life figures endowed with seemingly sovereign powers—that is, with the freedom and agency that sovereigns supposedly possess.[57] As a white female with financial resources, and from a musical background unusual in the context of the calypso scene, Plummer defies the normative profile of calypsonians and the politics of aesthetics and authenticity that have informed calypso as a musical practice. As a calypsonian, she arguably helps expand the definition of who can participate in and represent national culture.

Yet, simultaneously, she has conformed to many of the requirements of the calypso culture and music industry. Like most other calypsonians, in addition to entering competitions, Plummer has also performed in calypso tents from the outset—for many years in Kitchener's tent. She has produced her own yearly recordings. Once the Carnival season is over, she travels to overseas Carnivals and special fetes to perform. Unlike most calypsonians, however, Plummer benefits from having her sister attend to all the technical aspects of her career—interviews, contracts, rehearsal schedules, and travel arrangements. In Ottley's words, "Her singing career is operated as a business. . . . The singing is all that Denyse has to concern herself with."[58]

Her dream "to see calypso music as a category in the Grammy Awards and carry it out there, like what Bob Marley did with reggae," in her view, would benefit every one in the calypso music scene.[59] As the one who would like to open doors for other calypsonians, in 1993 she sang the song "Higher Heights" (written by calypsonian Bomber)—a self-promoting composition boasting her virtues and superiority in the calypso arena. Typical of the bravado style of calypso sung by scores of calypsonians over the past century, this song won several nightly encores in Kitchener's tent. But it angered some calypsonians too. Luta wrote a reply called "Denyse" for Tigress to sing: "You say you are a born calypsonian / But how come you take so long to start? / In my opinion, you really don't have no love for the art / And is because you failed as a pop singer / You run and grab up the soca . . . " And: "The songs you sing are really mediocre / Even though you are very good performer." In my view, this critique highlights how loyalty to the calypso tradition is an important issue in the calypso milieu, and conversely how musical experiences "outside" that tradition are not only construed with suspicion but also dismissed. However, this rebuff of her song, according to Plummer, was caused by "race problems." As she explains,

> You will never get rid of race problems, all over the world. . . . So even though the majority of Trinidadian people respect me and they don't look at me as a white person anymore, they look upon me as someone who is here to do the job, an ambassador to their country . . . there is still jealousy. . . . The only time this nonsense manifests itself is in competition, "Who she feels she is" and "the judges are biased because she white and she blond." . . . But you know, I don't have a problem in Trinidad at all. But I know, racism will continue as long as we live. And the time I take to allow it affect me, when I do see it happening, I could be further along the road getting something outstanding, you know? That is a waste of time.

Since her entry into the calypso music scene, as a white calypsonian, Plummer has challenged the racial politics informing calypso and, by extension,

of national culture. As a woman, along with Rose and other female calypsonians, she has also helped destabilize the notion that only masculin-
ized musical practice can be emblematic of the nation. Simultaneously,
she has prompted hostility inside gender lines in ways that highlight how
the racialized body politics in calypso overpower gendered ones.

In claiming calypso culture as her birthright, Plummer reinforces the
notion of national culture as the exclusive inheritance of Trinidadian
citizens. Regardless of her intentions, her emphasis on patriotism, nation building, education, and tourism in her songs and in her interviews
with me implicitly endorses Creole nationalism. When Dr. Eric Williams came to power in 1962, he advocated not only the strengthening of
culture as part of the nation-building process, but also its exploitation as
one of the national riches of Trinidad and Tobago.[60] Williams's modern-
izing speeches also frequently invoked self-discipline and professionalism as crucial to national development. Plummer's resolute insistence on
such practices of professionalism also constructs "national culture" as a
marketable resource for international consumption as well as an index of
Trinidad's modernity.

In line with Creole politics, Plummer also conceives Trinidad's national recognition and economic boost in relation to the United States.
However, while her practices implicitly endorse Creole nationalism, they
simultaneously challenge the notion of an authentic culture as mapped
exclusively to Trinidadian territory—hence her refusal to be confined
strictly to singing calypso and to adhering to its normative notions.
Plummer's understanding of nation not only includes Trinidadians living
in various parts of the world, but also insists that "authentic culture" be
defined as including more than one musical practice.

Crazy: Embodying a Unique Part and Product of the Mix

Crazy: The Lovable Lunatic
His first calypso moniker was Wong Ping. His next sobriquest was the Mighty Arawak. Finding these two names lacking the punch his personality required, Edwin
Ayoung was given his third calypso name by Fred Farrel and since then has been
known internationally as Crazy.

The Official Calypso Revue '88

Only a miracle can prevent Crazy from registering his first Road March victory this
year. The "lovable lunatic" of calypso, after knocking at the doors for a long time,
has finally come up with a song which seems to have the entire nation under a
spell. . . . Since entering the calypso arena, Crazy has always had at least one song

challenging the frontrunners for Road March laurels. Among these were *Dustbin Cover, Madness is Gladness, Uncle Crazy* and *Soca Tarzan.* From all indications, *Suck Mih Soucouyant* is the one most likely to do the trick for him.

Sunday Express, 12 February 1985

Crazy's singular story as a calypsonian reveals how through self-fashioning, musical skills, and business acumen, this non-Afro-Trinidadian artist made his way into calypso conventionally understood as the national musical practice carried on mainly, if not exclusively, by Afro-Trinidadians. It also shows how this artist's musical persona has been greatly influenced by the legacies of this racialized tradition, and simultaneously exploited by him.

Edwin Ayoung was born in 1944 into a family of eleven children. His first calypso moniker, Wong Ping, alluded to his paternal Chinese ancestry. His next, the Mighty Arawak, may have been selected to evoke his Amerindian heritage, deriving from his Venezuelan immigrant mother. His third calypso name, Crazy, given to him by his friends Fred Farrel and Doran Hector, is the name by which he has been known internationally. Compared to other calypsonian sobriquets, such as the Mighty Terror, Roaring Lion, and Black Stalin, selected to evoke power and pride, the name Crazy is unusual. However, Ayoung credits the name for giving him freedom. As he explained to me, "With that name, I can do anything I want."[61] He added that, unlike the two previous sobriquets, Crazy gave the punch his personality required. While Ayoung claims acquiring freedom by adopting this name, both his adopted sobriquet and his tendency to perform wild antics onstage conform to the ways that other artists of Chinese ancestry have gained access to the calypso stage. As mentioned in chapter 2, singers of Chinese ancestry, such as Rex West, Chiang-Kai-Shiek, and Dr. Soca, deliberately performed in a comic style, exaggerating body movements and adopting mannerisms in ways that entertained, but simultaneously confirmed their estrangement from the performing style considered emblematic of calypso and the prerogative of Afro-Trinidadians. Unlike many of his predecessors, however, Crazy has achieved feats in the calypso music scene that to this day, regardless of race, remain rare achievements. His achievements have won him recognition and respect among calypsonians. His participation in calypso competitions has helped signal the presence of the many ethnic groups living on the island. Yet he has also been the sole calypsonian of Chinese ancestry to succeed in that scene over the past four decades, reaffirming the marginality that individuals of Chinese ancestry occupy in the articulation of national culture in Trinidad.

The colonial legacy of calypso's racialization as Afro-Trinidadian has been reinforced not only by Afro-Trinidadians' leading roles in the artform. It has also been reinforced by non-Afro-Trinidadians' own refusal to be associated with what has been historically construed to be a practice assembling people of low class and disreputable behavior. In such a context, it was not surprisingly against his father's wish that Crazy in his teens began singing calypsos of the famous artists of his time—his two favorites being the Mighty Spoiler and Lord Blakie. During the day, he worked as a customs clerk, then as a mechanic, and, later on, as a salesman. At night, however, he performed calypso. From 1962 to 1968, he was the lead singer in Mano Marcelin's band. From 1968 onward, he began singing at parties, still performing other calypsonians' songs. In 1972, Crazy was invited to sing one of his own compositions in Sparrow's calypso tent, the Original Young Brigade. The song, called "Chinaman," is written in a party song style and describes a man rubbing his penis with a tiny little brush before having sex in order to last longer. This was the first song that Crazy recorded on a 45. Even though he performed songs that raised serious sociopolitical commentaries in succeeding years (including, in 1973, "No African Name for Me," about Afro-Trinidadians changing their English names for African ones during the Black Power movement, and, in 1974, "Modern Carnival," about the need to stop "all this fighting on the streets"), Crazy achieved his first important success in 1975 with "Electrician," a double-entendre ditty about electricians' work, tools, and appliances—the style that was to become to a great extent his trademark. From then on, as one journalist put it, "The local public, and indeed Crazy's fans abroad, eagerly looked forward to hear, and see, what he had to offer." [62]

The operative words here are not only to *hear,* but also to *see* Crazy onstage. In addition to his witty songs with sexual double entendre and his great vocal skills (precise intonation, great vocal range, and ease in several musical genres), Crazy also made his reputation through eccentric, outrageous outfits and acrobatic performances onstage. At a show I attended in Skinner Park, Crazy performed his song with only a diaper, holding a baby bottle. In many of his shows, he climbed up on the support stanchions of the stage during his performance—one of the first artists to do so in Trinidad. His spectacular physical agility was demonstrated when he also climbed the statue of Captain A. A. Cipriani at the corner of Frederick Street and Brian Lara Promenade (formerly known as the Independence Square) to advertise his CD. He also used his long, free, curly hair as part of the prop embodying his persona as "Crazy." As a result, Crazy has been known as a consummate entertainer in the calypso scene, as an artist who can not only sing, dance, and make people laugh, but also play with the limits of the socially and morally acceptable—how literal sexual references can be, what scandals can be described, and what taboos teased out. Taking advantage of his mixed ancestry, he explores with impunity the stereotypes of Trinidadians of all types, exaggerating to such extremes that they cannot be taken too seriously.[63] In so doing, he arguably has helped Trinidadians laugh at these stereotypes and see them as construc-tions, while reinforcing these stereotypes by singing about them.

Whether or not encouraged by his marginal positioning in the calypso scene, Crazy's emphasis on the "entertainment" part of calypso led him to attempt developing his acting skills and experiment with theater from 1982 to 1984. He began by performing the star role in a play directed by Helen Camps that was taken on a European tour. He was selected to play the role of a crazy man which, Crazy explained, "is a role I used to act good. I even used to sing a song about it, 'I am Chief Crazy' without a horse [in reference to 'Chief Crazy Horse' in the United States]." Crazy performed in a few other plays, including Cinderama and Snow Cone and the Seven Dwens written by Derek Walcott.[64] He also appeared in the movie Bacchanal Times in 1982. Crazy dabbled in acting, in his words, "to get more experience in the entertainment business. I wanted to do it to see where that would take me."

Apart from this brief theatrical experience, Crazy followed the nor-mative rites of calypsonians. After singing calypso with bands and per-forming in calypso tents, he entered competitions. His first major hits came in 1978 with "Dust-Bin Cover"—which Crazy describes to me as "one of my signature songs"—and "A Message to Joffre Serrette."[65] With these two songs in 1978, he competed in the finals for the first time in his career and placed second runner-up to Calypso Rose; he also placed second in the Road March competition. In 1985, Crazy won the Road March with the song "Suck Mih Soucouyant," with its overt sexual dou-ble entendre, ear-catching melody, and driving rhythm—a tune which, regardless of the jury's moral standards and opinion, created a stir and won the public's support that year.[66] In the following years, Crazy placed in the calypso competitions finals several times—an enviable position that earned him recognition as one of the major figures in the calypso scene, albeit in a category all his own.

Unlike most calypsonians, Crazy further consolidated his reputation through his musical innovations—which, by design or not, highlighted his Venezuelan, or what is called locally his "Spanish," ancestry. In 1979, he helped establish a new musical genre, parang soca—which mixed pa-rang, the Venezuelan Christmas musical tradition accompanied by several instruments among which the cuatro and maracas figure prominently, with soca, the upbeat, driving rhythm musical offshoot of calypso that will be discussed at length in part 2 of this book. His bold release that year of his "Parang Soca" on the same album with his calypso compositions (coincidentally the first LP he released in his career) made it a novelty that sold twenty-seven thousand copies—a record sale rarely attained in those days.

With profits from that album, Crazy moved into another venture: the music business. Very few calypsonians have had the financial resources to buy musical instruments and create their own bands. This, however, is part of what makes Crazy's career distinct from most others': in 1979, he created Chandelier. The band, however, broke up two years later, after Crazy had hired someone who, instead of simply managing the band, mishandled the funds. Undaunted by this experience, Crazy continued his music business venture. In 1981, he became a calypso producer, which in Trinidad combines the roles of both the sponsor and the musical director of recording projects. He produced several well-known calypsonians, including All Rounder, Lady Wonder, Delamo, Luta, Designer, Pink Panther, Brother Marvin, King Austin, M'ba, and Brown Boy. And, simultaneously, he started his own record label, called Crazy and Company. To ensure that his projects would be financially viable, he produced (and continues to produce) compilations, instead of a whole album for each artist. Unlike all other producers, he performs songs recorded by his own artists. As an astute businessman, he explained, "Yeah, 'cause when your record sells, is I gonna make the money. So, I have to sing my people's things."

Crazy's musical skills combined with his keen understanding of music business have prompted him to be actively engaged in maximizing his chances of artistic and commercial success. Crazy has been among the few calypsonians of his generation who have unashamedly sung compositions written in collaboration with other artists, including Merchant, Superblue, and Brother Marvin. In the same untraditional vein, against the general tendency among many calypsonians to leave arranging to the arranger, Crazy has played an active role in "over*hearing*" the overall sound of his recordings. Following the marketing strategies typical in the calypso music business, he has produced what he calls "variety albums," featuring calypsos that are sociopolitical commentaries as well as party music. According to Crazy, "When you're making an album with six songs, you must have your party song, that is for you to go out there and work so you could live." In the same business vein, he usually plans the release of his two annual recordings separately, each for the appropriate season: the parang soca, or Christmas music, in the first week of November, and his calypso and soca album immediately after Christmas when the Carnival parties are just about to begin.

Crazy's reputation as a hard worker, as someone who is reliable and, in his words, "lives good with everybody" (gets along with everybody) has earned him respect and confidence in the calypso music community. For nearly the past two decades, he has been on tour nearly all year long, often performing his two songs of the year in more than one venue during the same night. In 1989—the year in which he produced a big hit with his song "Nani Wine"—Crazy boasts that he broke a record in New York by performing in twelve different venues in one night—a feat apparently never surpassed since then.[67]

In one of my interviews with him, Crazy established a connection between himself and Byron Lee, from Jamaica, who is also of Chinese descent—thereby reinforcing a diasporic connection among Chinese Caribbean artists and their distinct positioning in Caribbean musical scenes. Inadvertently echoing the stereotypical coupling in the Caribbean of Chinese with business enterprises, Crazy has viewed Byron as his music business mentor. Among Jamaican artists an exceptional figure doing calypso, Lee, according to Crazy, is the richest man in the calypso music business. In his opinion, Lee's financial success is due to discipline: he has no girlfriends on the road. Girlfriends are costly and lead one to return empty-handed after the tour is over. Lee requires contracts to be signed before a show, a sum of money to be paid in advance when the contract is signed, and the balance to be paid before he goes onstage to perform. He agrees to perform only if he judges the amount of money offered acceptable in relation to his professional experience. Applying these sound financial habits to his own career, Crazy also prefers skipping a year in order to avoid overexposure and public saturation. As he puts it, "I don't go in one place too often." The result is that Crazy is financially well off: he now owns three houses in Trinidad. With many hit songs to his credit and several properties as part of his assets, this calypsonian named Crazy is anything but.

As a seasoned and renowned calypsonian, Crazy has expanded the permissible differences performed on the calypso stage. In a category all his own, his participation in the national cultural forum of calypso does not destabilize the domination of Afro-Trinidadians in the articulation of the nation, but signals the presence of minority groups as also part of it. Crazy's mixed ancestry—well known locally—effectively embodies four minority groups on the national stage: the Chinese, the "Spanish," the Amerindian, and the "mixed." According to Aisha Khan's thesis on the historically complex ethnic politics and social hierarchy of Trinidad, Crazy's "Spanish" ancestry acts as a positive modifier of the lower position historically assigned to the descendants of indentured Chinese. In turn, the Amerindianizing of his Spanish heritage (through his mother's mixed background) carries "vestiges of Trinidad's original, 'authentic,' and somewhat romanticized past, in the form of aboriginal blood."[68] In combination, his ethnic positioning as "synchronically 'mixed' and distinctive"[69] has offered him the possibility of creatively using these ambiguities to advantage in the racialized body politics of the national culture of calypso.

Through eccentric performances and blunt lyrics, Crazy has tested and at the same time stretched the boundaries of the acceptable in calypso—and thus of national expression—both in aesthetics and morality. Like Plummer, he has challenged the myth of single authorship in calypso practice, acknowledging publicly the collaborators with whom he has worked on particular projects. Unlike her, however, he does not perform musical genres other than calypso, soca, and parang soca.[70] In so doing, he uses his calypsonian artistic persona to perform what is conceived as national culture, that is, musics construed as emerging from the land—reinforcing the imagined correlations between calypsonian, national culture, and territory.

As cultural entrepreneur, Crazy renders visible the entanglement of national culture with business. He also reinforces the interracial collaboration that has been vital for the materialization of national culture. His creation of a band, his work as producer of several Afro-Trinidadian calypsonians, and his participation in the Spanish- and Afro-Trinidadian scene with his parang soca all have focused on expanding the outreach of calypo audiences (calypso here used as the generic label encompassing soca). Crazy's emphasis on professionalism (e.g., reliability), discipline (e.g., no girlfriend on the road), and "living good" with people inspired by Jamaican Byron Lee highlights a Chinese Caribbean diasporic connection and contribution that is rarely made in the calypso milieu. It also redefines to some extent the traditional profile of the male calypsonian as "easy living off immoral earnings and elaborate masking and self-evasion."[71] I say "to some extent" because, as a calypsonian, Crazy articulates a particular national subject whose marginality on the national stage in a sense serves to accentuate who dominates. Yet his long artistic and commercially successful career attests to the recognition he has been granted by calypso aficionados.

De Mighty Trini: Claiming Birthrights and Cultural Citizenship over Race, Ethnicity, and Class

So I was always back stage with all the calypsonians. Every calypsonian of that era knew who I was and liked me very much because I wanted to be part of it. And if I am in a tent, every night, and if the tent is going to San Fernando Sunday night, I go with dem. . . . I became very close to Sparrow, very close.

In 1983, Sparrow attempted to carry calypso a step higher than Carnival. In the Hideaway, he introduced calypso out of season, away from Carnival. So of course, I was there every night, with my bottle of Johnny Walker Black, and one night, he was speaking to Composer, to Fighter, Power, and myself. Chalkdust was on the stage singing at the time. And Sparrow was complaining that Chalkdust don't want to sing for fifty dollars. He wants more money, and he can't afford it, because, you know, he's trying, he has expenses, to pay the band. But I said, "That's not right. Look at how much people in the place. You should pay him a better salary." He said, "Shut your Syrian mouth."

Although I am Lebanese, in Trinidad to all the black people, we're all Syrians. So, he said, "Why don't you shut your Syrian mouth." I said, "Man, you hold your ass. You all drinking and you're having fun. All your Grenadian ass"—because I know he is a Grenadian.He said, "What you know about calypso? You shut up." I say, "What I know about calypso?

"I know more about calypso than you. You could sing better than me, but I know more than you." He say, "You could sing anything?" I say, "What song you want to hear? You want to hear one of yours, one of Kitchener, what do you want to hear?" He say, "Sing any song you know." And I sang "Bed Bug." When I sang, he did like that. He heard Melody [a well-known calypsonian] in my throat. He said, "You could sing, you know the song." I say, "Very well." So he said, "When I go up to sing, I am going to call you onstage. What name to call you?" And I said, "Call me, 'Son of the Soil.'" So he went on the stage, maybe one hour after. He sang three songs, during the fourth song, I say, "He forgot me." After the fourth song, he says,

"Well, ladies and gentlemen, we have Indian people singing calypso, we have Chinee"—because Chinee was Rex West in those days—"we have Africans, and now we have a white man who wants to come and sing calypso. Put your hands together for the Mighty Whitee." [As explained in chapter 1, in Trinidadian popular parlance, both Lebanese and Syrians are considered "white."] Well, I got so upset . . . I got so upset. I did not want to hear that name at all. I went on the stage and he hold the mic, and I say, "Give me the mic. Ladies and Gentlemen, Son of the Soil, no Mighty Whitee." And the crowd clapped and all of that. . . . So he told the band, let me in the key F. From my throat, my voice, he's so smart, so sharp, he picked

up the key, and I started and he sang the chorus with me. I sang the whole song,
four verses.

De Mighty Trini, 17 January 2003[72]

De Mighty Trini's musical story reveals how participation in Trinidad's
national artform has involved a struggle over issues of race, ethnicity, and
class. It also shows how, in combination with the colonial legacies of
social hierarchy among diasporic groups, resources and expectations as
well as tensions in well-to-do families have deeply influenced the difficulties of access and recognition of artists from such milieus in calypso.
Robert Elias was born in Woodbrock, Trinidad, in 1943, the seventh child
in a family of eight children. Both of his parents were born in Lebanon.
In 1929, soon after their marriage, they moved to Trinidad. Najib Elias
was a shoemaker, and his wife, a seamstress. After a modest start, Najib's
business grew to include not only a shoe store, but also a hardware store,
leading the Elias family to become wealthy. As was typically the case in
most middle- and upper-class families, during his teens, Robert was not
allowed to play in a steelband, because in those days in Trinidad, "if you
played in a steelband, or you sang calypso, you [were] considered 'low
class.'" In spite of these connotations and his father's wish to keep his son
out of these activities, Robert bought a cuatro in hiding and began to
learn calypso songs.

From the mid-1960s to the early 1970s, Robert developed a large
calypso repertoire to entertain friends. While such an endeavor can be
seen as stemming from his love for the artform, it could also be linked to
his desire to be integrated into the Afro-Trinidadian groups with whom
he played sports and with whom he associated calypso. From 1966 to
1972, as a team member of the first division of soccer in Trinidad and
Tobago, the Malvern Sports Club—he was then the first white-skinned
man to play on the black team of that country—and in the late 1960s as
a member of the field hockey team named the Casuals, composed mainly
of white players, Robert traveled throughout the country and also in
various parts of the Caribbean and Canada. During the tours, in between
games, Robert had many opportunities to sing and to memorize tunes.
Singing calypso became not only his favorite pastime, but also a way to
participate actively in what he saw as the national culture.

The constraints and possibilities that Robert's father's business entailed
had unanticipated tangible effects on Robert's singing career as a calypsonian. Even though he wanted to go to England to become a pilot,
Robert stayed in Trinidad to work in the family business. And inadver-

tently, through the family business, Robert became further immersed in calypso. As several other businessmen did at the time, Robert's father hired calypsonians to advertise his shoe and hardware stores. In so doing, he developed close relationships with many of them, and most particularly with Lord Melody and the Mighty Sparrow. As calypsonians were coming regularly to visit his father at his stores and at home, Robert got to know them well, too.

Not by design, Robert's father further helped him to learn about calypso through his real estate ownership. In 1962, one of the Elias family's tenants and neighbors was Syl Taylor, the manager for Sparrow's tent. Through this connection, Robert could go to the tent without paying. As a result, "every night, Monday to Saturday, I was in the tent, backstage."

Robert's initiation into the calypso stage was made possible not only through hanging out with calypsonians in his free time, but also by knowing some of the most important calypso figures of the day, including Sparrow. It was also made possible by Robert's fiery refusal to be excluded from what he considered national culture. His first public objection to being marked as "white," and thus different and estranged from calypso and hence national culture, occurred when the Mighty Sparrow called him "the Mighty Whitee" onstage. His reply that he was "Son of the Soil" rather than "Mighty Whitee" claimed his birthright as one who belonged as a citizen and as a full participant in the national culture.

Robert's refusal to be marginalized is illustrated by another incident that helped spark his first venture as a calypsonian. After work, Robert used to go to a club where the port workers assembled and played a game called "rummy."[73] In Robert's words, "Again, the only little white boy among all black people." One evening, as he made a mistake in playing cards, he was called a "damn Syrian fool." As he argued with the card player that rather than a Syrian he was a Trinidadian, someone in the attendance—the former president of the Seamen and Waterfront Trade Union, Vernon Glean—suggested to him that he should start singing calypso to "tell dem, you're born Trini." After Robert confessed that he did not know how to write calypso, the owner of the club, Andrew Boyce, proposed to write the song for him and to see Art de Coteau—one of the most famous arrangers of the time—to "put it together." In Robert's words, "And so said, so done": "I was born in Woodbrook / Don't care how I look / . . . I know good mango by smellin the leaf / I know bout the steelband, breakin dey call beats / . . . So tell dem, let dem know it's true / I born in this country just like all you / Ah rob, dey say, calling me Syrian everyday / Tell dem, tell dem ah sad / The way that dey treat me in Trinidad / Tell dem tell dem for me nothing can change / I born Trini."

Before asking Sparrow to hire him to sing this song in his tent, Robert wanted to find an appropriate sobriquet for himself. Glean suggested "the Mighty Trini," which immediately appealed to him. However, Robert changed the spelling of "the" into "De," in his words, "to decorate it in broken English"—De Mighty Trini.

De Mighty Trini's insistence on not being called Syrian or white comes from his own views, mediated by widely circulated perceptions, about both Syrians and whites.

> Syrians were not liked in this country and they are still not liked. They are
> wealthy . . . you know? And white people are racist. They tend to look at
> black people as niggers, and I don't like that. Not all white people, and I
> hope that you're not, but people are people, people are human, and you
> judge people, their character, their integrity, their honesty, and you judge
> a person like that; you don't judge a person by the color. I went to school
> in a black school. I sat . . . we were forty in the class, with thirty-nine black,
> and myself. I grew up with black people. I don't like that word "nigger"
> and "coolie." I don't like that. So I did not want Whitee; I did not want
> Syrian.

Like most calypsonians, De Mighty Trini began his calypso career by performing in calypso tents. He first sang in Sparrow's tent from 1984 to 1986, at Spektakula during 1987 and 1988, with William Munroe in 1989, back at Spektakula in 1990 and 1991, then in Kitchener's tent in 1992, and back in Spektakula in 1993. In 1994, he joined the Kaiso House, the only calypso tent sponsored by the state, where he has been performing yearly ever since.

Even though calypsonians have traditionally been expected to be the authors of their songs, like many other calypsonians, De Mighty Trini does not comply with this norm. Instead, he has hired some of the best calypso lyricists and composers in the country: Winsford "Joker" Devine, Merchant, and Gregory Ballantyne. I was struck in attending several of his performances by hearing De Mighty Trini, unlike many other calypsonians who benefit from the work of collaborators, publicly acknowledge them whenever he performed their songs.[74] He also acknowledges the arrangers with whom he works—a fact all the more remarkable since arrangers are rarely mentioned. His desire to be "true, true" to the artform and to his public has been translated into his insistence on being as transparent as possible and respectful of the people he admires.

In his own account, De Mighty Trini on the one hand portrays his experience just like that of other calypsonians, simultaneously projecting thereby his identification with, and sense of belonging to, the calypso milieu. De Mighty Trini's first hit was in 1986 with "Soca Your Woman," a song composed by Winsford "Joker" Devine. (At that time, the musical style soca was still not recognized as a separate entity, but rather was considered a variation of calypso—in that historical moment, a hotly debated issue.) In 1987, he performed another song by Devine, "Curry Tabanca," which became a hit in the overseas Carnival markets. However, even though, according to De Mighty Trini, the song was number 1 during Carnival in Trinidad, "yet I did not see the Savannah [where the finals are held], I reached only Skinner Park [for the semifinals]." The reason? Because, he explained, he was paying his dues: "This is what they say. It is a slang here. You are paying your dues."

De Mighty Trini explained that he also went through what most other calypsonians singing sociopolitical commentaries experience at some point or another during their career: censorship. In 2001, De Mighty Trini sang "Trikkidad," a calypso about Gypsy and William Bill Chaitan that accused them of fixing the elections held during that period by hiding their double citizenship. In his view, this song was kept away from entering the finals because of censorship.

> *De Mighty Trini.* I made it to Skinner Park, but according to Sparrow, Sparrow said, "Trini, if I had those two songs you had this year, I would not have only reached the Savannah, I would have win the crown." But the government paid the organization to keep me out of the Savannah. The song would have destroyed the UNC [United National Congress]. It was . . .
>
> *J.G.* How did you learn that they had paid the organization to trick the results?
>
> *De Mighty Trini.* Informers came to me. And when I saw the score sheet, my name and birth certificate, my first name is Robert, my middle name, dash, no middle name. Elias. In the score sheet, they have my name Michael Ellis. I questioned it. I got nowhere. I questioned my scores, the scores they give me. They did not even give me the quarter of how I was worth. Two of the judges, they put me right down. And when I investigated who they were, they were from the UNC government. And they were placed in Skinner Park in the semifinals to block me and Lady B when she had a song called "Tobago Not for Sale." She and I were blocked. Were you in Trinidad in 2001? I sang that song every night in the tent and I got two or three encores every night.

De Mighty Trini's explanation of the competition results reveals how, in his view, calypso competitions are often rigged through censorship and political bias. As the quote below indicates, he also believes that his own success in calypso is deeply mitigated by issues of class and ethnicity. As he explains,

> I'm the son of a wealthy man. And calypso really belongs to poor people, and there are people who say that about me, I should not be singing calypso, and I'm blocking a poor man from making a living. If I wasn't there, some poor man would be in my place. You know? But like last night, Delamo? I was speaking to him. And he said to me, "Trini, you are an icon." He said, "You are the only Syrian, white-skinned man singing calypso for the last twenty years. And you have done it on your own"—of course, with the introduction of my godfather, the Mighty Sparrow. But I fought; I really fought hard. I went through a lot of problems. Things I wouldn't tell people, a lot of dirty things were done against me, but I kept trying and trying, you know.

In 1994, De Mighty Trini gained a much-sought-after recognition among calypsonians: he was selected in the Calypso Monarch competition finals. Even though he did not win, he remarked, this feat alone gave him a sense of artistic achievement and a sentiment of national belonging. And while his biggest hit to date, "Curry Tabanca," did not take him to the calypso competition finals, it did spark tours, in his words, "to New York every weekend, Canada, Miami, every weekend"—confirming his recognition among, and connection with, several Caribbean diasporic communities in North America.

However, if calypso gave him the opportunity to fight his way to feel part of the national culture and to become a renowned artist, his activities as a calypsonian and as a performing artist did not go over well with everybody—and, in particular, with his family. According to him, his wife left him because of his involvement with the calypso music scene and his too frequent absences. When I asked him how the rest of his family viewed his career as a calypsonian, his answer went as follows:

> Personally, in the past I knew that they did not support. Now whether they pretend to, or they naturally do, they show it, because of my popularity. Remember, all of my family has business in this country. And who puts a dollar in your pocket? The black man, the black woman who goes into your store and they spend their money. So when people go to their store, Trini is my nephew, you know. Trini is my brother-in-law. Trini is my cousin. . . . So

everybody uses me as a passport or a visa, but some of dem may be genuine. I
have a couple nephews who like what I do, and they respect me for it. But I
maintain a respect, because I maintain a standard throughout the twenty years.

Very few other Lebanese performers have performed in the calypso music scene. When I asked De Mighty Trini why, in his opinion, this is the
case, he answered by referring to family pressure and lack of involvement
in "true" kaiso. He mentioned two other Lebanese singers who have appeared on a calypso stage. Master Tone (Anthony Salloum) sang in a tent
for a year or two, but gave it up because, according to De Mighty Trini,
his wife wouldn't allow him to continue. Salloum's brother (Michael),
known under the sobriquet Zoom, sang with Spektakula, imitating El-
vis Presley in a calypso style—hence not what De Mighty Trini consid-
ers "real kaiso." Otherwise, in his account, De Mighty Trini stands as a
unique figure in the calypso music scene to this day. His recognition as a
calypsonian, he remarked, was confirmed in 2002 when he was elected as
one of the two trustees to the executive of TUCO.

In spite of such achievements, De Mighty Trini emphasizes how his
participation in the calypso scene—as Lebanese, so-called white, and a
member of the upper middle class—still remains an object of contention.
As he puts it, "I often hear hurtful things said about me." Perhaps as a way
to counterbalance the way he has been negatively positioned in the calypso
scene by some, he boasted about how Delamo, a well-known calypsonian
and former Calypso Monarch, replied to him about such "nonsense":

> He said, "Trini, tell dem what you did. You carry the flag. You don't need
> to sing calypso." I don't need the money. But I have done well. I have suc-
> ceeded. And there are calypsonians who over the period of fifty or forty years'
> singing never went to Skinner Park, never see the Savannah, and I've done it.
> So I achieved popularity. The videos I have done are very popular; I walked
> the streets, everybody knows Trini, everybody. If you go with me now, and we
> walk around the block just once, at least thirty or forty people, "Hey Trini,"
> and they scream out. Everybody knows me. I'm very popular. But I am also
> very outspoken, and that is a problem in this country when you are very out-
> spoken; people don't like that. I speak my mind. I don't hesitate.

Interestingly, by ending the description of himself with a focus on being
"outspoken," De Mighty Trini reiterates his profound alignment with
what calypso is believed to be about.[75]

In figuring on the calypso stage, De Mighty Trini accomplishes many
things. As a member of the Lebanese ethnic minority, he makes room for

the recognition of another national subject. Through both his family history (hiring of, and personal friendship with, calypsonians) and his own history, he publicly renders visible and audible the intimate economic and social relations between male members of the upper middle class from minority groups—in this case, Lebanese—with black male lower-class calypsonians. Through his musical journey, he renders tangible the artistic involvement of members of the upper middle class in the official arena of national culture. As a male calypsonian, he provides one more instantiation of the dominance patriarchy maintains in the performance of the national practice.

Like Plummer, De Mighty Trini's claiming calypso as his culture by virtue of birthright tellingly shows how he constructs calypso as national culture. Yet, except for a few appearances by Plummer, neither she nor De Mighty Trini—as is generally true of non-Afro- and non-Indo-Trinidadians—has exercised this birthright by choosing to be active in the musical scenes of Indo-Trinidadians, who constitute half of the Trinidad population. De Mighty Trini's emphasis on having the Mighty Sparrow, in his words, as "his [musical] godfather" helps him legitimate his participation in calypso. Such an emphasis, combined with his childhood and adult immersion in a black milieu, also reinforces the historically widespread belief—as well as fear and resentment, for some—that access to the platform of national culture has only been possible through the adoption of the Afro-Trinidadian musical practice of calypso.

As a calypsonian, De Migthy Trini's appearance on the national stage has aroused racial tensions—tensions that confront whiteness and the upper middle class as symbolizing imperial (colonial and neocolonial) rules and, by extension, De Mighty Trini's legitimacy "to carry the flag" of Trinidad and Tobago. In the authenticating space of Carnival, where the national is articulated, racialized body politics and class trump ethnicity: De Mighty Trini's association with whiteness and the upper middle class supersedes his minority status as Lebanese. In relation to his own family, his calypso career has created tensions (with his father, his wife, and other relatives) around his participation in an activity considered low class and associated with disreputable behavior. Yet, in addition to his personal gain in popularity, self-esteem, and sense of belonging, his involvement with calypso has also produced financial benefits for his extended family.

By focusing on Black Stalin, Calypso Rose, Denyse Plummer, Crazy, and De Mighty Trini, I have tried to provide a window on the range of constructs, beliefs, and claims that have been made in the name of calypso. Taking for granted calypso's centrality in enunciating the nation in Trinidad and Tobago, these artists have privileged calypso as a means to assert their cultural citizenship and sense of belonging. In doing so, they have reinforced the role calypso has historically played in the production and (re)presentation of the national subject. From contrasting racialized groups, socially gendered roles, and socioeconomic positions, they have embraced calypso not solely because of shared musical sensibilities. They have embraced it, too, as a practice enabling artists to win fame nationally and to effect changes, often by directing attention to social, economic, and political problems in Trinidad. From the variety of their distinct subject positionings, these artists have promoted a variety of political projects: social justice, gender equality, self-pride, recognition, and cultural citizenship.

By situating these performers and their practices in multiple fields of power, I have foregrounded the consequential effects—both material and discursive—of these artists' practices rather than their stated intentions. This strategy has helped me historicize the artists' experiences by positioning their cultural politics in relation to calypso, nation, and diaspora. Despite the diverse, oppositional impulses of these calypsonians' performative practices, the hegemony of Creole nationalism continues to shape their sounds, styles, and political significance. Artists alone do not control the productive power of their work. From national elites to transnational tourists, from Pan-Africanists to Lebanese merchants, appropriation of calypso's cultural politics has produced contested subjectivities as well as profits.

5

Independence, Innovation, and Authenticity

> It is not at all accidental that in the very same decade that the West
> Indian artists are finding West Indianism, the native popular music and
> the native popular song find their most complete, their most vigorous
> expression and acceptance.
>
> C. L. R. James, "The Mighty Sparrow"[1]

Like most musical genres, calypso has eluded airtight definitions.[2]
As I indicated in chapter 1, the form, tempo, instrumentation,
melodic contours, and even rhythmic complex of calypso have
greatly changed over time. Several versions of it (e.g., lavway and
ballad–calypso) have often been featured during the same period
and sometimes even within a single song. While many scholars
have provided detailed descriptions of calypso's changing sounds
during the colonial period, fewer have written on the subject
after independence.[3]

This chapter focuses on calypso's changing expression in the
two decades following independence (1962)—not, however,
with a view to provide an exhaustive recording of all its in-
stantiations, but rather to illuminate the audible entanglements
that have been produced, privileged, and excluded during this
period. In the aftermath of independence, the sound(ing)s of
calypso became an important site in which to articulate received
notions of modernity, authenticity, originality, and "cultural" in-

135

dependence. In this chapter, I investigate the technologies that have been instrumental in forwarding these notions in the sonic conceptions and productions of calypso as national culture.

Whereas the body politics in calypso have been most vividly manifested in competitions sponsored by the state, its sound politics in the 1960s and 1970s, I contend, were mainly controlled by individuals, most notably arrangers, and a small number calypsonians. In the main, local arrangers produced the normative values defining the sound of calypso during that period. Acting as cultural brokers, they were responsible for creating sounds that simultaneously produced familiarity locally and accessibility to markets internationally. Arrangers set the "tones" so that calypso could provide sources of identification and marks of distinction, while keeping abreast of new musical expressions in and outside the region. In this chapter I examine arrangers' ways of thinking about sounds and their actual arrangements, both as musical technologies and technologies of power.

In the first section, I foreground the historical conditions that have led arrangers to play such a prominent role. I then introduce the musical life stories of Afro-Trinidadians Frankie Francis and Art de Coteau, two arrangers who have dominated the music scene and shaped the sounds of calypso in the two decades following independence. In highlighting the musical values, audible entanglements, and sonic sediments informing their arrangements, I reflect on how the soundings of calypso were not only raced and gendered, but also imagined in relation to an aesthetics associated with modernity, class, and alterity.

In the next section, I examine how during the 1960s and 1970s the sounds of calypso were also normalized by three powerful mediations: star figures, critical acclaim, and calypso tunes composed for specific material conditions—Road March competitions and steelband instruments and arrangements. I describe how star figures such as the Mighty Sparrow and Lord Kitchener—arguably then the two most influential calypsonians—used their fame to control and to influence calypso productions during those years. I show how critical acclaim for novel musical approaches, brought forward not only by these two calypsonians but also by Shadow (then a newcomer in the scene), defied certain calypso musical conventions and lent support to a redefinition of calypso's relationship with specific diasporas and regional and international music scenes.[4] Last, I highlight how the writing of calypso tunes for Road March competitions in tandem with Panorama—the annual steelband competitions held at Carnival—by one calypsonian in particular, Lord Kitchener, encouraged the production and normalization of particular sounds, forms, and calypso arrangements. Throughout the chapter, while emphasizing their individual contributions, I show how both arrangers' and calypsonians' agency in shaping the sounds of calypso articulates with audiences' and competition juries' endorsements.

Musicians' Arrangements of National Sounds

In popular music studies, the work of musical arrangers is rarely mentioned,[5] but in the calypso scene, arrangers receive a great deal of attention.[6] The public media and the press recognize them as being influential—at times even more so than the composers and performers—in making calypso part of the cosmopolitan music scene. There are at least two different ways of understanding arrangers' critical role in the calypso music business. One is historical, having to do with the tradition of calypso itself. At the beginning of the twentieth century, calypsonians relied on stock tunes for which they composed their own texts, and they were backed by instrumentalists using predictable harmonic progressions, formulaic rhythmic patterns, and standard melodic riffs in their accompaniments.[7] Following this practice, calypsonians and musicians developed a particular understanding of each group's task: calypsonians were responsible for the lyrics, musicians for the musical arrangements.[8] The two parties thus spent little time working together. Even today, very few calypsonians have worked extensively with the same group of musicians. (Notable exceptions include the Mighty Sparrow and the Troubadours, Black Stalin and Roy Cape All Stars, and David Rudder and Charlie's Roots.) It could be argued that this division of labor has given each role an authority of its own. Hence, while some calypsonians are to this day criticized for relying too much on arrangers to "do something" with their songs, it has also been acknowledged that many musical arrangers accept very little input from calypsonians. To quote one calypsonian, "You can't say, 'I don't want that line there,' no, you can't tell them that. You know, they tell you: 'Listen, you sing, I do the music. So, let me do the arrangement.'"

The key role arrangers play in the finished product of recorded calypsos is illustrated by the text of the song "Two Chords and Leston Paul," written by Hollis "Chalkdust" Liverpool in 1988. The song recounts how calypsonians often give arrangers only the bare outline of a song, expecting arrangers to turn it into something. The result, Liverpool points out, is that when one listens to calypsos, one hears mostly the music of the arranger—in this case, Leston Paul (one of the most famous calypso arrangers of the Caribbean)—and hardly any music by the recorded calypsonian. As a critique of calypsonians who do not take the time to, or cannot, craft their own songs, "Two Chords and Leston Paul" definitely shows how arrangers often end up being as prominent in the recording as the calypsonians singing the songs and how, in the process, they leave indelible marks of their own specific styles on calypso productions.

Another way musical arrangers have gained public recognition has been their close ties with the calypso tent tradition. Until the early 1980s, the tents' management hired a single arranger to write the arrangements for all the calypsos performed in their particular tents. Given that there were seldom more than four or five calypso tents in the whole country and that these tents featured the most prominent calypso artists of the island,[9] the tents' arrangers exerted great influence over calypso soundings.

The extent of the arrangers' influence, however, largely depended upon how the songs they featured were received by calypso tent audiences. Until the 1980s calypsos were usually recorded *after* being successful in the tents or in competitions—and not the other way around, as is the case today. Following the audiences' acclaim of a given song, the arrangements written for it by the tent's arranger were then featured on the airwaves, reaching a wide array of audiences. Conversely, since today recordings are used primarily as a means to promote calypsonians in both the tents and the competitions, the arrangers associated with songs that have either won past competitions or been successful among calypso tent audiences in preceding years are the ones sought after by most calypsonians. The more arrangements they write, the more these arrangers increase their chances of working with the top calypsonians and therefore of being associated with the soundings dominating the calypso scene.

As will be discussed below, the influence that Sparrow, Kitchener, and Shadow exercised on the sounds of calypso during the 1960s and 1970s was exceptional. The originality and boldness with which they infused their songs were bolstered and constantly reinforced by the unique support they received from their audiences. Interviews I have conducted over the past ten years, however, leave no doubt that most calypsonians continue to leave the arrangements of their songs entirely in the arrangers' hands. Whether that is because they have complete confidence in the arrangers they choose or because they are intimidated by them, the end result is the same: over the years, musical arrangers have played a critical role in shaping the sounds and styles of calypso.

Arrangers' Hegemonic Sounds

In my interviews with Trinidadian musicians, calypsonians, and calypso aficionados, Frankie Francis and Art de Coteau stand as the chief contributors to the calypso sounds of the 1960s and 1970s. Several record collectors told me that an overwhelming percentage of the LPs released in the late 1950s and early 1960s were produced with musical arrangements by and under the direction of Francis and in the 1970s under that of de Coteau. Several calypsonians have also noted the prominent role both played in local bands and in the tents as instrumentalists and arrangers. In this section, I examine the two arrangers' musical journeys and practices, as described by the musicians and calypsonians with whom they worked, family relatives and friends, and, in Francis's case, with the arranger himself.[10] Art de Coteau died in 1987 before I began this research project.

Frankie Francis

Frankie Francis was born in 1924, and learned the musical rudiments by going to the cathedral on Sunday evenings and singing with the church choir. He taught himself to play flute and piccolo at the Belmont orphanage where he grew up. While in the British navy, he started to play alto saxophone with bands on Fridays and Saturdays and gained experience with a small combo ensemble, featuring trumpet, alto sax, guitar, bass, drum, and conga. During this time, he learned instrumental versions of the hits that he heard on the radio and the tunes that were played at dancehalls and for other special occasions, such as christenings and birthday parties. In 1944, Francis left the navy to play music full-time. Considered one of the best saxophonists of his generation in Trinidad, he played in all the most important calypso tents of the time, including the Victory tent, the House of Lord, the Young Brigade, and the Old Brigade.

Thus far in his musical journey, Francis would have earned respect by having developed remarkable skills on saxophone. However, Francis's formidable reputation, I contend, also rested on his exceptional skills in reading and writing music—skills that in the context of colonial and postcolonial regimes are still seen in the Caribbean as the most, if not the only, legitimate musical knowledge that one can obtain. In the fifties and sixties, he was famous for his faultless sight-reading and for transcribing full arrangements in record time. He was also famous for being able to write new musical arrangements anywhere, without the help of any musical instrument—it is well known that his favorite place for such work was at a rum shop in the midst of people, drinks, music, and noise.

Francis started writing his own musical arrangements in 1947. Until then, he, like all the other musicians, had played the standard calypso arrangements by ear. Only occasionally would there be an arranger who would write so much as the chord symbols for the piano, guitar, and bass, and the music for the brass section.[11] Interestingly, said Francis, while scores for calypso songs were rare, scores for the musical themes of the latest American movies were readily available, as they were delivered along with the films at the local cinemas. Hence in the 1950s and the 1960s, musicians used scores to play foxtrots, Spanish waltzes, and jazzy tunes, thanks to one of the main providers at the time—the Globe Cinema—but played by ear local music, including calypso.[12]

Tired of the monotony of head arrangements[13]—which he considered mere repetition—Francis started to write out parts for the brass sections of the bands he played with, exploring the idiomatic possibilities of these instruments. Although other arrangers had used scores before he did, Francis is regarded as the arranger who started systematically to write out parts for musicians from 1947 onward.[14] Given his wide range of musical experiences and skills, Francis saw scoring as the most expedient way to get the brass section to play what he wanted to hear. Because he made such extensive use of musical notation, Francis is credited with helping several calypso musicians develop their reading skills and expand their understanding of harmonic language.

From then on, Francis's reputation as a musician grew by leaps and bounds. He was hired to write musical arrangements for some of the most prominent dance bands, such as Cyrill Diaz's and Mano Marcelin's bands, as well as for famous calypsonians of the time, including Terror, Lord Pretender, and Melody. In the 1950s, he accompanied the celebrated Calypso King, the Mighty Sparrow, on tours to Guyana, Grenada, and Barbados, usually for a week at a time, playing at cinemas—the typical sites where musicians would perform. Renowned for his novel arrangements, Francis was then offered a post where he could make a genuine difference. From 1959 to 1963, he worked at the recording studio named TELCO; during this time he ruled over who would be given a chance to record. At TELCO, he played the role of arranger, musical director, saxophone player, and artist and repertoire (A&R) head: in concrete terms, he was the person formally responsible for selecting new acts and material. In one night, he would make one recording with three different calypsonians performing two tunes each—a feat he repeated twice a week. His influence on the musical calypso scene at the time was major, to say the least.

Until the late 1970s, many of the most famous musicians, including Francis, came from orphanages, where they were encouraged to sing in church choirs or to play an instrument. From their early exposure to classical and hymnal music, they developed musical values associated not only with these practices, but also with received notions of modernity: musical skills, often assessed in relation to "perfect" intonation (i.e., the playing of notes in relation to Western tempered tuning), and musical technique, often translated as thorough knowledge of an instrument's capacities, and mastery of the instrument and tone quality. Importantly, as Francis's example illustrates, many among them also learned to prefer musical innovations over repetition—one of the hallmarks of many Trinidadian musical practices, including calypso, largely influenced by African-related musical traditions.[15] Along the same lines, they viewed musicianship as synonymous with the ability to read and write musical scores. And, adopting the classical music model, they conceived of scores as a means to prescribe and to control the sounds of calypso, and to ensure their exact reproducibility.[16] Instead of having to teach by rote the parts to each section of the band, they used their written arrangements as a means to "save time" during rehearsals in tandem with notions of efficiency. Not from conditions of their own choosing—growing up in an orphanage, being exposed to church music—musicians like Francis hence placed calypso within a modernist frame, looking to "improve" the sounds and performance of the artform. As a leading arranger and musical director and the head of the TELCO recoding studio, Francis propagated these views in his own practice. He hired musicians who possessed these skills over those who did not, and helped several calypsonians to sing more successfully in tune.

Francis eventually left Trinidad to seek better job opportunities, and he lived in New York from 1964 to 1974. From the time of his arrival until 1971, he played tenor sax with Syd Joe and his Caribbean All Stars—a cosmopolitan band, including musicians from Panama, St. Vincent, Barbados, and other countries as well. With this band, Francis related, he played regularly Latin American musics, including mambo, bolero, samba, and cha-cha and American music, especially foxtrot, waltz, quickstep, and swing tunes. During his time in New York, he further developed his arrangement skills. While Francis was in charge of writing calypso arrangements, Syd Joe wrote the arrangements for all the Latin American and American music played by the band. In addition to his cosmopolitan experience growing up (he was born in the United States, but raised in Cariacou, Grenada, and he lived in Trinidad for a few years in his early twenties), Joe had learned to write arrangements from a Cuban musician living in New York. While playing with Joe, Francis expanded both his musical repertoire and his musical skills in terms of voice leading and harmonic language. In addition, while in New York, he took music theory lessons by mail with the Berklee School of Music in 1970. This musical training complemented his early exposure to jazz and familiarity with written-out big band arrangements. He received his diploma in 1971.

Even while playing with Syd Joe and as a backup player whenever he could, Francis had to supplement his income. He worked for Merrill Lynch, the big financial corporation, starting at the mailroom and moving on to a better clerk position after he attended high school. After five years, however, Francis pointed out, he left the company because of racism. He then worked in a record store in Harlem and was exposed to a great variety of musics, including rock and roll and jazz. Around this time he started to play and arrange for recordings in New York, including a Christmas 45 with Lord Nelson, for whom he arranged two tunes and played the alto sax, and two tunes for Sparrow, including the featured selection "Wood in the Fire." In 1974, Francis returned to Trinidad, playing with and writing arrangements for some of the most prominent bands of the time. With the gradual demise of big bands by the late seventies, his role as both a player and arranger of big bands also began to diminish. However, he continued to work as an arranger for several calypsonians—including Kitchener (even though for only three tunes, including "Green Fig"), Black Stalin, Duke, Crazy, Cro Cro, the Original de Fosto, and Sugar Aloes—and, even though his prolific output had been dramatically reduced over the past few years on account of his health, he continued to do so until he died in 2005.

Calypso bands in the late 1950s and 1960s typically consisted of reeds, brass, and a rhythm section.[17] Two saxophones (alto and tenor), two trumpets, and two trombones generally constituted the norm. (During Carnival or in dancehalls, the bands played with three saxophones, three trumpets, and three trombones to add volume to their energetic sounds.) The rhythm section generally included a guitar, a piano, a bass, drums, bongos, and two congas.[18] Typical of most Trinidadian bands playing calypso live or in recordings in the 1950s and 1960s, Francis's bands were all male; 80 percent of the members were Afro-Trinidadians and the other 20 percent of mixed descent. While some instrumental bands at times hired singers for guest appearances (usually one male and one female singer), most bands, including Francis's, did not.

In Trinidad, as is the case throughout the Caribbean, women instrumentalists did not play in calypso bands (or, for that matter, in any other type of popular music band), and only from the 1980s did a few begin to be included.[19] From the late 1970s, when I started to do research in the Caribbean, until the present, the few female players I have seen onstage have been members of the police bands.[20] As members of an institutionalized state agency responsible for the enforcement of the law, these women have been able to perform on their instruments alongside men since the early 1990s without fear of endangering their reputations.[21]

Music bands have been historically associated with excess in drinking, the use of drugs, and illicit sex—with behaviors considered by the Christian church and its adherents (many of whom were part of the middle and upper classes) immoral, and thus unsuitable for women. Their reputations being at stake, women have thus been pressured to refrain from playing music in such contexts. Women trained in classical music have typically played in church choirs and concerts, appeared as soloists or choir accompanists, and taught their instruments in private lessons. Those who have learned to play by ear have usually performed at home or in small informal settings. Nevertheless, in spite of being "confined" to those particular spaces, women have been from a distance most influential on the popular music scene. What has been most striking in many interviews I have conducted with male musicians and calypsonians is that, whether they have learned by ear or through formal training, their mothers have not only passed on their love for music, but have also often been their first "teachers." [22]

Raised at the Belmont orphanage, Frankie Francis did not fit the mold of growing up around musically talented women. According to the musicians who worked with him, Francis's arrangements were most heavily influenced by his listening to jazz on radio in the early part of his career and also by his knowledge of the written musical tradition and experience with Latin American music and American dance bands, which typically included improvised solos. His favorite musicians, black or white, were all jazz musicians. They included Stan Getz (tenor saxophone) and Paul Desmond (alto saxophone) as well as big band leaders of the swing era such as Benny Goodman and Artie Shaw from the United States and Ted Heath from England. As a saxophonist, said Francis, he particularly liked the lyrical style of Getz's and Desmond's improvisations. He tried to emulate Getz's "floating tone." Influenced by jazz and the sound of big band ensembles, Francis was known in Trinidad's musical community as "the Duke Ellington of calypso." Fittingly, this title embodied Francis's aesthetic ideal, which, like Ellington's, combined sophisticated musical knowledge and unique arrangements. It also conferred on Francis some of the cultural capital associated with Ellington as a master of African-American music, famous for his stylishness, grace, and craft. It furthermore signaled how in his musical practice Francis featured arrangement techniques and stylistic devices borrowed from the great African-American jazz figure. [23]

In his arrangements, Francis had a predilection for the "horn" section—also called locally the "brass" section to refer to both reed and brass instruments—rather than for the rhythm section. [24] He did not write the

Example 1a
"Old-time" bass used by Frankie Francis in "Never Again," by Sugar Aloes (2004)
Transcription by Sylvon Sylvester

bass part. Instead, he kept the "old-time" bass—a Trinidadian expression referring to a bass line played on the beat, simply outlining the chord progression—and continued to require the typical calypso riff on the guitar throughout the entire tune (see ex. 1a).[25] As the bass and guitar players therefore did not need any guidance to play their parts, he provided the guitar and bass only with the lead sheet featuring the chord progression (see ex. 1b).

In contrast, Francis wrote parts for each instrument of the horn section. He was famous for his wide voicing in the brass section, spanning two or three octaves. As Trinidadian saxophonist and musical director Roy Cape put it, "He does not crowd the voices."[26] While he typically had the brass and reed instruments move in parallel motion, he also often featured tensions (through suspended or added notes) in the chord structures. Occasionally, he would then produce "fat" chords with sevenths and ninths or quartal harmony (see ex. 2).[27] Francis was also well known for writing an alto saxophone melodic line to accompany the singing of the calypsonian. In the chorus especially, he continued to use the traditional device of opposing trumpets and trombones against saxophones in the call and response typical of calypso arrangements. Written in 1985, Francis' s arrangement for Stalin's song "Wait Dorothy Wait" illustrates this tendency clearly.[28] (See ex. 3.)

Francis's musical legacy was recognized through several awards. To name only a few, the Carnival Development Committee (CDC) granted him an award for his contributions to calypso in 1983; the Sunshine Calypso and Steelband Music Awards Committee elected him as a member of the Hall of Fame in 1992; and the T&T Folk Arts Institute gave him an award as a Music Maker Extraordinaire in 1999.

Art De Coteau

Remembered as the calypso arranger who "ruled the roost" in the 1970s, Art de Coteau grew up in a milieu where calypso was discounted for its

Example 2
Frankie Francis's arrangement of "Never Again," by Sugar Aloes (2004),
featuring a four-part harmony for the reed and brass instruments
Transcription by Sylvon Sylvester.

association with low-class people. Born in 1928 in Belmont, he was from
a well-established middle-class family. His parents owned the land and
the house where he was raised, and they had a piano—a sign of a well-
to-do family at the time. From an early age, Art developed a passion for
music. However, as his long-time partner, Daphne McIntosh, who met
de Coteau at the age of eleven and subsequently became the mother of
his two children, recalled, "He did not want to have anything to do with
calypso." [29] As she explained, "Calypsonians then were not seen as decent
people, so as people from a certain bracket, we did not want to deal
with calypso." So both de Coteau and McIntosh used to listen to Bach,
Handel, and George Gershwin. Early in his teens, de Coteau decided to

Example 3
Frankie Francis's arrangement of "Wait Dorothy Wait," by Black Stalin (1985),
illustrating the call and response between the brass and the reeds

devote himself to music. He quit high school and, unlike most musicians
of that period, who had to supplement their incomes by taking on side
jobs, he spent his entire life working as a musician.

De Coteau began writing musical arrangements for singers in clubs.[30]
As an arranger who played bass, piano, and guitar, he was hired in the late
1940s to play in a small combo every weekend in a club in Guyana. After
five years there, he returned to Trinidad, where the status of calypsonians
and steelbands had begun to change under the new elected government.
Now recognized as chief exponents of national culture, both calypsonians
and pan players were held in greater esteem than before.

In this context, during the midfifties, de Coteau began to play the bass
pan and to arrange for the Casablanca steelband—gathering the type of

players whom members of the middle and upper classes had previously regarded, in McIntosh's words, "as outcasts and vagabonds." Calypsonians (including the renowned Lord Kitchener) were now writing new tunes for steelbands, and de Coteau decided to use his skills as an arranger to feature possibilities the new instruments offered. In so doing, he became one of the first arrangers to write for steelbands—a fact celebrated in 1996 when he received posthumously an award from the Steelband Festival "in recognition of your sterling contribution to the steelband movement."[31]

By the late 1950s, De Coteau had become directly involved with calypsonians through recording studios and calypso tents. With the state's initiatives now promoting "national culture," independent cultural entrepreneurs opened studios to record calypso. Shortly after the TELCO studio hired Frankie Francis to supervise all recordings—including selecting the calypsonians, writing the arrangements, and hiring the musicians— the Christopher recording studio hired de Coteau part time to do the same, though for production on a smaller scale. During that same period, he also wrote arrangements for calypso instrumentals and also various dance pieces for the police band. In the early 1960s, de Coteau formed his own band—the Art de Coteau Orchestra, which remained active into the midseventies—to play calypso instrumentals and to accompany calypsonians. In 1964, with Frankie Francis's departure to the United States and his own growing fame as one of the best arrangers in Trinidad, de Coteau began receiving more requests from calypsonians than he could handle. He stopped working for steelbands and began writing arrangements exclusively for calypsonians—not only from Trinidad, but also from other islands, including Short Shirt, from Antigua, and Alston Becket, from St. Vincent. In addition to providing calypsonians' musical accompaniment for their recordings, he arranged all the tunes performed in the calypso tents where he also directed the band— including Lord Blakie's Victory tent and Kitchener's tent, where he would often perform as many as three shows in one night.[32] Furthermore, he traveled with his own band, accompanying some of these calypsonians on tours throughout the region and also in New York. Through both recordings and performances, his name became associated with artistic and commercial success. From the late 1960s to the late 1970s, according to most of the calypsonians I interviewed in Trinidad, Barbados, and Antigua, Art de Coteau became the most sought-after calypso arranger in the region. In the words of one musician, "At the time, anyone who dealt with arrangements had to repeat the same arrangements as Art de Coteau's."

De Coteau's career in calypso was dedicated to bringing local musicianship to a high standard. Like Francis, de Coteau derived his musical taste from his experience with classical music and associated notions of modernity. He was known for strict discipline and insistence on musical precision. He showed nothing but scorn for anyone who was late to rehearsals, who did not have his scores in place when the rehearsal began, who did not play in tune or, worse, who made a mistake after having been corrected once. Almost every musician I met who had worked with him had an anecdote of this kind to recount. De Coteau did not try to please, nor did he compromise. His goal was to elevate calypso music to international standards.

Even though "the man was trouble," as many put it, he was also greatly admired. The arrangements he wrote and the sounds his bands produced attracted people to the rehearsals he conducted every Tuesday and Thursday; they also brought him respect and fame among calypsonians. As McIntosh recounts,

> Yes, that man was so popular. Madam, at one time, I did not even know what to do. When you see the season coming for calypsonians, I tell you, the house where we were living in wasn't so big. We were living down by the seaside, and there was a big shed by the sea. So they [the calypsonians] all used to go and sit down under the shed. And so when four or five come out [of the house], then four or five will go in, including Kitchener. Everybody had to come to my house. Because it is the first time, they are going to get their music right. They never heard about getting . . . you know. [Before] they would get a guitar, play anything, sing out of key, in key, whatever, and people clap, and that's it.

As the most influential arranger of the late 1960s and 1970s, de Coteau set musical norms. If a calypso tune submitted to him was missing a beat, for example, in one verse, he would add one to make all the melodic phrases of equal length. As for overall sound, he would refrain from using trumpets in the high register or from having them play loudly, so as not to detract from the calypso melody and the singer's voice, and also to avoid sounding like Latin American music or jazz. In the same vein, he would not hire, to use his words, "a parang singer in my chorus," meaning a backup vocalist singing in the high register: in his mind, calypso should not sound like "Spanish" music. He favored instead what he construed as calypso's own musical idiomatic expression, emphasizing the middle register and a specific rhythmic bounce. His aim was to ensure that calypso as national music could stand on its own, and project a unique sound.

Accordingly, de Coteau was fiercely opposed to reproducing sounds or musical gestures (e.g., particular phrasings or musical riffs) associated with "foreign music" in calypso. Even though he liked hearing many different types of music, he would immediately snap at musicians if he heard them play something he did not judge to be calypso. McIntosh reported one such incident as follows: "He would say: Do not bring jazz in calypso. Jazz is American music. Calypso is calypso, jazz is jazz. So if he would hear a trumpeter play a few notes in a jazz style, he would tell him, 'Is there anybody here named Eddy Calvert [in reference to the acknowledged English jazz trumpeter]?'—and tell him, don't come back if you're going to play that. Stay out. I'll get somebody else." Fearing, perhaps, that solo space would encourage players to improvise in the jazz style—through imitation rather than appropriation—de Coteau left little room in his arrangements for improvised passages by solo instruments.

According to Roy Cape, one of the most famous band directors in the Caribbean, de Coteau's calypso arrangements became normative for the sounds of calypso during the 1960s and 1970s.[33] His views about what constituted calypso's melodic structure and "authentic" sound, his rejection of what he considered mere musical imitations or quotations of foreign musics, and his emphasis on distinctive calypso rhythmic patterns informed the musical thinking and behavior of many calypsonians and musicians during that period—a kind of musical thinking and behavior that allegedly became the standard against which the musical offshoots of calypso were later to be judged.

The Art De Coteau Orchestra included the following instruments: one or two trumpets, two saxophones (one tenor and one alto), one trombone, piano, guitar, bass, drum set, and percussion instruments, including congas. De Coteau was well known for producing what local studio musicians refer to as "a rhythmic bounce." "When you listen to Arthur," said a recording studio musician to me, "listen to the bounce. It's always calypso. Arthur will give you pulsation and rhythm."[34] De Coteau achieved this feel by making the rhythm section clearly audible in the recording mix (see ex. 4).

Characteristically, he gave the guitar, piano (whenever used), bass, high-hat, and bass drum rhythmic patterns to play continuously throughout the tune (see ex. 5a). To infuse the section with rhythmic drive, he used distinctive piano strums (inspired by "guitar strums"—a Trinidadian expression referring to the playing of repeated chords on the piano) that became regarded as his signature (see ex. 5b). In turn, he featured the bass as it was then commonly played, on the first beat of each bar and emphasizing the notes of the triadic chord progression, until he adopted Shadow's innovative use of a melodic and syncopated bass line (discussed at greater length below).

Example 4
Art De Coteau's arrangement of "Nothing Ah Strange," by Black Stalin (1975)
Note the great rhythmic activity in this introduction.

(*continued*)

Example 4
Continued.

Example 5a
Art De Coteau's 1978 arrangement of the rhythm section for
"Market Street Jam," by Calypso Joe (Joseph Hunte)
Transcription by Lambert Philip.

De Coteau typically used the "brass" section at the ends of phrases
for punctuation. In his introductions, he often alternated the saxophones
playing in unison or in parallel thirds with the trumpets and trombone
playing short melodic phrases in a three-note chord harmony, then
brought together the whole brass section fully harmonized for a few bars

Example 5b
Two other typical keyboard strums used to accompany calypso
Transcription by Lambert Philip.

before he featured once again a call-and-response pattern between the saxophones and the trumpets and trombone. He did not like repetitions, and thus often used a melody for the band chorus different from the main melody of the given calypso over the same harmonic background. At other times, he would feature the main calypso tune in his band chorus introduction, but only by means of a few selected and reinterpreted lines. As was typical both then and now, de Coteau did not write the backup vocals' parts. Instead, he taught the vocalists their lines during rehearsals, or left it to the calypsonian to teach them the lines he or she wanted to hear during the course of the song.

According to Frankie Francis, de Coteau developed his preference for three-note chords with his piano teacher, Norman Simmons, who also played at church. Like the guitar, the brass section featured only plain triadic harmony. De Coteau used a simple musical language, Cape notes, to keep his sound ideal, not to "crowd the voice," and to stay as close as possible to the melody's own features.

De Coteau felt that many arrangers were paying too little attention to calypso's distinctive character and were going astray from it. Several musicians I interviewed remembered him saying such things as: "Frankie [Francis] does listen to jazz; Joey [Lewis] does listen to Latin; [Ed] Watson does listen to Haitian, you see?" Art de Coteau proudly considered his music to be "all calypso." He would listen to a calypso tune several times before writing the arrangement. As Cape put it, for him the goal was to "lift the song itself" with an arrangement making use of its particular qualities. De Coteau's adamant position against what he considered "foreign sounds" deeply influenced the Trinidadian calypso scene: by the mid-1970s, few arrangements prominently featuring jazz elements were being heard.

De Coteau continued to write arrangements until he died in 1987. Like Francis's, his tremendous influence on the calypso sounds of the 1960s and 1970s was acknowledged by many awards, most of them posthumous. In 1996 alone, in addition to the award given by the Pan Trinbago Steelband Week Festival, he was recognized by the Institute of Music for his outstanding contributions as a musical arranger.

Sound Mediations

Power through Fame

The influence of Francis's and de Coteau's arrangements on the calypso sounds of the 1960s and 1970s was propagated through the many recordings on which their work appeared and the live band performances of scores accompanying the calypsonians with whom they worked. It was also furthered through the band members they directed and trained during rehearsals and live performances. In turn, some calypsonians exerted a strong influence on calypso sounds by resorting to the power they acquired through fame—earned by winning competitions and by saturating the market with new compositions and major hits every year. Such was the case with the Mighty Sparrow and Lord Kitchener. Both became legendary figures for their remarkable feats in calypso competitions, unforgettable hit tunes and onstage performances during and outside the Carnival seasons. Following the local manner of describing how these calypsonians became star figures on the Carnival circuits, here are some of their prominent achievements.

Beginning with his first calypso competition in 1956, the Mighty Sparrow won the national Calypso King/Monarch crown eight times, the Road March title seven times, the King of Kings crown twice. As Ottley writes, he also achieved "the unique double of winning both the Calypso Monarch crown and the Road March title in the same year, 1956, 1960, and 1972, a feat still to be matched by another calypsonian."[35] In his turn, Lord Kitchener earned his fame by winning the National Road March competitions ten times, in 1946 before he left for England and nine other times between 1960 and 1979 (I stopped here to limit this description to the period concerned in this chapter). After his return to Trinidad in 1963, his pan calypsos were featured by twelve Panorama-winning steelbands in seventeen years between 1963 and 1979. He also won the Calypso King/Monarch Competition in 1975.

Unlike many winners whose songs were soon forgotten, both Sparrow and Kitchener produced winning tunes that were adopted overnight as "classics" in the calypso repertoire. In addition, many of their tunes not featured in competitions became well known through their stage performances in calypso tents, guest appearances at local fetes, shows on tours, and recordings—rare exceptions to the rule that most calypsos become part of the repertoire through exposure in competitions. In both Sparrow's and Kitchener's musical careers, the more competitions they won, the more opportunities they had to perform; the more money they made, the easier it was to produce a full LP album every year; and the more LPs they made, the more they could saturate the local, regional, and international markets with their tunes, and thus with their musical tastes and values. This is best illustrated by Sparrow, who, between the late 1950s and 1979, released some fifty LPs, with an average of ten songs on each.[36]

The Mighty Sparrow is credited with having helped consolidate older trends and initiate new ones. In his view, calypso has remained alive by achieving a balance between tradition and change and embracing different people and rhythms. In contrast to many individuals who defined calypso by a set of rules (illustrated below by Kitchener's stand on the issue), he argued that calypso's distinguishing feature as national culture was precisely its ability to absorb change and variety. As he explained,

> You see calypso is about life. It is about sex, violence, love, social and political commentary, it is about jobs, about shelter, about world issues. And you have different kinds of people singing it, people from different backgrounds, from different levels of education, giving the art all its infinite variety. Different styles. Some people are so grammatically correct, others go in for the common, every day parlance. There is as well, all the variety in tempo. Like Reggae it is a Caribbean music but it is able to embrace a far greater variety of rhythms. And to think it all started . . . way back in the days of slavery.[37]

Sparrow cultivated a calypso style of his own. From the time of his entry on the calypso stage, he composed his songs mainly in the major mode (e.g., "Jean and Dinah" and "Mr. Walker"), in contrast with many of the classic calypsos written in the minor mode during the previous decades. Many of the musicians interviewed remarked that while such a trend already existed in the thirties with calypsonians such as the Roaring Lion, the success of Sparrow's songs in competitions and record sales encouraged many writers to adopt it as the new standard from that time onward. As the interviewed musicians indicated, by the sixties, Sparrow's influence was so massive that the expression "Sparrowmania" was used to refer to the general attempt to "copycat" the songs and styles of the famous calypsonian.

In his illuminating historical reconstruction of the main trends during this period, Gordon Rohlehr (2004c) writes that Sparrow's "Jean and Dinah" expanded what was conceived up to the midfifties as the conventional structure of calypso: a sixteen-bar stanza and an eight-bar chorus.[38] Inspired, according to Rohlehr, perhaps by the musical structure of the foreign Alpine melody "The Happy Wanderer" (also known as "Valderee, Valdera"), which, to the discontent of many, had won the 1955 Road March, Sparrow wrote his 1956 winning song with a stanza and chorus of equal length: sixteen bars. Using this format from that point on for most of his compositions, Sparrow inspired many other calypsonians to follow suit.

Sparrow's musical experiments during that period, however, were not all well received. The song "Rose," which he performed in the 1961 competition, was criticized for its unusual form (which Rohlehr describes as a story line interrupted by repeated refrains within the stanza).[39] Allegedly for that reason, he lost that year's competition. His attempts to fuse calypso with twist, boogaloo, and cha-cha in the 1960s were also severely criticized by many, including his most serious rival, Lord Kitchener.[40] While both were recognized as trendsetters (as will be shown below in the case of Kitchener), each was also known for his attempts to control calypso's musical orientations during his heyday.

In the 1960s, Kitchener maintained that in order to continue to perform "authentic calypso," to use his own words, calypsonians had to stay away from foreign influences. In the aftermath of independence, his view that cultural independence could also be achieved if people focused on their roots was widespread. Such an endeavor (encouraged in fact by the former colonial powers and their notion of what constitutes a modern nation-state) could only be fraught with contradictions for a local population formed of several diasporic groups. Nonetheless, Kitchener used various tactics to make his views on this issue known to the entire calypso community. In 1967, he wrote a song entitled "No More Calypsong" admonishing Sparrow to stop singing "tango, carol, classic and ballad" and hence trying to fool the folks from Trinidad about what calypso really is. He then offered his own recipe for true calypso rhythm, tempo, melodic structure, harmony, linguistic accent, and content, specifying too that it should call for participation. Both Sparrow and Kitchener used their positions as star figures to promote "good kaiso" by hiring and firing calypsonians in the calypso tents where they performed.

In exercising this power, both effectively defined and assessed "talent" in aspiring calypsonians—as when Kitchener encouraged and helped young Black Stalin learn about the artform. From such positions of authority, the two calypsonians could also take risks by featuring unusual candidates in their tents—as was the case when Sparrow gave a chance to De Mighty Trini to perform on the calypso stage at his Hideaway, and when Kitchener hired Denyse Plummer to perform at the Review at the very beginning of her career in calypso.

As star figures, Sparrow and Kitchener also used interviews to judge new musical orientations in calypso. As reported by Rohlehr, both commented publicly during the second half of the sixties, on radio programs, in newspapers, and in interviews on the issue of tradition (then advocated by Kitchener) versus change (promoted by Sparrow).[41] Through these interviews, they loudly voiced their opinions on the issue of "serious" calypsos versus party music, referring to the emergence of soca in the late 1970s and its controversial place in calypso competitions. While by then Sparrow was complaining not about musical change, but the lack of lyrical content of the new "calypso for partying," Kitchener was using the media to communicate his new view on calypso's relation to change. In 1978, Kitchener insisted in many interviews that soca was simply an offshoot of calypso, a variation on the same theme, as it were, as had happened many times before. Calypso's capacity to absorb foreign influences meant that calypso by definition had always been, to use LeRoi Jones's expression, a "changing same."[42] As Kitchener put it on the radio broadcast *Evening News* in January of that year:[43]

The Calypso was once sung in patois; Lion was in those times. The Mighty Growler then added a swing in Calypso. . . . Growler's styling continued until Sparrow took over with a ballad type of Calypso in 1956 and the people loved it. Now Lord Shorty, who has been experimenting for years, has come up with the soca beat. . . . God bless Lord Shorty. . . . I am warning those calypsonians who feel the "soca" is not Calypso to watch the waves. Those who cannot ride on the crest of the waves will have to fall by the wayside. For years they have been clamouring for a change in Calypso and now it is here they have failed to recognize it.

The "soca" beat is the only beat to fight against The American 'soul' and Jamaican Reggae. We should be proud of the "soca" instead of trying to cry it down. I Kitchener say "soca" is Calypso and I should know because throughout my life I have identified myself as a calypsonian and nothing else. No one can tell me what is Calypso or not.

Around the time he was sharing his view on soca, Kitchener used his knowledge and definition of calypso to fire two arrangers with whom he had been working—one allegedly for featuring too many jazz elements, the other for too much disco influence.[44] For Kitchener, the limits within which the "changing same" of calypso could produce authentic national culture were always negotiable.

Critical Acclaim

If fame enabled calypsonians such as Sparrow and Kitchener to "normalize" certain calypso sounds, critical acclaim allowed new voices with hardly any musical pedigree in the Carnival music scene to defy some calypso conventions of the time and make an impact on the "artform." Such was the case for calypsonian Winston Bailey, known under the sobriquet Shadow. Shadow first stepped onto the calypso stage in Sparrow's Young Brigade tent as a backup vocalist in 1970. During the next three years, he entered competitions in the bold attempt to defeat the two reigning stars, Sparrow and Kitchener, since 1963 the only two winners of the Road March competitions. In 1974, Shadow won the Road March, ending that monopoly with his song "Bassman" (about how Shadow cannot do anything but hear in his head day and night the lines of a bass player). That he won the Road March competition with this song was significant. It showed the power of the public to challenge existing norms and styles, including those sanctioned by the judges.

"Bassman" foregrounded a melodic bass line in ways never heard before in calypso arrangements. It granted new importance to the rhythm section as opposed to the reeds and brass. The song's first eight bars consisted of a bass line doubled by guitar with only the drum set, cowbell, and conga as accompaniment; the full ensemble led by the horn section filled the next eight bars. Shadow's first verse opened with the usual eight-bar phrase, but the second phrase was divided into two parts: four bars of text followed by eight bars of vocables over the same bass line, doubled by guitar and accompanied by the drum set and other percussion heard in the introduction. The third and fourth phrases of the verse each unfolded over the usual eight bars. Compared to the then dominating ballad calypso, the melodic structure of the four-lines stanza, with its unconventional number of bars (eight plus twelve; eight plus eight) was unorthodox, but not entirely new in calypso (e.g., Sparrow's "Melda" and Kitchener's "Mas in Madison Square"). The foregrounding of the bass line and its break away from the text delivery in the second phrase of the verse, however, were revolutionary.[45] (See ex. 6.)

Example 6
Introduction of "Bassman," by Shadow
Transcription by Carla Brunet.

(*continued*)

While the chorus presented four melodic phrases of equal length (i.e., with the regular eight bars), it presented yet another uncommon feature: half the chorus was sung with vocables over the bass line heard in the introduction. The lyrical content of the song was also atypical. After featuring new text in the first two phrases, the second and third verses repeated the text heard in the third and fourth phrases of the first verse. Placed against the narrative ballad, this economy of words offered a stark contrast—one that, together with the newly featured melodic bass line, greatly appealed to the public. While the repetition of text in "Bassman" did not become a characteristic of calypso, but rather of soca in the 1990s, its bass line brought a musical metamorphosis in calypso sounds from the time it was heard in 1974.

Example 6
Continued.

Both the brevity of text and the emphasis on a melody carried by a highly rhythmic bass line in "Bassman" resonated with musical forms of the past as well as with new musical trends in the present. Nineteenth- and early-twentieth-century lavway songs were based on a minimum of text; the new Jamaican musical genre, reggae—already popular throughout the Caribbean—was known for its prominent bass line. In addition to such audible entanglements with local and Caribbean soundscapes, the widespread adoption of Shadow's new conception of bass line in calypso was made possible, I contend, partly through Shadow's own formidable presence onstage and partly through his arranger, Art de Coteau. According to Art de Coteau's band musicians, Shadow transformed the arranger's

Example 6
Continued.

(*continued*)

treatment of the bass line. Before Shadow composed "Bassman" (1974), de Coteau used to write scores for the brass section only. With Shadow's innovations, de Coteau started to write a part for the bass. As one musician put it, "Before Shadow, a bassman just had to have ears, and once he had ears, he could follow a tune. But after Shadow, you had to get eyes, because you needed to read." [46]

Following the resounding success of Shadow's song, Art de Coteau began using bass lines similar to the one in "Bassman" in arrangements for other calypsonians. Note, for example, how he drops all the other instruments and uses solely the bass and the guitar in unison to effect a break before the last line of each verse in Lord Relator's song "None So

Example 6
Continued.

Sweet" (1973); how he features the bass in unison with the brass and then
with the backup vocals in the Mighty Terror's "Pan Talent"; and also how,
on the same LP recorded by the Mighty Terror, *Calypso Hits* (1979), he
foregrounds the bass in the introduction of "Chinese Children."[47] The
resemblance to Shadow's bass line is striking.

Writing Tunes for Road March and Panorama

In addition to the influences I have been discussing, musical demands
made by steelband arrangements also influenced the sounds of calypso
of the 1960s and 1970s. Some calypsonians composed their songs with
these demands in mind for at least two reasons. One is that, on Jouvert
morning and on Carnival Tuesday, steelbands used to provide the instru-

mental versions of the most popular calypso tunes of the season and thus were literally instrumental in making a calypsonian win the Road March competition.[48] The other is that, from the moment it was instituted in 1963, Panorama provided another means for calypsonians to achieve recognition. Being selected by a steelband gave their tunes further exposure, thus confirming their public appeal, at least from a musical point of view.

To be played by steelbands, calypso tunes had to stand on their own, without the lyrics. Particularly for Panorama, tunes with varied rhythmic patterns, distinctive melodic riffs, and catchy hook lines had the best chance of being chosen by steelband players and arrangers.[49] Kitchener, recognized as one of the first calypsonians to write tunes with steelbands in mind, unquestionably understood well steelbands' strengths and weaknesses. He catered to the specific qualities of the pan instrument—its percussive sound, bell-like tone, lingering resonance, and various sizes and colors—and he wrote tunes with melodic and rhythmic motifs that lent themselves to elaborate instrumental arrangements. Between 1963 and 1979, twelve of the Panorama competitions were won by steelbands playing arrangements of his tunes. Through their appeal among steelband players and arrangers—who, by including up to one hundred players in each band, constitute in and of themselves a large audience in Trinidad[50]—and their success in Panorama competitions, Kitchener's compositions became well known in and out the country and contributed greatly to establishing the sounds of what became known as "pan calypso."

Conceived in tandem with the Road March competitions, Kitchener's pan calypsos were performed in an upbeat tempo—in the 1960s equivalent to $\quarternote$ = 112, and in the mid-1970s, reaching $\quarternote$ = 126, as is well illustrated in the original recording of "Pan in Harmony."[51] In the 1960s his Road March songs maintained the traditional form of a narrative ballad (a verse of sixteen bars followed by a chorus of the same length), but in the 1970s Kitchener placed a much greater emphasis on the chorus, further distinguishing the "serious lyrics" calypso from the Road March and pan calypso. In so doing, he increased the importance of backup vocals and public participation, while creating more possibilities for interactive playing between the various steelband sections. Hence, during that decade, while he continued to use a sixteen-bar verse, he usually featured a chorus of thirty-two bars (in the exceptional case of "Pan in Harmony," the chorus lasts forty-eight bars). In the first half of the 1970s, in line with the Carnival songs of the nineteenth and early twentieth centuries called lavways,[52] his choruses alternated between him as the song leader and the backup vocals every four bars, and always in the same order. By the second half of the 1970s, Kitchener had quickened the call and response to every two bars, and sometimes to every bar, and not always in the same order. In the same song, the first part of the call and response featured Kitchener; at other times, the backup vocals, creating further dynamic interplay and variety in the performance of the song. The number of different parts assigned to the backup vocals dramatically increased, providing richer material for steelband arrangements to explore—as was demonstrated by "Tribute to Spree," the 1975 calypso that not only earned Kitchener the winning titles of the Road March and Calypso King competitions, but also led the steelband playing an arrangement of that tune to win the Panorama competition.[53]

As a means of generating more dramatic excitement, Kitchener's pan calypsos often employed syncopated accents in the form of shouts and yells that could easily be reproduced by some sections of the steelbands. He also sang onomatopoetic sounds to explore and imitate the particular registers and colors of steelband instruments. His tunes typically incorporated breaks, described by Dudley as "an important device for creating excitement and rhythmic energy"[54]—particularly welcome to instruments with percussive qualities, such as steel pans. As yet another means to play with rhythm and texture, Kitchener contrasted dense lines of text performed in a rapid delivery over a few bars with a sparse use of words in the next musical phrase. Kitchener's pan calypsos greatly contributed to the consolidation of calypso's partnership with the national instrument.[55] As most steelbands up to the eighties were still made up mainly of male Afro-Trinidadians from the lower class, the partnership between pan and calypso arguably reinforced further the foregrounding of a very specific subject in the (re)presentation of Trinidad and Tobago as a nation.

During the 1960s and 1970s the cultural politics of calypso were deeply entangled with projects that forged distinctively Trinidadian national subjects. Leading arrangers, stars, and their audiences all engaged in struggles over markers of authenticity and the boundaries of permissible innovations that would still be recognized as legitimate calypso, understood by all as a distinctively Trinidadian cultural artform. De Coteau pursued contradictory impulses: on the one hand, he prohibited his musicians from imitating any recognizably "foreign" musical styles; on the other hand, he sought to standardize calypso by adding a beat to a measure in order to make this artform commensurable with his understanding of international standards. Francis, from an older generation, felt comfortable drawing on varied genres such as jazz and Latin American sounds without worrying that calypso would be in any way diminished. For him, national pride became translated into projects of improving musicianship, notably by encouraging musicians to read and perform from scores. These skills, which he took to be markers of progress, would usher calypso into modernity.

In their turn, stars fought over the extent to which calypso could absorb "outside" musical influences without losing its distinct Trinidadian qualities. Sparrow believed that calypso's vitality stemmed from its ability to absorb change and variety, a point on which Kitchener took him to task. While Kitchener viewed change as integral to calypso's history, he insisted that some specific musical elements needed to be present for a music to qualify as Trinidadian calypso. From this nationalist perspective, he wrote steelband compositions helping to promote the recognition of the pan as a national instrument. In so doing, Kitchener nurtured pride among musicians and audiences by helping them valorize this instrument as a creative invention unique to this nation-state.

Audiences also exerted influence on how calypso should be defined by making and breaking the stars, who themselves greatly depended upon the craft and skills of their arrangers. Shadow's audiences challenged what competition juries held to be the defining characteristics of calypso understood as the emblematic national music by making Shadow a Road March winner the same year he lost the Calypso Monarch competition. Sparrows' acclaim derives from the tangible support his audiences consistently demonstrated by buying his recordings, attending his shows in great numbers, and endorsing his music with fervor enough to produce "Sparrowmania." In myriad ways, audiences spurred dynamism in calypso, conferred prestige on performers and arrangers, and supported Trinidadian artists. Through such cultural politics, calypso became a means of identification for listeners and music makers that marked them all as distinctively Trinidadians.

Calypso's Musical Offshoots

Postindependence, Proliferation, and Permissible Traditions

This chapter begins part 2 of the book, focusing on postindependence Trinidad, by examining the proliferation of the new music styles—soca, chutney soca, rapso, and ragga soca. Two goals guide my analysis: to highlight the cultural claims these new styles make in relation to the politics of nation and diaspora; and to investigate the struggles over authenticity and permissible traditions waged by the groups associated with these new musics. This chapter examines how the new Carnival musics, making audible the presence of heterogeneous constituencies, have redefined the terrain on which national culture is debated. It also shows how these musics have sparked a rethinking of the expression, representation, and positioning of the nation and its discrepant diasporas.

By the 1990s, the proliferation of new styles had led to confusion both on and off the islands. Like many other readers, I was struck sometimes to see that no fewer than three different music styles could be attached to a single artist. Take for example, the following excerpt from a Trinidadian newspaper. Under a headline reading, "Toronto's *Soca* Star Guney Cedeno 'Inside' with . . . *Ragga Soca* Groove," the opening paragraph presents the artist as follows: "Stockily-built calypsonian/composer Guney Cedeno is another 'son of the soil' who is achieving great things on the Canadian/North American '*kaiso*' scene."[1] It is common knowledge in the Caribbean that the terms "kaiso" and "calypso" mean the same thing, but to conflate these musical terms also with

169

"soca" and "raga soca" seemed to suggest that there were no meaningful musical distinctions to be made among these terms. At a time when artists from the English Caribbean were trying to consolidate their position in the world music scene, such confusion could be disastrous in terms of marketing. That "soca," "ragga soca," and "kaiso" were—and continue to be—used indiscriminately at some times but not at others could not be simply ascribed to a lack of musical knowledge or to sloppy journalism. The differentiation between the terms—and the lack of it—had to be looked at, as Tina K. Ramnarine suggests, in relation to "the histories claimed for them."[2] In this vein, I set out to examine how the various music styles are constructed in relation to, and positioned against, the hegemonic discourse of calypso.

Since Trinidad's formal independence in 1962, the historical period normatively termed "postindependence" has had multiple moments. During the 1970s, disillusion set in. A majority of the population grew increasingly frustrated over the inability of the independent nation-state's elected officials to fulfill their promises, and a strikingly large number of people began migrating to the United States and Canada. In the early 1980s, Trinidad's local economy crashed, following the worldwide fall of oil prices, and the structural adjustment policies then imposed by moneylenders such as the International Monetary Fund (IMF) led to the loss of bureaucratic jobs and a large increase in the unemployment rate. Here I focus on the 1990s, the period that dramatically transformed Carnival musics' relations with the state and their later articulations of nation and diaspora. This historical moment also marks my own ethnographic immersion in the calypso scene.

In the early 1990s, the state government led by the PNM (which in 1986 had lost the elections for the first time, regaining power in 1989) no longer focused on nation building, but on economic issues brought about by the rise of chronic unemployment and the lack of funding for basic national services. In the wake of Thatcherism's policies in Britain, Trinidadian state agencies implemented neoliberal measures that increased privatization, redirected state objectives and funding, and encouraged the rise of new entrepreneurship and the creation of new networks and alliances. In its efforts to create the conditions for the so-called freedoms of market, self, and citizenship—the hallmark of neoliberalism—the state administration, for example, dramatically reduced the tariffs on musical and electronic equipment, thereby enabling musicians to outfit their studios with state-of-the art equipment purchased overseas.[3] It relinquished its exclusive control over radio and television broadcast and granted licenses to individuals and private organizations to operate their own stations.

In this context of neoliberal privatization, other dramatic transformations took place. Following the new emphasis on the free market, Carnival state-sponsored activities were now placed in open competition with the private sector's own initiatives. After more than half a century of monopoly, the state-sponsored calypso competition saw the emergence of new Carnival competitions for the musical styles of soca, chutney soca, and ragga soca. Held during the Carnival period and only a few days apart from the calypso competition, adopting its format with semifinals and finals, and placing a jury in charge of establishing competition criteria and choosing winners, these competitions helped calypso's musical offshoots gain both recognition and legitimacy. Crucially, globalization and commoditization—both as discourses and economic processes—figured prominently in these politics of recognition. Scores of musicians, fans, journalists, and academics vehemently debated the implications of globalization for aesthetics, morality, and national identity, with some charging that the process reduced cultural creativity.

I stress the emergence of new competitions here, but not to suggest, as noted in chapter 3, that they are the only site from which the social, cultural, political, and economic importance of new Carnival musics may be judged. The growing presence of rapso—another musical offshoot of calypso using a chanting style that emphasizes Trinidadian rhythmic speech patterns over calypso rhythmic accompaniment—during Carnival, in spite of having no competition of its own, has nonetheless been noticeable since the 1990s. Some self-proclaimed artists, rather than entering competitions, have performed on Jouvert morning, at fetes, and at shows; others, while not identifying themselves as rapso artists, have performed in the rapso style in soca and ragga soca competitions and on other musical occasions as well. Making claims of its own through practice, rapso has helped to undermine the normative construction of Carnival music defined through calypso. Yet by institutionalizing the audible entanglements of soca, chutney soca, and ragga soca, and by emulating the calypso competitions that served historically as the "authenticating" spaces of national culture in Trinidad, the competitions that emerged in the 1990s have been particularly significant. They have openly challenged, on its very terrain, calypso's hegemonic articulation of the tensions within the nation, between nation and diaspora, and within and among discrepant diasporas. For that reason, I give these cultural politics special attention.

In the first section, I focus on the origin stories of each of these new styles. As they seek to authorize and legitimate authentic traditions, origin stories are not politically innocent: they establish the terrain on which traditions are debated, challenged, and defended. From this perspective,

I examine the new styles' origin stories with two goals in mind: to highlight the particular claims of each and to examine how each one constructs its audible entanglement with distinct musics, technologies, and
ethnic, racial, and gendered social groups. Then I examine both the issues
of representation in national culture and the tensions that the new styles
have helped to foreground: between the African and Indian diasporas,
within groups, between gendered roles, across generations, and among
classes.[4] In the last section, I concentrate on the diasporic circuits in
which these musics are (re)produced and travel in order to address how,
within these contexts, the new musical styles perform their own versions
of nation and diaspora.

Origin Stories of the New Music Styles

Soca

The term "sokah" (later spelled "soca") was coined by Ras Shorty I (Garfield Blackman, formerly called Lord Shorty)[5] in Trinidad around 1973,
following his musical experiments in mixing Indian elements with calypso.[6] In an interview with Roy Boyke, published in the *1979 Carnival
Magazine,* Ras Shorty described the circumstances that prompted him to
put forward a new music style and a new sound:

> I was trying to find something because the talk was that calypso was dying
> and reggae was the thing. I thought the musicians in the country had a right
> to get together and use their minds to renew or improve calypso somewhat.
> Everybody was putting it down. . . . Calypso was dying a natural death. And to
> come up with a new name and a new form in calypsoul [calypso + soul] was
> what Sparrow was trying to do all along. Sparrow tried to add a lot of things
> to calypso and it didn't work. I felt it needed something brand new to hit
> everybody like a thunderbolt. . . . I came up with the name soca. I invented
> soca. And I never spelled it s-o-c-a. It was s-o-k-a-h to reflect the East Indian
> influence.[7]

If one of Ras Shorty's goals in creating sokah was indeed to "renew or
improve calypso," another was "to unite the Indian and African peoples."[8]
At his home in Piparo—a remote village with narrow and bumpy roads
where he retreated with his family, and where I first met him in 1997—
he explained to me his belief that through music he could help fight
"racialism" among Indians and Africans. In his view, "the fusion of the

music can do that."[9] Another goal was to encourage the young people of Trinidad to listen to their own music. Around that time, he remarked, young people preferred to listen to Jamaican reggae. Furthermore, they had come to believe that one had to go to the United States to accomplish anything. His aim, in creating a new sound, was to fight these tendencies and cultivate national pride by motivating Trinidadians to believe in themselves and to support their own music and musicians.

The term "sokah," Ras Shorty explained, comes from the combination of two syllables: "The 'so' comes from calypso. And the 'kah,' to show the East Indian thing in the rhythm, right? . . . . I selected the syllable 'kah' because it represents the first letter of the Indian alphabet." Mungal Patasar, a renowned Trinidadian sitar player trained in Indian classical music, noted the appropriateness of Ras Shorty's selection of the syllable "kah" as a symbol of Indian rhythm, since, as the first letter of the alphabet, it signals the start of a movement. In addition, "kah" is also the first syllable of the name of the beat "Kaherwa."[10]

Though not his first experiment in mixing East Indian and African musical elements, Ras Shorty's song "Indrani," recorded in 1973, represents a key moment in the commercial unveiling of the music he chose to call "sokah." Reactions to the song, however, were mixed in both communities. As Ras Shorty explained, because the lyrics talked about an East Indian woman who, after drinking rum, would lure her man into the bedroom, the Indians thought he was disparaging their women and, by extension, their music as well. Moreover, because the arrangements of the song featured instruments that Trinidadians associated with Indian traditions—the *dholak* (a double-headed barrel drum played with bare hands), the *dhantal* (also spelled *dandtal*, "a metal rod struck by a U-shaped clapper"),[11] and the mandolin—the Africans thought he was spoiling their music—namely, calypso.

Despite these complaints, in 1974 Ras Shorty produced an album entitled *The Love Man,* which continued in the same vein as "Indrani" and, except for one song, featured a *dholak* on every track. After this album was again criticized for using Indian instruments, Ras Shorty decided to change the instrumentation for his 1975 recording. In his new arrangements he removed the Indian instruments but kept the Indian rhythms, assigning them to traditional Western instruments—in particular, the drum set and the guitar.[12] According to Ras Shorty, some of the musicians, including the keyboard and conga players, found the new rhythms too difficult to play and reverted to those they knew best—the traditional calypso rhythmic patterns. The mixture of the new rhythms and the traditional ones on Western musical instruments stopped the controversy about "Shorty playing Indian." It also proved a commercial success for his album *Endless Vibrations*.

At precisely the time when the changes of instrumentation took place, the spelling of "sokah" was changed to "soca" by a journalist who, according to Ras Shorty, began his story on him with the headline: "Shorty Is Doing Soca." The interpretation of the term "soca" no longer referred to the Indian contribution. Instead, it came to be seen as the contraction of the musics believed to be at its foundation—namely, as the fusion of soul (so) and calypso (ca). Could it be that this change of spelling was done in the same spirit as the change of instrumentation, to make the new style more acceptable to the core audience at Carnival celebrations—that is, calypso aficionados? Ras Shorty did not protest; the new spelling stayed.

In Ras Shorty's account, the new rhythms and arrangements of soca were picked up for the first time in late 1976 by another artist, the renowed calypsonian Maestro (Cecil Hume), with the song "Savage." Many other artists then followed suit, but not until 1978 did soca become firmly established as a style. The key moment came with "Sugar Bum Bum," by Lord Kitchener, the song which apparently sold more copies than any of the other songs in his vast repertoire.[13] According to Ras Shorty, from that time on, soca became synonymous with party music and, in his words, "moved back" to a less sophisticated rhythm section and less politically conscious lyrics. By then, the chief exponents of the music as originally conceived had disappeared from view. Maestro had died in a car accident the year before at a premature age, and Ras Shorty had withdrawn from the music scene.

In Ras Shorty's view, after "Sugar Bum Bum" the new soca has continued to carry the Indian rhythms through the drum set and "to punch out the bass line on the drum set." At the same time, he believed that many new elements have contributed to the continual transformation of soca, including "a lot of sampling with zouk, with plenty American influences, plenty funk. . . . A lot of things went on."

By the 1990s, compared to calypso, soca not only enjoyed the greatest media exposure in both press and radio, but was also the music generating the most important incomes during Carnival. In spite of its musical appeal and commercial success, however, it was still shunned by the calypso competitions, because, instead of featuring "conscious" lyrics, it focused nearly exclusively on pleasure, dance, and sexualized bodies. (Soca lyrics will be discussed at greater length in the next chapter.) Dance and in particular "wining" became central to soca's expression and attraction. "Wining" is one of the dominant dance movements typical of many

African-derived musical traditions in the Caribbean and is characterized by winding or gyrating the hips. Performed alone or in close physical contact with a partner, wining can be done in an erotic or a more casual manner.[14] The propulsive rhythms of most soca songs, with their frequent calls to wine and execute other moves, conjure up a festive and playful mood. Capitalizing on soca's massive outreach in parties and fetes and its commercial value, William Munroe, chairman of Caribbean Prestige Productions International (CPPI), created the Soca Monarch competitions in 1993.

In line with its initial mission to bring the Indians and the Africans together, soca songs in the 1990s competitions continued to draw the voices of new subjects into the Carnival scene. Influenced by the growing prominence of women in other Caribbean popular musics, such as dancehall and zouk, and transnational practices such as rap, soca featured a significant number of solo female artists and frontliners. Along with these relatively new musics and the new importance of female singers, soca thus provided a space for Trinidadian female artists to join regional and international movements while also participating as song leaders or mass leaders in the prominent public sphere where the nation was audibly articulated.

Featuring the voices of new subjects, soca also forged new relationships with tradition. Old musical techniques (like repetition, call and response, and rhythmic patterns typical of traditional Carnival characters like Jab Molassie or Jab Jab) were featured in new songs, including "Jab Molassie," by Superblue (1994), and "Jab Jab," by Machel Montano (2000). Old calypso songs were not abandoned, but reconfigured, as when Maximus Dan's 2002 song "Vampire" featured excerpts of Black Stalin's song "Vampire Year," recorded in 1982. The rearticulation of traditional material with contemporary sounds from multiple cultural and national locations was not a new strategy in the Caribbean, where mixes and remixes have always been common. But placed against the prohibitions of using "too many foreign influences"—the sign for nationalists of commercial co-option—soca's open celebration of the creolization process in the 1990s made any claim that the nation could be defined exclusively in terms of a fixed tradition harder to sustain.

In the same vein, soca foregrounded new music technologies by means of "cultural reconversion"—an expression coined by Nestor Garcia Canclini to stress the active agency involved in appropriating various elements in musical production.[15] Such cultural reconversion took place, for example, when band musicians used the drum machine to make soca sounds palatable to contemporary audiences. It also took place when

Machel Montano appropriated a Jamaican dancehall rhythm to create a break in his fast-paced 1997 soca song "Big Truck," providing a breathing space before returning to his fast soca section with a renewed intensity. Similarly, when by the late 1990s soca artists were relying on "riddims" (derived from a well-known Jamaican practice, fixed, prerecorded instrumental rhythm section tracks created by producers or arrangers that are used by different artists) to create their own soca songs, they did not fear that this imported compositional technique would endanger the local cultural heritage.[16] Rather, as Machel Montano explained, "It simply shows who we are, and what we listen to."[17]

Like calypso, soca continually appropriates new musical elements. As Gordon Rohlehr explained in his article "Calypso Reinvents Itself," when "ragga soca" emerged in the Carnival music scene in the 1990s, it was only the last version of "the long and sometimes unacknowledged interface and intercourse between Calypso and Jamaican music from Mento to Dancehall."[18] (♪ CD track 3, "Daddy Axe," by Machel Montano and Xtatik.) The difference between the 1990s and earlier times, I would argue, however, is that a far greater number of elements from Jamaican music—dancehall, in particular, and what Rohlehr has described as its earthier version—have been integrated into soca.[19] So unlike in the 1970s and early 1980s, when, say, the offbeats of the reggae guitar could be heard occasionally in the accompaniment of some calypsos (e.g., Lord Superior's "Cultural Assassination"), since the late 1990s, the tone of voice, vocal delivery style, and melodic riffs typical of dancehall have often been fused with soca (e.g., in KMC's and Bunji Garlin's recordings, to name only two obvious examples of this new tendency). The great popularity of dancehall music in Trinidad and elsewhere in the Caribbean, combined with the worldwide trend of foresounding musical fusion have provided the conditions of possibility for ragga soca to create a wide appeal among fans who listen to soca and/or dancehall musics. In 1999 ragga soca's appeal was such that cultural entrepreneur Veejay Ramlal created a yearly National Ragga Soca Monarch competition during Trinidad's Carnival hoping to boost its commercial success. In turn, these competitions gave ragga soca official recognition in the calypso music scene. In spite of their institutionalization through competitions, however, ragga soca and soca songs have continued to be admitted in either one of the two competitions or simultaneously in both, suggesting that soca has become, like calypso, a generic term of its own.[20]

All the imported technologies in soca and ragga soca—technologies here meaning practices, products, and techniques—as Canclini would argue, helped rearticulate the local cultural heritage by putting at the forefront a multiplicity of subjectivities and senses of belonging that interconnect the local and the global, the national, the regional, and the transnational.[21] Made audible in nationally held competitions during Carnival, soca and ragga soca sounds became an effective medium for witnessing how the bonds and boundaries of national culture were negotiated.

Even before being sanctioned in competitions, the audible entanglements foresounded in soca songs paved the way for other formulations of the tensions between nation and diaspora, within the nation, and within and among discrepant diasporas, notably through chutney soca.[22] By the mideighties, after its initial mixing of Afro- and Indo-Trinidadian sounds was almost no longer audible, soca (then predominantly heard as an Afro-Trinidadian music) was (re)appropriated by the Indian community to produce chutney soca, a fusion unmistakably merging the sounds of the two musical traditions—and, furthermore, those of other traditions.

Chutney Soca

The music style "chutney soca" emerged among Trinidad's East Indian population. As the expression indicates, it refers to the fusion of the musics chutney and soca. Even though this musical fusion had already existed for some time, its recognition as a musical style was firmly established on the market in 1987 with Drupatee Ramgoonai's appearance in Spektakula—one of the most attended calypso tents in Trinidad—with the song "Chutney Soca." Unlike that of soca, the origin story of chutney soca in my interviews was not linked to one single individual. Instead, it was consistently recounted as proceeding from an evolution marked by three distinct phases: the tracing of chutney as a folk music practice from India, its subsequent transformation in Trinidad, and its ultimate fusion with soca.[23]

Mungal Patasar, an outstanding performer (sitarist) of Indian classical traditions and a leading artist in fusion music (mixing Indian, Indo-Trinidadian, Afro-Trinidadian, and jazz), as well as one of the judges of chutney soca competitions, spoke to me about the "evolution" of chutney soca: "First, to understand chutney soca," he began, "you've got to know what chutney is and what soca is."[24] In reference to Indian food, "chutney" is a Hindi word referring to "a spicy sauce that one takes with one's meals, in small quantities, to add the right taste or flavour. It is made up of small proportions of many herbs and spices ground together to form a paste—one which adds an 'extra tinge' to the routine meal."[25] In Trinidad, Patasar explained, this term also refers to the music that has emerged from the mixture of Indian folk music traditions associated with weddings and childbirth celebrations—celebrations performed by women.[26] The hybrid offspring has been called "chutney," because, as someone explained, "the music is hot . . . [so] people started calling it chutney."[27] Traditionally performed at Hindu wedding ceremonies in Trinidad, chutney songs were sung in Hindi and Bhojpuri—the main language of Bihar and Uttar Pradesh, the regions where most of the immigrants came from—and accompanied by *dholak, dhantal,* and *manjira* (hand cymbals joined by a string).[28] The songs were characterized by fast tempo, simple refrain-verse structure, and light, erotic texts. During the maticor, also spelled matkor (on the Friday night of the wedding), the singing was typically accompanied by erotic dances performed with playfulness and ribaldry to initiate the bride into the rituals of conjugal life.

According to Manuel, however, the musical legacy of chutney cannot be traced exclusively to these single musical traditions performed by women. Rather, it comprises "a variety of genres, such as wedding songs, birth songs (*sohar*), devotional Hindu *bhajans,* narrative *birha,* seasonal songs (*chowtal, hori, chaiti*), Urdu/Muslim *qawwali* and *qasida,* and idiosyncratic versions of Hindustani classical and light-classical genres which form the core of neo-traditional '*tan*-singing' or 'local [here meaning Guyana, Suriname, and especially Trinidad] classical music.'"[29] Along these lines, historian and songwriter Ken Parmasad suggests that while the themes of East Indian men's drinking songs at rum shops and women's songs performed at wedding ceremonies contrast with each other, their musical structures were virtually identical.[30] By incorporating musical elements from these different musical genres, chutney can be said to have enacted a family resemblance for a wide musical repertoire. Its distinct characteristics became associated with a set of melodic structures in combination with a fast, "hot" tempo inciting dancers to "breakaway" (let go).

In the late 1960s and early 1970s, the songs performed at wedding ceremonies underwent profound transformations. They were taken from the private cooking nights where they were performed exclusively by women before the wedding and transmuted into a public dance phenomenon.[31] By then, traditional prohibitions against women performing in public, and inhibitions about men and women dancing in the same space, had grown more relaxed. Many Indo-Caribbean weddings were now including chutney-style dancing performed by women and a few men, as Manuel specifies, "not necessarily in couples, but in the same space and in merry disregard of prior taboos."[32] As these dances gained popularity, cultural promoters Sham and Moean Mohammed began to promote chutney in several public events, Indian Cultural Pageant competitions, Indian radio shows, and fetes. By the late 1960s, chutney was no longer sung exclusively by women, but also by men.

Recognizing that several singers and musicians contributed to the emergence of chutney as a popular musical style, I interviewed Sundar Popo, commonly acknowledged as a leading exponent of chutney (as it is known today), to learn his version of the genre's origins. Popo began with information about his background and childhood. He was born in 1943 in Lengua Village, Princesstown, into a family of musicians. His father was a tassa drummer for East Indian weddings, and his aunt, who raised him after his mother died, was a renowned chutney singer who also played the *dholak*. When he was a young boy, his aunt took him to the "cooking nights" (the night before the wedding during which chutney music is performed), and there he learned the melodies associated with this musical tradition. Even though Popo did not mention to me being exposed to these melodies elsewhere, it is likely, according to Gregory M. Diethrich, that "the songs he heard as a young man in rumshops and other contexts influenced him as much as the songs of private women's ceremonies."[33] In all cases, his interest in learning this repertoire was encouraged by the radio program transmitting Indian-Caribbean music initiated by Moean Mohammed in 1947 and Mohammed's creation of the televised talent-scouting competition, Mastana Bahar, in the late 1960s.[34] In his early twenties at the time, when many efforts were being deployed to encourage the revival of Indian musical practices, Popo became interested in being part of the shows organized by the Mohammed brothers and began composing melodies based on the repertoire he had learned through his aunt. To these he added new texts in English—a relatively novel feature which, he explained, created strong appeal at the time. One of the first songs Popo sang in that vein, the most remembered and commercially most successful of his songs, was "Nana and Nani" performed in 1969 and released on record in 1971.[35]

In performances of the late 1960s and early 1970s, Popo was usually accompanied by the *dholak* drum, *dhantal,* and harmonium. Later on, influenced by the growing popularity of soca, his musical accompaniment added to the traditional instruments those associated with soca bands: bass, guitar, drum set, a synthesizer (which, by imitating its sounds, often replaced the harmonium), and occasionally a brass section, plus four or five male or female backup vocalists. This, he explained, is what marks the difference: "When you sing a chutney melody with just *dholak, dhantal* and harmonium, that's chutney; when you have chutney with a big band, that's chutney soca."

Despite all these transformations, said Patasar, chutney songs can still be easily identified. While the texts may be new, they nevertheless follow standard Indian folk song themes. Peter Manuel describes these standard themes as "portraying Krishna teasing the cowgirls, or the young wife complaining of her in-laws, pining for her absent husband or lover, or ambivalently relating an erotic encounter."[36] Similarly, even today the melodies remain stereotypical in their structure, based on stock tunes, or variations thereon, from a diverse yet homogeneous set of Indo-Caribbean repertoires.[37] As Patasar explained, "Chutney has always been a sort of fixed repertoire, a fixed number of melodies. And this fixed number of melodies comes back to us according to how the artist interprets it. And he may change some parts of the melody, but the basic structure of the melody remains the same because these melodies really originate in the ragas. So the feeling of the melody is very strong. So you find that somebody may take this melody and change up the whole thing, yet you know, I know that that belongs to that song."[38] In the early 1980s, chutney soca music typically featured a melody in a chutney style in combination with the rhythmic patterns and instrumentation associated with soca, as a way to create the widest possible appeal among both Indo- and Afro-Trinidadians. As Manuel describes, "Chutneys use scales that correspond to the Western major or Myxolydian modes (Indian Bilaval and Khamaj thats). A few use the minor third degree and Phrygian-type modes (Bhairavi). Most are centered on the ambitus C-D-E-F (sa re ga ma)."[39] They are easily recognizable by their typical refrain and, according to him, by their common use of what he refers to as the ur-melody of Indo-Caribbean song (see ex. 7).[40]

Just as soca sounds made audible the entanglements of Afro-Trini- dadian musicians with other African diasporas in the Caribbean and North America, chutney soca relayed the entanglements of its artists with the Indian diaspora in various parts of the world. Since the time of its emergence, some chutney soca songs have incorporated (and new ones continue to incorporate) musical phrases and lyrics from songs featured in Bollywood movies,[41] thereby relating not only to Indo-Trinidadians,

Example 7
Chutney: typical refrain melody (a) and ur-melody (b) of Indo-Caribbean Song
as featured in chutney "Nand Bāba."
Source: Peter Manuel 2000b: 176.

but also to Indian audiences in London, New York, and Toronto (e.g., Rikki Jai's "Hamareh Galeeyah").[42]

In Patasar's view, after the arrival of chutney music on the market, the fusion of chutney and soca was "inevitable," because "Trinidadians have always been looking for ways and means to get an Afro-Indian integration.... Calypso was the popular form. So everybody was trying to make their form popular. So they tried to integrate with the calypso to become more and more acceptable in the common stream." This view that such fusion was "inevitable" may be misleading by suggesting a history with only one possible choice instead of a terrain of struggles. The emergence of pichakaaree in the 1990s—an Indo-Trinidadian music defined by many East Indian singers and scholars as the first one to center on themes of social commentary—could also be conceived as an East Indian response to calypso and an attempt to compete with the Afro-Trinidadian-dominated artform and its market. According to Diethrich, "While acknowledging the influence of calypso, rumshop songs and Phagwa songs from Trinidad and India provided alternative Indian models for pichakaaree's social commentary."[43] Pichakaaree's active engagement with contemporary politics and explicit social criticism show that calypso did not monopolize socially conscious lyrics. However, Patasar's construction of chutney as an "inevitable" fusion conveys how calypso—and by extension, soca and chutney soca as its musical offshoots—has been perceived by some East Indians as the music authenticating them as part of the nation. It also indicates how musics like chutney soca, through their alliances with calypso, have been thought to be in the position to help redefine national culture.

The musical fusion between chutney and soca, as several scholars have argued, has been part of several Indian movements seeking more recognition and power in the national sphere. Celebrations of the 150th anniversary of Indian arrival in Trinidad in 1995 aimed to reaffirm the presence of Indo-Trinidadians not just as immigrants, but as part of Trinidad's colonial and postcolonial formations. To this end, efforts were undertaken to document Indo-Trinidadian socioeconomic and cultural practices and to describe their contributions to Trinidad's nation building. In tandem with these new incentives, group organizations were mobilized, academic studies were produced, and artistic activities were sponsored. In addition, Balliger names three factors that, in her view, contributed to the historic victory of the United National Congress (UNC), formed mainly of Indians, in 1995 and to the growing acknowledgment of Indo-Trinidadian music as part of the nation:

First, Indo-Trinidadians had been gradually achieving more power in state and business spheres since the 1970s; second, there was dissatisfaction with the PNM among its Afro-Trinidadian constituents, especially in the context of the oil bust; and in 1993, the new power of an all-Indian radio station thrust Indian culture into the national public sphere with tremendous energy—exemplified by the popularity of chutney soca music. Simply put, globalization and privatization have much to do with the rise of ethnonationalist expression in Trinidad.[44]

In 1995, with the support of an elected government headed for the first time by an Indian prime minister, the sounds of chutney soca became more audible. With the launching of yearly competitions during Carnival in 1996, organized by the Southex Trade Show and Promotions headed by show producer George Singh, Jr., chutney soca took its place in the authenticating space of national culture and acquired legitimacy. Together with soca competitions, chutney soca competitions thus arguably redrew the map of Carnival space, reframing the question of who and what, in ethnic and diasporic terms, constitutes the nation. In Trinidad, these competitions audibly linked the Afro- and Indo-Trinidadian diasporas in unprecedented ways. Beyond the competition stage, chutney soca also helped forge new relations between what had historically coalesced into high and low castes; some members of the high caste now embraced the folk chutney culture.[45] (In Trinidad, high and low castes have been redefined largely in relation to occupational activity and education, i.e., between those with professions and those without.) In addition, this new musical practice elaborated emergent entanglements with India and its multiple diasporas. The complex cultural politics embodied in chutney soca complicated standard definitions of authentic national culture understood as rooted and bounded by Trinidadian geographic territory.

Rapso

In an interview with Isaac Fergusson, a Trinidadian journalist living in New York, Lutalo Makossa Masimba, better known as Brother Resistance, explained rapso music as follows: "We define Rapso as the power of the word in rhythm. . . . Musically we emphasize the African vibrations within the music."[46] In an interview with me in Port of Spain, Brother Resistance gave a lengthier explanation. Recognized as one of the chief exponents of rapso, he was accustomed to giving interviews to researchers and was kind enough to spell out once more how it emerged from the melody and rhythm of local speech patterns: "A network of rhythms

where the rhythm of the voice blends with the rhythm of the drums. . . .
Rapso is not poetry to music. . . . Anyone could do poetry to music. . . .
[Rapso] comes out of the way in which we just talk in Trinidad. . . . If
you listen carefully . . . there is a melody. . . . So we use a drummer and
the percussion to help develop . . . this musical force of ultimate poetry."[47]
During our meeting, Resistance traced rapso's origin back to Africa—an
imaginary Africa, unitary, strong, and undefeated by colonialism. More
specifically, he described rapso as being derived from the African tradition of the griots, or praise singers, who, despite their many incarnations on the African continent, are believed in the Caribbean islands to
share distinctive artistic traits and lyrical orientations. (West African singers are recognized for their verbal and singing skills and their focus on
daily news and sociopolitical commentaries.) He recounted how, having
survived the "Middle Passage" shipboard experience and plantation slavery, the griot tradition was passed down through the chantwèl—a French
Creole term still often used today to refer to a song leader—from whom
came calypsonians. He further depicted how in the 1960s, Lancelot Kebu
Layne was inspired by the portrayal of the Carnival characters called the
Midnight Robbers and the Pierrot Grenade and their ability to deliver
"fast lyrics,"[48] and transformed it into the popular genre known today
as rapso.

The first rapso hit, "Blow Way" (before the style was invented), which
Layne recorded in the early 1970s, said Brother Resistance, inspired him
and other youths at the time to compose in this vein. Around the same
period, Cheryl Byron became known as "the mother of the movement,"
to use Brother Resistance's expression, by performing what she then
called "poem songs" (poems accompanied by drumming). According to
Byron and several other rapso artists I interviewed, she was the first artist
from the emerging rapso movement to be invited to perform in a calypso
tent, initially in Brooklyn, New York in 1975, and the following year in
Trinidad in Lord Shorty's calypso tent, the Professionals. After returning
to New York, where she had moved permanently in 1974, Byron continued to promote what became known as rapso through her live radio
performances and appearances in street fairs and festivals not only in
New York, but also in Barbados and Guyana.[49]

Along with Brother Shortman (Everard Romany), Brother Moopsman
(Wayne Blackman), and a few other friends,[50] Brother Resistance turned
to rapso in the early 1970s, seeking to do something about the ghetto
conditions affecting their lives in the disadvantaged areas of Laventille,
Port of Spain. Following the traditions of the chantwèl and the calypsonian, they saw their roles as both educators and historians. As Resis-

tance explained, "Community work was the heartbeat of everything. . . . Influenced by the Black Power movement, we aimed to lead people to appreciate the self . . . to appreciate our own way of talking . . . our drums as instruments . . . the steel pan and many other things. . . . There was a whole new breeze blowin' in the land . . . and it is from there that we really got our teaching, our training, our philosophy, our outlook of the world."

Brother Resistance is here referring to the Black Power movement and the youth movements of the late 1960s and 1970s that were spreading worldwide. Combined together, these movements were inspiring black youth groups to organize locally and engage in activities aimed at recovering self-esteem and black pride.

In the early 1970s, Shortman, Moopsman, Resistance, and other friends formed De Network Riddum Band. At first, the band included mainly percussion instruments (traditional drums and a steel pan) and occasionally a bamboo flute, and emphasized rhythms borrowed from the Orisha yard (an African cult practiced in Trinidad)[51] and Baptist services. The soloist typically delivered his lyrics in a chanting style, enunciating clearly the text over only a few notes, sometimes in the "fast-lyrics" Midnight Robber and the Pierrot Grenade style (i.e., using a flood of words over just a few musical bars), at other times in a slow tempo to mark emphatically the meaning and phonetic resonance of some words. By the late 1970s, the sound of the band had been transformed by adding electric instruments (a bass guitar and a rhythm guitar) and a saxophone, as well as by including rhythmic patterns and melodic riffs associated with soca.[52] However, rapso's resemblance to soca stopped there. Unlike most soca artists and musicians, the band members bore what has been considered a Rastafarian look, wearing loose-fitted clothes made of local batik or other fabrics with African-inspired designs, and with caps protecting long dreadlocks. While they danced to the beat, they characteristically avoided any of the wining movements and pelvic thrusts associated with soca performance and dancing. The lyrics spoke of class inequalities and struggles and contested the existing political order inherited from colonial empires.[53]

Rapso initially found little public support, as it corresponded to neither of the two artforms from which it drew inspiration: poetry and calypso. Brother Resistance explains:

We were told by the poetry authorities that what we're doing is not poetry, so, we say what we're doing is what we're doing, so we just gonna find a name . . . to follow nobody's rules and regulations. . . . So we say "rhapsody" and the definition was very close to what we was doing . . . but it wasn't that.

"Rhap" . . . we'll shorten it to "rapso" . . . because the people hear we rehears-
ing and thing, or they hear we in a session and they say, 'Hey, how you can rap
so!' . . . "Rap so," that was it.
    And it [what we were doing] could not be called calypso, because
rapso is . . . freedom style. Because there's less rules and regulations within
rapso. . . . In calypso there's a melody . . . and if you don't have a melody, to
me, it can't be a calypso. Right? . . . In rapso, now, you can do anything you
want to do. . . . We don't use steady rhyme. We have something to say . . .
we want to say it live and direct . . . because it is a militant stance. . . . That,
calypso did not accommodate.

Along with its protests over neocolonialism, rapso's militant stance promoted an Afrocentric identification that calypso, as national music, could
not promote. Unlike calypso, it avoided songs about sex or relationships
and, adopting the militant stance, avoided humor in its texts. Nevertheless, Brother Resistance stressed how calypso was fundamental to rapso's
development. In his words, "[Calypso] formed the root. . . . What we have
developed is simply a branch . . . it doesn't make us different . . . not separate . . . but it has its own identity, yes. But always with that link. . . . This
is talking after the fact now . . . but if you look at what's happening today
and see African rap relative to soul and funk . . . Jamaican dub, relative to
reggae. Yes we see that [rapso] was the best moves we could have made.
And it was not a conscious move. . . . It was just organic kinda thing,
right?" In this perspective, rapso's distinctive musical orientation joined
a widespread African diasporic movement that, musically, emphasized
African-derived traditions and, politically, focused on lyrics decrying the
(neo)colonial legacies of poverty, racism, and unequal power relations.
After several years of being nearly ignored, rapso gradually took root in
the musical scene of Trinidad after the relentless efforts and achievements
of artists such as Brother Resistance and Karega Mandela—an original
member of De Network Riddum Band who later developed his own
rapso style. Many of their activities contributed to the promotion of rapso
in and outside Trinidad: their crucial role in having rapso artists provide
the first act of the tent called People's Kaiso Court around 1977–78; their
participation as delegates of Trinidad and Tobago in Carifesta and other
cultural festivals, their resounding visible and commercial success with the
song "Ring de Bell" in 1985, their entrance onto the Carnival scene in
1988,[54] and their subsequent appearances at highly visible venues around
the world (including S-O-B's[55] and the Apollo Theater in New York).
    Along with its growing visibility, rapso received official recognition
through key events. These included special invitations, such as Prime

Minister Maurice Bishop's request that De Network Riddum Band perform for the first festival of the People's Revolution in 1980; prestigious
awards, including Brother Resistance's Trinidad Silver Hummingbird
Medal for his contributions to culture in 1992; and the selection of rapso
songs at world events—such as Karega Mandela's "Free Up Africa" as the
theme of the Poets against Apartheid movement and Brother Resistance's
"Mother Earth" as the theme song for the Earth Day and World Environmental Day and observances by the United Nations Environmental
program in 1994.[56] Furthermore, rapso has gained particular momentum
since 1991 through the celebration of what the leaders of the rapso movement then called the National Day of Rapso and the Oral Traditions.[57]
This title attested the organizers' desire to affirm rapso's organic relationship and side with the resilient, orally transmitted, African-derived practices and, in their view, the indomitable spirit that infuses them in Trinidad. Thanks to the mobilization of the media on that day, rapso enjoyed
greater exposure, and thus developed a stronger foothold in the artistic
community. On this occasion, live shows involved, and they continue to
involve, rapso artists from other Caribbean islands as well as Trinidad.

From the time of its inception, rapso has had a strong presence among
"radical" intellectuals and educated black youth. During the 1990s, rapso
was musically transformed to attract a larger audience. Still using the
fast-delivery speech of the Midnight Robber, it now incorporated musical features from a wide range of sources, including Nigerian Afro-beat
(e.g., the 1996 version of "Cyar Take Dat," by Brother Resistance), soca,
and, at times, dancehall (the 1993 version of "Blow Way," by Kindred).
(♪ CD track 4, "Cyar Take Dat," by Brother Resistance.) In so doing,
rapso developed a strong fan base among what is dubbed in rapso songs
the "boom generation," that is, the generation that experienced the music of the African diaspora, like Jamaican dancehall and American rap. As
Robin Balliger indicates, "while rapso is marginal to national forms like
soca music, it influences those forms musically and politically."[58] Several
artists in the calypso music scene who do not call themselves rapso artists today compose their lyrics and perform in that style, typically using
chanting and/or its typical delivery of "fast lyrics" over a few bars, usually in a fast tempo. Stalin used such techniques in some sections of his
song "Revolution Time" (1991). David Rudder composed several of his
songs in the rapso style, including "Another Day in Paradise" (1995),
"The Madman's Rant" (1996), and "Bigger Pinpin" (2001). For reasons
that still need to be investigated, very few female artists have recorded
any rapso, unlike the situation in the American rap or Jamaican dancehall
music scene.[59]

Drawing on what Brother Resistance described as its initial mission, rapso has continued to feature a militant stance. He, as well as other rapso artists, still aims to promote rapso's emphasis on black pride, self-esteem, and appreciation of Trinidad's local resources through community organizing, visiting schools, and providing mentorship to younger artists. Through their songs, they continue to critique neoliberalism and its fomenting of individualism and to celebrate the collective subject and communal spirit. In the context of economic depression and neoliberalism, band names like Kindred and Home Front in the early 1990s further emphasized how personal relations and youth solidarity for rapso artists are central to the politics they want to embrace and cultivate.[60] While over the past few years rapso has furthered its African diasporic connections by featuring musical traits associated with American rap and Jamaican dancehall (i.e., melodic bass lines and, at times, a breakdown section), it is locally recognized as a Trinidadian creation. Rapso enacts its allegiance to calypso and soca by using many of their sounds (accompanying rhythmic patterns, the use of horns, and tempo), yet distances itself, to use Balliger's wording, "from the overly conformist and competition driven aspects of those styles."[61]

As explained by Brother Resistance, rapso artists have refused to hold their own competition because, in his view, competition stifles creativity, while also perhaps compromising the integrity of the songs. The rapso artists who take part in soca or ragga soca competitions feel relatively more free to do so because, unlike their soca and ragga soca counterparts, they do not rely on these competitions to earn their reputation as rapso artists. In my view, by not having its own competition yet sharing the Carnival space as its main performing venue, rapso has criticized the normalizing and limiting format through which national culture has been traditionally authenticated. At the same time, rapso's identification with transnational black youth culture—musically through Jamaican dancehall and American rap, and politically through the Black Power movement, class struggles, and black resistance culture—has promoted an African diasporic frame, aside from the national one, to express in Trinidad other subjectivities and senses of belonging.

Policing New Music Styles under the Sign of Tradition

The new musical styles in the Carnival musical scene have brought forward new notions of identity that have themselves stirred controversy. The cultural politics these styles embody have raised polemics about how globalization and commoditization have affected the cultural values informing

national expressions. They have generated heated arguments on themes
that have historically been used to distinguish various groups in Trinidad's
multicultural society: race, religion, and gendered relations. They have
also prompted fiery discussions about the tensions between members of
different generations and classes within various ethnic groups. They have
also provoked animated debates about creolization and the issues it poses
in defining and representing national culture. In short, the cultural politics
these new music styles embody have incited discourses on the parameters
used to define and position Trinidad's nation and its different constituencies. Each of these parameters deserves special attention.

Globalization and Commoditization

The globalization- and commoditization-based complaints have been
raised mainly in relation to soca of the 1990s onward. Most of the criticism has centered on soca's reliance on technology and commoditization
and its incompatibility with traits of calypso—more precisely, with traits
construed by social activists, journalists, and academics as representative
of national culture.

During the 1970s and 1980s soca songs were absorbed into calypso
competitions. A majority of the more than one hundred interviewees
(including musicians, show organizers, and calypso artists) to whom I
have spoken report that soca during these years was perceived as a musical
experiment: a variant of calypso involving certain changes in the rhythm
section. In their opinion, the format of the lyrics—the element through
which calypso was and to a large extent continues to be defined—
remained close to the format of traditional calypso: three verses alternating with a refrain. Thus, even though soca lyrics were party oriented,
they were still regarded as a type of "calypso" that concentrated on one
of the four main streams of the artform (i.e., sociopolitical commentaries, humor, Road March, and party songs). Through its association with
calypso, in which aesthetic values depend mainly on the lyrics, soca music
was judged in relation to calypso's traditional criteria. To be acceptable in
the Calypso Monarch competitions, therefore, the tempo of soca songs
could not be too fast and the voice in the final mix of the recording
needed to be foregrounded so that the lyrics could be heard.

By the 1990s, most soca songs contrasted with calypso so much that
they could no longer qualify for calypso competitions. In the words of
columnist Burton Sankeralli, "We may now speak of 'traditional' soca and
a new kind of youth soca which probably ought not to be called soca
at all, as it is in a sense fundamentally discontinuous."[62] By 1993, when

the first National Soca Monarch competition was held, soca lyrics in fact had abandoned the verse-refrain form of traditional calypso, resorting mostly to short lines, repetition, and call and response. By using only a few words, they typically emphasized an emotion rather than telling a story. As critics who opposed soca charged, at that point its songs and their musical arrangements had changed not only the rhythmic patterns and tempo of calypso, but also its lyrics' format and content. Along with these changes, soca's great reliance on technology—drum machines and digital samplers—led from their perspectives to both a lack of original-ity and craftsmanship and a focus on creating commercial appeal that disregarded moral values and accountability. According to those who defended calypso under the sign of "tradition," soca challenged the very notions of modernity, authenticity, originality, and cultural independence that calypso aesthetics had embodied.

"Bring the Rhythm Down," an article by Mark Lyndersay published in 1998 in the Commentary and Analysis section of a leading daily Trin-idadian newspaper, is symptomatic of many public discourses on soca from the late 1990s onward. Its detailed list of soca's "problems" is reveal-ing and worth including here.

Driven by frenetic drum machines cranked up to dozens of beats per minute, technology makes possible a rhythmic heartbeat that exceeds anything a hu-man drummer could be expected to keep pace with.

Crowds of loyal citizens, long trained to keep their wine to the beat and laugh at hapless tourists who just don't get it are worked up into a lather just trying to keep up with this frenzied pace. . . .

Burgeoning advancements in the science of recording aided and abetted this new phenomenon. Incorporating digital samples of other songs became easier with desktop audio systems. With the coming of affordable CD record-able systems, anyone who wished to become a soca artist could put something together on the desktop and burn ten or so CDs for the radio stations.

Faster and faster. Leaving less and less time to think, to reflect, to contem-plate this festival we are creating.

There was a time when the calypsonian thought long and hard about the events of the day and fashioned songs which used irony and parable to tell stories richly flavoured with their opinions.

Now we have what tourism officials call a Carnival product, something which is generated rather than created and which matures with increas-ing intolerance for the pockets of tiresome handwork which resist modern trends. . . .

The people might well seem to be getting the Carnival they deserve.

And yet . . .

In the fetes leading up to the festival and I guarantee you on the Monday and Tuesday of Carnival itself, they will make their choices. For all the arguments about a soca mafia and payola, no DJ who wants to keep his work will play songs which do not move his audience and that audience, sweating with exertion, humming with the endorphins of hot rum with pelvis itching to rotate makes its preferences heard clearly.[63]

Placed against calypsonians and calypso—described nostalgically by the author as richly flavored songs created through long, hard reflection— what is at issue here is how soca artists, hoping to penetrate the international market, have allegedly fallen prey to the global market's "rules," turning original musical compositions (here meaning traditional calypso or "traditional" soca songs) into cultural commodities ("youth" songs, also referred to as party songs) and adopting foreign aesthetics at the expense of local musical values. In this critique, soca songs exhibit the symptoms of commoditization, resembling many and any other popular musics. They are described as simplified, homogenized, and, to use Rohlehr's wording, as "a kind of fast-food, mass-produced, slickly packaged, and meant for rapid consumption and swift obsolescence."[64] They are said to resort to gimmicks involving both self-advertising and the adoption of the basic methodology of all advertising: repetition. Echoing the views of many, including Lyndersay, Rohlehr concludes: "Soca has in two decades moved from being a trade name for a variety of calypso-crossover rhythms to a fairly rigid song form with standard chord structure, melodic lines, and lyrics."[65] In this view, soca artists' attempts to penetrate global markets have diminished their narrative power through the loss of storytelling skills, a decline of humor in song compositions (a unique feature of many Trinidadian calypsos), and the replacement of local ways of saying things with other people's ways of talking.

Lyndersay's article, after deploring a loss of aesthetic values, goes on to complain about soca on moral grounds. By imputing an "increasing intolerance for the pockets of tiresome handwork which resist modern trends" to those who use technology to create a so-called Carnival product, he suggests some disturbing correlations: when musicians use modern technology, they develop not music, but a product that (a) lacks creativity, (b) can be easily reproduced ("generated"), (c) adopts an inhuman tempo, (d) leaves no time to think, and ultimately (e) gives rise to intolerance for other musics or products not operating within the same parameters. The article further hints at the "negative" effects soca's speedy tempos have on people by caricaturing, criticizing, and admonishing the audience enjoying this music.[66] Astutely, it does so by associating the audience with two elements traditionally assumed to lead to degeneration: rum and sex ("humming with the endorphins of hot rum with pelvis itching to rotate").

Lyndersay's discourse, in fact, resembles that of the colonial powers at the beginning of the twentieth century, which was used to discredit the recently freed slaves and their songs and dance traditions. Here, for example, is how the *Port of Spain Gazette* reported the singing and dancing at Carnival time in 1907: "There was a noticeable degeneracy in character as well as in songs, and current topics which have been accustomed to afford opportunities for the local song-maker were entirely discarded and in place thereof was substituted a monotonous chorus of ribaldry, and meaningless jargon to the strains of which maskers of the feminine sex in particular, wrought themselves into contortions, sufficient to explode the already accepted theory of vertebrae and the human machination."[67] Discourses have the power to position things, and to elevate some while debasing others. The songs and dances performed in 1907 would no doubt have been described differently had their descriptions been written by their performers. Likewise, critiques of soca are usually less about musical characteristics than about positioning soca as a musical outcast within the regime of values evolving from calypso's "tradition." At issue is the new modernity that soca artists embrace, including not only new notions of musicianship and aesthetics that have emerged with new music technologies, but also their redefining of what constitutes "the nation" and "the political" in an era of globalization. Refusing to limit politics to formal political organizations, electoral contests, and the normative definitions dictated by nationalist formations, soca has shifted the terrain of politics itself. Soca and its affiliated practices have challenged the regulatory policing of bodies and permissible pleasures, articulating new affinities that remap relations among communities and spaces of belonging not reducible to the Trinidadian nation-state.

Racial and Ethnic Relations and Creolization

In 1997, a symposium on calypso, soca, chutney, and pichakaaree held under the auspices of the ISER (Institute of Social and Economic Research) at the University of the West Indies gathered elected officials, academics, and artists to examine concerns emerging from the transformation of the Carnival music scene over the past few years. Papers prepared for this event and public interventions made during the symposium were later published. In this publication, several participants viewed the creation of soca competitions, followed by the creation of other competitions (such as chutney soca and ragga soca), not only as a fragmentation of the Carnival music scene, but also the result of commercialism, "niche marketing," and political maneuvering, leading in turn to a further ethnicization of the discrepant diasporas on the island.

Along these lines, some participants accused local political leaders of being responsible for the absence of any policy for radio broadcasts that could help prevent the alleged denial of airtime to a variety of musical styles. (Some envisioned, for example, a quota system in which a certain range of musical categories would have to be represented to hold a license to operate a commercial radio station.) Many seriously questioned the role of political leaders, accusing them of seeking to capitalize on the hypersensitivity to race and ethnicity that has always existed in Trinidad—a hypersensitivity accentuated by both the election of the first East Indian prime minister in 1995 and the fragmentation of the hegemonic calypso music scene. As has long been true of calypso in relation to Afro-Creole Trinidadian culture, chutney soca now serves as a means to legitimize East Indian culture and even, on some occasions, to "consolidate Indian nationalism and mobilize Indians of almost all classes, castes and religions at the political and social levels."[68] Addressing this context in a special journal issue devoted to the Trinidad and Tobago Carnival, Rohlehr describes the ethnic interface through chutney-soca crossover music as facing a particularly fierce contestation of space, "in which little quarter is being given on either side."[69]

The complex relationship between Indians and Africans has been the subject of many publications, including, more recently, some focusing on sociomusical issues.[70] As revealed in some, the controversies chutney soca has raised involved the Indian traditionalists' sense of identity not only in relation to what stands musically as national culture (i.e., calypso or soca), but also in relation to their own musical traditions as an ethnic group. In other words, these controversies have been as much about the tensions within the Indian diaspora as they have been about the tensions between the Indian and African diasporas. As Ramnarine explains, since "there is no single conception of an Indian-Caribbean [in our case, Indian Trinidadian] . . . the reception to chutney and to its place in national culture has [thus] been varied."[71]

In the Indian community, the issue of creolization—also referred to as hybridization—posed by chutney soca has brought forward several contrasting perspectives. For the liberals of the Indian community advocating the "unity in diversity" definition of nation put forward by the PNM, the hybrid music of chutney soca sends a message of solidarity to the two main cultural groups. In the words of Drupatee, the Indian singer acclaimed for her crucial role in the national recognition of chutney soca, this genre has been a way of making a contribution to the two cultures. As she explains, "I think I have a contribution to make to calypso. If I choose to sing songs based on Indian culture then I think I am perfect because I will not mis-pronounce any Indian words ... Calypso is a Trinidad 'ting.' ... Is it wrong for an Indian to fit into calypso without losing his/her identity, providing the merger allows for a healthy diversity with the range of unity?"[72] In the same vein, for many of its supporters, chutney soca has taken its rightful place next to calypso in ways that recognize the importance these two musics have for different ethnic groups while acknowledging the roles they play in the distinct historical experiences of the nation-state's citizens. Ramnarine quotes Daphne Philips, minister of culture and gender affairs of Trinidad and Tobago in 1998, declaring of chutney soca and calypso that "culture and our creative art forms have now become a dynamic forum for equity and national unity."[73]

For their part, chutney soca's fans boast about how the new musical fusion has helped to shatter limiting stereotypes about Indian artists. In a 1992 newspaper article entitled "Rikki Shows His Motion!" Senath speaks of Rikki Jai's most recent album as "a prime example of Rikki's unique versatility as an artist, contain[ing] a mixture of up-beat, cross-over and laid-back soca, destroying again, all stereotypes marking him as simply an 'Indian Calypsonian.'" According to this piece, Jai should be viewed as a Trinidadian calypsonian—creed and race apart—not only for his own sake but for a better, more integrated Trinidad.

For Indian ethnonationalists, however, chutney soca is the product of assimilation by the so-called dominant African culture.[74] It is the emblem of a sociocultural "callaloo," a stew of ingredients with the potential of bringing cultural oblivion. From this perspective, chutney soca thus poses serious issues about racial and ethnic assimilation and acculturation, and it produces feelings of alienation.[75]

Echoing patterns throughout the Caribbean, creolization has been central to articulations of identity and culture for both Afro-and Indo-Trinidadian groups at different times in their histories in Trinidad and Tobago.[76] According to Reddock, the term "Creole" historically has been used to refer to descendants of Europeans, born in Trinidad and Tobago, who still dominate the local economy. Indian conservatives especially have used the term to designate people of African descent whose desire to have their cultural practices valorized and accepted by Europeans have muted expressions of more authentic traditions.[77] Creole cultural hegemony, promoted and reproduced through nationalist politics, has marginalized Indians and other ethnic groups. On the one hand, Indian ethnonationalists have differentiated themselves from so-called Creole culture, criticizing perceived assimilation, emphasizing distinct community values, and enunciating opposition to political subordination attributed to Creole hegemony. On the other hand, black radical critics have positioned authentic African traditions over and against Creole cultural nationalism. Opponents of chutney soca thus share with Afrocentrists a political critique of musical traditions perceived as assimilation of Creole culture.

According to André Vincent-Henry, a major reason some East Indian leaders advocate maintaining the purity of ancient ethnic forms is that, for them, "the cultural purity argument is a means to mobilization and to the maintenance of traditional particularistic patterns of communal power."[78] Their hostile response to chutney soca, in other words, is not exclusively spurred by the African versus East Indian paradigm; they fear the gradual erosion of the powers some individuals and groups of people have historically held over others in the East Indian community. In that sense, the purity argument, as Vincent-Henry notes, is a means for some members to defend their views against others about the spirit of Hinduism and to maintain the existing hierarchy and socially gendered roles already normalized under the sign of tradition.

Religion and Social Gendered Relations

In support of the status quo, some East Indian see chutney soca as a threat to what, in their views, defines the East Indian community, its religion and moral values. For them, the sensual wining in public that accompanies chutney soca violates the spirit of Hinduism. It goes against Hindu notions of honor and modesty, making songs performed to devotional texts unforgivably blasphemous in character.[79] In several interviews, Siewdath Persad, Drupatee's husband, and other chutney soca supporters in conversations with me have traced these accusations to orthodox critics with dogmatic views about Hinduism: "The mere mention of the holy names of Sita, Parvati and Radica have been considered a degradation to the Hindu religion because they represent goddesses (pure persons in Hindu mythology)."[80] As Manuel reports, chutney soca defenders react to such value judgments "by pointing to the tradition of sensuality and pleasure in Hinduism" and stressing that "it is ultimately impossible in many Hindu arts to separate the spiritual and the secular realms."[81] So despite the intense critiques lodged by representatives of conservative associations, chutney soca songs about Krishna and other deities continue to be composed and abound in the market.

As in the case of soca, the critiques addressing the sensual dancing at chutney soca events are aimed exclusively at women—demonstrating that what is contested is the social, public behavior of women. Called "vulgar," "inelegant," and "disgusting," women's chutney soca dancing, as it occurs in public performance spaces, is perceived as a threat to morality, according to representatives of the Hindu Women's Association, "lead[ing] to the breakdown in family life and encourag[ing] the development of extra-marital relationships." [82]

As several authors have pointed out, much of the criticism against chutney soca has been mitigated by factors of socioeconomic class and residential status. [83] "Women who participate in chutney dancing, or even in chutney singing," writes Ramnarine, "are described as being low or working class from rural areas . . . although no statistical data seem to be available in support of such claims." "Such a perception," she adds, "may stem from the somewhat disparaging view of the 'folk' and their music, evident in much music scholarship in Trinidad." [84] Characteristically, chutney soca's most severe critics come usually from the Hindu Women's Association and the Sanatan Dharma Maha Sabha (SDMS), which are composed of professional middle-class and upper-class people who, rather than being representative of Indian women and men, are marginal to the East Indian community as a whole. To these critics, as Manuel reports, the populist columnist Phoolo Danny had this for a response in one of his articles' headlines: "The People Will Wine!" [85] Chutney soca's mass appeal among East Indians, as crowds of thousands of people attending Chutney soca's parties attest, [86] has gradually forced many of its detractors into retreat or made their comments appear out of touch with today's reality.

Since the 1990s, many East Indian Trinidadian women have viewed and used chutney soca as a medium to express themselves in the power struggles that occur over gendered roles and gendered spaces. In the words of Ramrajie Prabhu, "Chutney is modern and it is a liberation for women. . . . We no longer hide behind doors to dance as we want." [87] Such a narrative, Balliger reports, "lends credence to Indra Ribeiro's argument that chutney fosters the 'growing emancipation of East Indian women in Trinidad,' along with education and increased economic independence; and that most women who support chutney are 'mature . . . and working class.'" [88] Even though Ribeiro's thesis may be, according to Balliger, "overly romantic about chutney as the vehicle for women's liberation," it nonetheless signals in my view how chutney soca's supporters see this music as reflecting as well as helping to effect changes within the East Indian community.

In tandem with the increased presence and power of East Indians in state and economic sectors and, with the issuing of new licenses, on radio and television broadcasts, chutney soca, according to several authors and artists I interviewed, is one of the sites in which definitions of local and national culture are contested. As Rhoda Reddock explains, Indian nationalists argue that chutney soca has enabled Indo-Trinidadians to perform Indian styles of dance in public, allowing the explicit display of embodied pleasures in social gatherings. This development has linked cultural communities and individual expressions of enjoyment in ways precluded in discos and clubs. Afro-Trinidadians' perception of Indian public expressions embodied through chutney soca has encouraged a recognition of commonality that cuts across cultural difference: a shared sense of bacchanalian celebration of music, transgressive regulations of the sexualized body, and spontaneous expressions of self and community. In particular, Indian women's prominence in chutney soca—onstage and dancing in the audience—has helped Afro-Trinidadian women recognize across racial and ethnic differences a common gendered politics pivoting on the public expression of sensuousness and sexuality in social spaces historically regulated by patriarchal conventions. For working-class Trinidadians, chutney soca has challenged the elite's imposition of permissible cultural expressions and has fomented a political affinity that foregrounds common experiences of class subordination spanning the discursive divide between Afro- and Indo-Trinidadians.[89]

Soca's, Chutney Soca's, and Ragga Soca's Articulations through Several Diasporas

In 1996, when the competition was renamed the International Soca Monarch competitions, soca competitions were given a wider scope to welcome not only participants from other countries, but also Trinidadian migrants. Over the past few years, for example, in addition to Trinidadian artists, the competition has included participants living in Barbados, Grenada, St. Lucia, Miami, and Toronto.[90] As a result, the Afro-Caribbean diaspora in terms of bodies and sounds was not only acknowledged, but also welcomed as an economic opportunity for both the public and private sectors. At the state level, the new importance given to the Caribbean diaspora as consumers was clearly expressed in Henry and Nurse's report to the Tourism and Industrial Development Company (TIDCO). The report suggested, for example, that one possible strategy to improve the Trinidad and Tobago music industry was to exploit further the diasporic West Indian market (which numbers over ten million)—not only in North America and in Europe as "outside" market niches—but also as part of cultural tourism "back home."[91] At the private level, this suggestion was followed up by the local entrepreneurs' decision to turn soca competitions into an international forum to widen public outreach, and to institutionalize the ragga soca competition as an international competition from the outset. If what prompted the change of politics and policies in Trinidad toward the Caribbean diaspora and Caribbean diasporic aesthetics was economics, I would argue that what these politics and policies generated was, however, far more than income.

The formal inclusion of the Caribbean diaspora and Caribbean diasporic aesthetics[92] into the national space of Trinidad and Tobago through soca competitions suggests several interventions in redefining nation, diaspora, and Trinidadian identities. First, it allows the recognition of local identities constituted by transnational experience. In musical terms, the institutional recognition (granted by international competitions) that soca, chutney soca, and ragga soca embody West Indian diasporic aesthetics "allows," as Gayatri Gopinath suggested in another context, "for a far more complicated understanding of diaspora, in that it *demands a radical reworking of the hierarchical relation between diaspora and the nation.*"[93] On the one hand, soca's incorporation of diasporic sensibilities from different Caribbean cultures and communities "which intersect both with one another, and with the national spaces that they are continuously negotiating and challenging," creates a network of alliances that "displaces the 'home' country from its privileged position as originary site."[94] On the other, soca's performance of diasporic aesthetics in the nation-state reconfigures the very terms by which the nation-state is constituted, by making the diaspora both culturally and financially part of its economy; moreover, it reconfigures the ways in which the nation-state is inscribed as part of discrepant diasporas and, to a certain extent, as defined by them. The acknowledgment of the new musical offshoots of calypso as embodying diasporic aesthetics also enables appreciation of the ways in which they constructed their audiences: that is, as being formed by both national and diasporic subjects whose identities are "not singular or monolithic and [are] instead multiple, shifting, and often self-contradictory . . . made up of heterogeneous and heteronomous representations of gender, race, and class."[95] Second, rather than conceptualizing nation-state and global political economy as separate categories of analysis, the inclusion of the Caribbean diasporas in the nation-state—and vice versa—articulates how both local and global political economies are constitutive of each other.[96]

Third, the inclusion of the Caribbean diasporas and diasporic aesthetics in the authenticating space of national culture problematizes the isomorphism between culture and space and, in so doing, foregrounds politics over the construction and location of "authentic culture." It brings to view (and hearing) the mutual entanglement of cultural politics and the geographies of both belonging and exclusion.

Many publications have documented the importance of overseas Carnivals for Trinidadians and other Caribbean population groups in diaspora and the crucial role popular culture—most particularly music—has played in such contexts. But few have addressed the specific role the new music styles have played for West Indian audiences in diasporic spaces. What kinds of identities do they perform and for whom? In their transnational circuits, do they reinforce or abandon the notion of nationhood?

By entering the long tradition of overseas Carnivals (the first overseas Caribbean Carnival began in the late 1920s in Harlem),[97] soca and ragga soca—not chutney soca for reasons to be discussed below—have taken on the overseas Carnivals' original mandates: namely, to assert a pan–West Indian cultural identity and to provide a means of resistance in an otherwise alienating environment.[98] Yet soca performers reach Caribbean diasporic population groups markedly different from those of the early twentieth century. The frequency with which many migrants can now travel back and forth between their new homes and their mother countries and the ease with which they can exchange daily news with friends and relatives still living in the Caribbean have given a new twist to the meaning of migration. West Indians in diaspora now actively participate as consumers in many musical activities held in Trinidad. With today's access to mass communication and modern technology, the traditional meaning of "home" defined by a specific place or locality has become ever more blurred and indeterminate.

Paradoxically, despite these changes, immigrant population groups' efforts to maintain ideas of cultural and ethnic distinction have become more salient than ever.[99] In the face of adversities such as racial discrimination and ethnic ghettoization, visible diasporic minorities have felt pressed to reinforce their collective identities so that they can fight for political spaces. For Caribbean population groups abroad, and for Trinidadians especially, the means of reinforcing this sense of collective identity has been through Carnival, through calypso, and, over the past fifteen years, through soca.

In fact, as Percy Hintzen has noted in relation to New York's West Indian diaspora, "Country-specific identities do not disappear on Labor Day [when West Indian Carnival is celebrated in New York] but are reflected in patterns of participation at the Carnival festivities that publicize national rather than regional identity. On the day of the parade, a profusion of flags represents the various countries, and designated sections of the parade route have become country-specific gathering places."[100] These remarks apply equally well to most other West Indian diasporic communities. Therefore, the question is how soca and ragga soca have catered simultaneously to both a pan–West Indian and Trinidadian identity. The answer, according to Nurse, is that they have done so by being hybrid in form and influence—like overseas Carnivals themselves—and simultaneously embodying a culture of resistance and one of co-optation—thereby defying the simplistic notion that these two cultures are by definition opposed to each other.[101] Soca's and ragga soca's trademarks of sounding multiple cultural and national locations and embodying various musical sensibilities undoubtedly stem from appreciating the new kinds of audiences they aim to reach and, to use Stuart Hall's words, "the dialogic strategies . . . essential to the diaspora aesthetic."[102]

Even though soca and ragga soca artists have aimed to reach a "heterogeneous" audience, in the Carnival space they have mainly attracted people considered "Afro-Caribbean."[103] Hence, heated debates have emerged over whether the Carnival that soca helps to articulate should be simply portrayed as a "black" or Afro-Caribbean thing instead of a "Caribbean" festival.[104] What is at stake, particularly for the ethnonationalist members of the Indian community, is the issue of racial and ethnic representation in the diasporic celebration of the nation and the region, and what music and whom the overseas Carnivals continue to privilege.

Just as soca and ragga soca (re)produce in diaspora some of the tensions from "home" when performing the nation, both musics also experience in diaspora the same marginal positioning that "home"—and the nation they represent—has historically held vis-à-vis so-called first world societies. They face the legacies of postcolonial conditions: lack of access to political and economic leverage and insufficient organizational capability to control their circulation and to maximize their commercial returns (e.g., those enabled by legal copyright protections). Soca and ragga soca are racially marked, and thus heavily confined to predefined markets and possibilities. Just as Keith Nurse has written about overseas Carnivals, the limitations faced by soca and ragga soca "are systemic in nature in that they relate to large-scale, long-term processes such as colonialist discourse . . . and imperialism."[105] Yet, together with the expansion of overseas Carnivals beyond the confines of the immigration populations they represent, these new musics have reinforced some old alliances and created new ones—racially, ethnically, culturally, economically, and politically. In "this act of transnational, transcultural, and transgressive politics," to borrow Nurse's wording,[106] soca and ragga soca may be said to have strengthened both national and pan–West Indian identities at home and abroad.

While the new soca and chutney soca competitions have openly challenged the restrictive construction of nation and diaspora nurtured by the calypso competitions since independence, they have not provided any commitment to further equal representation and equal rights to all Trinidadian citizens. Taken as a whole, they still perform a selective number of identities. To take the most glaring omissions, they still exclude members of the gay community, white women and men, and artists from other racial and ethnic groups living on the island. In the same way, artists who are not from the lower class are still under pressure in the calypso arena. And while the competitions examined here share the same temporality—Carnival—they are still held in divided spaces. Strikingly, soca competitions still bring nearly exclusively Afro-Trinidadians, other members of the Afro-Caribbean communities, and whites (local and visitors), and the chutney soca competitions gather mainly, if not exclusively, an Indian-based crowd of performers and participants.[107] So even though the mix of Indo- and Afro-Trinidadian musical practices may be heard through soca and chutney soca, they have yet to be seen onstage. In Stuart Hall's terms, the cultural politics that these musics make audible are thus "without guarantees."[108] Complex and syncopated, these musics remain historically contingent and contested through their embodied and spatial practices.

New Cultural Formations around New Music Styles

In 1998, the state's relation to calypso competitions held during Carnival was dramatically altered.[109] In tandem with the neoliberal policies adopted earlier by the PNM and the proliferation of music competitions set up by private entrepreneurs, the new political party in power, the UNC, relinquished its control over calypso competitions and handed it to the Trinbago Unified Calypsonians Organization (TUCO)—which de facto became responsible for the organization of calypso competitions and the selection of the jury members. The new party in power even planned to reduce gradually the financial sponsorship provided to calypso competitions since independence and to replace it with minimal subsidies. (Even though this did not happen, the change of state policies produced tangible effects on TUCO's organization. These effects will be discussed at length in chap. 8.) By placing the onus of responsibility more than ever before on TUCO for both its artistic and financial success, it could be suggested, the new state government placed calypso competitions on a different footing from the other competitions, but symbolically in a position closer to them. (After decades of monopoly, calypso competitions did not lose overnight their privileged status or the prominent role they have historically played in Trinidad's cultural politics.) What such a change in cultural politics did, however, is to make the calypso competitions' articulation of nation and diaspora now a matter of open contest.

Soca, ragga soca, chutney soca, and rapso have radically altered the Carnival music scene since the late 1980s. Their deployments have set into motion new "cultural formations" that have remapped collective identities while reformulating in fundamental ways what is taken to be authentic in national culture. Through these new musics, a constellation of new social relations, shifts in sensibility and desire, strategic use of new technologies, and involvement of dominant institutions and infrastructures have come together in transformative ways.

Some of the social, political, and cultural moves these new formations have encouraged stand in contrast to traditional dominant ideologies locally and have been met with resistance. In addition to rethinking the bounds and boundaries of the nation—who it includes and excludes and what geographic spaces partake in its embodiment—the new cultural formations enacted through soca, ragga soca, chutney soca, and rapso have embraced a diasporic aesthetics and identity politics that have posed vexing questions about the ethics and politics of representation. However, like calypso in distinct historical moments, the soundings and embodied practices these new musical styles have foregrounded have occurred under very specific discursive conditions and social relations. As Herman Gray argues in relation to contemporary African-American musics, the circumstances in which the new Carnival musics have emerged "set the limits of possibility for imagining, producing, and circulating different kinds of representations."[110] In the next chapter, I examine the cultural politics and musical practices enacted by two of the most influential artists of the new Carnival musics, emphasizing the neoliberal conditions informing their careers.

Soca, Nation, and Discrepant Diasporas

The most important thing we brought is the will to transform.

Machel Montano, 3 August 2003

Over the past two decades, soca and chutney soca have transformed the Trinidadian Carnival music scene. Beyond the origin stories and the polemics they have generated, both have succeeded—albeit to various degrees among the discrepant diasporas—to expand the range of permissible expressions and experiences during Carnival. In this chapter, I examine the musical practices, aesthetics, and cultural politics of these two new musical styles as enunciated by two of its most important leading stars: Machel Montano and Rikki Jai.

In recent years, I have closely followed these two artists' works and the musical scenes in which they circulate. When I interviewed them, I was as much interested in detailed questions of musical analysis as in querying sweeping statements I had heard or read about their musics. While our exchanges explored a wide range of topics—from issues of gender, race, and diaspora to the roles they play in recording studios—I encouraged them to discuss their own work in detail. What aspects of their music did they find most important? Socially and politically, what contributions did they hope to have made—and still aim to achieve— through their musical practices? How did they position their musics in relation to calypso hegemony? In what terms, and in relation to what, whom, and where did they articulate their cultural politics?

I selected Montano and Jai not just because their names unfailingly come up in discussions of soca and chutney soca on radio broadcasts, in academic publications, among fans, and in the announcements of the most sought-after Carnival shows and parties. I selected them too because their contrasting yet sometimes overlapping journeys help to foreground the new subjects and multiple subjectivities that animate the new scene. Montano is of African descent; Jai of Indian descent. Even though Montano (born in 1974) is younger by ten years, he has had a longer musical career than Jai: Montano began singing in public at the age of seven, Jai at twenty-four. Montano is known as a key trendsetter in the new Carnival musics; Jai as a successful exponent of existing trends. Both are well known for performing songs in different musical genres, and both are renowned as winners of competitions and other prestigious awards.[1]

My aim in examining Montano's and Jai's musical practices is to probe what it means for them to be Trinidadian in a global world and a multicultural state at this particular historical time. By emphasizing the multiple senses of belonging they express musically, I show how "nation" for them is a contested formation. Similarly, by examining how they relate to the selective traditions enshrined as representative of their own communities' past, I acknowledge how they define their notions of authenticity and loyalties in tandem with their own historical time and its particular possibilities and contingencies.[2]

Several conceptual premises guide my analysis. I view Montano's and Jai's musical practices as performing cultural work—work that, on the one hand, requires material and discursive labor and, on the other hand, produces consequential effects and inaugurates changes. As leading artists, Montano and Jai influence how other artists compose, perform, and think about their own practices. They incite others to reflect on, and experiment with, musical fusion and technology; they also encourage them to express their affinities and loyalties. Through their own accomplishments, they help shape the ways soca and chutney soca audiences are construed and constituted, and how the performance circuits for these musics are imagined and established.

I also assert that Montano's and Jai's songs, recordings, and performances are not solely the result of their work as individual artists but rather, as Keith Negus has argued in his research on music industries, the culmination of collaborative efforts with "a range of occupational groups and with specific social milieus."[3] While my emphasis does not aim to belittle these artists' creative input in their musical practices, it seeks to challenge attempts to understand their creative work as emerging from a self-sovereign subject or rare, isolated genius.[4] I stress the complex collaborations in which the two artists are engaged to produce and perform their work, situating what they do as embedded in multiple communities of practice. Their collaborative labor with sound engineers and arrangers as well as with dancers and cultural promoters, to name only a few, constitutes a lively circuit constantly repositioning them as artists.[5] I was struck by Montano's and Jai's politics of acknowledgment of their collaborations in their interviews with me—a politics departing from calypso's long-standing de-emphasis on collaborations, while also revealing the ways these two artists conceive their work in both soca and chutney soca.

Their own appreciation of such collaborative cultural work encourages me to investigate at once their various subject positions—the various knowledges and senses of belonging that inform their vantage points.[6] As many argue, artists never think and act as artists only. Along these lines, I contend, both Montano and Jai conceive and evaluate their work as alternating constantly between different embodied perspectives—as music makers and as audience members, as producers and as consumers, as singers and as dancers. Their different subjectivities interact and inform each other in ways that allow them to innovate and at the same time to stay in tune with their imagined audience, in recording studios as well as onstage. This analytical perspective allows me, first, to challenge the assumption that artists and audiences form separate categories and must accordingly be studied separately and, second, to legitimate my focus on these two artists as enacting many of the experiences, contradictions, and solidarities articulating the musical practices of soca and chutney soca.

Rather than providing exhaustive biographies of Montano and Jai, I orient my analysis around what these two artists identified as having contributed to their cultural politics, musical knowledges, and interventions in the Carnival music scene. They stressed formative experiences ranging from London music clubs to an Ohio sound engineering school, from South Trinidad bazaars to specific performances in Port of Spain. In turn, I situate their experiences in a larger context by drawing on newspaper articles and academic essays. I also draw on personal observations gleaned from my own attendance at their shows and conversations about their work with other artists, deejays, and fans. This approach enables me to place Montano's and Jai's distinctive contributions within the wider contours of the soca and chutney soca music scene.

Machel Montano

Winning as many as four competitions in the same year at the age of nine—including the National Junior Calypso Monarch competition—and composing and singing with his own band ever since have given Machel Montano vast experience in both music and business. I wanted to interview him, but was not able to do so in Trinidad. As is often the case, most artists in the islands have less time for interviews when they are "at home" than when they are on the road. Family obligations, social engagements, rehearsals, recording sessions, the scheduling of tours, and technical preparations all leave little time for interviews dealing with more than factual information. After seeing Montano perform in several countries—Trinidad, Barbados, Antigua, and Canada, in both Montreal and Toronto—I was finally able to meet him in Northern California the day after his show at "Reggae on the River" in August 2003.[7]

Montano's Construction of Soca through Youth Identity

Determined to spare him from having to repeat some of the basic information about his feats—including the list of the competitions he won and awards he received—and the titles of the songs that earned him fame and commercial success, I asked him from the outset to speak about his main contributions to the Carnival music scene. Montano without a pause answered, "The most important thing we brought is the will to transform." The "we" here refers to the friends with whom he formed his first band and with whom he came to the conclusion that, in order to connect with people of their own age—young people—"they needed to do something fresh." As he explains,

> When we decided to form a band, we looked around at the bands that were existing and realized that we're young and our band is not the same crowd as the calypso with the older heads. We would go to shows and there would only be old people around us. . . . We went to all the major producers—Leston Paul, Pelham Goddard, the best—they were older guys and we had to listen to them. . . . In 1997, I said, "Look fellows, we need to do something new." This was at the time of the Barbados invasion, [what was referred to as] the Bajan invasion, in 1996, with Edwin Yearwood and Krosfyah. We were already popular in Barbados with these bands, and we knew what they were coming up with. So we decided we needed to come up with something new and to do it all on our own.[8]

In Montano's assessment, the associations of old people with calypso and of young people with new music, combined with the pressure created by the Bajan band's success in Trinidad, played a role in motivating the band to create new music. All these issues—the gap between age groups, the difference in musical tastes, and "outside" competition, to use a local expression—had to do, in Montano's opinion, with a problem of identity. And according to him, this problem could only be addressed by living, working, and bonding together as a group. In setting up a studio and working collectively day and night, they hoped to come up with something with which they could identify themselves, something that, in Montano's words, "must be a reflection of us." The "us" here referred not only to themselves as performers, but also to the many other ways in which they thought about themselves as audience members, as youth, as Trinidadians, as West Indians, and so on. The "us" also referred to the particular historical moment in which they grew up and the particular musics and new sonic technologies to which they had been exposed and that, not of their own choosing, had influenced their musical tastes and informed how they thought musically. Montano and the group members' efforts in 1997 to create something that would embody their own sensibilities led to the production of the CD *Big Truck,* named after the winning title of the Road March song of that year. Montano explained how that CD, in his view, marked the beginning of a new musical era:

> People liked it and the album took off. It was a new movement. It was like, here are the youth, here are the young people coming forward making their own type of music. We actually lived through it. I can close my eyes and see from year to year the image of the crowd changing to younger people, people in sexy clothes, to youths who never liked it [soca] before, high society people. I can see throughout the years how it has changed.

As he indicates, this musical era involved a transformation of the audience in terms of age group (younger people), class (including people of high society), outreach (new fans), and look (greater emphasis on wearing sexy clothes or, to put it differently, on exhibiting "sexiness").[9]

Challenging Calypso Conventions

To write, sing, and perform their own material, Xtatik group members had to transgress several calypso conventions; as Montano put it, they had "to break a lot of rules." Xtatik's transgressive musical gestures can be seen as inspired by the musics the group members listened to, most particularly, Jamaican dancehall, rock, pop, and hip-hop from Anglo-American mainstream. For instance, they used several singers to sing different sections of one song—which, he argued, had never been heard before in soca, and challenged soca competitions' prior judging of solo artists only. They composed tunes that, for some people, did not have "enough melody," and lyrics that, others maintained, offered too little serious commentary. They also used melodies composed by others, such as in "Footsteps" in 1998, even when they entered Road March competitions—a daring move, says Montano, that created an uproar by countering the usual expectation (based on traditional ways of thinking about "true kaiso") that the songs entered in competitions be composed by the competitors themselves. Montano's band also experimented with sampling, bringing sound bites, for example, from American rap artist and producer Puff Daddy's and legendary R&B singer Barry White's tunes into many of their compositions.[10]

As Montano's own description suggests, his band's notion of authenticity profoundly differed from the ways calypso had been traditionally defined. It was more a matter of resonating with their particular experience than being faithful to an established tradition. From this perspective, authenticity therefore required neither the performers to be necessarily the composers of the songs they performed nor the songs to feature only material composed in the land—the sampling of artists from the United States being a case in point. In Montano's view, what made their songs "authentic" was that they were a "reflection of us"—a reflection of the new visual and sonic environments they experienced on a daily basis. In his own words, "This is what was new; this is what we looked at. We looked at MTV, we looked at BET, and as far as I can remember I looked at Solid Gold. So I was always fixed on the pop market, and we were trying things that they were trying."

The musical knowledge and values inherited from listening to these programs and from being exposed to the musics produced and performed in the islands influenced not only the music Montano's band produced, but also the ways they viewed their musical practices and artistic careers.

Authenticity, Music, and Money

In spite of being criticized by several calypso pundits for using too many Jamaican and Anglo-American sounds in his band, Montano adds, "The main thing is that it [the music] always had great impact in the fan base and people always support the music. . . . We were trying to get people to go out and buy the albums, read the booklets. We needed to sell CDs. Before soca and calypso would not sell anything, just two thousand copies, which is like complimentary now for your first party. So we really needed to do something like that [to change and try new things]." In other words, the new notion of authenticity brought forward by Montano and his band members demanded not only that musical practices be recognized as emerging from multiple musical practices, places, and people. It also demanded a rethinking of music not only as an act of love but also as a product of labor, and a rethinking of money not only as commercial profits (or commercialism) but also as payment for services—and tangible confirmation of enjoyment and acceptance. In short, it required addressing the rapport between music and money in new terms—terms that recognize creative acts as involving labor and thus legitimize artistic pursuits as a career, worthy of financial rewards.

This insistence on the need to earn income from the music one produces must be situated in relation to both Trinidad's harsh socioeconomic conditions and the political economic moment of neoliberalism in which Montano and his band members live. In addition to the fact that before the 1990s there were far fewer calypsonians who attempted to live exclusively from their art, the few calypsonians who did could often count on a social safety net. Older calypsonians often helped younger ones artistically and materially at the beginning of their careers. Black Stalin, for example, lived with Kitchener during his first years of apprenticeship. As I learned in many interviews, many calypsonians could count on friends or lovers to support them in difficult times. In the 1980s, I was told, Trinidad underwent a severe economic crisis following the fall of oil prices and the devastating impact that the structural adjustments imposed by the IMF had on employment—making it harder for many people to survive and to help others. By the 1990s, calypsonians remarked that a "popular mentality" changed in the wake of these reforms. Translated into my own words, since the 1990s, neoliberal practices and institutions in Trinidad have encouraged people not only to maximize profits, but to attribute market values to activities hitherto not thought of in these terms. In this context, activities such as music making already viewed in terms of market value and income have been conducted increasingly with a business-approach, as Montano and his band exemplify.

Consistent with neoliberal reforms and vocabulary, Montano's attempts to reach a wide musical market required, in his words, "putting a package together." One of the first steps was to improve the sound quality of recordings. It meant using the latest recording equipment, developing a wide palette of sounds, and incorporating new musical elements—in order "to cross the generation gap," "to break musical barriers," and "to sell." At first, Montano recounts, his band went to the biggest studio in Trinidad at the time, Caribbean Sound Basin (CSB), then to ACF (in New York, on Long Island) where the Jamaican dancehall artist Shaggy started to record. They spent extravagant budgets on expensive studio rentals, "up to five hundred thousand dollars, which we weren't making back, nothing near that, to the point that we were ending up paying back right through the whole year for our recording." The first-rate sound recordings from Jamaica, the United States, or Britain they listened to, and wanted to compete with, incited them to find other solutions. In order to achieve the same sound quality and to save money, Montano focused on acquiring new knowledge and greater control over their own sound:[11] he, and subsequently several members of his band, went to a recording-engineer school in Ohio to learn about recording and mixing technologies.[12]

> We realize time after time, you have to compete with the big guns. We have
> to develop the professional studio, because there is a war between small studios
> setting up in Trinidad. We have the tendency, say, this year this guy works
> in the studio set up in his bedroom. So it keeps getting smaller and smaller,
> instead of coming together and getting bigger and more professional. . . . We
> have to go to professional studio level, use professional equipment, use the
> studio. . . . We really try hard with the vocal especially. We try to produce the
> vocal to the maximum, use all the techniques and all the effects we can use to
> make it right.

Two other projects that, according to Montano, helped the band develop a new sound involved working with other Caribbean artists. One project was to learn from those who had more experience with recordings, and the other was to collaborate with artists from the neighboring islands on performing and recording songs together. Referring to his recordings with Jamaican dancehall artists, Montano noted,

> We are fans and we are friends—for every combination we made. [For exam-
> ple,] we stepped in the studio with Red Rat; we did not speak to a manager
> or an organizer, we just went to the studio. . . . We respect each other's work.
> We said, "Let's do something," and we started to write. [The same thing hap-
> pened with Shaggy:] Shaggy came in; he heard us writing "Toro, Toro" and
> said that he loved it and wanted a piece of that action. I jumped on. He came
> in, helped us write, we sat down and did it together. It just basically grew out
> of a friendship. [It was the same thing] working with Tony Kelly, Dave Kelly,

and Danny Brown from Jamaica—these are top producers: it was all friendship and love. In the end, we realize that what we were doing was bringing people together: we were breaking musical barriers. . . . And I think it is important because the quality of music in Jamaica is a lot higher. . . . We try to get the best quality in soca music, but the only way to do that is to learn from those who are more professional than us, from those who are more advanced.

Montano mentioned "musical barriers" in reference to the tensions that have long existed among several Caribbean islands—not only between Trinidad and Jamaica, but also between Trinidad and islands from the Eastern Caribbean—over claims of musical origins and ownership, and about the musical hegemony exercised by some islands over others. Montano's philosophy was that there is much to gain both in learning from others and in engaging in collaborative work. Even after meeting some resistance, he and his band members worked to develop new collaborations with artists from different islands—with bands (such as Burning Flames, from Antigua) as well as producers (including Nicholas Branker and Peter Coppin, from Barbados, and the aforementioned Tony Kelly, Dave Kelly, and Danny Brown, from Jamaica, to name only a few).[13]

One impetus for appropriating some of the sounds and musical techniques of reggae and dancehall that Montano did not mention—and yet which must also have played a role in his songs—is that Jamaican music is now part of the global market and has to a large extent become emblematic of the West Indies, as calypso was up to the 1970s. By mixing some of the newer elements of Jamaican music with soca, Montano not only continues a longtime exchange between the two countries, as Rohlehr remarked (2003), but he also arguably increases his chances of penetrating the global market.[14]

In contrast with the politics of purity guarding kaiso against "diluting" or "polluting" influences, discussed in chapter 5, the challenge in foresounding new mixes into his band's music, according to Montano, is to know how to blend the different musical elements. In his words, "We have to figure out the best way to put integrity and sincerity behind it [the music]." As I understand this statement, for Montano mixing different musics is not about losing his identity, but rather about constructing it in ways that acknowledge his multifaceted, ongoing musical experience of the past and the present. The challenge is to avoid losing himself in any one of these experiences and end up merely mimicking others. Conversely, the sincerity and integrity with which he wants to infuse his music require him to respect the uniqueness and the sum of his experiences and his multiple senses of belonging. Out of these challenges arose the notion of workshop: as Montano recounted, when he set up a studio in 1997, all members worked together to come up with new ideas. The motto was, "We must write, we must sing, we must perform, and just having that will and that urge to do that."

Revisiting "Originality"

For Montano, developing new musical ideas involved changing traditional perspectives on originality in the calypso music scene. Instead of defining musical originality as a composition entirely new or borrowing from nothing else, Montano conceived originality as a composition whose overall result is unique.[15] Inspired perhaps by American hip-hop musical practices, Montano's philosophy of collaborative work involved not only working with other Caribbean artists, but also dipping into Caribbean musical resources as a whole. Hence, at times, the production of an original song for him meant "blending new songs with old calypsos to bring out a fresh sort of a minstrel."[16] In 1998, it meant reinterpreting Lord Nelson's old song "We Like It" (1982): adding a soca rhythmic accompaniment and including samples from the original recording as well as a long instrumental bridge typical of today's remixes, focusing on the drum sounds foregrounding sound effects and the chorus part. It meant featuring two soloists, not one, as in the past. The song's reinterpretation also featured two different delivery styles side by side. In one, Montano enacts many gestures now associated with soca: singing with interjections of spoken words such as "Can you see it?" "Yeah," and "Oh, gosh," over the chorus, and using commands such as "Sing," "Everybody," thrown at the backup singers and at the audience. In the other, following a more calypso style, he focuses less on the backup vocals and on interjecting comments throughout, and more on the words and tune of the song.

In other new compositions, Montano incorporated several distinct musical elements and techniques associated with different historical moments. In 2003, for example, together with Dean Williams and Peter C. Lewis, Montano produced "The Collectors Riddim," which employs the recently appropriated Jamaican musical technique of prerecording a rhythm section track over which several singers compose their own tunes.[17] In "What She Want," Montano performs sections of a tune that he recently composed in alternation with his cowriter, Calypso Rose, who sings, in a medley style, lines of text selected from many of her hit songs of the 1970s (including "Give me Tempo" and "Fire"). By featuring Calypso Rose with him in this recording, Montano brings together calypso and soca and two generations of artists, quintessential figures of distinct musical eras. Furthermore, by performing this song over a rid-dim, he fuses the creative sounds and techniques of Trinidad and Jamaica.

Elsewhere, producing new original songs has encouraged Montano to draw his inspiration for both the music and lyrics of his songs from old calypsos. His 2004 "Love Fire," for example, draws on Black Stalin's 1987 song "Burn Dem." Cowritten by Montano, Stalin, and Antonio Theodore, "Love Fire" uses a minor mode, as does "Burn Dem." Instead of speaking as in the old calypso of burning fire as the punishment awaiting people's oppressors in hell, Montano speaks of fire not as an external punishment, but as the fire of love that can bring people together. In addition to performing the song with two other band members, Farmer Happy and Fresh Life, Montano sings the song in the company of Stalin, rendering all the more audible the entanglements that produce the song.

For Montano, changing perspectives on traditional ideas of original-ity has also involved learning about new instrumental techniques and technologies (e.g., turntable effects and sampling). It also entails a readi-ness to share knowledge. Contrasting this philosophy of music making with that of many calypsonians, Montano told me that those unwilling to share knowledge or to make changes have dwindled away, and in the end did nothing to preserve the culture. In order to keep culture alive, he explained, "We try to keep some history there and at the same time try to keep ourselves modern. We try to make a profit, to make a way, and encourage people everywhere. [The goal]: to bring in new people, to turn over, and give back to the community." For Montano, music making is irrevocably entangled with history, modernity, and capital. While music must conjure up the past and simultaneously "progress" with the times ("keep modern"), it must also produce tangible returns so that its makers can continue to create and attract new audiences.

Concept Albums and "Sound Formats"

The method of composing music employed by Montano and his band members reveals how they work to integrate their varied musical expe-riences. In contrast with many other soca bands and artists, since 1997 Montano, as the bandleader, has envisioned the band's CD productions as concept albums, each with its own theme around which at least some songs in the album are composed. According to Montano, his tendency to plan comes from his upbringing and his parents' focus on being or-ganized: "Ever since I started, it was always about getting your focus on what to do, and understanding what you are asked and required to do. Every year I always sit and think what I am going to be, what I am going to do, what I am representing, and what is my job. If you focus on this, being a performer and being lonely, you start listening to your inner spirit and . . . listening to the atmosphere." Each concept brings forth, in his words, "a little universe." It guides the decisions that must be made, including the themes on which the songs will focus. He explained his 1997 album *Heavy Duty* in this way:

> This year is about heavy duty; just imagine we name the album *Heavy Duty*. We need to do a lot of hard work, extra work, over time. Then we had *Heavy Duty*. I had this "Big Truck" idea, and usually all the idea we come up with is like a little universe. All we have to do is just to focus and you get the CD; you get your album cover; you get the idea of what you're going to wear; you get the idea of what you're going to sell—merchandising, to make the people part of your whole image. It just kind of flow from there. We did the *Big Truck* concept; it was all about the *Big Truck*, riding the *Big Truck* for Carnival in the different countries.

The exploration of concepts for their various albums (*Charge* in 1998, *Any Minute Now* in 1999, *Circus* in 2003, and *Road Marching Band* in 2004, to name only a few) led the group to break other rules, as Montano pointed out, in relation to what he calls "sound formats."

> We did basically what we were familiar with in the beginning. Then we were limited with sound formats. In our country it was always verse, chorus, band chorus, verse, chorus. . . . [But] I have been exposed to a lot more, reading books, trying new songs. And we have been just blessed with the fact that there is a lot of youths coming in the scene every year. They recognize soca as a way to get professional and make money in their own country. Every time one comes, he is coming from a different background that may be rap, and he would put some rap in the soca. And the one who listens to dancehall would put some dancehall in there. I think that's what is happening in terms of the format. You can sit down and break it down to students, and explain the different styles and why and how calypso has changed.
> For me, however, I kind of let it come, and try to organize it after. . . . Sometimes it may be a song without a chorus, a chant. But I know what the standard formats are. If it is too far off, I will try to bring it back to something people can relate to . . . but I don't want to be standard.

While Montano stresses his desire not to be confined to "sound formats," he simultaneously acknowledges how his freedom in writing songs is nonetheless conditioned by his audience's listening habits and expectations.

Soca Lyrics, Dancing, and Interactive Composing

Regardless of whether they are mostly listened to or danced to, Montano's band's songs share one thing with most soca songs: the lyrics center on feelings rather than social commentary. As Montano explained,

> It is more of a Superblue approach because Superblue is the guy—I always watched him onstage —he has the vibes and his songs, his vocals started to go into the spiritual feeling inside and the spirit would be rising, and we like that.[18] We try to be entertainers and not calypsonians. Calypsonians are basically commentators: they come out there to say what they have to say. We try to come from the inner [soul]. We try to bring energy. This song makes you feel like doing this, this song makes you feel like doing that: it is more a feeling type of basis. . . .
>
> So good lyrics for me means that I could be listening to this song and start singing these words and it can represent me. . . . We never use person-to-person feeling. I kind of think it is missing in the Caribbean. In America there are so many ways to say that I love you. . . . We all look at that; we never put that personalized touch in our music and more and more you see it coming out.

Montano's lyrics focus on everyday life, affect, and affinities developed through personal experiences and feelings.[19] Like many other soca songs of the 1990s onward, the texts aim more to evoke than to recount. They favor spontaneous expression, as Montano pointed out, in the manner of extempo in contrast with the carefully crafted humorous and sociopolitical commentaries of calypso.[20] Occasionally, some soca songs include a story line in the traditional alternation between verse and chorus associated in Trinidad with calypso form (e.g., "Harry Krishna" on Machel and Xtatik's *Charge* [1998]; "Doh Tell Meh" on *The Xtatik Parade* [2004]; and "You" on Machel Montano and the Xtatik Experience [2005]).[21] (♪ CD track 5, "You," by Machel Montano and Xtatik.)

**"You," cowritten by Machel Montano
and Winston Montano**

Introduction
Eh you [whistle] come here
Yeah Yeah you, here we go, here we go
You You,
Yeah You
Breathe, you got to breathe (3 times)

Verse 1

Ready to defend in the toughest time

Right down till the end

Standing by my side

When I need a friend I depend on you and you

And you and you and you and you and you

Nothing could rise above my feelings for you

I give you all my love and that times two

The strength to go all day

I get it from you

And you, and you and you and you and you and you

Refrain

You give me a reason to jump for joy—Yeah You

You give me the reason to live—Yeah You

You give me the vibe

And keep me alive

Make everything right

Yeah You, Yeah You

It's you got me feeling to jump around,

It's you make me feel to go on and on—Yeah You

Say through every season, you are the reason,

Yeah You, Yeah You, Yeah You

Verse 2

When I am down you pick me up like a newborn

You replenish my cup, you make me feel strong

I could never get enough, enough of you, and you

And you and you and you and you and you

You are a diehard

You down with the crew

You always represent when I call on you

No matter where I go, I'm sure to see You

And you and you and you and you and you and you

Refrain (2 times)

Breathe you got to breathe, breathe you got to breathe (Repeats)

Bridge

You know I love the things you do for me
Every touch I get I go crazy for ... YOU ...
And I'll do anything, anything you want me to
Everything you want I'll do, for you and you and you and you and you

Refrain

However, most of the songs focus on an image, a moment, or a feeling amplified through word repetition and often also by the chorus, intervening after each line sung by the song leader (e.g., "Powder Puff Part 2," "Madman," "Fireman," "Wide Road," and "On The Road," on *The Xtatik Circus* [2003], to name only those on one CD). By focusing on widely shared human experiences, the lyrics, it is hoped, will reach a wider audience than those concentrating on local party politics or incidents. (♪ CD track 6, "On the Road," by Machel Montano and Xtatik.)

"On the Road" by Machel Montano

Introduction

On the road (×4)
When we tell you wave your flag, everybody wave your flag
When we tell you wave your rag, everybody wave your rag
Take out your flag and take out your rag (×2)
And wave, wave, wave, wave, wave it, wave it, wave it, wave it,

Refrain

Wave it up and down, jumpin' up and down (×2)
Celebration time on de road, festival again on de road
Everybody gets on de road, everybody jump on the road

Verse

Jump up, we on the road, we on the stage, we in the band
Jump up, we come to fete, we're getting wet, we're havin' fun
We love to follow Digo Man, so when we hear de instructions
Everybody in your band, jump up, jump up
When I tell you to take a jump, everybody must take a jump (×2)
When I tell you to take a wave, everybody must take a wave (×2)
When I tell you to take a jump, everybody must take a jump, jump,
   jump . . .

Dancing, central in soca, is, in Montano's view, another means of bringing people together: Montano is particularly well known for his energetic and "sexual" dancing onstage. In all the shows in which I saw him perform, he jumps and "wines" and uses key moments in the songs (music breaks, chorus parts) to perform, in complete synchrony with the music, incredibly fast, repeated djouk movements (pelvic thrusts); or along with a slower rhythmic-paced song, he very slowly "goes-down-low," bending the knees, gyrating his waist in sensual motions. His charismatic presence onstage and dynamic performance enthrall most of his audiences, typically with thousands of fans packed as closely as possible to the stage. Most dance energetically, arms raised in the air waving their rags, responding to Montano's dance moves.

In my interview, Montano related his way of thinking about dancing to "something African," to the "feeling of fighting war when the war was just a dance: you dance and I dance; we back each other up till we fall. We get that feeling." He emphasized too how deeply music touches him sensually, and how dancing helps him to convey this feeling and energy to his "young and sexy" audience. He further explained that this is the difference between singing about love in a general way, and performing what he calls "sexual music"—in his words, "like the guy in the party wanna make love to you tonight."[22] Comparing these two performance styles, he adds, "They [calypsonians] will never think of that [of expressing their sexual desires as directly]. . . . All that is part of our life, and we just let that come through."[23] In his performance, the focus is placed on immediacy, embodied expression of feelings, and contact with a young audience whose own "sexiness" in looks and dancing further encourages Montano's expression of sexuality onstage.

Montano's particular ways of thinking about lyrics and dancing, he explained, come from his approach to listening and music making—as a composer and audience member, as a producer and consumer—in all cases, as an embodied experience. In his words, "I see music. When I listen to a song, I already perceive how the people will react to it—what they will be doing, what I will be doing. I does write in three dimensions. Sometimes I will want to write from lyrics, sometimes I will write from the response, sometimes from the movements, but it happens in different ways all the time. . . . Usually we get the beats and make up songs with topics that jump out with the music. I like working in completion." Montano's expression "working in completion" refers to composing in an interactive mode, in reaction to an existing beat, in tandem with a band member's idea or, as he put it, "along with the vibes." For Montano, collaborative work is present at all times. From the moment his memory is at work evoking melodic lines from different times or spaces, or he hears some rhythmic patterns or views the bodily movements of his imagined audiences, he mentally responds by composing new lines, beats, or moves.

As is typical in soca, Montano's band places the focus on producing dynamic and powerful soundings. In their 1997 major hit "Big Truck," Xtatik featured the five-piece wind section (two trumpets, two saxophones, and one trombone) characteristic of the 1980s soca bands as well as the bands accompanying calypso during the 1960s and 1970s. Over the past five years or so, most soca bands, including Montano's, have considerably reduced the number of wind players, often leaving only one trumpet and one trombone. In tandem with his emphasis on energy, movement, and participation, I asked Montano to explain how he arrived at his new band instrumentation.

> This is an ongoing saga. We have a lot of brass men. Brass men in our country is an ongoing institution. . . . We [his band Xtatik] had a brass section, but then we decided to break down the band. It was more like, songs being created in soca have less horns. So the horns were playing a very small part, and we'd be doing that unison thing and short riffs, so it [their use] was limited.
>
> When we name the band Xtatik 5.0, we wanted to focus on the five-piece [band]. We were downsizing, but we were upgrading. It is an upgrade in the Xtatik experience—like how you would upgrade your [computer] system from 4.1 to 5.0. Everybody was running the Xtatik program, like you are accustomed to getting your regular Xtatik, and now you get Xtatik 5.0.

Montano's conception of soca sounds using "less horns" can be related to widespread musical trends in the Caribbean since the early 1990s, spurred among other things by Eddy Grant's arrangements of calypso and soca at his Ice Record studio as well as by Jamaican dancehall. Montano's use of computer imagery to describe the changes in his band is telling not only about himself, but also about the audience he hopes to reach: techno-savvy users and consumers—in particular, the younger generation.

The core components of his band now include bass, guitar, keyboard, drums, and vocals. "Then we have to put in the percussion there, and we have to put in samples which we may consider, whenever we get to that point. . . . We do things like Sting: we have five members; and we have the alternate band for tours." Along with this new orchestration, the band concentrates on developing its own sound and, instead of featuring several soloists in one song, on placing the focus on only one singer. "We try to align ourselves to international standards and try to make it simple." He added,

M.M. We have a trumpeter, a young kid who stuck around. And in the end, we didn't have use for horns—the keyboardist will play the horn. He was just there with the one trumpet. So we found a way to make the one trumpet sound like a horn section.

J.G. Do you use double tracking?[24]

M.M. Yes. For that, the other horn player said, we will burn in hell, we will never see our way. But he stuck around and he also became a producer and produced the song "Mo Luv."

Montano's band, like many bands undergoing changes, was transformed after a series of events not all of his own choosing. In 2001, after signing a contract with Atlantik records, Montano stopped performing with the band as he attempted to pursue an international career as a soloist. For reasons still not clear to me, his plans changed and he resumed his activities with the band the following year. However, by then several members had already opted for other musical endeavors. One of the main singers, Roger George, was now with Byron Lee's band; two other lead singers, Sean Caruth and Wayne Rodriguez, had decided to go solo. Montano thus formed Xtatik 5.0 with a reduced number of players.

Montano's explanation of why he transformed the band from a thirteen-piece band to a core of five members, however, was not in relation to particular contingencies but rather in relation to three more general factors: marketing, change of musical values, and efficiency. During his stay in London, he realized that it would be easier to develop a quickly identifiable sound and an image for international marketing with a smaller band and only one lead singer. Like most other soca bands over the past few years, Xtatik did not make major use of the horn section and thus did not require horn players to be part of the band, as they had before.[25] Hindsight also revealed that the band had spent much time, money, and energy in the recording studio trying things out before they were ready to record. Working with a smaller number of core members on compositions before going to the studio became for Montano an attractive solution, emerging as much from experience and a new focus on efficiency as from the ad hoc circumstances of band members' having decided to leave.

As the stories about the transformation of Xtatik reveal, the group's new musical constitution and orientation emerged from a series of contingencies involving not only local, but also regional and international events, new musical values, and marketing strategies. As in 1997, the band's changes, instrumentation, arranging style, and new sound were part of a particular articulation that is not reducible to a commercialism argument, as some observers and authors have proposed.[26] Montano's contract with the international firm Atlantik, his experience in London, and his understanding of successful marketing as requiring a particular sound and image combined with the departure of some of his band members, the use of new musical technology, and the decreased reliance on horns in soca bands in Trinidad and in other islands: all have played a role in the creation of the most recent version of Xtatik's sound and image.

Gender Politics

Over the past decade, the upsurge of female soloists in the Caribbean musical scene (e.g., in dancehall, zouk, and soca) and the unprecedented success and influence, in particular, of Alyson Hinds—who, after being one of the lead singers in Barbadian soca band Square One, became the group's main voice—incited many, if not most soca bands to add a female lead vocalist. With this in mind, I asked Montano how Xtatik had so far resisted this new trend. He replied:

> "Resisted" is the perfect word. I would love to see some female singing background vocals—if we could get some real professional girls. Before the idea was: keep them out, keep them out, keep them out by all means. Because when we started, we had three girls in the band: a girl playing guitar, one playing cuatro, one playing tambourine. . . . In 1984, 85, 86, 87, we had three female vocalists: Melanie Hudson, who is now a Broadway performer; we had Camille Greenidge, who since retired; and Rachel Fortune, who sang with us for a long time. Now she is in a duet with one of Ras Shorty's daughters, Abbie. They were vocalists with us. [But] we had problems with the females going on tour; they were young and lots of trouble.
>
> At one point, we decided we are going to be a boy band. That's it. And we just went that way. And there were times when it was tough, as we would have great woman songs but we would not be able to sing them. Then there was the year when we had "River"; it was a Road March. Who would sing "River"? Then we would have to sing it. If Roger George could be there, he could do it; some other day, someone else would do it; sometimes it would not be appropriate to do it. Then I would wish we had a girl, but we always wanted to stay kind of guys. [But] now we are into the world concept: so if we have a female in the band for the purpose of female things, now I am even contemplating having an East Indian singer, a classical East Indian singer just to do riffs. I always wanted to have that Indian and African influence in the band at the same time. So we have different ideas. We're not going to lock into any one concept, we're trying to find ourselves. It may happen, it may not happen.

Montano's perspective on women in the group suggests particular gender politics. Women are constructed as others, young, and the ones bringing trouble—a conservative vision of women that has been circulating as commonsensical for decades, but that has been greatly revised among several groups over the past few decades.[27] Furthermore, their difference as others is racialized—African or East Indian. The fact that Montano views the addition of a female singer as one of the best ways of merging the two ethnic influences in his band is in itself a significant consideration: For many in the East Indian community, the presence of an East Indian female singer among Afro-Trinidadian males would be seen as endangering the preserved domain and embodiment of Indian culture that has been contested since Indian arrival in Trinidad. The consideration of such an inclusion in an African-dominated soca band signals how, through chutney soca, the sound and physical presence of East Indians has become part of the imagined Carnival music scene.[28]

In the meantime, while Xtatik is still a "boy band," Montano has nonetheless recorded songs with several female singers over the past two years. In "What She Want" (2003), as mentioned above, he cowrote and performed a song with a female singer, Calypso Rose, while remaining the main soloist. At other times, he cowrote a song with a male singer, but performed it with a female singer, leaving her the main part, as in "Love Is" with Trini Jacobs (2004) and "Carnival" with Destra Garcia (2003). Indeed, the inclusion of a female voice in a soca band has arguably now become one of the conventions. In the case of Xtatik, even when lacking an embodied presence, it features an audible one. In August 2003 at the dance club Ashkenaz in Berkeley, California, I was surprised—and at the same time impressed by such audacity—to see Montano and Xtatik perform the song "Carnival" in the absence of Destra Garcia onstage. The band wholeheartedly accompanied and danced to her recorded solo before Montano began singing his part. While this performance could be indicative of Montano's and Xtatik's continuing resistance to a female singer in their midst, it simultaneously suggests how unavoidable the incorporation of female voices in soca bands has become.

Reimagining the Nation through Soca Soundings

More than most other soca bandleaders, Montano has worked hard to make Carnival music the terrain on which people from different diasporas, generation groups, and different Caribbean countries can meet. His many attempts to promote and, in Rohlehr's words, "to celebrate the myth of racial harmony and inter-racial love" have been instantiated through many of his songs, recording projects as a producer, and annual concerts.[29] His 1998 song "Harry Krishna," though criticized for alluding to a Hindu deity, was nevertheless about the merging of the soca and chutney musical cultures and, by extension, uniting the people with whom these two practices are associated. While audibly mixing soca with melodic lines and instruments (such as the harmonium) associated with chutney music, "Harry Krishna" humorously dealt with an Indian deejay's mix of soca and chutney and his success in making Africans and East Indians "come together in unity." Montano's 2000 song "Real Unity" was another attempt to promote unity by having Drupatee— "who had braved the contempt of the Hindu purists to help create Chutney Soca a decade before it became politically correct," as Rohlehr nicely puts it[30]—record the song in duet with him. The lyrics inviting anyone in the audience to "jam" on any member of any race typically referred to physical interaction through dancing to evoke and convey this utopian, multicultural, egalitarian vision of Trinidad's "united nation."[31]

Montano's eighteenth annual concert—the megaconcert named after the "Real Unity" song that took place in 2000 at Chaguaramas Heliport—was organized along these lines, aiming to assemble onstage stars who embodied the diversity present in his imagined united nation—from which Montano draws not only his inspiration, but also his sense of multiple belongings. By inviting not only older calypsonians (Sparrow and Lord Nelson), an Orisha priestess (Ella Andall), an East Indian singer (Drupatee), soca artists (Sherwin Gardner and Wayne Rodriguez), but also dancehall superstars from Jamaica (Red Rat and Shaggy), Montano proposed a reconsideration of the notion of nation. His show was designed to feature symbolically a nation not confined to the physical territory of an island but emerging out of the Caribbean and its multiple diasporas as a whole.[32]

Montano has resorted to various means to further this view of nation. Over the past few years, as a producer and composer, he has worked with artists encompassing a wide range of age, experience, and musical affinities, and of different races (best illustrated by the CD *The Collectors Riddim* [2003]). His own contributions to recordings featuring Jamaican riddims and Jamaican artists provide more examples of the ways he construes his music as being entangled with the many resources of the Caribbean populations. Montano's idea of music making goes hand in hand with his expanded notion of nation, and with his expanded notion of audience. As he explained:

> I grew to learn that some people like to be recognized as Trinidadians or
> Grenadians, and they fight to stay together, especially when they go to a place

like England. You would see all the Jamaicans together, all the Trinidadians together. . . . But now we perform [for everybody] like Barbados, Grenada, New
York, Jamaica, England: it is all the people, it is the whole Caribbean. . . . It is
a catch-22 for us because I think we will gain more being Caribbean people
and people of the world trying to come into the world.

For Montano, the catch-22 is the tensions between the Caribbean as a
nation and Trinidad's place within it and the complex cultural politics
these multiple, competing senses of belonging entail. Montano's attempts
to make these multiple senses of belonging central to his cultural politics
led him, in our talk, to address his identity as being simultaneously West
Indian, Trinidadian, and also African.

> Basically. . . . I try to suppress a lot of the African in me . . . but when I was
> introduced to Fela Kuti's music in 2001 . . . I went through a whole spiral of
> emotions, and I would start crying and I feel the connection and I want to
> do a lot of African drums.[33] But where we come from, a lot of people don't
> accept Africans so much; they scared of them. They think it's something voo-
> doo; they think it's something ritual, not commercial or normal. We have a
> plan, we have an idea: eventually . . . I will like to end up to totally revolution-
> ize the African song. . . . Eventually we see soca being popular in Africa. We
> know we can do it; it is our ultimate goal.

Along with his expanded notion of Caribbean nation and multiple senses
of belonging, Montano conceives Africa in modern terms, not as fixed
in time but instead as simultaneously part of his own identity and global
market.

Rikki Jai

> I like to be called "Trinidadian." I am Indian of East Indian descent, but I like to
> be called a Trinidadian. Because if I go anywhere else in the world, I am not an
> Indian; I am a Trinidadian; I don't fight this Indian or African thing. I believe in
> Trinidad and being Trini. The reason is that I was born in this country. I don't want
> to alienate myself from that.
>
>   Rikki Jai, 15 January 2003

When I met him at his home in South Trinidad in 2003, Jai (born
Samraj Jaimungal in Friendship Village, San Fernando) had just finished
recording the song "My Brother, My Friend" with Black Stalin. This
song, composed by both artists, features both calypso and chutney soca

and, interestingly for me, sums up Jai's entire musical career and the very reasons I wished to meet him. Jai is one of the best-known chutney soca artists in the Caribbean, but he is also renowned for his deep affinities with and performance of a wide range of repertoires. Having listened to his music over the past decade, I was intrigued by his obvious commitment to collaborative work with artists from different backgrounds, and the unique position he has earned as a result. How, as an East Indian artist, has he succeeded in developing his own niche in the Carnival music scene and engaging its complex cultural politics? How have his musical transgressions (singing calypso) and fusions (involving at times not only soca and chutney, but also dancehall) been received by the local media and distinct communities? As a means to situate his musical tastes and his embrace of several musics, Jai highlighted for me the main events that led him to his musical career.

Contrary to many assumptions that artistic careers are the result of planning or telos, Jai did not initially aim to be a "versatile" artist in order to attract a wide audience. Rather, as he explained, he slipped into this position through a series of unanticipated circumstances. He always knew, however, that he wanted to be identified as Trinidadian.

During his entire career, Jai never liked to be pigeonholed into set and separate categories according to ethnicity, religion, or skin color. Accordingly, he felt free to sing songs from any musical repertoire. Unlike many East Indian singers at the time, he refused to become a local imitator of the great movie singers from India. He preferred instead to emulate those closest to him, the stars who were best known locally—which explains why, as he put it, "my focus was more on calypso."

As Jai's insistence on being "Trinidadian" suggests, his sense of national belonging resonates with Eric Williams's vision of Trinidad as a nation based on unity and unambiguous loyalty. Yet Jai's identification and identity as Trinidadian is not entirely a decision of his own. In large part, it follows the ways in which people in this modern era are "placed" in relation to the pervasive paradigm of "nation-state" ("if I go anywhere else in the world"), and perceived in tandem with the stereotypical associations of being a national of that place.

Gifted with a facility for memorizing songs, Jai and his friends would learn the hit songs of the calypso season every year and create a little stir in performing them at Naparima College. After he quit school to work at the Ministry of Finance, Jai's intimate knowledge of calypsos provided him his first opportunity to sing in public. At a bazaar in a predominantly East Indian community in 1986, he heard Naya Andaz's orchestra from Princesstown perform instrumental versions of the most recent calypso hits and asked the bandleader if he needed a song leader. Interested in hiring a singer to perform with the group at weddings and private parties, the bandleader set an audition, and shortly thereafter Jai was hired.

While calypso had been performed instrumentally for years before Jai began his singing career, only rarely had it been sung by an East Indian. Even though the first time he performed in public Jai's nervousness caused him to forget words, or to sing them at the "wrong places," as he recounts, "people did not care. For the most part they were amazed, surprised, but also eventually pleased. It was very strange to see an East Indian sing calypso then." This incident reveals how calypso has been crossing the so-called ethnic divide far more frequently than has usually been acknowledged, while suggesting the variety of ways (instrumental and vocal) and contexts (bazaars, weddings, and parties) in which it has been reproduced, other than on the calypso competition stage. In this context, by adding an East Indian embodied voice to the calypso sounds already being reproduced, Jai helped to expand further a practice already taking place in East Indian communities.

From 1986 to 1989, Jai performed calypso with Andaz's orchestra at small-sized events within East Indian communities. In 1989, he joined one of the most famous East Indian bands in Trinidad—Trevini, from San Juan—and began performing at all the big fetes of Port of Spain (e.g., WITCO, WASA, and Soca Village).[34] The major change for him was the size of both these new performing venues and the audience. As Jai indicated,[35]

> There I was thrust into a new environment where there were only black people in front of me. Previously I had been singing in venues where there were more East Indian people. Now with Trevini, the first set of party we start to go to was pro-African, Afro-Trinidadian crowd. It was little daunting at first, but we went down well each night. We went out so well that it kind of build my confidence. . . . It also gave me a chance to learn from the major players in the game at the time: Carl and Carol Jacobs, David Rudder, and Tambu [the sobriquet of Chris Herbert], and from all these other bands. We would open for all these bands, and after when we opened, I would stay. I would stay and see how these people work the crowd, and how they swing their repertoire—little things that make the difference.

As Jai explained, to perform in front of an Afro-Trinidadian crowd was all the more daunting because, even though he sang sometimes one or two songs drawn from Indian films and some songs from Sundar Popo, he was hired mainly, in his words, "to bring the calypso part." Defying expectations in the context of Trinidad's ethnicized cultural politics, he improved his skills by watching seasoned Afro-Trinidadian performers, while further developing his sensitivity to Afro-Trinidadian singing and performing styles.[36]

Following the challenging learning experience of performing for an Afro-Trinidadian audience, Jai still aimed to improve his performing skills. As Trevini usually performed last in East Indian events and thus had to wait for hours before going onstage, Jai decided to become an emcee. This gave him a chance to learn how to establish a rapport with the crowd and, in his words, "to make people comfortable." In 1990, Jai left Trevini to begin his career as a soloist. At this point, Jai had performed for both Indo- and Afro-Trinidadian audiences. While he focused on calypso, he also occasionally performed songs from East Indian musical repertoires, including not only local musical genres, but also movie songs from India—embracing the various musics that were all part of what constituted his Trinidadian soundscape.

Concordant with his focus on calypso, Jai hired some of the most re-spected calypso composers to write songs for him—including Winsford Devine, Gregory Ballantyne, Wayne "Cassman" McDonald, and Delamo. However, he quickly abandoned some because of their strong emphasis on sociopolitical commentary. His interest was in party songs. A focus on party music, in his view, is what distinguishes him from other East Indians, such as Hindu Prince, Raja, and Sheik, who performed calypso before him:

> The difference between me and them is that they always maintained a sort of a social and political aspect to their music. Their music was always based on social and political issues. . . . [However], you will see the party music always take the forefront to the social music. The social music has gone back into the tent. You will hardly hear it on the radio, and the political comes to the front only at competition time. I didn't want to get involved in that at all. I dabble in social issues now and then just to compete, but I don't interfere in politi-cal issues at all. When I have to jump into a situation, it has to be in the party point of view.

By "political aspect," Jai here means issues involving political parties fighting over state governmental powers. However, his choice of per-forming almost exclusively "in a party point of view" does not remove "the political" from his performance. That choice could be seen as both strategic and political by enabling him to move across and among groups historically polarized into racialized voting blocks by politicians from

Afro-Creole and Indian political parties. In that sense, his decision to focus on party songs in order to enjoy more "freedom" to perform among distinct communities has contributed to the shaping of, and has itself been shaped by, the cultural politics central to soca, which aim to bypass state issues, focusing instead on creating and reinforcing solidarities among people.

While Jai professes not to be interested in focusing on the political, he conceives the choreography that accompanies his performances according to highly ethnicized conventions. For instance, when he participates in competitions, he often hires female dancers—the proverbial formation that accompanies East Indian male singers—to perform set choreographies while he sings and takes a few dancing steps. While in the chutney soca competitions the group of female dancers is usually composed of East Indian dancers only, in the soca competitions it tends to include both East Indians and Afro-Trinidadians. In the same vein, the choreography the dancers perform tends to feature in chutney soca songs movements mainly associated with East Indian traditions (involving particular steps or arm gestures). When accompanying a soca song, a mix of East Indian and Afro-Trinidadian dance movements (including "wining," not exclusive to Afro-Trinidadian dancing but in Trinidad associated with those dancing styles) may be expected.[37] Even though set choreographies performed by female dancers are by no means exclusive to, or exhaustive of, the Bollywood movie tradition, the great number of dancers, the large space they occupy onstage, and their particular lineup around Jai strategically appear to establish a connection with that tradition. In competitions, Jai integrates female dancers into his performances in line with artistic and gender conventions. At the same time, he chooses his female dancers in relation to the ethnicized spaces in Trinidad in which he is performing. While over the years he has performed with East Indian female dancers in chutney soca competitions, he has included Afro-Trinidadian dancers when he has entered soca competitions to facilitate his participation in an otherwise Afro-Trinidadian-dominated performance context. Conversely, the few Afro-Trinidadian performers who have been participating in chutney soca competitions have usually included East Indian female dancers in their presentations.

In 1993, Jai enjoyed his first "big hit" with "Wine On Ah Bumsee" and went on tours. As he put it, "There was not a place that I didn't go in that year. . . . Once there was a pocket of Trinidadians, I touched that place: Toronto, Montreal, Vancouver, the Caribbean, down the Bahamas straight to Grenada." While on tour he spent much time with Preacher, a seasoned Afro-Trinidadian calypsonian who encouraged him to compose his own material. To learn the tools of the trade, Jai wrote his first song in collaboration with Preacher. Even though the song they wrote together, "Turn Yuh Waist," had, according to Jai, "a fair amount of success," it did not help to further his career. Rather, it signaled the beginning of his decline in popularity; as Jai said, things "went down hill for me in calypso" from 1995 to 1999, the period when he was learning to write his own songs alone.

In his interview with me, Jai attributed what he calls "his decline in calypso" to his lack of writing skills, without ever mentioning the political events that were then unleashing new sources of resentment and creating new anxieties among the Afro-Trinidadian communities. In 1995, for the first time in Trinidad's history, an East Indian politician was elected as prime minister. Combined with the flourishing of East Indian social, academic, and artistic activities spurred by the 150th anniversary of Indian arrival in Trinidad, celebrated the same year, the new elections displacing the Afro-Creole party from its seat of power created an unsettling atmosphere for many Afro-Trinidadians. Jai's writing skills notwithstanding, such a context was not propitious for an East Indian aiming to transgress ethnic boundaries and to sing calypso, especially for Afro-Trinidadian audiences.

As his popularity in calypso declined, Jai fell back on East Indian community organizations. In line with his insistence on being Trinidadian and, by extension, on being a legitimate heir to several musical traditions, Jai turned his attention to East Indian musical repertoires and began performing chutney and Bollywood songs. Yet his entrance onto the chutney musical scene during the midnineties, as in the case of calypso, was not a result of self-conscious planning. As a well-established artist in Trinidad, he was called to take part in one of the shows in the then fast-growing "chutney industry," as Jai termed it.

Jai's entrance into the chutney soca competitions provided him with new artistic opportunities and recognition as well as occasions to be involved in what became a family and community process. Jai entered the first chutney soca competition, held in 1996,[38] and came in second. Because, according to Jai and also other competitors, the criteria of the newly created competition were still poorly defined, the following year he did not qualify for the semifinals, for his song was judged to be too calypso oriented.[39] From 1998 to 2002, he won every chutney soca competition except in 2000, when he lost by one point to Rooplal.[40] His outstanding achievements in competitions gained him performing engagements not only in Trinidad, but also in the Caribbean region, the United States, Canada, and England throughout the years.

Following the clarification of the judging criteria for chutney soca competitions in 1997, to qualify as chutney soca, songs had to include either melodies written in the chutney style or lyrics typical to the chutney repertoire or referring to East Indian affairs, or to be sung in the languages traditionally used in Chutney, usually a mixture of Bhojpuri and Hindi. To be able to feature songs that would comply to these criteria, soon after he became involved with the chutney scene Jai began working closely with his mother, who, as a regular singer at the maticor on the Friday night of Hindu weddings, possessed an extensive knowledge of chutney songs. He worked in collaboration with her not only to draw on several traditional songs to create new chutney compositions, but also to learn about the meanings and pronunciation of the lyrics in Bhojpuri and Hindi, which, like most chutney soca singers, he does not speak. In the same vein, his participation in the yearly chutney soca competitions drew the support of, and drew him closer to, a large community of family relatives, friends, and fans. His winning or losing became a community affair. This is how he described the night he lost the crown by one point to Rooplal in 2000: "It was a very sad day because I have a very big camp here. And when the Soca Monarch competition comes, there is about forty, fifty people who come at home, right here. That night, people were devastated. . . . There is something inside of us when this competition comes around. This, for the people, is like heart, soul, and blood." In spite of (or because of) his resounding success in nearly all the chutney soca competitions in which he took part, Jai still did not want to be identified as a singer confined to one musical category. In 2001, he aimed to challenge the local stereotypical image that East Indians sing only East Indian things. He entered six competitions that year in several different categories:

> I won the Chutney Soca Monarch; I tied for first place with Bunji Garlin for Young Kings; I won the South Calypso Monarch; I won the National Unattached Calypso Monarch; I made it to the final of the Soca Monarch; and I made it to the final of the Dimanche Gras, placing seventh at the end of the day—the first East Indian to make it to the finals. 2001 was a great year for me in calypso, because apart from the one chutney competition, I had entered five other competitions.

Jai's determination to perform musically his sense of multiple belongings was motivated, in my view, by more than personal pride. It fulfilled his definition of being "Trinidadian," enacting not only the sum of his musical experiences, but also the manifold ways he defines himself as "Trini."

It also followed the musical trends set by Afro-Trinidadian soca. Apart from entering different types of competitions, he tried to achieve such fulfillment through several other practices, including his performance and recording of a wide range of musical styles and engagement with various collaborators. I invited him to describe the songs on his CD *Chutney Vibrations* (2001)—a compilation of his most important hits over the years—as a means to map his involvement with many musical genres and artists, and to assess the audiences he hoped to reach while recording and those he had reached in the past.[41]

Many of the tracks foresound Jai's entanglements with the musics emerging within the East Indian communities in Trinidad, from other Indian diasporas in Britain and North America, and from India. The CD begins with the chutney song "Hamareh Galeeyah," allying Jai from the outset with the members of the older and younger generations who continue to participate in the traditional wedding-night gatherings. The cultural work this song accomplishes is important: it voices Jai's respect for and knowledge of the East Indian musical repertoire of chutney and his affinity with a large segment of the East Indian population. "Hamareh Galeeyah" is performed with traditional instrumentation, including a harmonium, *dhantal,* and *dholak.* Jai selected this instrumentation to affirm the return in East Indian communities to the use of traditional instruments instead of the synthesizer and drum machine that had recently replaced them. The song is performed in the typical mixture of Hindi and Bhojpuri and features a love story—about a man who is heartbroken after his wife leaves him to go abroad. Love stories are characteristic of most of his songs, Jai explained. "I try to fashion the chutney the same way the Indian film industry fashion their music, mainly around love scenes. There is more expression, more mood. When I do love song in chutney, the people who understand it feel good about it. I try to stay away from derogatory topics and, even if I put a touch of double language [double entendre] inside there, it is very subtle." Jai's privileging of love songs in his repertoire is thus no accident. His understanding of both the sensibilities nurtured in Indian films and the ways in which such sensibilities are exploited as commodities by the Indian film industry outlines Jai's close ties to the East Indian communities and also to the Indian material culture that is pervasive throughout many Indian diasporas.

Several songs on the album feature Jai's collaborations with members of the East Indian community. "Koyal Bhole Peecha Wadawa" and "Chamaka Chale Jatee" introduce two traditional chutney songs whose words and melodic phrases he and his mother have modified slightly. Both songs

are performed with a soca arrangement. In the case of "Koyal Bhole Peecha Wadawa," the introduction, played in a strict soca style before the
tune begins—a chutney melody and Bhojpuri and Hindi lyrics—presents
an unusual instrumentation: strings, hardly ever used in chutney soca
songs, combined with a keyboard. I asked him to speak about the ear-
catching introduction: "We were trying to vary the introductions for all
the songs. . . . Every time a song starts, people know it is that song. It has
a distinctive identity."

Jai's account of the contrasting introductions of the various songs included on the CD is telling: it emphasizes how, while he borrows from
various idioms (traditional chutney tunes and standard soca arrangements) and thus brings forward the familiar, he is also mindful of marketing distinction—his own musical creative intervention. In other words,
Jai's musical thinking, performances, and recordings are informed by his
understanding that music making is always enmeshed simultaneously
with the issues of identity, sense of belonging, and marketing.

Jai's engagement with other members of the East Indian community
is demonstrated through his use of several songs by well-known chutney
singers. In each case, Jai transforms their songs through particular arrangements that clearly foresound his audible entanglements with several
musical genres. For example, "Sting She" is based on the chorus originally
recorded by Sundar Popo; in this version, Jai sings in the company of an
Afro-Trinidadian singer called "Double D." (♪ CD track 7, "Sting She,"
by Rikki Jai.) I asked him how he would label his rendition of this song:

> *R.J.* "Sting She" is kind of a ragga soca mixed with chutney in it. I would say
> it is a form of ragga soca chutney because it has that rap. We could call it
> rapso chutney because there is so many things happening.
>
> *J.G.* There is a Drupatee's signature in it. There is also a vocal styling that
> reminds me of dancehall, and then there is the "patang patang" of old
> mas [a Trinidadian expression referring to "traditional masquerade"].[42]
> And then there is the chorus that is harmonized. This is very special, be-
> cause you don't hear harmony like this that often. I was not too sure if
> you were going into a rapso style.
>
> *R.J.* The ragga part would be heavily reggae influenced, dancehall reggae
> fused in with soca and then fused in with chutney. We use the tone quality
> where Drupatee would go weeeeeeee because, in the industry, people tend
> to associate certain things with what we term as chutney or Indian, and
> Drupatee's trademark in the industry is one of those. Her high-pitched
> song that she makes is "weeeeeeeee" and "hah." It translates to the public
> as something Indian and something chutney.

In his recorded version of "She Wish She Was a Virgin," also a song by Sundar Popo, Jai sings in a way close to the original version, but with two notable exceptions. The song is performed with an additional "rapping" part sung by Afro-Trinidadian singer Major Yankee and is recorded over a riddim the latter produced called "The Plantation"—linking Jai to two of the most recent trends in soca, the use of riddim and inclusion of dancehall vocal styling.

In "Nazaria," Jai features another chutney written by a composer of an older generation, Basdeo Jaikaran. While this time he hardly alters the chutney vocal delivery style, Jai uses the arrangement to render audible his affinities with soca and his collaboration with musicians with still other musical tastes. In addition to the typical instrumentation and arrangement of the rhythm section in the soca style used to accompany the chutney tune, one of the players, saxophonist Gerald Rampersad (a member of the Trevini orchestra), adds some jazz-influenced melodic lines to the mix.

On this CD, Jai also recorded a tune to pay tribute to an East Indian composer who has influenced his musical orientation. Here he made few changes to the tune, the vocal delivery style, or the arrangements. As Jai explained, "'Indian Singing' is a tune by Yussuf Khan, an East Indian who was doing what I am now doing . . . and nobody was noticing him in the national scale . . . but he really and truly did what I am doing." This song, recorded in the 1970s, in Jai's words, "moves so cleverly between calypso and the Indian melody. [The verse draws on typical calypso features—diatonic melody performed in a narrative delivery style over simple harmony.] In the chorus, he just changes and goes back into the old chutney style. I always liked this song. These people influenced me in the early days. I wanted to record back some of their work to be part of my repertoire."

In addition to enacting his musical affinity with local East Indian composers and local repertoires, Jai includes two tunes on the CD that demonstrate the circulation of various musics among Indian diasporic groups. Most particularly, these selections show how his soundscape in Trinidad links him to Bollywood sound tracks. "Mohsafir," Jai said, is one of his favorite songs: "It is the original song from one movie done by Kishore Kumar. He is one of the legends of Indian music. He is like a giant. I just love the song." Jai decided to record it in a chutney soca style, with the typical riffs played on the synthesizer imitating the horn section and a solo on saxophone. Similarly, "Juma," which Jai performed in a chutney soca style, is a song drawn from the well-known Indian movie called *Hum* released in the late 1980s.

While Jai's rendition of Bollywood songs illustrates his engagement with musics from various Indian constituencies, three other songs on the CD exemplify his simultaneous attunement to distinct musical demands in Trinidad: local competitions. For example, the third track on the CD presents a chutney soca version of the chutney song "Hamareh Galeeyah" found on the first track (♪ CD track 8, chutney version of "Hamareh Galeeyah," by Rikki Jai). In contrast with the first version, the chutney soca rendition features the typical instrumentation of chutney soca songs, including bass, drums, synthesizer, and brass sounds produced by the synthesizer (♪ CD track 9, chutney soca version of "Hamareh Galeeyah," by Rikki Jai). Jai's two versions of the same song, he noted, were produced to cater to two different performing venues and markets in Trinidad: "What it is, is that the first one [the chutney version] plays on the radio more regularly, but the third one I will use for competition. But what was happening is that I had the two versions playing at different times. So around chutney soca time, number 3 was playing, and afterwards the other one will play all year." The track entitled "The Hammock" provides another illustration of how Jai's compositions are imagined in relation to competitions. To my ears, "The Hammock" sounded like a soca song, but Jai corrected me and, in so doing, explained some of the cultural politics involved in his compositions: "The music is more soca, but the melody is [still] between Indian and soca. That is what I must try to maintain in order not to be 'ex out' in the competition. So if you do a melody which is pure soca, you will not be judged properly."

Jai also wrote "Chutney Soca Time" with a view to competitions, not for himself but for somebody else—revealing another dimension of his musical activities and wide artistic network in Trinidad:

> R.J. I wrote that song, but it was not me singing it. I wrote it for a guy called Daddy Chang. . . . Over the years I have been doing music for a couple of artists very silently to help them. Sometimes I see a coming artist and I throw a little bit of support their way. So this guy was entering a competition. He did not have a second song, so he came to me and he said he wanted a song. . . .
>
> J.G. "Chutney Soca Time" is sung in English. Can you tell me. . . .
>
> R.J. The way the melody of the song runs is very East Indian in flavor. I just made a song around him, because I wanted to create a presence: for he is not Indian, he is a Chinese Negro Indian in an Indian industry. So this "Chutney Soca Time," it was like I might do this, I can do like this. [Meaning Daddy Chang's multicultural ancestry could theoretically have allowed Jai to incorporate various musical elements associated with the

various ethnic groups with which he is associated; however, to emphasize Daddy Chang's Indian heritage, Jai chose to compose a melody "very East Indian in flavor."]

Jai's affinity and collaboration with Afro-Trinidadians and other members of the African diasporas, particularly in Jamaica and New York, are exemplified in many of the songs in the album. On the CD the song titled "Sumintra" is accompanied by a parenthesis that reads "Spanish Riddum."[43] As Jai recounted, "Sumintra" was originally composed by Afro-Trinidadian calypsonian Gregory Ballantyne in the late 1980s and performed in a chutney soca style. In 2002, the producer of the Spanish riddim, KMC (Ken Marlon Charles)—also well known as a soca artist—fell in love with that calypso/chutney soca song "Sumintra" and invited Jai to redo the song over his riddim—itself influenced by the huge success of Montano's Spanish-tinged song "Toro."

"Dayida Moreh Layla" foresounds yet another amalgam of musics, connectig Jai, this time, with the African-American musics of the 1970s. In this song, Jai explains, "I wanted to capture that soca breakdown into that soca jam. Me and my colleagues from Trevini, we all like the music of the seventies, [the music, for example, of] Earth, Wind, and Fire. You will definitely find some of the horn spread out with a calypso beat, but you're right: you will get some of that pop feel and some of that seventies music right there."

The last song on the CD, called "East Indian in New York," is based on Sting's song "Englishman in New York." The song is not performed on a calypso or soca rhythm, but instead on a fusion of rhythmic patterns and sonorities. In addition to what Jai described as "banghra feel," one can also hear the dry-sounding drum rolls associated with reggae in the verses' last phrase, leading to the refrain, the upper notes of what sounds like a sitar, and the ringing sounds, seemingly, of a *dhantal* in different sections of the song. Meanwhile, the driving bass line is sonically and stylistically resonant with Sting's soft-rock-ballad (also referred to as "alternative-pop-ballad") accompaniment.[44] Besides Jai's singing his new lyrics over Sting's tune, the song incorporates a dancehall vocal styling section performed by Major Ranks—an Afro-Trinidadian singer whose voice strikingly resembles that of Jamaican star Shabba Ranks (from whom he undoubtedly derives his name)[45]—accompanied at times by a syncopated, high-pitched chorus reminiscent of Bollywood movie songs.

Jai's comments on this song indicate how his multiple senses of belonging are constantly negotiated along with particular desires and situations and a complex circuit of musical references. Jai's main goal in doing this song was, in his words, "to get a foot into the Indian market in New York." "Indian from India," I asked? Jai's answer went as follows:

> R.J. Yes. I could have said I was a "West Indian in New York," but then it would have been lost in me being an Indian. I toyed with words to come with. . . . Musically it was not fitting, I am a "Trinidadian in New York": it was a little too long and then I am a "Trini Indian in New York" was not working. So I figured the best thing was "East Indian." I was really trying to approach the Indian people who were already the deejays in New York, who were jumping and meddling already with dancehall rhythms in their Indian songs. The young deejays were already mixing dancehall styles with Indian songs. So they will take the rhythm and fit their Indian songs on the rhythms. I really like that song "English Man in New York." And then Shinehead did it over, "I am a Jamaican in New York."
>
> J.G. Shinehead ?
>
> R.J. A Jamaican artist. A reggae artist. He did it over. Then I decided I am going to do it over too. I figure it was going to have a kind of mass appeal for the East Indians, not only from Trinidad or from India, but East Indians from everywhere—New York being the center of the world kind of thing. Everybody kind of gravitate to New York for some reason. So I said, it might have picked up in a way. It didn't pick up the way that I expected it to, but for personal satisfaction I still love that song.

When I heard Jai's song "East Indian in New York," I was struck by how some of the lines in the lyrics, identical to Sting's version, fitted Jai's positioning on the issues of identity and authenticity perfectly. On the one hand, his song title, "East Indian in New York," chosen to highlight his affiliation with other Indian diasporic groups, enabled him to reiterate his politics of difference in relation to both other Indian diasporas and Americans, emphasizing his pride in his own identity and refusal to become assimilated. On the other hand, the line "Be yourself, no matter what they say" went hand in hand with his insistence on fighting stereotypes, and with his desire to render musically his affinities with different musical expressions—in resonance with Montano's notion of authenticity. Furthermore, the line "I'm a legal alien" allowed him to emphasize his legal rights in spite of his difference—in terms of race and ethnicity, culture, and religion. Even though in sharp contrast with most of the other tunes performed in a chutney soca style on the CD, this song characteristically embodies the complex musical networks and desires that animate Jai's professional career.

❖

Both Montano and Jai have been actively engaged in musical practices that foreground their own definitions of what constitutes Trinidadian national subjects. Their compositions and performances have challenged received notions of musical authenticity that derive from nationalist discourses about calypso. By integrating sounds and artists from different nation-states into their music, they have deployed a notion of authenticity that is not bounded by Trinidad's territory. Rather, they have claimed musical authenticity as emerging from their unique sum of experiences, which in turn has led them to enact distinctively Trinidadian soundings and subjectivities. Montano's listening to American hip-hop on MTV and Jamaican reggae and dancehall on Trinidadian airwaves combined with his participation in the National Junior Calypso Monarch competition in 1984 have led him to compose and think about music in ways that are peculiar to the particular soundscape he inhabits and to dip into the numerous musical repertoires that have informed his musical sensibility. Jai's exposure to Trinidadian calypso and chutney along with Jamaican dancehall and Bollywood hit songs has in the same way enabled him to feel "at home" with, and to perform, all these genres.

The claims Montano and Jai make about their sounds as embodying who they are and as being "authentically" Trinidadian have been enunciated, however, against different musical genres and in relation to different constituencies on the island. The positioning of Montano as Afro-Trinidadian and of Jai as East Indian has conditioned the types of claims they have been able to make. Montano defended his soca compositions against charges that he transgressed how the artform has been traditionally conceived by calypso artists and aficionados since independence. In contrast, Jai has been defending his "right" to sing calypso and, in so doing, to be among the national subjects representing the nation-state. His desire to be accepted among Afro-Trinidadian audiences has meant more than just expanding his performing circuit. It has had to do with redefining the cultural politics of national inclusion in the very space—calypso—where they have been elaborated.

Both Montano's and Jai's notion of originality speaks about their musical experiences and knowledge in this particular historical moment. It embodies not only the audible entanglements that link them to several musical scenes simultaneously. It also shows how selective musical practices prominent in their environment (e.g., bhangra and hip-hop) have contributed to the ways they think about their musics as distinctively Trinidadian: as a mix of varied musical influences and elements that are articulated in ways that are unique to their musical knowledges and access to a particular array of musics. Jai's artistic combination of Bolly-

wood melodies with a chutney soca rhythmic accompaniment incorporating brief sections of Jamaican chanting style speaks about his unique
positioning as an East Indian Trinidadian and with a particular sensibility.
When Montano recorded his fast-tempo soca song with Haitian Jean
Wyclef, who lives in New York, the track included sound bites of American rap. This creative composition articulated soundings and African diasporic connections in ways that are unique to Montano's positioning as
an Afro-Trinidadian. Jai's "East Indian in New York," based on a song by
British-born artist Sting, instantiates a differently racialized experience
of alienation in this U.S. metropole. For both Montano and Jai, their
sensibilities emerge out of a mix, but a mix that does not give equal value
to all musics involved. By privileging Trinidadian English and distinct
rhythmic patterns and brass arrangements strongly associated with soca,
these artists—in articulation with Carnival circuits, audience identifica-
tions, promoters' efforts, and marketing campaigns—make the mix Trinidadian. By featuring songs in musical styles associated with Trinidad, they
make the mix distinctively Trinidadian, linking sounds and communities
as diverse as those associated with London, New York, Bombay, Kingston,
Port of Spain, and San Fernando.

Some journalists, academics, and audience members have criticized
such new musical mixtures as being too technologically mediated because
of their use of drum machines, synthesizers, and samplers, among other
devices. In my view, these new innovative technologies combine contemporary knowledge, materials, and possibilities that did not previously exist. In the same way, during the late 1930s, the steel pan became an instrument that expanded opportunities for musicians and arrangers to explore
novel calypso compositions. The emergence of the steel pan also provided opportunities for many Trinidadians to develop musicianship, technical skills, and income. In such ways, previous musics have been not less,
but rather differently technologically mediated than those of the present.

In other words, musicians are both enabled and constrained by the tech-
nological possibilities of the present. Similarly, while artists actively position themselves in relation to audience demands, market dynamics, and
musical traditions, they are also subjected to them. For instance, when Jai
participated in the 2004 soca competition, he included not only East Indian, but also Afro-Trinidadian female dancers to facilitate his acceptance
in a space racialized as Afro-Trinidadian. In the same vein, both Jai's and
Montano's gender relations with women follow normative hierarchies of
Trinidadian gender politics. Similarly, these artists' entrepreneurial efforts
are both influenced by and contribute to neoliberal practices, constraints,
and possibilities. It is to the workings of neoliberalism that I now turn.

Cultural Entrepreneurship under Neoliberalism

We have the responsibility to develop as a country, in terms of professionalism, in terms of management, marketing, in terms of videos, and that's what we're doing for soca.

Machel Montano, 3 August 2003

In the 1990s, the Carnival music scene took a new turn. In less than a decade, private entrepreneurs organized three new national competitions during Carnival: the Soca Monarch competition in 1993, the chutney soca competition in 1996, and the ragga soca competition in 1998. In 1998, the relationship between the state-sponsored National Carnival Commission (NCC) and the Trinbago Unified Calypsonians Organization (TUCO) was also radically transformed. According to TUCO's secretary, Brother Resistance, the new state policy now regarded Carnival as a national festival that needed to be reorganized along the lines of a business venture. In the hope that it could decrease its financial support to national organizations involved in Carnival,[1] the NCC required all of them now to be in charge of their own affairs. From that point on, it encouraged them to increase their focus on entrepreneurship. Meanwhile, several individuals launched new music business ventures—setting up recording studios, offering their services as managers, and organizing new fetes during Carnivals. The Carnival music scene in the 1990s

239

was thus transformed not only by the proliferation of emergent Carnival spaces and practices, but also by the reconfiguration of social and
economic relations among state agencies, interest groups, and individual
entrepreneurs.

In this chapter, I investigate the changing style of governing that has
accompanied neoliberal politics since the 1990s and its implications in
the Carnival music scene. Governing here refers to the "conduct of
conduct," after Foucault's much-cited maxim.[2] It concerns the tactics
of management and methods—the micropractices of power rather than
its institutional forms—construed "to shape, guide, direct the conduct of
others."[3] Defined this way, the new style of governing could be looked
at in relation to bandleaders, the director of a radio station, the owner
of a recording studio, or a band manager. It could also be examined in
relation to individuals, such as Machel Montano or Rikki Jai, in terms
of self-management: the ways they govern themselves to achieve certain
ends. From this perspective, my focus on the new style of governing in
Trinidad since the 1990s is thus not limited to the state or to political
parties. Whereas the state was conceived as central in earlier investiga-
tions of power in Caribbean Carnival studies,[4] it "now appears simply as
one element—whose functionality is historically specific and contextu-
ally variable—in multiple circuits of power, connecting a diversity of
authorities and forces, within a whole variety of complex assemblages."[5]
In this chapter, while investigating Trinidad's new cultural policies in the
1990s, I also examine national Carnival organizations' new initiatives and
individuals' new enterprises. Concomitantly, I explore how the technologies deployed to manage these new initiatives and enterprises have
worked through the emergence of new fields of expertise. In so doing,
I show how the entrepreneurial use of expertise has contributed to a
growing marginalization of the state in the Carnival musical space—the
space that has historically served to authenticate national culture. I also
show how the nation-state's new cultural policies, together with new
private initiatives and enterprises, have produced unintended outcomes
that cannot be traced to particular intentions or causes.

In the first section, I concentrate on the neoliberal rationality and the
reframing of economies of Trinidad's new cultural policies instantiated by
the new style of governing dealing with Carnival musical activities.[6] I use
the term "rationality" here to refer to the form of reasoning that since the
1990s has brought many new technologies and practices to the Carnival
music scene.[7] In the next three sections, I focus on the views and practices
of three individuals involved in different aspects of the calypso and soca
music business. I focus on the experiences of three individuals to address

contrasting aspects of the calypso and soca music business not because I believe their experiences tell the whole story, but because together they richly evoke the wide range of new practices that have emerged in the wake of neoliberalism.

To investigate the practices and concerns that govern the national organization of TUCO during this historical moment, I interviewed Brother Resistance, who, in addition to being a rapso artist, has been the secretary of TUCO since 1996 and has been deeply involved in transforming the association's activities since 1998. To assess how individual soca artists and bands are conducting their own business in relation to local and global markets, I interviewed Liz Montano, who, since Machel Montano began his musical career, has acted as his manager, and subsequently as the manager of his band. Finally, to examine new forms of cultural entrepreneurship and expertise that help link political objectives and personal conduct,[8] I interviewed Alvin Daniell and George P. Singh, Jr., who, since the 1990s, have initiated several projects focused on music business activities in the local Carnival music scene. In this last section, I explore how, in this era of neoliberal politics, the new targets in Carnival music practices, and the technologies deployed to address them, bring transformations and new problems to the scene that change the political terrain of struggle in Trinidad.

The National Carnival Commission's New Mandate

In an article entitled "Imperatives of Caribbean Development for the 21st Century," published in 1989, economist Compton Bourne from the University of the West Indies in Trinidad predicts that the economic crisis in the Caribbean, including Trinidad, would persist and deepen unless development strategies and policies were fundamentally reshaped. Echoing the rationale advanced by leading industrial countries, he attributes Trinidad's economic crisis to the anticompetitive and antientrepreneurial activities of the state itself. As Rose put the matter in relation to England, the problem was "the form of government that had associated the optimization of social and economic life with the augmentation of the powers of the state."[9] The solution? The state must redirect its mandate and only maintain the infrastructure of law and order. The people must ensure their individual and national well-being by assuming their responsibilities and developing their own enterprises. As Bourne explains, "The new orthodoxy strongly advocates deregulation, the dismantling of protective and incentive systems, and privatization."[10] Accordingly, he writes, "the longrun development of the Caribbean nations will ultimately depend upon the *sustained effort, creativity, productivity and thrift of individuals and enterprises* within the framework of stable supportive and facilatory government policies. A more liberal stance by international financial agencies and foreign governments should make the transition more manageable."[11]

Sharing the premises of neoliberalism, Trinidad's state-sponsored National Carnival Commission developed a new rationale to guide its relation to the national organizations taking part in Carnival. The fact that this new rationale was developed precisely when the UNC was in power may not have been a coincidence. As some PNM supporters have suggested, the UNC may have used neoliberal arguments to divert the privileged attention formerly given to activities led by Afro-Trinidadians during Carnival. In all cases, as a state agency, the NCC would no longer be acting as a provider—as in the "social state"—but as a facilitator—as in the "enabling state."[12] Resembling Margaret Thatcher's explanations for the reallocation of state funds in Britain, the rationale was "The state can never have the information to enable it to judge and plan each micro-event in a free-market society. Only individual economic actors possess the information to enable them to make the best judgments on risks and potentials in order to guide their conduct; they must be freed to choose according to the natural laws of the free market on the one hand and human nature on the other."[13] Significantly, such explanations not only pointed out that the state's control of national economy and culture has always been a fiction. They also recognized that, in the wake of global political economy, the state had even less control than before over domains central to entrepreneurs.

Accordingly, the NCC's mandate in the 1990s contrasted greatly with that of the Carnival committees of earlier times. In the late 1930s and 1940s the Permanent Carnival Improvement Committee tried to "improve calypso's lyrics" and purge Carnival of its unsavory elements and, in the late 1940s, to centralize all competitions, thus gaining more control over all Carnival performance practices and spaces; from the late 1960s onward, in the aftermath of independence, the Carnival Development Committee (CDC) was designed to foster participation in the nation-building project. In the 1990s, however, the NCC aimed to promote youth and educational activities during Carnival and otherwise encourage the national organizations, including TUCO, to operate along commercial lines. As the Trinidad and Tobago Chamber of Industry and Commerce insisted, following the logic of the market, such organizations must act "with a profit motive driving their business plans."[14]

The NCC's new form of management, while ostensibly passing power to the national organizations to direct their own activities, actually rendered those activities governable in new ways. As Rose explains it, "In the new public management, the focus is upon accountability, explicit standards and measures of performance, emphasis on outputs, not inputs, with rewards linked to performance, desegregation of functions into corporatized units operating with their own budgets and trading with one another, contracts and competition, and insistence on parsimony maintained by budget discipline. This required a shift from an ethic of public service to one of private management."[15] For TUCO and the other national organizations, this shift meant not only greater autonomy but greater liability.

TUCO's New Initiatives

On behalf of its calypsonians' membership, TUCO has always had some say in how the calypso competitions were run. Its representatives would propose and lobby for the adoption of certain judging criteria, or the installation of performing facilities, or the hiring of specific individuals. The NCC's hegemonic rules were thus constantly negotiated. With the implementation of neoliberal policies, TUCO's autonomy increased, but only to a relative degree. While it took charge of devising its own activities, financially it was still dependent on state subsidies to remain afloat. However, what did change, together with the NCC's redefinition of institutional responsibilities, was TUCO's ways of conceiving its own management in terms of market economy.[16]

TUCO was now responsible for selecting the judges and organizing seminars for them to promote agreement on the competition criteria. The object of TUCO's management, however, was to make the competitions attractive and lucrative. Such a focus entailed not only deciding which competitions to run, but also changing the format of their presentations. In 2002, after a brief transitional period, TUCO launched its first series of new major initiatives: Calypso Fiesta and the creation of the Calypso Queen and the Calypso King contests.

For several years, in the calypso semifinal competition held at Skinner Park in San Fernando, South Trinidad, each participant presented his or her two songs in the same sequence—one sociopolitical commentary followed by a song with "lighter" lyrics. This format, however, was now losing its audience. After receiving complaints that the show was "too slow, too long and too laborious," TUCO decided to replace it with another competition called Calypso Fiesta, presenting more varied elements: the final competition of calypso by different categories. As Brother Resistance explains, "So we had the twelve most humorous—supposedly the twelve most humorous songs—twelve social commentaries, twelve political commentaries, and twelve party songs. . . . And that worked quite well. . . . The response from the public and from the media and so on was really, really nice." [17]

Out of its desire to draw a large audience and generate income, TUCO deployed new programming strategies. Instead of presenting all songs in sections, TUCO asked the participants to use a random draw to avoid a long, monotonous sequence of the same type of song. Financial preoccupations, however, had to be combined with artistic ones. Several calypsonians had expressed a fear that the power and energy of the party songs would dilute the social and political commentary songs. Therefore, TUCO decided not to leave the programming of party songs to random sequence. Instead, it scheduled them in sections during key moments of the show: six party songs before the intermission, and another six at the end of the show. Moreover, TUCO did not include the party songs as part of any competition. Brother Resistance gave two reasons for this decision: "One, we didn't really directly wanna compete with the Soca Monarch [competition]. And two, the caliber of artists that we wanted to attract were not interested in competing, you know. So people like Machel Montano, you know, these people were not interested in competing. And we wanted them there." The inclusion of leading soca stars, it was hoped, would boost ticket sales, and the strategic programming of their performances would help TUCO address both its financial and its artistic concerns.

The creation of Calypso Fiesta, replacing the calypso semifinal competition, entailed the creation of another show to choose finalists for the Calypso Monarch competition: the Calypso Queen and Calypso King contests. Before this new initiative, TUCO had launched a Calypso Queen competition in 2000 aimed at increasing the number of women singing calypso. [18] However, that competition stirred protests among male calypsonians who felt that women now had more opportunities than men to win major prizes during Carnival. Women were eligible to enter both the Calypso Queen and the Calypso Monarch competitions, whereas men could compete only for the Calypso Monarch crown. In 2001, Denyse Plummer's winning of both the Calypso Queen and the Calypso Monarch competitions proved that the competitions' setup turned to women's advantage and led TUCO to create the Calypso King competition. In 2002, for the first time in the history of calypso, the Calypso Queen and Calypso King competitions were organized and, in the hope of drawing a large audience, were held on the same night.

1. The Mighty Sparrow at the calypso tent Spektakula, Port of Spain, 20 July 1985. (Courtesy of *Trinidad Guardian*.)

2. Lord Kitchener accompanied by "Professor" Ken Philmore, 27 December 1985. (Photo by Krishna Maharaj, courtesy of *Trinidad Guardian*.)

3. Black Stalin at the state memorial service of C. L. R. James, who figures in the background painting, Port of Spain, 28 June 1989. (Photo by Noël Lalderde, courtesy of *Trinidad Guardian*.)

4. Black Stalin singing at the Calypso Monarch competition final at the Savannah, Port of Spain, 1997. (Photo by the author.)

5. Calypso Rose, the first female calypsonian
to win the Calypso Monarch competition
in Trinidad and, for the second time in a row,
the Road March in 1978. (Press release in
1997, courtesy of Calypso Rose.)

OPPOSITE

6. (*top*) Denyse Plummer, often called "the
queen of the calypso music scene" for having
won more competitions than any other
woman in the business. (From the album
cover of Denyse Plummer's *Carnival Killer*
[1991], Dynamic Sounds, DY3466.)

7. (*bottom*) Calypsonian and historian Hollis
Liverpool, a.k.a "Chalkie," with Crazy
(undated). (Courtesy of Edwin Ahyoung.)

10. De Mighty Trini. (From the album cover of *De Mighty Trini: "Sailing?"* [1988], JW Records TR003.)

OPPOSITE

8. (*top*) Crazy performing at the Calypso Monarch competition semifinal at Skinner Park, San Fernando, 1996. (Photo by the author.)

9. (*bottom*) Crazy in the midst of acting his song at the Calypso Monarch competition semifinal at Skinner Park, San Fernando, 1996. (Photo by the author.)

11. Arranger Frankie Francis with his saxophone, leaning against the ramp on the right of the photograph, at a hotel in New York, circa 1966. (Courtesy of Frankie Francis.)

12. Arranger Art de Coteau at the Christopher recording studio on Nelson Street, Port of Spain, 1962. (Courtesy of Daphne McIntosh.)

13. Shadow at the Biggest Universal Calypso King Show (BUCKS) at the National Stadium, Port of Spain, 4 May 1985. (Courtesy of *Trinidad Guardian*.)

14. Ras Shorty I, pioneering figure of
soca, with his wife and children at
their home in Piparo, 6 February 1997.
(Photo by the author.)

15. Drupatee Ramgoonai, the singer who helped firmly established chutney soca through her appearance at the calypso tent Spektakula in 1987. (From the album cover of *Drupatee's Mr. Bissessar* [1988], IMPredisco, C.A. D002A.)

16. Sundar Popo, one of the most well-known
chutney singers. (From the album cover of
Sundar Popo and Classic JMC Triveni [1994],
J.M.C. Records JMC1082.)

OPPOSITE

17. *(top)* Brother Resistance, one of the
leading figures in rapso, performing
at the launch for Clive Telemaque and
Audio Stars, 19 March 1989. (Courtesy
of *Trinidad Guardian*.)

18. *(bottom)* Rapso artist Karega Mandela
in performance, 1 February 1988.
(Courtesy of *Trinidad Guardian*.)

19. Young Machel Montano recording "Now Is the Time" at the K&H recording studio, 18 September 1985. (Courtesy of *Trinidad Guardian*.)

20. Machel Montano in performance, 25 February 2000. (Courtesy of *Trinidad Guardian*.)

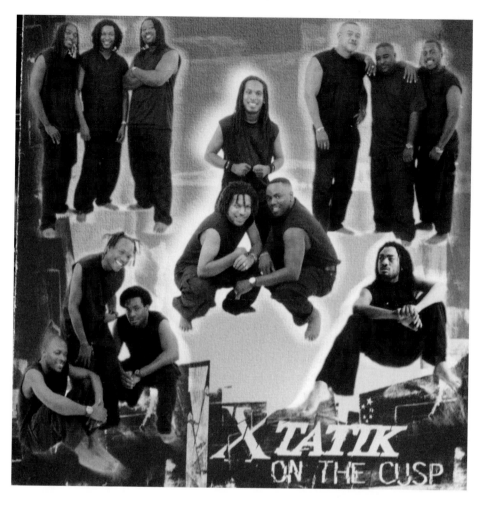

21. The group Xtatik. (From the
album cover of *Xtatik on the
Cusp* [2002], Mad Bull Music
X24-11-74-27, JW Productions
JW-235-CD.)

22. Rikki Jai. (From the album cover of *Rikki Jai: Calypso Music Vol. 1* [2001], Spice Island Records DMTU 1342.)

23. Rikki Jai. (From the album cover of *Rikki Jai: Chutney Vibrations* [2001], produced by Rikki Jai.)

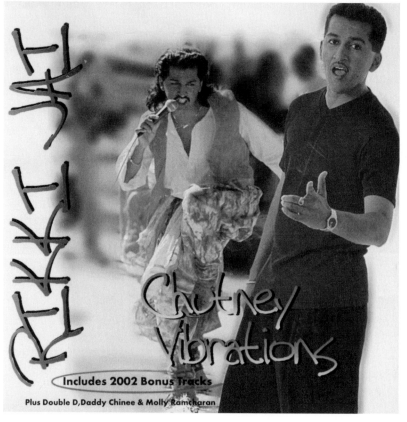

The neoliberal policies adopted by the state and the restructuring of national Carnival organizations that followed produced several unintended outcomes. In its attempt to make the Skinner Park show more financially profitable, TUCO featured prominently and rendered more audible the various categories of the calypso "artform" (humor, social, political, and party-oriented songs). In creating a new show to feature both the Calypso Queen and King contests, TUCO addressed gender issues, both in its representation and in its equal opportunities for both female and male calypsonians. By holding the Calypso Queen and King contests on the same night and using the same panel of judges for both competitions, it also—inadvertently or not—provided the conditions enabling the same criteria to be used to select the winners in both cases. By featuring from the outset a nearly equal number of female and male participants in the two final competitions and then choosing on the basis of points scored the contestants for the Calypso Monarch competition show, TUCO projected a renewed commitment to equitable gender representation. As in many business enterprises, some of the new projects succeeded and others did not. As the Calypso Queen competition organized by TUCO did not draw a large audience and did not produce the visibility the female calypsonians were hoping for, in 2003 many of them entered both the TUCO and the NJAC Queen competitions—making the number of competitions they could enter unequal with those available to men. As a result, the new set of competitions created by TUCO was cancelled in 2004.

By conceiving its own management in terms of an economic market, TUCO was prompted to distinguish between activities earning revenues and those designed as developmental projects. On the one hand, the developmental activities, including the Junior Calypso Monarch competitions and the Unattached Calypso Monarch competitions, were considered investments in the future: they might not bring in revenues at present, but they would nurture the artists and cultivate the consumers of the next generation. On the other hand, the Dimanche Gras show was not viewed as a moneymaking enterprise, since, says Brother Resistance, it was not a "TUCO product": it shared the benefits among the three national organizations, "TUCO, the Mas Fraternity, and the Steelband Fraternity." Therefore, it was decided that the major opportunities for TUCO to generate revenue revolved around the Calypso Fiesta and, potentially, the calypso tents it also ran—which, in 2003, included four in Trinidad and two in Tobago. The calypso tent audiences, however, had been dwindling over the years.

To maintain its commitment to provide artists with opportunities to perform and earn income during the Carnival season, TUCO continued—and still continues—to run the calypso tents for five weeks, in contrast with the usual four-week period of the privately owned tents during the Carnival season. As Brother Resistance explained, "The longer the season, the better it is for the artists in terms of the earnings by weekly contract. But from the point of view of the businessperson, it's not worth that. [You still have] the same running costs, but you don't necessarily have the audiences."

For TUCO, Brother Resistance added, the dilemma was to create a balance "between doing business and making sure that the artist is all right, because we are an artists' organization." Instead of reducing the number of weeks during which the TUCO calypso tents operated, TUCO emulated the strategies used by the private owners of other tents. It now organizes three big shows to increase its revenues. Resistance described how these shows are typically organized: "So on the nineteenth [of January], we open in Skinner Park [South Trinidad]. And we use some of the Kaiso House cast, and we bring guest artists—some of the popular songs of the top artists, like Bunji Garlin or KMC. We're still trying to tie up Machel Montano. So we're gonna do a few shows like that before the start of the season." As Brother remarked, TUCO is trying "to do more business. That's the idea." However, "we have problems." Tellingly, the problems to which he referred were not musical, but were described in business terms: "We are a good organization, we got a good heart and spirit, but we have not enough of the business acumen, not enough of the business attitude, not enough promoting knowledge.... I think as an organization we need to work a lot more with established promoters." The problem, according to Resistance, is pride: in his view, entrepreneurs in Trinidad typically avoid asking for help, fearing that such requests render public their lack of skills in particular domains, making them vulnerable to competitors. That the moral economy of respect is at odds in Trinidad with the political economy of competition has had detrimental implications not only for TUCO, but also for calypso artists in general. Brother Resistance's call for "experts"—to promote shows and products locally and internationally, to develop marketing strategies, and to gather information on various aspects of the music industry (including copyrights)—on behalf of institutions like TUCO as well as of individual artists foregrounds a new way of thinking among TUCO's membership that shares many of the assumptions of neoliberalism. This distinct way of thinking entails not only a new conception of the different domains of knowledge to which TUCO's management must now address itself, but also new ways of allocating its management tasks among various entities, experts, sponsors, associations, volunteers, and artists.

Concomitant with Trinidad's new cultural policies and new style of governing, Brother Resistance's recourse to the vocabulary of incomes, allocations, costs, and profits reflects the new importance of accounting discourse in the calypsonians' association. In addition to introducing a new vocabulary, TUCO's focus on accountability has also entailed a series of new processes and procedures. As Rose explains, "Government by audit transforms that which is to be governed. Rendering something auditable shapes the process that is to be audited: setting objectives, proliferating standardized forms, generating new systems of record-keeping and accounting, governing paper trails."[19]

While revising its mode of functioning, TUCO has attempted to move away from the classical network of state patronage and, like entrepreneurs, to focus on increasing the number of paid admissions at the gate as a measure of the success of its shows.[20] Its goal is to produce consumers and to cultivate a desire for consumption. Its representatives' emphasis on promoting its shows to earn revenues is not new. The technologies they deploy to do so (e.g., the hiring of experts to do promotion), however, signal how they now imagine many of their activities in tandem with self-management, new forms of knowledge and authority, and organizational responsibility.

Individuals' New Musical Enterprises

Until recently, calypso managers hardly existed in Trinidad. Typically, however, several people—oftentimes family relatives—worked "behind the scenes" to help calypsonians organize their stage performances. Although these people performed a variety of tasks, from overseeing the timely preparation of stage outfits to planning the artists' touring schedules, they were rarely viewed as managers. Consequently, they were not paid. There were simply considered stout supporters of the artists they served. While lesser-known calypsonians, soca artists, and bands continue to rely on this informal support system, many of the more prominent ones have recently formalized such working arrangements, in response to their new working conditions, by hiring managers. With the proliferation of overseas Carnivals, competition winners and veterans of the calypso scene have enjoyed greater opportunities to perform locally and internationally, increasing their financial incomes, in turn making it possible for these artists to hire managers. Together with this material reality, however, the incentive for hiring a manager has also emerged from the new global emphasis on market economies, global competition, and the gradual formalization in Trinidad (and elsewhere in the Caribbean) of certain musical practices. These include written performance contracts (as opposed to the traditional verbal agreements) and the legal reinforcement, at least in some cases, of copyright laws. In this new context, artists have been encouraged to hire managers not only to help touring schedules, but also to deal with the different types of knowledge required to function in this increasingly regulated music business environment. The new conditions have also led several small music ventures to be converted into registered privately owned enterprises. To illustrate the emergence of the new managerial class in the calypso music scene, I focus on the experience of Liz Montano as manager of the Xtatik soca band and as one of the major forces in the creation of Machel Montano's diverse music companies and other business investments.

Liz Montano began as the stout supporter of her child Machel's becoming a performer. As a parent, she aimed to help him nurture his musical interests. As a school teacher and professionally trained guidance officer, she used her skills to help him balance his burgeoning musical career with his school studies and homework. When at nine years old, after winning the Junior Monarch title with his song "The Letter," Machel was invited to sing in New York at Madison Square Garden to celebrate *Actual Magazine*'s fifth anniversary, she accompanied him, receiving her first experience of show business. Typically, the amount of money offered by the promoter for Machel's performance was small; Liz Montano negotiated and obtained higher fees for her son's performance. From that time on, she devoted herself to protecting her son's interests.

While this story is in some ways unusual, involving a parent as her own child's manager, it illustrates the informal circumstances that in Trinidad have often drawn relatives into the music business. The involvement of women in this domain, though rarely acknowledged, has been a long-standing feature of the calypso music scene. While wives (through marriage or common law) have typically helped their husbands to pursue their careers locally by taking care of details (overseeing the preparation of show outfits and local arrangements), several women, part of the Caribbean diasporic groups established in various locations in Europe and North America—often lovers, but also female friends as well as unrelated individuals—have played an active role in organizing shows and tours in the areas where they now live. As Percy Hintzen wrote in his illuminating study *West Indian in the West,* they have often taken on the role of managers (often unofficially) and cultural promoters as a way out of their social isolation and into the diasporic community. Most calypsonians and soca artists I interviewed have mentioned—usually in passing—how such and such a woman in Toronto organized a show for the association to which she belongs and invited him to perform; or how another in London organized a tour for him to perform in various English festivals taking place in a particular time of year. However, most of these women usually act as cultural promoters only sporadically, as a side activity to their full-time employment. And when they assume the role of manager for one artist—as a fan or lover—many remain publicly unacknowledged.

Similarly, even when Machel Montano's career with his band had become well established and involved in widespread touring, Liz and Winston Montano (Machel's father, who was also part of Xtatik's management for several years), as family members, would continue to work for the group behind the scenes.[21] However, by 1989, the group's promise was so strong that Liz Montano quit her teaching post and officially became Xtatik's manager and administrator. While hardly any other band can afford a full-time manager and administrator, as Xtatik can[22]—in many ways, Machel's and his band's achievements remain unique on the island—Liz Montano's experience with Machel and Xtatik band members helps to reveal some of the technologies deployed in Trinidad over the past few years to transform the style in which music business is run.

From the outset, Liz Montano encouraged the development of expertise in the domains that interested Machel and the Xtatik band members. When Machel decided to quit school in 1993, she and her husband sent him to a recording-engineer school in Ohio. After that, she explains, "We sent the other boys to the same school we sent Machel. So we sent Ken, we sent Samuel Jack, Ken Holder, Rodney Daniel, and we sent Marlon John. We sent the three of them to school. So they came back again all engineers. So we have *that expertise.*"[23]

With their new skills, Machel and the Xtatik band members began to record on their own. Besides the Rufnex recording studio based in Siparia, a mobile studio named Ruf Rex recording studio was set up in 1997 to bring greater flexibility to the band's recording venues. In Liz Montano's words, "It was basically a studio to produce our music. . . . If we were in New York, we took the studio to New York. And if we were in Siparia, we had it in Siparia. If we want to go anywhere, [say] Jamaica, we took it to Jamaica. And we would set up the studio and we would record. Like 'Big Truck,' for example, was recorded at our studio, but it was when we had carried it to New York." After the success of "Big Truck" in 1997, the decision of the management team—then including not only Liz and Machel, but also Winston Montano—was to transform the main studio into a commercial enterprise.[24] One step toward this end was to move Ruf Rex recording studio, based in Siparia, to an easy-to-reach location in Port of Spain, at the corner of Edouards and Gordon streets (from which the name of the new recording studio, EdGordon, took its name). At the time of my interview with Liz Montano, in 2003, I was told that, in addition to now having access to what has been described as "a state-of-the-art digital setup with analog capabilities,"[25] they intended to instrumentalize the various domains in which Machel and his band members had acquired expertise. One of the Montano family's tactics and greatest assets—which has greatly contributed to the success of their commercial enterprises—has been not just to develop expertise, but also to demonstrate their capacity to orchestrate different types of expertise. Hence, some of the new services now offered by the EdGordon studio include training in recording techniques, recording other artists' songs, and, in addition, producing video clips for music videos or for publicity ads with the help of Peter Lewis, whose company Red Boys Entertainment was brought in as part of the EdGordon recording studio.[26]

Influenced, I suspect, by American hip-hop music industry, Liz Montano and Machel made coining names to map and mobilize Machel's own expanding range of activities and markets one of their new managing devices. Following the standard practice of recording studio owners, Machel Montano gave a name to his first recording studio: "Rufnex Recording Studio." As required by law, he also named his recording label "Macho Music," later changed to "Mad Bull Music." However, unlike other Trinidadian music entrepreneurs at the time, he also named various groups of people with whom he collaborated. As Liz Montano explained, "And so we had what you call the 'Mad Bull Posse': it was a group of young people that Machel produced, a lot of young artists that he had put on a CD. And we get them work and manage them and things; so they were called the 'Mad Bull Crew.'" The "Mad Bull" term affixed to Machel's recording label, posse, and crew astutely accompanied the launching of one of Xtatik's most commercially successful CDs in 1998. Entitled *Machel and Xtatik CHARGE,* the CD began with an interlude called "Mad Bull Intro" followed by the song "Toro, Toro."

In addition to using naming devices both to manage and to advertise Machel's multiple activities and markets, Liz Montano and Machel created companies to protect them legally. In line with the neoliberal style of self-management and assumed responsibilities to protect his own rights, Machel now owns three registered music-related companies: Xtatik Limited, Ruf Rex Productions Limited, and Masuso Publishing. Speaking about the Masuso Publishing company, Liz Montano explained this name:

L.M. Yeah, that is his publishing company, using his name. His name is Machel Jesus, like Jesus, Montano. So, Masuso. MA in Machel, SU Masu, SUS from Jesus, O from Montano. And it's with BMI.

J.G. So, Ruf Rex is a recording studio?

L.M. Ruf Rex is for anything he's recording, like our CDs, recording people, anything, doing jingles, anything with studio and recording is Ruf Rex. That is the production. And Xtatik Limited is for live recording, like the performing of the band and things. Masuso Publishing is for the publishing. And then he has MJM and EVA Properties Limited . . . MJM is his name, Machel Jesus Montano, and we say E-V-A, but it's Eva, that was my mother's name. MJM and EVA Properties [are the companies] that deal with all his properties.

As Rose remarks in describing neoliberal self-management, even when such initiatives as the creation of music companies and the naming of various musical activities are driven by marketing objectives and musical rights protections, "these practices use techniques that take up and disseminate the idea that the consumer is an ethical citizen; consumers can and should consciously seek to manage themselves and their conduct in an ethical fashion according to principles that they have chosen for themselves."[27] In Trinidad as anywhere else, the notion of "ethical citizen" in regard to musical rights has, however, remained a problematic and contested issue.[28] The widespread sentiment that music belongs to everybody has been such that little attention has traditionally been paid to intellectual property.[29] This sentiment, combined with conditions of poverty for many, has meant that piracy and disregard for copyrights laws, though condemned in theory, have remained an everyday practice until recently, dramatically diminishing artists' revenues. The question, then, of who defines ethical behavior in regard to musical recordings remains an embattled ground.

Although state legislation in Trinidad and Tobago in 2003 reformed its copyright laws, the way these new laws were formulated made them difficult to enforce. As Allison Demas, the director of the Copyright Organization of Trinidad and Tobago (COTT), explained, before they could make an arrest, the police had to prove that sellers of illegally dubbed recordings did not know that the recordings they were selling were duly registered intellectual property, protected by the law. This fact proved extremely difficult to demonstrate. Demas indicated that proposed reforms of the copyright laws—which she hopes will be passed before the end of 2005—will enable the police to arrest anyone selling, or in possession of, illegally dubbed recordings.[30] Until then, however, illegally dubbed tapes and duplicated CDs continue to be sold daily on street corners in broad daylight throughout the country. In the almost complete absence of police enforcement, artists have lost and suffered the most from the failure to enforce musical rights. In the meantime, COTT representatives and publishers involved in negotiating copyright claims have intensified their lobbying efforts to neutralize the problem of piracy.

In this context, the challenge for managers such as Liz Montano, and for musicians and musical entrepreneurs such as Machel and Xtatik band members, has been to cultivate among audiences awareness of and respect for musicians' rights and to make infringing these rights more difficult. In 2003, Liz Montano explained, they chose not to launch their CDs during Carnival because piracy reaches its peak during that season, with its large number of tourists and thus prospective buyers. Release came instead on Ash Wednesday, just before tourists leave, so that the pirates would not have time to dub and sell their illegal copies. In March 2004, the band turned their attention to the public and launched an antipiracy drive. They organized tours in malls around the country and had their visits advertised in the media. With sound systems and music videos featuring their latest songs together with merchandises to be sold, they aimed to mobilize people's attention with the slogan "Support the Local Artists: Buy the Original CD" printed on their T-Shirts. Instead of rehashing the "Don't do illegal dubbing" message, they rewarded those who bought their CDs by giving them a large poster with the inscription "I Bought an Original XTATIK CD" that Machel and the band members signed. As a means to further their outreach, they also distributed to record shop owners and media personnel T-shirts advocating the buying of the original CD.

The transformation of informal practices (e.g., reliance on supporters) into formal ones (e.g., the employment of managers), the more widespread use of written contracts, the gaining of expertise (e.g., training as sound engineers), the instrumentalizing of these new knowledges in commercial services, the invention of a new vocabulary to designate activities and markets, the proliferation of registered music companies, and attempts to educate people about musical rights and protect one's own represent a few ways in which the music business in Trinidad has been reconfigured over the past few years, and also how it is now regulated. In the next section, I examine the constitution of a new field of expertise in Trinidad, the main focus of which is to explore the possibilities and new problems the reconfiguration of the music industry now entails.

New Fields of Expertise

Music entrepreneurs have always been an integral part of Carnival music activities. Even though this subject may be peripheral to their main interests, several authors have traced the roles of many individuals in the production, promotion, and circulation of Carnival musics. Hence, we have learned that, since the early 1900s, music hucksters such as Lionel Belasco have been actively involved in developing calypso music markets both in Trinidad and in New York, for example. Moreover, over the past century, some calypsonians established their own calypso tents as a means of increasing both the number of performing venues and their own revenues. From the 1930s, several Indian businessmen and entrepreneurs have contributed directly to the calypso music scene by helping to finance recording projects, organize tours, and provide venues to hold competitions and, since the 1990s, they have been financially responsible for the chutney soca competitions and many other events.[31]

Since the 1990s, entrepreneurs have multiplied in tandem with the proliferation of the new Carnival musical styles and the new conditions of possibility they have provided. As new music styles have appeared, many new artists have entered the Carnival music scene, bringing a greater number of recording projects. In turn, growing record production has encouraged the establishment of new recording studios. Concomitantly, show promoters who specialize in specific music styles, focus on particular venues, and organize tours for particular communities in and outside the Caribbean have emerged.[32]

What distinguishes the market-based economy of Trinidad Carnival music activities since the 1990s, however, is not only the greater volume of the business. It is also the emergence of new types of entrepreneurship and new types of authority that constitute at once new services and new means of regulation. In this regard, Alvin Daniell and George P. Singh, Jr., provide particularly outstanding examples of individuals who have ventured into new musical areas in Trinidad.

Alvin Daniell

An electrical engineer by profession, Alvin Daniell owns a successful and well-established business enterprise. He first became involved in music only as a hobby. During his student days at the University of the West Indies in St. Augustine, Trinidad, Daniell combined his course work with his active participation in calypso-related activities on campus. He helped organize shows and began to compose, in his words, "the odd tune and to give it to someone."[33] After graduation and several years of involvement in the calypso music scene, continuing to combine his two main interests of engineering and composing with an occasional stint as a member of calypso juries, he noticed that hardly any published music transcriptions of the hundreds of calypsos created each year existed. In 1992, he launched his first new music venture: publishing, with computer notation, musical transcriptions of the melody, bass line, chord progression, and lyrics of some of the Panorama tunes of the season. His purpose, says Daniell, was "to preserve the music."

As he explained to me, he later became a music producer not by design, but in response to the circumstances he faced at the time. After composing some tunes, he looked for singers to perform them and for "a genuine executive producer willing to put out money." In Daniell's assessment, however, executive producers hardly existed then, because the production of CDs "did not seem like a lucrative department." With his income, Daniell decided to become a producer himself and to turn this business venture into a profitable one. In addition to being an executive producer who took a cut of the revenues from the CDs he produced, he also became a publisher, "where I did own the rights: being a co-writer, I had both assigned to me." In addition, he began "managing the very artist who would sing the songs. So I got something out of the live performances. So when I added the three incomes together, it became very lucrative."

From 1994 to 1998, Daniell served as the director of COTT. Having learned about copyrights, he realized there was a "big hole" in the Trinidadian music business. As he explained, "I saw the void of artists not being properly managed, not understanding the meanings of contracts, assigning their work, giving away their copyrights, things like that. I became a civil consultant in the area of copyrights to artists. And the fact is that, right now, my more lucrative area is actually as a contractor working on behalf of artists whom I don't even manage. They bring their problems to me, I sort out their contracts. . . . I call it 'contract management.' " Interestingly, the powers of this new field of expertise, like those explained by Rose in his discussion of the growth of new experts in the nineteenth century in Britain, have been "based on beliefs about the competence provided by knowledge and training, and also about the ethical values imparted by professional identity."[34] In the same vein, Daniell's experience as COTT director lent credibility to both his expertise and sense of ethics in the domain of "contract management." While helping artists earn their due, as an "expert" in music contracts Daniell has simultaneously participated in the new style of neoliberal governing by providing some of the means by which musical activities are regulated among and by active individuals in accordance with the new ethical responsibilities devolved to them—taking care of themselves and of others.[35] Equally important is that, in this new style of governing, all individuals involved in Carnival music activities are defined as ethical subjects: not just producers (like the Montanos) and consumers (including record buyers), but also music experts such as Daniell.

In his interview with me, Daniell explained how he understands the various types of managers and how this knowledge has enabled him to act in these various capacities in ways that have helped artists gain the greatest benefit from contractual arrangements. His explanation went as follows:

> A general manager would be the person who sees the overall management of the artist, decides on the bookings, negotiates recording contracts, and chooses who finances the recordings. He is the one who collects all his incomes and makes the payments back to the artist. A personal manager would be the one who does the promotions, advertising, and that sort of thing. And then you can have a legal manager, who is a lawyer. But you see, there are not many lawyers in Trinidad who understand copyrights. So that's why many of the artists need what I call a "contracts manager," who understands the nick about the law, but who also understands more about the ratings happening in the real world.
>
> A guy comes to you: "I wanna song. Take it, ah. Do what you want with it." The song gets a hit, now the guy comes up and says, "Hey you only gave me five hundred dollars for that song, and that is a big song." "Yes, that's all I needed to give you." "No, I want more than that." And this is when you have a big surprise. . . . What do you do to keep these things from happening? This is where the contracts manager comes in and, from the outset, you say, no, let's do things the right way.

Daniell spoke of other cases when a contracts manager is most useful. He gave the example of a song from someone in Tobago who was in negotiations with the tourist board (TIDCO) for promotions to advertise Tobago. As he indicated, "As long as they are talking directly to the composer, they're always going to undersell it. They know he does not know how much his song is worth; he has a sentimental value to it. And he would do it for nothing, just to have a chance for people to hear it. And they play on that." Interestingly, Daniell's description of how his role as "contracts manager" becomes beneficial reveals how his expertise is based on his subjective assessment of the song's market value—which, through his negotiations, he helps also to define. In his words, "An old, but well-known song, say, could go from twenty-five thousand dollars to one hundred thousand dollars. But a lot depends. . . . I said I have to listen to it. I have to evaluate it from its strength, what I think . . . if I think it says something, or has a feel in it, that the client must use it, he has no choice, then I can argue."

As a contracts manager, Daniell points out, he uses his knowledge of the various musical rights sanctioned by law to assess the claims to which his client is entitled. In other words, his knowledge of musical rights combined with his own estimate and construction of a song's value on the local market gives him the power to raise the stakes in the negotiating process and, in so doing, to play an active role in the management of both products and people. He defined these various rights as follows:

> Adaptation rights: The song has its own lyrics and its own melody. But you want to change part of the lyrics: instead of "I love you," you say "I love KFC." That is "adaptation."

> Transcription rights: this is a song that is used straight as is on radio—not as background music, and with no changes, just to be used on radio.

> Synchronization rights: that is if you use the music with images, for film or television.

Based on this knowledge, Daniell then uses his negotiating skills to obtain the best possible financial agreement for his client. In negotiating musical rights, he takes into account several factors: the popularity of the singer or composer, the setting in which the song will be used (e.g., if in a commercial, its value may be irrevocably "cheapened" and it may be rendered useless), the audience to which the song is directed (e.g., if a song is selected to attract tourists, its value might then actually increase), the length of time during which the song will be played (whether on radio or television, in a film, or as part of advertisement). As Daniell explains his tactics: "You need to emphasize how many things you are getting. . . . Only for radio? For one year? Five thousand dollars. Then we go for television, and then seventy-five thousand dollars is not so much after all." He adds, "There is no fixed formula. You have to judge the parameters."

While he has explored the multifaceted aspects of managerial work and sold musical transcriptions of Panorama tunes, Daniell's shrewd sense of entrepreneurship has led him to seize other opportunities, including those provided by music publishing.[36] As he noted, publishing has always been part of Trinidad's music business. However, he has realized that the publishing business could become big business with the single hits of newcomers entering the Carnival music scene. He is well aware that artists with only one "big" song could not join COTT: "COTT has a law that you have to have three commercial items before you can become a member." Hence, says Daniell, "the only way they could get money was to join with a reputable publisher." So Daniell began signing up many newcomers to Trinidad's music industry.

I was struck during our interview by Daniell's use of the term "reputable," highlighting how, from a business point of view, belief in his own ethical behavior—accountability, sense of responsibility—in dealing with a large section of Trinidad's Carnival music milieu has brought him more clients, and more financial capital as a result. He explained: "When I say 'reputable,' because a lot of guys have been ripped off by people saying, 'Give me the song, I'll watch it for you,' and collect the money and don't pay them. I guess, the word spread that I was a bit more decent than the others." In the neoliberal context, where competition among entrepreneurs is increasingly heightened, Daniell's managerial skills, as his description suggests, will continue to be recognized as long as he meets the obligations he sets for himself and his self-management inspires trust and yields tangible results.

Daniell believes that a music publisher should oversee an artist's songs from the time of their inception to their circulation on the market. His goal should be to ensure that the songs generate as much revenue as possible. According to this definition, in his view, there have been very few "true" publishers in Trinidad. He described his work as a music publisher in this way:

> If I am your publisher, from the time you are thinking about composition, you should discuss it with me. The publisher will say: Is that the right type of song you should be singing at this time? Is it what the market is looking for? Where is it going to end up, in a compilation or as part of a full CD? So the publisher is someone who is working with you, either finding singers for you or finding record labels for you, and things like that. As the song develops, he then exposes the song on your behalf and monitors the use of the song. So if somebody wants to use the song in a film or in a commercial or a music video, the publisher will jump on it quickly if they did not get permission. And he will make sure that the proceedings are regularized. So the publisher does a lot for the song and maximizes what the song can earn. Because he works on a percentage, so things which the individual artists cannot do the publisher can do on their behalf.

Daniell has sought to boost sales of the recordings with songs he has published by making them more readily available. He created a Web site from
which orders can be fulfilled. At first, he confined his Web site to his own
catalog, but after receiving orders from abroad on a daily basis, Daniell realized that distribution through the Internet was another untapped market
in Trinidad. As he explained, "People wanted different products to be put
together in a package and sent to them promptly." He thus added the following sentence on his Web site: "If you are interested in any other local
artist and other products, please let me know." As a result, Daniell's Web
site, www.majorandminor.com, processes orders ranging from putting together a few compact discs in a package to shipping a steel pan to Brooklyn.

The more Daniell has worked as an entrepreneur in various music-
related domains, the more knowledge about the Carnival music industry
he has acquired. And the better known he has become for his "new field
of expertise," the more projects he has become involved with. His reputation as one deeply involved in many aspects of the calypso music scene
prompted me to set up an interview with him in 1995. Since then I have
discussed with him on a yearly basis some of the current highlights of
the calypso scene. Since the early 1990s, Daniell has indeed been a well-
known personality in the local media.

Apart from working as a producer, a manager in various capacities,
a music publisher, a publisher of musical transcriptions, a distributor
through his Web site, and between 1992 and 2000 the researcher and host
of the weekly one-hour *Calypso Showcase* program on national television
(Trinidad and Tobago Television),[37] Daniell is now acting as a private
consultant for such international organizations as the United Nations
Development Projects (UNDP) and the World International Property
Organization (WIPO), and for the state government. He reports on the
local music industry, assessing its revenues, identifying its problems, and
making recommendations, as he says, "to improve it." Daniell's work has
helped make the Carnival music industry increasingly a field of management by defining the targets for "improving" it, and the technologies for
regulating and making it more profitable.

Significantly, however, most of his activities have revolved around
members of the Afro-Trinidadian community. I now turn to George
Singh, a representative of the East Indian musical community, to contrast
the business side of chutney soca with that of the Afro-Trinidadian musical scene and to show how the challenges as well as the business opportunities offered by chutney soca since the 1990s incited him to deploy
new technologies to expand and manage this burgeoning music market.

George P. Singh, Jr.

Since 1996, George Singh has been one of the most important cultural entrepreneurs of chutney soca. After hearing about his crucial role in that scene, I interviewed him at his office, located in a large building complex in the southern part of Trinidad in San Fernando. Shortly after the receptionist announced my arrival, Singh arrived to greet me in the waiting room. In his own quarters, elegantly furnished with an impressive desk and several comfortable leather chairs, we sat in the front of the room around a conference table and began the interview.

Singh, a businessman who began to work for one of his father's businesses at the age of seventeen, became involved with chutney soca not because of his love of culture, but because he saw it as a business opportunity. In 1990, he created Southex, a company specializing in event management that started by holding an annual international exposition (trade shows and promotions) for companies dealing with products (furniture, fabric, garments, and others) from different parts of the world (including India, Pakistan, China, the United States, Canada, and the Caribbean). By 2005, this event was drawing more than one hundred companies and over fifty thousand people over the five-day period in October during which it was held.

In the mid-1990s, Singh recognized that the chutney soca music market was growing rapidly and that it offered new business opportunities. In 1995, chutney soca had known an unprecedented success in both the East Indian and Afro-Trinidadian communities with the song "Lotela," by Sonny Mann—a success furthered nationally by the PNM party's use of it as an election song. During the same season, other songs such as "Chutney Bacchanal" had also succeeded in crossing over into the Afro-Trinidadian community. Yet, Singh noticed, there was no organization to capitalize on these events to help chutney soca become a fully national presence. In his words, "because chutney music is so catchy and whatnot, I decided to bring this thing into Carnival. I came up with the name Chutney Soca Monarch; there was already a Chutney Monarch, but there was nothing for chutney soca. So I made up my proposal and I went to the media—radio stations, TV stations, and so on."[38]

Singh's decision to venture into managing a musical event such as the Chutney Soca Monarch competition during Carnival sprang at first strictly from a wish to expand his business activities and to make some money. In contrast to most other people involved with chutney soca, Singh commanded an infrastructure: a well-established office with full-time employees. He also had experience in overseeing big events. He believed that he was thus in a good position to make the competition a lucrative venture. His new business goal, however, became rapidly enmeshed with local politics.

Because it draws on several types of activities, knowledges, and services, cultural entrepreneurship is never "apolitical." The first media person Singh met told him not to bring the Chutney Soca Monarch competition into Carnival because this meant "putting Indian business in African business," and the two would not mix. After being warned that his venture would fail, Singh became all the more determined to succeed. From its beginning in 1996, the competition drew great support, and it has since enjoyed a steady increase of patrons. The finals now usually attract between fifteen and twenty thousand people. Even though the audience is still mainly East Indian (according to Singh, 90 percent East Indians, 10 percent Afro-Trinidadians), he told me: "What is happening with chutney soca is really phenomenal. Ten years ago, it was almost like an activity that was happening behind closed doors. It has now come mainstream. No longer African people think twice to dance and enjoy chutney soca. It has become totally part of Trinidad and Tobago."

As these words indicate, Singh views the success of the chutney soca competition not only in economic terms, but also in relation to the cultural work it has accomplished. The greater audibility and visibility of East Indians during Carnival, in his mind, has boosted their recognition in the national sphere and, simultaneously, increased their sense of national belonging.

Singh's understanding of cultural entrepreneurship's entanglement with politics led him to look for sponsorship. Sponsorship would provide bigger budgets to stage elaborate productions. In addition, by holding the Chutney Soca Monarch competition within the authenticating space of Carnival, it would also convince sponsors, whether from the private or public sectors, to recognize East Indian music as an integral part of national culture. And that, by extension, would make its artists national subjects. In 2005, Singh could boast as many as sixteen corporate sponsors, which, in addition to local and transnational big businesses, included the Ministry of Culture, TIDCO, and, as the title sponsor, the National Lottery Classic (also a state-run agency).[39] Having built this structure of support, Singh resolved to keep holding the Chutney Soca Monarch competition on his own terms. As he said,

> I have had many calls over the past few years, especially from the NCC asking me to bring the Chutney Soca Monarch finals to the Queen Park Savannah.

They felt that it was now a national event and maybe needed to be in Port of Spain, it needed to be in the Queen Park Savannah. I refused to take it to Port of Spain because that is not where my market is. Although it may be successful [if it is taken there], I feel I need to keep it where the market is; it is very successful at Skinner Park, and I don't want to change that thing now—at least not now. Also, it is the biggest event in San Fernando for Carnival. So if I take it out of San Fernando, I am taking out the biggest event [for East Indians?] and taking it to Port of Spain.

Singh's words show that his approach to chutney soca exhibits not only an acute understanding of business markets, but also a sense of ethical responsibility vis-à-vis the public that has supported him—that is, the public south of the Caroni river in Trinidad, from which San Fernando attracts.

Singh's decision to create not simply a show but a competition involved a new area of management: that of the music itself. Artists now had to ensure that their music featured not only soca or chutney musical elements, but a fair balance of both. Even though not under Singh's control, the judging criteria of the competition began to regulate what qualifies as a chutney soca song. Banking on presenting this distinct musical product, Singh was determined to make his competition a "good show." This meant that his team invested the resources needed to make this show attractive to a wide audience. It also meant that to make his investment profitable, Singh sought to exploit the performance's financial power to the fullest. Hence, as the musical performances in the Chutney Soca Monarch competition generated identities and subjectivities that emphasized the fusion of cultural differences, they also produced new entrepreneurial opportunities and incomes.

As well as creating the Chutney Soca Monarch competition, Singh began to produce both a video—and, subsequently, a DVD—of the Chutney Soca Monarch competition finals and, from 1998 on, a CD compilation of selected songs performed by the finalists to expand chutney soca markets. He has also licensed these two products in both the United States and Canada. Furthermore, since 2003 he has made the show available on the Internet on a pay-per-view basis. As he explained, he subcontracted other agencies—TIDCO the first year and TV6 the second year—to videostream the finals live in order to make it available on the Internet. "After that," he added, "you can order it, and you get to download it on the computer." The "product," to use his wording, is also edited into a two-hour version to be sold to television stations abroad.

New business ventures, like the Chutney Soca Monarch competition, gave rise to new demands and opportunities. They incited Singh to help formalize and regulate the channels by which the monies from such products are made. To do so, Singh created two organizations. First, he formed the Chutney Soca Organization of Trinidad and Tobago as a nonprofit organization. As he explained, "The organization's mandate is to promote and enhance chutney soca of Trinidad and Tobago, to promote its visibility and enhance the music. It is a representative organization for artists to deal with problems that may occur in the industry, to get things put in the media, and to explore and channel the directions in which we think the music should go."

This organization is now partly funded by Singh and partly by the Ministry of Culture, a significant political recognition of chutney soca's importance in the national sphere. Second, Singh has also helped chutney soca artists form another organization "for themselves," he says, equivalent to TUCO—a recognition that these artists need to learn more about the music industry environment and their musical rights. He has helped organize workshops to educate artists about the importance of being a member of COTT, the local copyright association, and of having their work registered so that they can collect royalties. In so doing, as the executive producer of numerous chutney soca ventures and a shareholder in their products (DVDs CDs, and television programming), Singh has worked to ensure that his as well the artists' share in the enterprise is legally protected and financially rewarded. As his efforts to promote a better understanding of copyrights demonstrate, Singh views the law as an instrument that can enable profits and accumulation.

As his initiatives with chutney soca have proved successful, Singh has continued to explore new possibilities within the East Indian music industry and to expand his activities. In 2004, he launched a new fete called Chutney Glow, after a newly created Afro-Trinidadian event called Glow held in Port of Spain. This show attracted eight thousand people. At these events, everyone in attendance wears white, so that when ultraviolet lights are projected onto the crowd all the participants glow and become themselves part of the show. In the same year, Singh also produced for other people two additional major events featuring chutney soca: Mela, an Indian word for party, for the local radio station 103FM; and a chutney soca fete for the tenth anniversary of the National Lottery Control Board. In each case, Singh was responsible for the entire organization, from programming and marketing the event, to hiring the stage manager, to arranging the security and catering services. Featuring four or five bands, both these events were free to the public. In Singh's estimate, each attracted around twenty thousand people. As Singh indicated, because these events succeeded, they are likely to become part of his annual calendar of activities.

Even though he has already significantly increased his business activities through chutney soca, Singh has bigger plans for the future. After having helped to make chutney soca part of the national music scene, he now aims to make it part of transnational events and programming. The vehicle, he believes, is Hindi pop and the Indian diasporic connections and circuits in which it travels. As he explained,

> Hindi pop is a young beat that mixes rap and Hindi lyrics and that kind of things. It is like pop rock with Indian lyrics. . . . Banghra is often referred to as Hindi pop. It is a genre of music that is extremely popular in India and in London. And from London, it crossed to New York. There are lots of underground parties in New York. So if we could bring chutney soca under Hindi pop where you have banghra, we could then turn around and promote chutney soca to the international community under the banner of Hindi pop.
>
> In 2003, so I introduce the Hindi pop festival. All the [East Indian] bands played in the festival, and all the bands [whether at some point or for the majority of the songs] played chutney soca music. It was a mixture of chutney soca and Indian music, a combination really. And it all went very well. And the terminology of Hindi pop in Trinidad is picking up. And people will begin to understand.
>
> [For marketing purposes,] I was trying to piggyback on the terminology of Hindi pop, rather than trying to reestablish and to reset a completely new genre of music called chutney soca and take it to the international public. Hindi pop is a very infectious type of music. My goal is that next time we have the festival—most likely in 2005—what we want to do is to bring one of the Hindi pop international acts and put them on the stage with the locals. And that way, the entire thing starts coming into one. I feel that, that way, we would have more chance to attract people like MTV India and DTV. It is a hard sale, [but this is] what we are trying to do.

Distinctively, Singh has capitalized on the fusion of stylistic differences that chutney soca enacts and the diverse sensibilities and the markets to which it appeals. He has reached audiences from the two separate diasporas by strategically marketing a cultural product that embodies musical traits of both Afro-Trinidadian and East Indian musical practices. Singh's strategic marketing has exploited distinctive spaces (Carnival and fetes) and places (Port of Spain and south of the Caroni river). At the same time, he has used the ethnicized social and cultural networks of a transnational Indian diaspora.

From a business perspective, George Singh's involvement with chutney soca has enabled him to expand and diversify his management company's activities and to increase his annual income. Simultaneously, in addition to creating job opportunities for a wide range of nonperformers (e.g., stage managers and sound engineers), his launching of numerous chutney soca events has created new sources of employment and greater visibility for chutney soca artists. Through wider national exposure, many of them have been invited to join tours in Guyana, Surinam, the United States, Canada, Britain, England, and Holland as soon as Trinidad's Carnival is over. Such touring has allowed these artists to bring back foreign currency, contributing, even if only in small measure, to raising the GNP. In many ways, Singh's activities in chutney soca have provided opportunities for disciplined, knowing subjects to be more competitive in the unforgiving political economy of neoliberalism.

Politically, Singh's creation of the Chutney Soca Monarch competition in the Carnival space has helped this music and its artists to be recognized as constitutive of the nation. By providing, in addition to the Chutney Soca Monarch competition, several other forums in which chutney soca is heard, Singh has helped "normalize" its sounds in the Afro-Trinidadian sonic environment. While much work remains to be done not only for sounds but for people from the two discrepant diasporas to mingle in public events, Singh's attention has turned toward expanding his business ventures even further by aiming to turn performances of chutney soca into transnational events. Singh's focus on establishing a market for chutney soca within and across Trinidad's discrepant diasporas, in his mind, is not antithetical to exploring its connections with the Indian diasporic networks. Together with neoliberal rationality, chutney soca's multiple affiliations—musically, ethnically, culturally, politically, and geographically, among others—make it for Singh all the more attractive financially.

In focusing on the Carnival music scene since the 1990s, I have shown how its distinctive articulation constitutes a problem-space that has been predominantly animated by neoliberal practices. Enunciated variously by the state, by privately owned enterprises, and by individual entrepreneurs, such practices contrast with those of nationalism prevalent during the period immediately following independence. Instead of placing the emphasis on nation building, I have demonstrated that it concentrates on questions of management, improvement, and ethics. Carnival music activities are viewed as cultural capital to be managed as part of a market economy. In this context, many aspects of musical activities have been assigned new commercial values and entailing rights. Hence, the notion of management that has emerged since the 1990s has meant not just the creation of new musical projects—for example, shows, recording studios, and publications of calypso and soca musical transcriptions—aimed at boosting commercial revenues. Nor has it been primarily concentrated on the invention of new technologies devised to "improve" existing activities by making them more profitable—for example, greater control of paid entrance. Rather, in addition to fostering such new practices, neoliberal conditions have produced new subjects whose ethics are constitutive of how they define themselves and are defined by others.

As an assemblage of practices, knowledges, and technologies, cultural entrepreneurship has demonstrated a profound understanding of the processes, both discursive and material, at work under neoliberalism. Entrepreneurs have exploited long-standing productive tensions between nation and diasporas that produce subjectivities and identities as well as products and profits. What makes such neoliberal entrepreneurship distinctive is its subjecting long historical patterns of practice to managerial expertise. At the same time, however, neoliberalism has subjected artists and entrepreneurs—categories that are not necessarily mutually exclusive—to forms of discipline that have also involved inequalities and exclusions.

CODA

In 2005, changes in the calypso music scene continued to proliferate. That January, in the midst of attending shows and interviewing artists in Port of Spain and San Fernando, I recorded how the scene was once more transformed. Here are some excerpts from my diary and newspaper clippings:

Port of Spain, Trinidad, January 2005

Frankie Francis died on Thursday, January 6. Lord Blakie (who gave Black Stalin his sobriquet) died on the next day. Black Stalin announced that he will no longer sing in calypso tents, but only do guest performances. Denyse Plummer sang about how the Chinese in Trinidad have been historically overlooked and need to be acknowledged for their contributions. Singing Sandra (the second woman in the history of calypso to win the Calypso Monarch competition) recorded a song in a rapso style. Machel Montano was announced as the emcee for the Soca Divas show "The Ladies Night Out" at the Jean-Pierre Complex on January 8, but the show was canceled because of rain. Rikki Jai began to sing Hindi pop and to produce chutney soca riddims. A chutney soca show was included for the first time at Mas Camp (a venue historically dedicated to calypso shows) in December 2004. After a resounding success, a second East Indian chutney soca show was held on January 6. Lady

Gypsy sang about how sweet her Indian man is, following Denise Belfon's
song last year, "I Want an Indian Man."

Following last year's tendency, the tempo of many soca songs is noticeably
slower than in the late 1990s.

According to Sugar Aloes, "Calypso tents are a dying art form. . . . Any tent
coming now, God has to be part of that cast, because we have seen people
with more collateral and business sense fail."[1] The pan kaiso competition
has ceased to exist. Trinbago Unified Calypsonians Organization (TUCO)
president Michael "Protector" Legerton told reporters that there will be a
chutney category in the calypso competitions this year and that it "will be
judged alongside songs dedicated to other niche genres like party, humour,
social and political themes."[2] In its second year of existence, the Massive
Gosine Roving Chutney Calypso Tent, organized by Nirmal "Massive"
Gosine, will include twenty shows during this season. The National Action
Cultural Committee is launching a new calypso competition for calypsonians who have been performing for thirty-five years or more, called the
Veteran's Calypso Competition.[3]

Throughout this book, I have attempted to show how such changes in calypso and in the calypso music scene have been the norm, not the exception. My point in highlighting how calypso and its musical offshoots have
been transformed in many different ways—in language, musical form,
rhetorical strategies, instrumentation, and arrangement, for example—
throughout their history was not only to show how such occurrences
unsettle notions that tradition is something fixed and stable. My point
was also to show how the construction of calypso as tradition emerged
from a selective process and constituted as much the stakes of Trinidadian
cultural politics as its product. From the start of the colonial period, musical practices in Trinidad—as most musical practices elsewhere—were not
conceived as "merely musical."[4] They were conceived as performative, in
and of themselves as performing deeds. Precisely because musical practices were understood as *doing* things, calypso by being performed during
Carnival—one of the most prominent spaces for the display and exercise
of power—was conceived at once as a target and an instrument of discipline, and as a terrain through which agency could be deployed.

Accordingly, this book has been about "governing sound." It has
sought to examine how, on the one hand, sound has been the object of
disciplinary measures to encourage specific forms of conduct and how,
on the other hand, it has enabled particular forms of conduct to prevail.

Personal conduct here refers not only to musical taste and knowledge, but to people's attitudes and behavior in regard to sexuality, gender relations, and morality. It has to do as much with propriety—the "right" choice of language, physical move, or lyrics at the "right" time or in the "right" space—as with a particular way of being and sensing the world. To use Foucault's often-cited formulation, it thus concerns not only knowledge, but also power—that is, who has the power to make one person's knowledge dominate that of others. From the time of its emergence, calypso, as I have tried to show, has provided an important site of struggles over such power.

In this book, I used the notion of "governmentality" to destabilize the common tendency to equate governing with the state. Hence, I have focused on myriad governing technologies deployed through the musical practices of calypso and its offshoots that have shaped the conduct of artists and their audiences according to particular aesthetics, moral values, and ethical practices. Concomitantly, I have examined the different types of agency possible at different moments in the histories of calypso and its musical offshoots. In focusing on governing technologies, I was more interested in identifying what they were and what they produced than in describing the intentions that have contributed to their deployment. As I have shown, distinct technologies—whether imagined in the form of bans, prizes, or new competitions, whether deployed by repressive or progressive institutions or individuals—often produced unintended outcomes that exceeded or failed to meet initial expectations.

In focusing on agency, I wanted to identify the specific constellations of practices, forces, and relations that shaped distinct outcomes in the calypso scene. I have conceived agency as resulting from a combination of material conditions, individual and collective actions, and historical events and contingencies *in their articulation*—that is, not orchestrated by an institution or a sovereign subject. I differ in my analytical use of "agency" from those who understand the term as the sole property of an intentional, willful, human individual or collective social group. Hence, while I related how in the late 1950s the Mighty Sparrow and Lord Melody led the boycott of calypso competitions to obtain more money prizes, making them more compatible with those awarded in the Queen competition, it was equally important to stress the conditions that encouraged them to do so: their boycott stemmed not exclusively from their own political visions, but together with the anticolonial-nationalist sentiments that were then fomenting and confronting the asymmetrical power relations between what were perceived as activities promoting white European aesthetics and Afro-Trinidadian ones. I also stressed how things previously unrelated but combined in specific conjunctures also produced tangible effects. In the introduction, I gave the example of how the U.S. sailors posted in Trinidad during World War II, the severe state censorship of the time, and calypsonians' performances at the military base, in their articulation, produced a distinct orientation in calypso compositions during that period.

While attempting to identify what produced agency in calypso and the calypso music scene, I was equally interested in exploring the forms it took and its tangible effects. Hence, while I showed that agency in calypso has been expressed as resistance against oppressive powers, I also referred to occasions seized by individuals to put forward certain activities or processes for personal gain—to make a career or earn a reputation or respect—and, at other times, to maintain the status quo—as certain judges did by privileging "traditional" musical forms, sounds, or lyrics over innovation.

With these things in mind, I examined calypso in relation to three historical periods—colonial, anticolonial/nationalist, and neoliberal. While this periodization at first glance may appear self-evident by suggesting a historical chronology, I conceived it on analytical grounds. I chose to frame my study around these three periods because they contrast with each other in their different arrangements of power, and they foreground the different hegemonic cultural politics that marked the conditions in which calypso and its musical offshoots emerged, changed, and mattered.

During the colonial period, I showed how the colonial administration and middle and upper classes understood cultural values and behaviors both as vital forces of production and as an index of modernity. In this view, musical values and behaviors were seen as inextricably linked with the ways people conducted themselves in other realms of activity and production. Accordingly, from the outset calypso was entangled with modernist projects shaped by discourses of improvement and moral conduct elaborated through a Protestant work ethic that valorized productivity and self-discipline. Early in the twentieth century, it became further implicated in capitalist economies by acquiring a commercial value through recordings, paying calypso tents, and tourism. During this period, calypso went through multiple and continuous transformations in musical forms, instrumentation, and lyrical focus. While many of these changes were imposed by both the colonial administration and the church in attempts to govern the conduct surrounding calypso, some changes in calypso took place through the calypsonians' own agency. Calypso sounds were transformed not only through the calypsonians' contacts with other musicians and new musics, but also through their rejection of, and responses to, colonial musical injunctions. These artists also transformed their sounds to suit their publics' tastes, attending carefully to audiences' demands made tangible as much through record sales as through the crowd's reactions at live shows. As foreigners began attending calypso tents early in the twentieth century, calypsonians focused their lyrics increasingly on international events and modified their diction to reach out their new audiences.

While assessing the cultural politics that dominated this period, I was equally concerned with tracing the tangible effects of these politics. As I have indicated, calypso during the colonial period made visible and audible the bodies and voices of the black population.[5] Its lyrics criticized the colonial regime and vented frustration. Yet the language calypsonians used over time gave way to English, the language of the British administration, over French Creole, the black lower-class vernacular until the late nineteenth century. From the early twentieth century, it privileged male perspectives and excluded women. Most particularly, it constituted a space for black male lower-class artists' creativity and expression, and provided work opportunities for them. In turn, through its market relations in North America, Europe, and Africa, calypso enacted a white-and-black dialectic. In so doing, it reinforced the divisions nurtured by the colonial administration, obscuring the contributions of East Indians. And while voicing anticolonial-nationalist sentiments, calypso also acted as a tourist attraction and a source of national income.

My focus on Trinidad and Tobago's historical period from independence in 1962 to the late 1980s aimed to highlight how, during that historical period, calypso became an object of other demands and desires. My goal here was to show how, in this particular conjuncture, calypso became inextricably entangled with the project of nation building. Following the worldwide movement of new independent nation-states, the new Afro-Creole political party in power set out to establish Trinidad and Tobago's distinct cultural identity. For decades involved with Carnival, the Afro-Creole leaders viewed calypso as their expression—which, from their hegemonic position, they constructed in practice, if not officially, as that of "the people." Along with the dominant cultural politics surrounding independence, however, came a conception of calypso that differed radically from those of the preceding era. As during the colonial period, calypso on the eve of independence and after it continued to change. However, instead of being viewed from a modernist perspective—as progress or improvement—its transformations within the nationalist perspective were constructed as a "changing same." A new focus on establishing continuity with the past emerged as crucial to the new aesthetics, not just for the state leaders, but for the followers of the Black Power movement spreading worldwide at the time. Simultaneously, such

politics of memory were thought to provide the very resources that legitimated the nation-building project and the recovery of black heritage
and pride. In practical terms, this veneration of the past meant that only
certain types of musical changes were now admitted in calypso competitions—those deemed compatible with the imagined inherited tradition.
Furthermore, as such an aesthetics of continuity within a perspective
advocating independence became inextricably linked with the new sovereign territory, only Trinidadian artists residing on the island could now
be included as calypso contestants.

As calypso became the site where the politics of national representation were elaborated, it also became a site of contestation within the nation and between the discrepant diasporas. As I pointed out, by remaining
the privileged space of Afro-Trinidadian, male, lower-class artists, calypso
continued to perform certain exclusions traceable to colonial legacies.
The tensions between Afro-Trinidadians and East Indians continued to
be enacted by the near absence of the latter on the calypso stage. Gender,
racial, and class politics continued to loom large, even as they were confronted by black women and by nonblack middle- and upper-class male
and female artists forcing their way into the authenticating space of the national subject. In this context, Afro-Trinidadian and East Indian audiences
remain for the most part two distinct entities rarely mingling together.

While various political technologies were deployed to highlight continuity with the selectively imagined past, calypsonians and musicians
transformed calypso—or "updated" it, to use a term in line with the prevailing aesthetics of continuity—by incorporating electric instruments,
new melodic bass lines, arrangements, and performance practices (e.g.,
the use of a score). They worked as cultural brokers, attempting to render
calypso into a musical artform readily identifiable with Trinidad, while
simultaneously aiming to make it attractive to the local market, and also
regional and international audiences. Viewed from a nationalist's and
black social activist's perspective, calypsonians and musicians performed a
double motion that Rex Nettleford has evocatively termed, in reference
to self-definition and effective action, "inward stretch, outward reach."[6]
In both cases, local, regional, and international audiences remain key to
calypsonians' endeavors, providing performers with national recognition
and conferring commercial value on their products.

In the second part of the book, I focused on the shift in regimes of
power brought forward by what I referred to as neoliberalism in Trinidad from the nineties onward. My goal here was to examine what is
hegemonic within this new formation and consequential for the new
generation of artists working in the calypso music scene. Within Trinidad's

neoliberal politics, politicians in power no longer saw the state as the sole purveyor of social welfare. Instead, they placed the onus of responsibility on self-discipline and entrepreneurship. As everywhere else, the neoliberal turn, however, did not involve simply economic reforms. As Wendy Brown has written: "[Neoliberalism] is not only about facilitating free trade, maximizing corporate profits, and challenging welfarism . . . rather it involves *extending and disseminating market values to all institutions and social action,* even as the market itself remains a distinctive player."[7] From this perspective, culture—even when it implicates "national culture"—is not conceived as antithetical to commodity. In Trinidad, this meant that state agencies as well as entrepreneurs viewed their involvements with calypso and its musical offshoots not just as support for local culture. They viewed these musics also from the perspective of market values and sources of income. This understanding of the rapport between music and money or, more specifically, of national emblems as commodities is certainly not new; remember the efforts of the colonial administration to get rid of Carnival's "ugly" features to attract foreign tourists. What is new is that in the nineties it became central to the political economic discourses of the day and was deployed into a new form of governmentality.

As I have shown, this shift in the "art of governing" in Trinidad took place in tandem with the introduction of several political technologies. In the late 1990s, the state transferred the management of the national calypso competitions to TUCO. While continuing to sponsor the competitions, it demanded a new degree of accountability for the subsidies it granted. In its turn, TUCO restructured the events it organized more in line with business ventures, so that they would be more lucrative financially. It also sought to create new shows to boost its incomes. Around the same time, more artists began to require contracts before they went onstage. An increasing number of composers now claimed their tunes as intellectual properties, registering them with the local Copyright Organization of Trinidad and Tobago (COTT). In their turn, private organizers of the new soca and ragga soca competitions and other show promoters moved away from the requirement in calypso competitions since the late 1970s that only contestants born and living in Trinidad be admitted. They "denationalized" the criteria for inclusion, recognizing popular music as a cultural practice that cannot be confined within the compass of the nation-state. They realized, in other words, that the music's best chance to remain significant culturally and nationally, and to thrive musically and commercially, was to make it part of a market as wide as possible. Whether real or imagined, audiences here influenced how soca and ragga competitions would both unfold and be marketed.

Within these conditions of possibility, the calypso music scene has radically changed. (I use the present tense here because the historical time from which I speak is still part of that same moment.) Promoters' new ways of thinking about the music competitions held during Carnival have since 1996 opened the soca, ragga soca, and chutney soca competitions to a wide range of artists—from various nation-states, in theory, opened to all. In practice, however, these competitions feature predominantly artists from the same ethnic group. In this climate emphasizing the market value of inclusion, the politics of gender onstage have changed. Women have ventured onto the calypso music scene from which they had been marginalized for decades. Their number as contestants in the calypso music scene, and as leading performers in soca bands, has dramatically increased.

Within the neoliberal "condition," soca, ragga soca, and chutney soca artists have foregrounded new politics of memory.[8] They have used excerpts from old calypsos not simply to establish continuity with the past, but also because these old songs provide new generative material in the present. Along the same lines, they have integrated musical techniques from other countries, too, and recorded with other local and nonlocal singers to create new sounds and new relationships. Moreover, they have reconfigured their expression of sexuality onstage in ways that reject colonial Victorian morality. They have explored sexual moves and sexualized outfits as part of commoditization and commercial attraction. Enacting what Brown has defined as a neoliberal practice, this new generation of artists in the calypso scene has extended market values to sentiments and pleasures. They have made these two aspects central to their music making, both as vital forces in community formation and also as forces of production.[9] When Iwer Georges shouts into the microphone "Anybody from Trinidad?" to a packed crowd at a Caribana fete, the response is thunderous. Georges not only capitalizes on this show of belonging, but furthermore counts on this sentiment to elicit consumer loyalty.

While artistic entrepreneurship in Trinidad historically preexisted neoliberalism, some entrepreneurial activities are peculiar to the "neoliberal condition" of their emergence. In the last chapter, I described new entrepreneurial activities that stemmed from placing market values on practices not previously considered in these terms in Trinidad. In so doing, I showed how some entrepreneurs now viewed certain knowledges in the music business as commercial commodities, as in the offering of new technical services, ranging from managerial assistance to training in recording studios.[10] I also referred to the rise of novel fields of expertise that provided new sources of incomes, while also becoming part of emergent disciplining technologies (e.g., the responsibilities of the contract manager). If neoliberalism has led more artists in Trinidad to copyright their songs, it has also led to the regulation of the conditions in which their songs are exchanged and performed. More generally, while neoliberalism may have encouraged the proliferation of musical activities, the participation of more people (e.g., in competitions), and the rise of new music business ventures, it also yielded new forms of management.

Neoliberalism, with its own "art of governing," has not emerged in a vacuum. The new musical practices it has brought to the calypso music scene have been enmeshed, and at times embattled, with those that dominated previous eras and are still in existence. Similarly, their emergent audiences cannot be dissociated from the selective and residual calypso audiences that dominated the colonial and nation-building eras.[11] While Machel Montano sought to expand the soca market by exploring different sounds and engaging in collaborations with artists from other musical scenes, he still operated within specific contingencies. While many of these contingencies had to do with the long-term hegemonic musical aesthetics of calypso, others concerned the hegemonic global soundings of the present. In addition, as he explained to me, he had to listen to his public, to hear his critics, and to tune in "with what they expect and what they want." Put another way, his awareness that his success depends not only on how he positions himself but also on how he is positioned by his audience has guided his artistic moves. Furthermore, the artists' own desires or new visions are often confronted by behaviors that have come to be "common" practice and ways of thinking. Hence, even though neoliberalism may have encouraged artists to consider their work as intellectual property, they are still subject to the long-term view in Trinidad (and elsewhere) of musical compositions as common property. In the same way, in spite of the efforts along neoliberal political lines to encourage wide participation, the legacies of colonial racial politics still inform many of the exclusions performed in the calypso music scene. While a lively traffic in creative intermixtures links Afro-Creole and East Indian musical productions, those who perform and consume these sounds remain for the most part spatially and racially segregated. In live shows, Montano's audiences remain predominantly black, while Jai attracts an almost exclusively East Indian crowd.

In 2005, in the midst of the political tension in Trinidad, intensified by the rivalry between the two main political parties, which embody—actually reinforce—the deep-seated divisions between Afro-Creoles and East Indians, the calypso music scene nonetheless still performs multiple audible entanglements and senses of belonging.[12] All in their own ways—calypsonians, and soca, rapso, chutney soca, and ragga soca artists—profess their social, political, and economic engagement with the nation-state and the discrepant diasporas to which they relate on and off the island—in the Caribbean, Africa, India, North America, and Europe. They each foresound musical sensibilities that connect them with different, yet over-lapping, pasts that have become increasingly linked to each other in the present—in music making, performance, touring circuits, and institutions.

To me, all these musical practices matter. Each has emerged histori-cally in response to particular demands and desires. Within their respec-tive conventions, all have produced gems of creativity as well as floods of banality. Regardless of the value attributed to these musical practices, they have enabled expressions of particular longings for inclusion and critiques of exclusion—whether as national subjects or as members of discrepant diasporic groups or other sociopolitical, economic, and cultural forma-tions throughout the world. In focusing throughout this book on *sound work,* my goal has been to show what calypso, soca, and chutney soca have accomplished, while calling attention to the work and material conditions that have enabled these sounds to emerge, thrive, and animate audiences.

As has been shown throughout the book, the generative power of sound work has been struggled over throughout Trinidad's history. A critical question for many today is, Where are the new Carnival musics leading? Or, put another way, what kinds of future might be envisioned through them?

In my view, rather than focusing on a particular telos, these new mu-sics are predominantly concerned with other issues: What experiences are people *now* willing to share and with whom? And how might a spirit of conviviality enable people's desires to be realized? I use Paul Gilroy's expression "spirit of conviviality" because it captures much of what is crucial to soca, chutney soca, and ragga soca: *a celebration of life and pleasure with people.* As the term "conviviality" suggests, it involves not only one's self-responsibility, but also one's relationship with others.[13] This perspec-tive shifts from the way many critics have viewed these musics, as pro-moting a hedonistic popular culture that has disavowed national party politics, working-class struggles, and political vision. Instead, it focuses on the opportunities these musics provide for reworking relationships between self and others. Such a view does not preclude being critical of what these musics privilege, dismiss, or exclude in the communities of sensibility they foster. It does not suggest that the types of musical elements, musical skills, outfits, lyrics, and relationships they feature and promote must be embraced indiscriminately. However, it requires an openness to the horizon of possibilities they conjure for people whose senses of belonging traverse nations and diasporas.

APPENDIX 1

Criteria for Various National Music Competitions during Carnival

Trinbago Unified Calypsonians Organization (TUCO)
National Calypso Monarch Competition 2000

30 points: Lyrics (development and depth of idea, structure—narrative
and coherence and organisation)

30 points: Melody (basic melody and compatibility with chosen
theme—use of rhythm)

20 points: Rendition (articulation, clarity of diction, voice quality, and
tonal pitch)

10 points: Presentation (stage presence and performance)

10 points: Originality (originality and treatment of theme, creativity)

Caribbean Prestige Productions International (CPPI)
The Carib International Soca Monarch Competition 2000

Note: no explanation of the criteria is given.

30 points: Lyrics
40 points: Music
30 points: Performance

Southex Trade Shows and Promotions
National Chutney Soca Competition 2000

10 points: Impact (effect on audience judged by audience response,
visually and aurally)

10 points: Crossover (marriage of East Indian harmonies and dialect and the rhythms of the soca beat; the assimilation).

20 points: Presentation (showmanship: how you present your song on stage)

20 points: Lyrics (good story, discussion, argument; interesting lyrics structured to make sense; same theme throughout, relationship between verses and chorus; good development, terms and phrases)

20 points: Rhythm (refers to the time aspect of music; music is rhythmical when there is a regular recurrence of pulse or accent in a given set of sounds; rhythm in music makes it possible to distinguish a waltz from chutney soca; the rhythm has to be even in relation to the type of music performed)

20 points: Singing techniques (singing is merely elongated speech on carefully chosen pitches to create a meaningfully and artistically interesting melodic line; intonation: the production of tone, either vocal or instrumental, a good, strong and steady tone; maintaining pitch accuracy: not singing flat, i.e., below the required pitch, not singing sharp, i.e., above the required pitch; diction: clarity of words, i.e., must hear clearly the words being sung)

Trinbago Unified Calypsonians Organization (TUCO)
The National Pan Kaiso Competition 2000

Note: The Pan Kaiso competition uses the same criteria as the National Calypso Monarch competition.

30 points: Lyrics
30 points: Melody
20 points: Rendition
10 points: Presentation
10 points: Originality

Trinbago Unified Calypsonians Organization (TUCO)
Extempo Competition 2000

40 points: Lyrics
25 points: Rendition
20 points: Originality
5 points: Presentation
10 points: Repartee

Carnival/Cultural Judges Association of Trinidad and Tobago (CJATT)
Carnival Ragga Soca Monarch Competition of Trinidad and Tobago 2000

30 points: Lyrics (the words of a song as distinguished from the music; lyrical content and verse construction; using lyrics to vividly relay a situation; storytelling skills)

30 points: Musical arrangement/rhythm (the way in which the production or arrangement of the music is constructed to give the feeling of the respective artform; utilizing elements such as dancehall samples, riffs, runs, rhythm and bass lines)

20 points: Presentation (the manner, style action, dress, facial expression, props or any other ingredients that make the performance more effective; creativity and imagination with regard to the portray of the "stage show")

List of Carnivals and Festivals

Source: *Carnival,* vol. 12, no. 1 (Winter/Spring 1998): 47.

NOTES

Introduction

1. T. Joseph (2002).

2. See Vianna (1999), Austerlitz (1997), and Savigliano (1995). For a related argument, see Gupta and Ferguson (1997).

3. I use the term "technologies" here to refer to an ensemble of techniques that pertain to a particular domain. I use "techniques" in contrast to speak about a particular expertise or method. Hence, "political technologies" refers to several techniques such as bans, censorship, and competitions used by the colonial administration, whereas bans refer to only one of the techniques used by that administration. Along these lines, the technologies used by the clergy would encompass techniques such as confession, excommunication, mass, and so on, that are peculiar to this entity. In this study, the term "technologies" is used in the plural to signal that the ensemble of techniques pertaining to a particular domain (e.g., calypso, the slave plantations, and morality) is not fixed. It changes and thus encompasses different ensembles of techniques (even though at times overlapping) at different historical moments.

4. Rapso, another musical offshoot of calypso, also became prominent in the 1990s. However, it is not commonly associated with the expression "party music," for reasons that will be explained in part 2 of the book.

5. As Keith Negus indicates in *Music Genres and Corporate Cultures* (1999), the announcement that a genre is dead is commonly made in direct relation to concerns about its gradually changing life. As he remarks, despite laments of their deaths, rap, salsa, and rock are heard by many of their fans as dynamic, changing, and continually transforming themselves (Negus 1999: 26).

6. In this study, I refer to class as a folk category that is used in Trinidadian popular parlance as well as in academic literature on the subject. From these perspectives, class usually designates a socioeconomic position, relative access to economic capital and political control, and presumed moral and aesthetic values.

281

Such formulations run the potential risk of homogenizing and essentializing an aggregate of varied interests, identities, and aspirations.

7. I use "genealogy" in Michel Foucault's sense. Rather than relating a history following a linear development, genealogy treats history as the product of not only contingencies, but also "'accidents,' 'errors,' and 'faulty calculations'" (Foucault [1971] 1977: 146). As Foucault puts it, "it must record the singularity of events outside of any monotonous finality; it must seek them in the most unpromising places" ([1971] 1977: 139). In *Governing Sound,* I trace calypso's transformations through unexpected places, processes, and practices—from competing imperial regimes of rule in the early nineteenth century, to diasporic routes traveled by musical arrangers in the 1960s, to cultural entrepreneurs under neoliberalism in the 1990s.

8. This does not exhaust what music does, but these are the dimensions that I attend to.

9. See, for example, Elder (1966a), Quevedo (1983), Rohlehr (1990), Liverpool (1986, 1993), Cowley (1996), and L. Regis (1999).

10. Bennett (1998: 70).

11. I translate Michel Foucault's expression "arts de gouverner" as "arts of governing," in contrast to many authors' reference to "art of government"—which can be easily misread as belonging to the state (as a noun). "Arts of governing" emphasizes instead that such practices are both dynamic and plural. I thank Donald Moore for sharing this insight with me.

12. Grenier (2005: 200).

13. Lovelace (1998: 56).

14. I refer here to "discursive formations" in the plural because, at different historical moments, contrasting discursive formations enabled calypso to be constructed as emblematic of Trinidad.

15. Grenier (2005: 201).

16. This quotation derives from David Scott's elaboration of MacIntyre's position (Scott 1999: 10).

17. R. Williams (1977: 115; italics in the original).

18. I thank Line Grenier for bringing to my attention this important consideration.

19. Hall ([1986] 1996: 141). For an elaboration of this notion, see Moore, Kosek, and Pandian (2003: 3–4) and Moore's discussion of what he terms "articulated assemblage" (2005: 23–25).

20. Negus (1997: 135).

21. Gordon (1991: 4). In contrast, others have deployed Foucauldian analyses to explore the "Powers of Freedom" in contemporary societies (Rose 1999).

22. In response to this criticism, Foucault wrote an essay entitled "Technologies of the Self" which he defines as "what permit individuals to effect by their own means or with the help of others a certain number of operations on their own bodies and souls, thoughts, conduct, and way of being, so as to transform themselves in order to attain a certain state of happiness, purity, wisdom, perfection, or immortality" (Foucault 1988: 18). In this study, I have translated "technologies of the self" as "cultural entrepreneurship," a particular type of agency that is central in musical practices—which, in the same way Judith Butler speaks about culture, are never "merely musical." For an elaboration of this argument, see Butler (1998).

23. See Guilbault (1997a: 39–40) for a critical discussion of agency—a notion, I argue, that should not be limited to human subjects.

24. Bennett (1998: 71).

25. Turino (2000: 13).

26. It should be stressed here that to speak of musics associated with nationalist discourses does not entail that these musics necessarily endorse the politics of such discourses. Rather, it emphasizes that the lyrics and mode of address are for the most part inextricable from the terms set by the nationalist discourses. For an elaboration of the subject, see Butler (2000).

27. Barry Shanks reported in Straw (1991: 373).

28. Straw (2001: 248).

29. In this book, I emphasize the relational and positional dimensions of diasporas in the plural. Conceptually, I draw on Stuart Hall's germinal formulation: "The diaspora experience . . . is defined, not by essence or purity, but by the recognition of a necessary heterogeneity and diversity; by a conception of 'identity' which lives with and through, not despite, difference; by *hybridity*" (1990: 235). Crucially, Hall's formulation of diasporic identity attends to the historical and geographic specificity of the Caribbean. Trinidad was the site of both arrival and departure for multiple migrations of African slaves and East Indian indentured labors and their descendants—identities radically inflected by exclusions. For helpful exploration of these processes, see Hintzen (2004, 2001) and Puri (2003a). More broadly, I build on Gilroy's insight that "the diaspora idea encourages critical theory to proceed rigorously but cautiously in ways that do not privilege the modern nation-state and its institutional order" (2000: 129; 1993). In this book, I explore the multiple subjectivities, translocal musical practices, and audible entanglements enacted through Trinidad's discrepant diasporas, African and East Indian—none of which precludes a sense of national belonging. For an insightful formulation on these dynamics, see Clifford (1994). Also relevant to Caribbean diasporas, see Basch, Schiller, and Blanc (1994).

30. Both Grenada and St. Vincent have been granted much recognition in the region for their important contributions to calypso. But for reasons of logistics, it was not feasible to include these two sites in my study.

31. "Mas" is the Trinidadian expression for masquerade.

32. For further information on how the Carnivals celebrated in various diasporic sites such as New York and San Francisco differ in many more ways than just size, see Hintzen (2001).

33. Puri (2003a: 7). Gordon Rohlehr provides invaluable historical documentation in this regard in his landmark book *Calypso and Society in Pre-independence Trinidad* (1990). See also Rohlehr's interview with Shalini Puri (Puri 2003b: 247–55), and *Atilla's Kaiso: A Short History of Trinidad Calypso,* by Raymond Quevedo (Atilla the Hun) (1983).

34. One of the reasons why this is the case is certainly economic. For the majority of people in the islands, the cost of recordings is prohibitive. However, economic reasons cannot be seen as the sole determining explanation. In the context of poverty, insecurity, and need for flexibility, it could be argued that the limited space where most people live does not easily accommodate collections. It could also be argued that, while the hit songs of the season greatly matter, they are played on the radio to such an extent that they actually saturate the market. One other reason might be that, for some people, the process rather than simply the product of competitions (the songs) ultimately is what counts the most.

35. In Toronto, a group of record collectors headed by George Maharaj was formed and included specialists in the most reputed artists, for example, a Mighty Sparrow specialist, a Lord Kitchener specialist, and so on. At this point, one of the most important calypso record and film collectors is Ray Funk, from Fairbanks, Alaska, who has developed one of the most—if not *the* most—sophisticated database about calypso artists' recordings, lyrics, performance appearances, and so on. I am indebted to George Maharaj, John White,

Fitzroy Richardson, and Tony Boissière in Toronto, Ray Funk in Fairbanks, and Shawn Randoo in Trinidad (the exception that confirms the rule that most record collectors live outside the islands) for their generous help during the course of this research.

36. Several authors have highlighted how *space,* understood not merely as location—outdoor versus indoor performance, the location and size of the venue, the dimensions of the stage—but also as social relations—among friends, family, or an anonymous crowd—plays a crucial role in the production and reception of music and the shaping of subjectivities. Conversely, it has been also argued that music greatly contributes to the construction of place. For further information on the subject, see Berland (1992), Stokes (1994), Feld and Basso (1996), Herman, Swiss, and Sloop (1998), and Forman (2002).

37. The fact that audiences often assemble members of the same diaspora (African or East Indian), does not mean that they do not perform boundaries of exclusion within that diaspora. For example, while chutney soca audiences assemble mostly East Indians, until recently they rarely included members of the East Indian upper class or orthodox Hindu practitioners. In other words, class or religion sometimes trumped ethnic affiliation, with tangible consequences for audience formation.

38. As James Clifford put it, "Intervening in an interconnected world, one is always, to varying degrees, 'inauthentic': caught between cultures, implicated in others" (1988: 11).

39. For an elaboration of the subject, see Hall (1997) and Bourdieu (1986, 1993).

40. While the term "commuting" may imply repeated travel between two fixed sites, my use of the term evokes the experience of traveling between several locations.

41. I refer to particular circuits of the transnational Caribbean space because such a space includes many different types of networks (established, say, through music, small trading, and family relations) and maps connections among several locations (England, Denmark, etc.) with which I am not familiar.

42. Personal conversation with George Lipsitz, at the University of California, Berkeley, 14 March 2003.

43. See Lipsitz (1994).

44. Many years before, in 1973, Peter Wilson produced an illuminating ethnography along these lines entitled *Crab Antics: The Social Anthropology of English-Speaking Negro Societies of the Caribbean,* in which he focused on a marginal figure in order to assess the limits of the socially acceptable on the Colombian island of Providencia, in the western Caribbean Sea.

45. I owe this insight to Shalini Puri's generative writing on cultural hybridity (1999: 13–14).

46. Stoler (2002: 7).

47. I coined this expression, "audible entanglements," to highlight the multiple musical practices and soundings assembled in a music such as calypso and the affective resonances these create for individuals and communities. As I wrote elsewhere, "As a critical analytic, audible entanglements thus *foresound* sites, moments, and modes of enunciation articulated *through* musical practices. So, far from being 'merely' musical, audible entanglements . . . assemble social relations, cultural expressions, and political formations" (Guilbault 2005: 40–41).

Chapter 1: Calypso's Historical Entanglements

1. I use here the expression "imperialist influence" in relation to the United States to emphasize how its cultural politics and political economy have assumed a domineering quality akin to the authority of a sovereign state over its dependencies.

2. For further information on the subject, see Marshall (1986).

3. Trinidad is endowed with rich natural resources, including lake asphalt (natural pitch), oil, and gas. The oil wells in Trinidad were among the first to be constructed in the Western Hemisphere. In addition, in the nineteenth and twentieth centuries, agriculture, and most particularly sugar, cocoa, and coffee, played an important role in the local economy.

4. The demographic figures I provide are drawn from the latest census, in 2006.

5. Liverpool (1993).

6. D. Hill (1993: 167).

7. This is acknowledged in several publications, including Quevedo (1983: 14–19), Rohlehr (1990: 140), Liverpool (1993: 507–8), and Cowley (1996: 178, 180).

8. Quevedo (1983).

9. See chapter 5, and in particular the section on arranger Frankie Francis, who is credited with having produced calypso arrangements continuously since 1947.

10. The expression "brass band" in Trinidad refers to bands including both brass (trumpets and trombones) and reed instruments (saxophones).

11. Unknown source, quoted by Rohlehr (1990: 328).

12. The first official Calypso King competition in Antigua did not begin until 1957; in St. Lucia, it was 1957; in Grenada, 1958; and in Barbados, 1959 or 1960, to name only a few. For further information on these competitions, see *Calypso Talk '86: Antigua Carnival* (1986: 36), *Lucian Kaiso 1990* (1990: 4), and McQuilkin and Panchoo (1984: 52). Note that whereas Best (1995: 29) refers to 1959, Marshall (1986: 28) indicates 1960.

13. On this subject, see Liverpool (1993) and also Nurse (2000b: 87–95).

14. Cowley (1996: 9).

15. Rohlehr (1990: 7).

16. For an elaboration of this subject, see Corrigan and Sayer (1985).

17. Brereton ([1979] 2002: 9).

18. Adderley (2003: 19). According to Rohlehr, however, given that the slave trade in Haiti had dramatically increased between 1779 and 1790—during these twelve years, 312,000 slaves were brought to the island, as opposed to 5,000 slaves for the previous fifty years—it can be safely assumed that many of the Haitian slaves imported into Trinidad between 1798 and 1802 were African born (Rohlehr 1990: 7).

19. Adderley (2003: 19–20).

20. Quoted in Koningsbruggen (1997: 93).

21. Koningsbruggen (1997: 13).

22. Quoted in Koningsbruggen (1997: 92).

23. Koningsbruggen (1997: 92).

24. While the expression "Creole Indian" has been used historically to refer to a person of Indian descent born in Trinidad, its use today is quite rare.

25. Brereton ([1979] 2002: 2–4). For further elaboration of the subject, see also Hintzen (2002).

26. Koningsbruggen (1997: 93).

27. Brereton ([1979] 2002: 177).

28. Koningsbruggen (1997: 93).

29. As Corrigan and Sayer (1985: 6) noted concerning England, moral discipline in colonial Trinidad was not neutrally about "'integrating society.' It was about enforcing rule."

30. This quotation from Corrigan's and Sayer's work (1985: 133) on English state formation and women's place in it is pertinent here, as it provided the model according to which the British colonies such as Trinidad were socially structured.

31. Koningsbruggen (1997: 117).

32. Puri (1999: 17).

33. Constance notes that "the 1960 census revealed that local whites received on average $500 per month in salary. For Africans it was a mere $104 and even less for Indians—a paltry $77" (1996: 12). The author indicates that "among the business elite of 1970 whites and French Creoles made up 87%, Indians 9% and Africans 4%," and in the same year, "of the people who were able to obtain employment without education beyond O Level, 71% were white and 28% were 'off white' " (1996: 11, 13).

34. Liverpool (1993: 185).

35. Gordon Rohlehr, quoted in Liverpool (1993: 186).

36. For an elaboration of this notion, see Pratt (1992).

37. Rohlehr (1990: 6).

38. George Washington Cable, "The Dance in Place Congo," published originally in 1886 and reproduced in Rohlehr (1990: 12).

39. Andrew Pearse, cited in Rohlehr (1990: 14).

40. Errol Hill, quoted in Liverpool (1993: 204).

41. Liverpool (1993: 204).

42. For an elaboration of the theories of the origin of calypso, see Rohlehr (1990: 386–91).

43. Who sang the first calypso entirely in English remains a controversial affair. See Rohlehr on this issue (1990: 59).

44. Rohlehr (1990: 213) indicates the "sans humanité," or oratorical, period to be between 1900 and 1920. For further information on this form of calypso, see Rohlehr (1990: 57–68), Liverpool (1993: 490–92, 508–9), and Cowley (1996: 138).

45. Trinidadian calypsonians and arrangers rarely refer to minor keys alone; they usually refer to songs as being written in "re, mi, or la minor." Given the sparse documentation on the subject, it can only be inferred that, as many calypsonians in the early twentieth century composed lyrics over a number of well-known melodies and sang them in the same key, tunes with particular melodic contours and chord progressions became dubbed songs in "re," "mi," or "la" minor, regardless of whether the song was performed in that key.

46. Rohlehr (1990: 61–62)

47. Liverpool (1993: 492).

48. Rohlehr (1990: 57).

49. Roaring Lion, interview in 1973 with Hollis Liverpool (Liverpool 1993: 501).

50. Liverpool (1993: 430, 448).

51. Liverpool (1993: 490).

52. Rohlehr (1990: 73–74).

53. Cowley (1996: 47, 62) and Rohlehr (1990: 38, 41).

54. Liverpool (1993: 432–33). Rohlehr (1990: 49–50) adds that in the Carnival rehearsal sessions in the yards, the music was supplied by "guitars, quatros, shac shacs, veeras and two short pieces of bamboo which they strike one against the other. Occasionally a stray violinist [was] seen among them." For further information on the subject, see also Cowley (1996: 180).

55. Cowley (1996: 124). On the same subject, see also Liverpool (1993: 479).

56. See the photograph of the Trinidad Banjo, Mandodine and Guitar Orchestra published in London in 1912 in Cowley (1996: 181).

57. Cowley (1996: 124).

58. From Liverpool on minstrel music (1993: 358–59, 475).

59. See D. Hill (1993: 141) and Rohlehr (1990: 100).

60. Michael Anthony (1989: 36). In referring to jazz playing in the 1922 Carnival in Trinidad, Anthony does not specify whether he is speaking about ragtime or New Orleans jazz. More research is needed to elucidate this question.

61. Anthony (1989: 46).

62. Jazz bands were not exclusively composed of black musicians. A Chinese jazz band led by A. Codallo won the Carnival jazz band competitions in 1927 and for many consecutive years thereafter (Anthony 1989: 64, 84).

63. Frankie Francis, interview with the author, Port of Spain, 19 October 1999.

64. Anthony (1989: 207). Even though Charleston was inaugurated in the United States circa 1923, the dance may have become popular in Trinidad only years later. As is the case in other islands, documentation on dance trends in Trinidad remains scarce. I thank Richard Crawford for helping me situate the emergence of Charleston.

65. Some of Nurse's arrangements can be heard on the CD *London Is the Place for Me: Trinidad Calypso in London, 1950–1956* (Honest Jones Records HJR CD2).

66. D. Hill (1993: 117). As Rohlehr (1990: 147) further indicated, "Between 1912 and 1934, American recording companies fostered the emergence of Trinidad's music primarily as an aspect of Latin American music. This is why Belasco almost indiscriminately recorded calypsos and folksongs as paseos. . . . If 'paseo' was the most acceptable trading title, then it made good sense to call most songs paseos. In the fifties, for similar reasons, Jamaican singers started calling their mentos 'calypsos,' while today, a wide variety of song-types is termed 'soca,' the current trading-name."

67. D. Hill (1993: 120).

68. D. Hill (1993).

69. D. Hill (1993: 141). As Hill explains in relation to New York as a key example, recorded vocal calypsos from the 1930s onward circulated in at least three distinct audiences: "West Indians in New York, Trinidadians at home, and non–West Indians, who by the late 1930s were mostly middle-class whites" (D. Hill 1993: 141).

70. Humphrey Regis names this phenomenon "cultural imperialism by reexportation" (1988). He uses this expression to highlight how, for example, local musicians from former colonies are given more recognition locally *after* they perform in countries such as the United States or England. This power of granting cultural validation that countries like the United States or England have had over many former colonies cannot be accounted for solely by the potentially huge socioeconomic markets they represent. In Regis's view, this power has more to do with the political power and, more precisely, with the "imperial power" these countries have deployed over the past centuries and the ways in which they continue to exercise their influence over—in our case—the aesthetic values of various musical practices in countries with which they have had historical ties. In the 1920s and 1930s, this "cultural imperialism by reexportation" worked locally in favor of calypso.

71. D. Hill (1993: 185).

72. Rohlehr (1990: 147).

73. *Trinidad Guardian,* 2 February 1937, quoted in D. Hill (1993: 130).

74. Several soca songs, including Lord Kitchener's "Sugar Boum" in 1978, had such an impact that several arrangers began mixing some of their musical elements in so-called traditional calypsos. For example, in the early 1980s, Superblue composed "Ethel" (1981) and "Rebecca" (1983) in the calypso style—together with a story line and verse-chorus form—with a soca rhythmic accompaniment.

75. Anthony (1989: 88).

76. Rohlehr (1990: 214).

77. Liverpool (1993: 493).

78. Liverpool (1993: 498).

79. Liverpool (1993: 498).

80. Rohlehr (1990: 308).

81. Liverpool (1993: 502); and D. Hill (1993: 84).

82. Rohlehr (1990: 459).

83. Rohlehr (1990: 357).

84. Rohlehr (1990: 124).

Chapter 2: Governing the Conduct of Carnival and Calypso

1. The term "African" refers exclusively to persons born in Africa.

2. For a critical elaboration of "traditions," see R. Williams (1977: 115—20).

3. While I use the term "problem-space" slightly differently from the way David Scott (1999) uses it, my analysis is indebted to his generative formulation of this term. I use the term to direct attention to the specific targets that have been imagined as crucial to "improving" the current situation and the distinctive technologies that have been deployed to manage and regulate them.

4. I want to clarify my use of the terms "foresound" and "Creole." I use the term "foresound" to highlight the audible entanglements, including the sonic dimensions of an analysis. The term "Creole" embodies a complex genealogy. In the late nineteenth century, it referred to persons born in Trinidad of European and/or of African descent. It also referred to those who may have had both European and African ancestors but regarded themselves or were perceived by others as white. To this day, "Afro-Creole," as Briget Brereton explains, "is used to describe cultural practices which fused African and European elements, and were kept up by black Creoles in Trinidad" ([1979] 2002: 3).

5. L. M. Fraser, quoted in Liverpool (1993: 296).

6. For further information on the white elite's parody of the slaves during Carnival, see Liverpool (1993: 296–97).

7. Liverpool (1993: 303).

8. Koningsbruggen (1997: 16).

9. For an elaboration of how music is a contested form of knowledge that brings forward issues of not only aesthetics, but also ethics and politics, see Paul Gilroy's "'Jewels Brought from Bondage': Black Music and the Politics of Authenticity," in Gilroy (1993a), Gilroy (1993b), Frith (1996a), Veit Erlmann's "Symbols of Inclusion and Exclusion: Nationalism, Colonial Consciousness, and the 'Great Hymn,'" in Erlmann (1999), and Radano (2003).

10. Peter Manuel (2000b: 5).

11. Jacob Elder, cited in Liverpool (1993: 367).

12. Cowley (1996: 52–53, 57).

13. Liverpool (1993: 404).

14. Rohlehr (1990: 27).

15. Balliger (2000: 44).

16. Those middle-class persons called "the jacketmen" acted as patrons to calypsonians and stickfighters and often had liaisons with the barracks women. The term "jacketmen" stems from the association of their clothing with that of the upper class. See Brereton ([1979] 2002: 163).

17. *Port of Spain Gazette,* 24 January 1890, quoted in Anthony (1989: 11–12).

18. See Corrigan and Sayer (1985) for an elaboration of how morality has been constitutive of English state formation.

19. Brereton ([1979] 2002: ix). For further information on the jamet Carnival, see Franco (2000), DeCosmo (2000), and Barnes (2000).

20. Cowley (1996: 73).

21. Liverpool (1993: 369).

22. Liverpool (1993: 370–71, 429).

23. Cowley (1996: 75). For an elaboration of the subject, see also Brereton ([1979] 2002: 167) and Trotman (1986).

24. Rohlehr (1990: 213). I thank Junior Telfer for his insights on the subject and for reminding me that Lord Kitchener began his singing career as a chantwèl for work gangs (interview with the author, Cascade, Trinidad, 4 January 2005).

25. Rohlehr (1990: 51).

26. Liverpool (1993: 292).

27. Rohlehr (1990: 55–56). French Creole, now considered by linguists a language of its own, contrasts greatly with French through its grammar and lack of gender. Furthermore, while many French Creole words derive from French, others come from African languages. For an elaboration of the subject, see Prudent (1989).

28. Rohlehr (1990: 43).

29. Rohlehr (1990: 51).

30. Liverpool (1993: 431, 479), Rohlehr (1990), Anthony (1989).

31. Liverpool (1993: 441).

32. Quoted by Rohlehr (1990: 89).

33. Jacob Elder, cited in Rohlehr (1990: 57–58). The individuals from the middle and upper class who attempted to "improve" Carnival included those with different ethnic and racial backgrounds, such as Patrick Jones, known as "Chinee Patrick," who was half African, half Chinese. On this subject, see Rohlehr (1990: 66) and Liverpool (1993: 469).

34. Liverpool (1993: 445).

35. Rohlehr (1990: 96).

36. Rohlehr (1990: 100–101).

37. Liverpool (1993: 485), Rohlehr (1990: 295). There were several Carnival Improvement Committees before, dating as far back as 1927. For further information, see D. Hill (1993: 76).

38. Rohlehr (1990: 328).

39. See Anthony (1989: 350).

40. On Marcus Garvey's political views, activities, and projects, see Campbell (1987) and Lewis (1987).

41. Rohlehr (1990: 278).

42. Rohlehr (1990: 108, also 284).

43. Rohlehr (1990: 284).

44. Liverpool (1993: 564).

45. In 1969, the National Folkore Archive was created to document the cultural practices of the nation. For further elaboration of the subject, see Wallis and Malm (1984: 227).

46. From 1967 onward, the Prime Minister Best Village competitions, including all categories of artistic expression (handicraft, steel drum, literature, calypso, dance, "drummology," and so on), were organized in each village throughout the country to encourage amateurs from all ethnic groups to develop their artistic talents and promote their cultural heritage. The term "drummology" was created at the height of the Best Village competitions in the late 1970s and early 1980s in order to include in this category not only drumming, but also chanting and other accompanying performing activities. I thank Joyce

Wongsang, one of the main administrators of the Best Village competitions from its very beginning, for sharing this information with me (interview with the author, Port of Spain, 5 January 2001). The Best Village competitions, initially called Better Village Program and created in 1963 under Prime Minister Eric Williams, were inspired by the Unemployment Relief Program (URP), initiated in 1957 to stop the violence in East Port of Spain. For further information on the various initiatives taken during this period to deal with poverty, see Rhoda Reddock's groundbreaking study *Women, Labor, and Politics in Trinidad and Tobago* (1994b). I am grateful to Ann Lee for bringing this clarification to my attention.

47. Koningsbruggen (1997: 2).

48. Koningsbruggen (1997: 254).

49. L. Regis (1999: 16). Like samba in Brazil, calypso in Trinidad was given pride of place in the " 'invention,' dissemination, and international projection of national culture" (Dunn 2001: 6). For an elaboration of the subject, see Dunn (2001); on tango, see J. Taylor (1998); and on merengue, see Austerlitz (1997).

50. James (1977: 199).

51. Quoted in Holder (2001: 142).

52. Quoted in Holder (2001: 145).

53. Rohlehr (1990), Best (1995), Liverpool (1993), L. Regis (1999). It is telling that, as in Trinidad, most national calypso competitions held in the other English-speaking islands are state sponsored.

54. According to Rohlehr, the Butler riots of 1937 "led to a reappraisal of Black/White relations" and a renewed interest in seeking independence (1990: 248, 386).

55. Quoted in Rohlehr (1990: 386).

56. See, for example, Charles and Atilla the Hun (1943), Patterson and Belasco (1943), and Belasco and Whipper (1944).

57. See, for example, Espinet and Pitts (1944) and C. Jones (1947).

58. See Pearse (1956).

59. Hicks (1940), Gorman (1945).

60. For lyrics, see Elder (1966b), Carr (1975), and R. L. Austin (1976). On the origin of the genre, see Crowley (1959) and E. Hill (1967).

61. Elder (1966a).

62. For an elaboration of the subject, see Elder (1988), Rohlehr (1970, 1975), R. L. Austin (1976), Liverpool (1986), Quevedo (1983), E. Hill (1976), Warner (1982), and Warner-Lewis (1984, 1986).

63. See Rohlehr (1972) and Roach (1972).

64. Quoted in Puri (2003b: 254).

65. In this regard, the Mighty Sparrow represents an interesting case. Grenadian born, he is nevertheless hailed as the king of Trinidad calypso. To understand how as someone born abroad he could hold such a title, we need to situate the historical conditions in which he earned it. The Mighty Sparrow won the calypso competition in 1956, the same year that witnessed the formation and election of a new party, the PNM, as the first party government in Trinidad and Tobago. During the transition period from 1956 to 1962, when the country became an independent nation, the Mighty Sparrow not only won several competitions, but also vocally gave his support to—and arguably helped other people rally behind—the new political party in power. It thus could be concluded that before the calypso competitions were nationalized, the Mighty Sparrow had acquired such a prominent position that his dismissal from calypso competitions after 1962 on account of his being foreign born would have been unthinkable.

66. Calypso Rose, interview with the author, Port of Spain, 14 January 2005. This regulation endorsed C. L. R. James's view in his lecture "The Artist in the Caribbean": "Local men [*sic*] playing for the local people. Every calypsonian who stays abroad too long loses the calypso's distinctive quality. . . . It is inconceivable to me that a national artistic tradition, on which I lay so much stress as an environment in which the artist must begin, it is inconceivable to me that this can be established by writers and artists, however gifted, working for what is essentially a foreign audience. I think I could prove that already their work is adversely affected by it. . . . I cannot believe that the last resources of West Indian artistic talent can be reached under these conditions" (James 1977: 188–89). This rule, however, is no longer in effect for other calypso-related competitions created in the 1990s, such as the Soca Monarch competitions. These changes will be addressed at greater length in part 2.

67. Quoted in Holder (2001: 149–50). Ironically, the name "Black Stalin" itself deploys a series of entanglements not only at the geographic, but also at the historical and political levels by referring to Stalin, the towering political figure in the Russian communist movement of the 1930s.

68. Malkki (1992: 31–33). Such a construction of the calypso musical scene resembles Derek Walcott's description of the native. In his Nobel Prize acceptance address in 1992, for instance, Walcott describes the opposition between the traveler and the native as follows: "Caribbean culture['s] . . . proportions are not to be measured by the traveler or the exile, but by its own citizenry and architecture" (Walcott 1993: 23). I was reminded of the distinction Walcott makes between the traveler and the native—thanks to Puri's incisive analysis of his Nobel Prize acceptance address. For Walcott, the exile cannot be viewed as a citizen of his or her native land and thus cannot claim any national rights. His statement that "the traveler cannot love, since love is stasis and travel is motion" makes it virtually impossible for anyone to develop a sense of belonging in more than one "land." By adding that "if he returns to what he loved in a landscape and stays there, he is no longer a traveler but in stasis and concentration, the lover of that particular part of earth, a native" (1993: 24), Walcott not only invests the local with a static quality, but also obscures any trace of the institutional hierarchies of power that characterize its history. As Puri remarks, by resorting to a highly poeticized version of the native with connotations of "love, stasis, and rootedness in the earth" (Puri 1999: 22), his strategy aimed at challenging "foreign domination" runs the dangerous risk of displacing the issue of inequality among natives and of protecting the status quo.

69. I owe the constructions of these disavowals to Donald Moore's insights.

70. Hesse (2000: 2).

71. L. Regis (1999: 11).

72. Puri (1999: 25).

73. Puri (1999: 25).

74. See Brereton ([1979] 2002) and Reddock (1994a).

75. In her (1994) article, Alexander discusses the politics of law, sexuality, and postcoloniality in Trinidad and Tobago and the Bahamas.

76. As Ramnarine reports, "Spottswood and Cowley's 'Discography of East Indian recordings from the English-speaking West Indies' (1996) indicates that there were very few recordings made under this category of musical performance during 1915–1939 by the main recording companies, Bluebird, Decca and Victor. During my field research, I found no commercially available recordings made before the late 1950s (although my search for such recordings was not extensive)" (2001: 17). Not until Alan Lomax's 1962 recordings could she find examples of Indo-Trinidadian musical performances. Even though as early as 1947 Moean Mohammed played an important role in featuring Indo-Caribbean music

Notes to Pages 52–54

through organized tours and radio broadcasts, it was only by the 1960s that, again thanks to the efforts of Sham and Moean Mohammed, more attention was given to Indo-Trinidadian music, with the televised talent-spotting competition Mastana Bahar (Ramnarine 2001: 71). Studies of Indo-Trinidadian music began to appear only in the late 1970s and until the 1980s remained sporadic. A rare collection of Indian folk songs in Trinidad was published by M. Samlal in 1972. The following year, a local publication focused on Dhrupad singing in the country (Bissoondialsingh 1973). Ten years later, a pioneering study documented Mastana Bahar and Indian culture in Trinidad (S. Mohammed 1982). Only in the 1990s, particularly with the celebration of the 150th anniversary of Indian arrival in Trinidad, did a steady flow of publications begin to emerge. While some authors (e.g., Myers 1993, 1998; Desroches 1996; and Diethrich 2004) undertook important research into Indian music, Ramnarine notes that "there is no general history of Indian Caribbean music, even though this music offers an interesting case study into the workings of musical traditions in diasporic contexts" (2001: 16). Most studies instead focus on particular musical genres, notably chutney (Ramaya 1990; Constance 1991; Ribeiro 1992; Manuel 1998; and Ramanarine 1996, 2001) and tan singing (Manuel 2000a, 2000b). One study focuses on the development of Indian classical music in general (Maharaj 1994), while another addresses the issue of identity and images of India in Indo-Trinidadian musical practices (Manuel 1997–98). One article concerns modern trends in Indo-Trinidadian music (Patasar 1995).

77. "Local whites" is a Trinidadian expression to refer to whites born in Trinidad. On the Chinese migrants, see Look Lai (1998b). In 2000, Robin Balliger wrote one of the first in-depth studies addressing the musical practices of various groups in Trinidad. For further information, see her doctoral dissertation (Balliger 2000).

78. For studies on the "Spanish" in relation to issues of race and ethnicity, see Brereton ([1979] 2002, 1981) and Khan (1993). On parang, see Fulton (1993). As in the case of Indo-Trinidadian musics, parang originally entered the media via live broadcasts from competitions around that time. It also began to be heard in radio commercials made for the Christmas season (Malm and Wallis 1992: 68).

79. Chiang-Kai-Shiek, who in the late 1940s and 1950s was among the earliest Chinese calypsonians, took the name of a famous revolutionary leader in China. Later on, apart from Crazy (Edwin Ayoung), three other Chinese calypsonians became well-known figures in the calypso scene: Rex East (other name not known), Rex West (Richard Chen), and Dr. Soca (Dr. Kong-Shiek Achong Low). I thank Michael Germain for sharing this information with me.

80. Koningsbruggen (1997: 229–30).

81. This dance movement, called "wine," has been the object of much debate in scholarly writings in relation to gender, aesthetic, and ethical issues. For further information on the subject, see Barnes (2000); Cooper (1993), in particular chapter 8, "Slackness Hiding from Culture: Erotic in the Dancehall," 136–73; Dikobe (2003); Burton (1997); Franco (2000); and Miller (1991, [1994] 1997).

82. I thank Black Stalin for sharing this information with me (interview, Cascade, Trinidad, 13 January 2005).

83. Sponsored by the state, calypso competitions granted calypso the stamp of official national culture and, concomitantly, gave it pride of place in official events and special broadcasts during Carnival on national radio and television early in the history of independent Trinidad. Michael Anthony reports that in 1963, the year after independence, Trinidad and Tobago Television made its first live transmissions of Carnival (Anthony 1989: 322–23).

84. Malm and Wallis (1992: 65).

85. See Malm and Wallis (1992: 65–83) for further information on the subject.

86. Balliger (2000: 65–66).

87. In 1970 and 1971, a series of weekly half-hour programs broadcast on state-owned radio focused on the history of calypso. In 1973, another weekly series of twenty-six radio programs with Gordon Rohlehr documented calypso history from the forties to the seventies; in 1975, he did yet another series centered in particular on the treatment of women in calypso. However, such programs were sporadic.

88. Balliger (2000: 66).

89. Koningsbruggen (1997: 239).

90. Wallis and Malm (1984: 262–63).

91. Please see and hear Lord Superior's "Cultural Assassination" (1980).

92. Malm and Wallis (1992: 67).

93. Quoted in Wallis and Malm (1984: 236).

94. Wallis and Malm (1984: 237). Many records by local calypsonians were pressed in the United States or Canada and then shipped to Trinidad.

95. Koningsbruggen (1997: 18).

96. Koningsbruggen (1997: 19).

97. Andrew Carr, cited in Liverpool (1993: 366).

98. Quoted in Koningsbruggen (1997: 19).

99. Shannon Dudley defines the term "picong" as staged confrontations between calypsonians in song duels. He adds, "The term *picong* also refers more broadly to derision and insults, including those traded between calypsonians, whether or not they share the same stage" (2004: 25). John Cowley uses the term "fatigue" as a synonym for "picong" (1996: 175).

100. Rohlehr (1990: 40).

101. Koningsbruggen (1997: 229).

102. Rohlehr (1990: 215).

103. Rohlehr (1990: 215).

104. Rohlehr gives the example of a calypso drama of 1934 that took a Shouter's meeting as its object of ridicule (1990: 138).

105. Rohlehr (1990: 125).

106. Liverpool (1993: 431).

107. See Blake (1995), Stuempfle (1995), and Dudley (1997, in press).

108. According to Ramnarine (2001: 15), several other influences contributed to steelband soundings: "Wood, referring to Simmonds's (1959) book on the steel pan, for example, suggested that it was probably through the drumming, the ritual function of the chamar caste that 'the drum-beats of India were drawn into the mainstream of Trinidad music. Their techniques are part of the inheritance of the steel bands' (Woods 1968: 144). In a study of the steelband, Stuempfle (1995: 219) similarly identifies several musical influences, including a tassa contribution: 'The steelband is essentially a culmination of a long process of musical creolization, a process in which diverse musical traditions have been locally re-created. Among the main sources of steelband music are Afro-Trinidadian tamboo bamboo, metallic percussion, and Orisha drumming; the calypso tradition of vocals and string-band accompaniments, which itself is a Creole synthesis of African, French, Spanish, and British musical elements; Indo-Trinidadian tassa drumming; European marching band and classical traditions; Afro/Latin dance rhythms and tunes; and North American popular songs and jazz.'"

109. Blake (1995: 272).

110. See Stuempfle (1995: 159–64).

111. Constance (1996: 13).

112. In his account of the politics of the seventies, Constance stresses the importance of using the word "black" instead of Negro or African since "black" was also used to include East Indians. The cooperation of Afro-Trinidadians and Indo-Trinidadians was indeed seen as critical to the success of liberation. This was similar to the situation in England described by Nabeel Zuberi, in which "[a] political rather than biological notion of 'black' emerged in the late 1960s and 1970s as a response to the rise of popular racism" (2001: 186). In the same way, Lisa Lowe describes similar coalitions in the United States during the same period: "The social movement of the 1960s and 1970s brought together Asian American struggles with those of African Americans, Native Americans, and Chicano-Latinos in a concerted demand for racial equality and social justice" (Lowe 1996: 22–23). However, as will be shown in later chapters, the notion of "political blackness" in Trinidad rooted in the late 1960s was short lived, as Indians not long after argued for their own spaces (Balliger 2000: 51). What remained central among the black political leaders and social activists during the seventies was that black people had to develop new ways of thinking about themselves. Then and only then, it was believed, could black people make choices suited to their unique world situation, culture, and history.

113. While the NJAC's organized competitions were initially perceived as being Afro-centric, they grew in stature to be embraced by everyone by the early 1980s.

114. L. Regis (1999: 86).

115. Foucault ([1978] 1990: 103).

116. I use the term "soundings" here to emphasize the resonances sounds produce—the ongoing physical and emotional reverberations sounds produce.

Chapter 3: Power, Practice, and Competitions

1. For a related argument, see Butler (1998).

2. I thank Michael "Protector" Legerton, the current president of TUCO, for sharing this information with me in an interview, Port of Spain, 14 January 2005.

3. For the use of other technologies deployed to govern sound, see Gage Averill's insightful study *A Day for the Hunter, a Day for the Prey: Popular Music and Power in Haiti* (1997).

4. Wald (2002). For an elaboration of the critical influences of calypso competitions, see Guilbault (2005).

5. Rose (1979: 59). This approach follows what Foucault has termed "genealogy," or the history of the present ([1971] 1977). Inspired by Nikolas Rose's use of such an approach (1979: 12), my aim is to trace calypso competitions' past in Trinidad, casting light on certain issues posed by the current dynamics of calypso while also, in part 2 of the book, examining how and under what conditions the calypso music scene since the 1990s has transformed its relationship to some of calypso competitions' historical sediments.

6. Rohlehr (1990: 74).

7. Rohlehr (1990: 74).

8. Cowley (1996: 136–37).

9. D. Hill (1993: 65).

10. Cowley (1996: 137).

11. Rohlehr (1990: 112).

12. It is noteworthy that, whereas in the 1920s such a lineup usually included five or six singers, in the 1990s it regularly featured as many as twenty, and at times up to twenty-eight singers in one evening.

13. Rohlehr (2001: 7).

14. Unknown source, quoted by Rohlehr (1990: 328).

15. Rohlehr (1990: 328).

16. Rohlehr (1990: 402).

17. In 1949, for example, the *Guardian* Carnival Committee (headed by the daily newspaper the *Guardian,* but otherwise a committee formed along the same lines as the Carnival Improvement Committee) brought onstage steelbands in competition, singing groups, and the police band, as well as a dance company to complement the Carnival Queen show, and leading calypsonians to participate in the calypso competition (Rohlehr 1990: 407).

18. In 1998, for the first time in Trinidad, the major Carnival organizations (steelbands, calypsonians, mas bands) were allowed to be in charge of their own competitions for reasons that are discussed in chapter 8. In most other English Caribbean islands, however, most national competitions during Carnival are still held under the aegis of the state.

19. Rohlehr (2001: 20).

20. Chouthi (2000).

21. Rohlehr (2001: 24).

22. Rose (1999: 10).

23. The list of criteria, which comes from Alvin Daniell's "De Judges Tief" (1992), remained essentially the same up to 1998. A point of clarification: rendition has to do with vocal qualities and the clear enunciation of words. Baron, for example, is well known for making his lyrics clearly audible. Presentation, in contrast, has to do with the ways in which the artists present themselves onstage, the outfits they wear, the ease with which they move, and the props they use during their performances. I thank Rhoda Reddock for clarifying these two terms for me.

24. Blood (1998; my emphasis).

25. This competition has been held only one other year, in 1985. The Mighty Sparrow won both competitions (Alvin Daniell, interview with the author, Port of Spain, 15 September 1998).

26. Jacob (1988: 27; my emphasis).

27. In his comprehensive chapter "Calypso Reinvents Itself," Rohlehr describes "Rose" as a composition whose story line is interrupted by repeated refrains within the stanza (2004a: 407).

28. R. Williams (1977: 115).

29. In Lovelace's words, "To claim the aesthetic you had to deal with the political" (1998: 56).

30. Koningsbruggen (1997: 244).

31. Koningsbruggen (1997: 244–52).

32. Rohlehr (2001: 10–11).

33. Rohlehr (1975: 84).

34. The significance of "wining" for both male and female performers is addressed at length in chapters 4, 6, and 7.

35. L. Regis (1986: 26).

36. As mentioned in chapter 2, the term "dougla" is a Trinidadian term referring to the mix between Afro-Caribbeans and Indo-Caribbeans and of their children.

37. Today, Road March competitions can be won either by calypso or any of its musical offshoots—soca, chutney soca, or ragga soca.

38. Koningsbruggen (1997: 244–45).

39. This was most clearly illustrated, for example, when Gypsy—a Trinidadian of African descent who that year had joined the UNC Party, formed primarily of Trinidadians of East Indian descent—appeared onstage for the semifinals at Skinner Park and faced a gross toilet paper reception; during the same event, however, the stout PNM supporter Sugar Aloes was embraced by the newly elected prime minister, who was the leader of the PNM. As Rickey Singh writes, "It is not that such PNMites are unaware that there are people of ethnicities in both the UNC and their own party. Rather, they seem to find it too difficult, too uncomfortable to appreciate a 'black' calypsonian, so popular and talented, being identified with the UNC as a parliamentarian and coming out to do what he probably likes best—sing and entertain for the Carnival" (Singh 2002). In this case, as a group of hecklers fiercely equated calypso and calypsonians with black politics and thus rejected Gypsy's performance as a calypsonian after he showed his allegiance to the UNC, jury members were pressured not to include Gypsy as a contestant in the final. In the end, they did not include him.

40. Panorama is the annual steelband competition held during Carnival time. For further information on the subject, see Stuemple (1995) and Dudley (2002, 2003, and 2004).

41. The Soca Monarch competitions will be discussed in part 2 of the book.

42. This argument was inspired by Judith Butler's discussion, "Sovereign Performatives," in *Excitable Speech* (1997: 94).

43. The program was suspended in 2000, after the television station TT&T underwent a review of all its programming and its financial resources.

44. There are sometimes exceptions to this rule. On a few occasions, some winners have not been invited to take part in tours because the focus of their lyrics has been deemed too parochial to be understood or not pertinent outside Trinidad. At other times, some winners have not performed much outside Trinidad because their day jobs did not permit them to take extended leave.

45. With the emergence of new local radio and television stations since around 2003, more local music is regularly heard. The new programming includes older winning calypso titles along with more recent releases.

46. H. Hoetink, quoted in Koningsbruggen (1997: 105). For an elaboration of the Calypso Queen contest, see Koningsbruggen (1997: 103–8), Rohlehr (1990), and Liverpool (1993).

47. Rohlehr (1990: 331).

48. Rohlehr (1990: 433) and Liverpool (1993: 487).

49. Rohlehr (1990: 456).

50. In September 1998, the exchange rate was approximately TT 6.2 = US $1. The details of the competition prizes are from Assang (1998).

51. The only exception to this rule was on St. Joseph's Day, during which calypso could be sung. As Father Christian Perrera explained, St. Joseph's Day is a festive day in the Catholic calendar in recognition of St. Joseph as the universal patron of the church and the guardian of Jesus Christ's body. As a result, the usual rules and observances were lifted on that exceptional day during the Lent season (in personal interview, 4 January 2001). I thank Monty Dolly for alerting me about this exception.

52. Henry and Nurse (1996: 15).

53. Over the past fifteen years, the greater ease of mass communication has made it possible for artists to travel more often to perform at special fetes organized by several Caribbean diasporic populations around the world.

54. For example, while Trinidad celebrates its Carnival just before the Lent season, usually in February or March, Jamaica celebrates its own Carnival in April, St. Vincent in June, and Antigua and Barbados at the beginning of August. And with increasing Carib-

bean population groups in diaspora, Toronto also celebrates its Carnival at the beginning of August, Notting Hill in London in late August, New York in September, and Miami in October, to name only the best known.

55. The figures quoted for the dancehall artists represent the all-inclusive price that is usually paid to cover the performance fee of the given artist and whomever he or she chooses to bring along and the local expenses. The point is that, even after taking into consideration the traveling expenses of those artists who leave Jamaica to perform in Trinidad, dancehall artists earn more money from their performances than their calypsonian counterparts.

56. The few notable exceptions would be in the case of the Mighty Sparrow, who is considered "sure value" on the market, or some of the soca bands, such as Xtatik, from Trinidad, Krosfyah, from Barbados, and Burning Flames, from Antigua, who have on some occasions sold as many as fifty thousand copies of a given recording (Edwin Yearwood, interview with the author, Bridgetown, Barbados, 6 August 1997; and Toriano "Onyan" Edwards, former member of Burning Flames, from Antigua, interview with the author, St. John's, Antigua, 24 July 1997).

57. Quoted in Fox (1986: 292).

58. For further information on *bachata*, see Pacini's informative study *Bachata: A Social History of a Dominican Popular Music* (1995).

59. In terms of the music industry, "the formal economy of the country" refers here, for example, to the officially registered and regulated mass media and retail outlets.

60. It should be stressed that "calypsonians" here refers only to artists of so-called traditional calypso. As will be discussed in part 2, artists of calypso musical offshoots such as soca function under slightly different rules.

Chapter 4: Calypsonians Onstage

1. James (1977: 185).

2. The debates about "experience" as an analytic category have been numerous. Like Ronald Radano, I employ it "with qualification" (Radano 2003: 288). Drawing on the writings of Joan W. Scott (1991), Eleni Varikas (1995), and Craig Ireland (2002), I write about "experience" here as being in need of explanation—not as an unmediated practice, but rather as the product of a particular conjuncture involving socioeconomic and political forces as much as specific material conditions. In Foucault's wording, I understand experience "as the correlation between fields of knowledge, types of normativity, and forms of subjectivity in a particular culture" (Foucault [1984] 1986: 4). My goal in referring to "experience" is thus to historicize it in relation to its conditions of emergence.

3. M. J. Alexander (1994).

4. I use the expression "body politics" to emphasize how politics of exclusion and of inclusion dealing with issues of citizenship and national culture have been elaborated and performed through the construction of racialized and socially gendered bodies. For critical studies on the subject, see Butler's book by the telling title *Bodies That Matter* (1993) and M. Jacqui Alexander's article "Not Just (Any) Body Can Be a Citizen: The Politics of Law, Sexuality and Postcoloniality in Trinidad and Tobago and the Bahamas" (1994); *Confronting Power, Theorizing Gender,* edited by Eudine Barriteau (2003); and *Interrogating Caribbean Masculinities: Theoretical and Empirical Analyses,* edited by Rhoda Reddock (2004). For studies focusing on the issues of race and ethnicity in national formation, see Premdas (2002), Allahar (2003), Ramdin (2000), Premdas (1993), and *Trinidad Ethnicity,* edited by Kevin A. Yelvington (1993).

5. Premdas (2002) describes at length the prejudices and stereotypes about the "other" informing both African and East Indian communities. "To the African," writes Premdas,

"the Indian is not to be trusted. Selfish, the Indian is seen to be overly preoccupied with the pursuit of business goals and family interests in a clannish way that undermines public and community participation and obligations"; "to the Indian, the African is lazy, undisciplined, brutal, spendthrift, happy-go-lucky, promiscuous and thieving" (2002: 181–82). For a literary evocation of how the Chinese figure in the national imaginary of Trinidad, see Chen (1988). See also Look Lai (1998a) for one of the first comprehensive book-length studies of the Chinese histories in the Caribbean and A. Wilson (2004) for detailed studies of the experiences of the Chinese in various parts of the region.

6. The issues of race and ethnicity have been addressed extensively in the literature on Trinidad. Some of the major works on these issues include Premdas (2000), Yelvington (1993), and Smith ([1984] 1990).

7. Steedman ([1986] 1994: 12).

8. To be the son of a Grenadian father does not make Stalin stand apart from other Trinidadian calypsonians. Few may have a parent born on another island, but the majority of interviewees had some family connections in various parts of the region. For further information on immigrants' experiences, see Rohlehr's interview with Puri (Puri 2003b). See also Rohlehr (1990), Quevedo (1983), and D. Hill (1993).

9. Black Stalin, interview with the author, Port of Spain, 12 July 1994. In the remainder of this section, I use quotations without references whenever the text stems from that interview unless otherwise indicated. I use the same practice for the primary people interviewed in the other sections.

10. For more information on the subject, see Maureen Warner-Lewis's illuminating work on the influences of Shango terms and melodies and of the Baptist Church on calypso, in particular, *Trinidad Yoruba: From Mother Tongue to Memory* ([1996] 1997). See also Frances Henry's comprehensive study *Reclaiming African Religions in Trinidad* (2003).

11. I placed the expression "African art of storytelling" in quotation marks to signal that, in Trinidad, storytelling is constructed as the hallmark of African art, even though storytelling is also practiced in many other parts of the world. In contrast, even though the "history and culture of Africa" is commonly referred to in the singular in daily speech, most interviewees at one point or another acknowledge the diversity and difference among various African cultures and their histories.

12. Ballantyne (1998: 40).

13. From Rohlehr (2004a: 85).

14. L. Regis (1986: 4).

15. L. Regis (1986: 6).

16. There have been a few notable exceptions, such as in the late 1960s, when the Mighty Sparrow broke this unwritten law by recording one of Lord Kitchener's songs. As of 2001, however, traditional calypsonians rarely performed cover versions.

17. Please see and hear Black Stalin's "Burn Dem" (1991).

18. From Koningsbruggen (1997: 246).

19. Koningsbruggen (1997: 247).

20. Excerpt from the *Sun,* 7 March 1979.

21. In one interview with me, Stalin explained that in fact it is because he was known for his emphasis on unity that in 1992 he was asked to perform in Los Angeles soon after what is known as the "L.A. riots" or "the Rodney King uprising."

22. L. Regis (1986: 12).

23. In 2005, after witnessing a gradual decline of calypso tent audiences over the preceding few years, Stalin quit the calypso tent and began performing only as a guest artist during Carnival and the rest of the year.

24. L. Regis (1986: 67).

25. Black Stalin, interview with the author, Toronto, 5 June 1995.

26. Ibid.

27. Many calypsonians, calypso fans, and journalists in my interviews refer to calypsonians as griots. This notion that calypso derives from "a West African musical form of telling the stories of life in song," as Opoku Ware simply posits (1997: 1), has been reinforced by countless academic efforts to document such a connection. Historian Hollis Liverpool referred to statistical returns of the Slave Registration Order of 1812 as evidence that most slaves in Trinidad came from the west coast of Africa (1993). Maureen Warner-Lewis in turn published several studies focusing on linguistic and musical connections between Trinidadian calypso and Nigerian musical practices (1984, 1986, [1996] 1997).

28. For an elaboration of Black Stalin's gender politics, see Dikobe (2003).

29. Calypso Rose, interview with the author, Port of Spain, 18 January 1997.

30. In his letter published in the *Trinidad Express* newspapers, 10 March 2005, Miguel Browne disputes the claim that Calypso Rose was the first calypsonian to hold the title of Calypso Monarch. Even though, in his account, she may have been the first woman to hold it, he reminds the readers that Chalkdust (Hollis Liverpool) was the first recipient of that title, in 1976. The reason for the change, he explains, had to do with the results of the Calypso King competitions of the previous year, 1975: "In that year designated 'International Women's Year' by the United Nations three females (Singing Francine, Calypso Rose and Singing Dianne) made it to the finals. Kitchener went on to win the competition by one point beating Singing Francine into second place, making her the first female to come closest to winning. Calypso Rose placed third. It was felt that a female was not given the nod over a male because the title was still 'Calypso King.' Hence the name-change in the following year, 1976." I am grateful to W. R. Holder for sharing this information with me.

31. Ottley (1992: 6).

32. Please see and hear Calypso Rose's "Come Leh We Jam" (1977).

33. Rohlehr (1975: 85).

34. Biographical accounts differ concerning the time during which she performed in tents. In Ottley (1992: 5), Rose indicated that she began singing in Kitchener's tent in 1964. In the interview I had with her, she reported beginning in 1963.

35. More specifically, her father belonged to the Coptic Baptist Church.

36. Quoted in Ottley (1992: 4).

37. Ottley (1992: 5).

38. Quoted in Dikobe (2003: 47).

39. Ottley (1992: 7).

40. Cadogan (n.d.); italics mine.

41. See, for example, Boyce Davies's illuminating study, "Woman Is a Nation: Women in Caribbean Oral Literature" (1990), in which she discusses the ways in which Rose's persona has often been construed.

42. Dikobe (2003: 46). It should be noted that the same tactic—accusations of homosexuality—is used to denigrate men.

43. Ottley (1992: 5).

44. From Boyce Davies (1990: 183).

45. Ottley (1992: 5).

46. As Marjorie Thorpe indicates in her introduction to Earl Lovelace's novel *The Wine of Astonishment,* the prohibition ordinance of 1917 was lifted only in 1951 (Thorpe 1982:

viii). For more information on religions practiced and banned at different moments in Trinidad's history, see Henry (2003).

47. I use the term "performativity" to stress the tangible effects produced by the reiteration of situated practices. For an elaboration of performativity, see J. L. Austin (1961), Butler (1993, 1997), Mahmood (2001), M. Joseph (2002), and Hollywood (2002).

48. As Sydney Mintz remarked, perceptions of color are usually not merely "a matter of observed phenotype but of observed phenotype taken together with many other factors" (cited in Kahn 1993: 181).

49. Denyse Plummer, interview with the author, Port of Spain, 7 August 1993.

50. See Dikobe's detailed analysis of that song (2003: 127–37).

51. Please see and hear Denyse Plummer's "La Trinity" (1991).

52. In 1991, Plummer sang a song called "Carnival Killer," which she portrayed by wearing an outfit reminiscent of those worn by masqueraders during Carnival Tuesday and created by one of the most celebrated mas designers from Trinidad and Tobago, Peter Minshall. See the plate featuring Denyse Plummer wearing this costume on her album entitled *Carnival Killer,* named after her hit song that year.

53. Ottley (1992: 85–86).

54. Dikobe (2003: 129).

55. Only in the eighties did it become public knowledge that the calypsonian known as the King of Calypso, the Mighty Sparrow, had hired Winsford "Joker" Devine to write many of his songs during the 1960s and 1970s. Most calypsonians until then hid the fact that they performed songs written by collaborators or composed with their help.

56. David Rudder started as a background vocalist in Kitchener's tent before entering the calypso scene as a soloist.

57. For further information on the creation of artistic personae and fame, see Grenier (2001) and De Cordova (1990).

58. Ottley (1992: 89).

59. Ottley (1992: 89).

60. See E. Williams (1993).

61. Crazy, interview with the author, Toronto, 2 August 1996.

62. From "Crazy: The Lovable Lunatic" (1988).

63. I thank Rhoda Reddock for bringing this aspect to my attention.

64. Both plays were based on children's stories. *Cinderama* was inspired by "Cinderella," and *Snow Cone and the Seven Dwens* by "Snow White and the Seven Dwarfs," made famous by Walt Disney's movie.

65. "Dust-Bin Cover" refers to the garbage receptacle in Trinidad. Around Carnival people would use dust-bin covers as percussion. Crazy sang about losing his dust-bin cover around Carnival. "A Message to Joffre Serrette" refers to the brigadier and first chief of the defense forces from independence to the late 1970s. In this song, Crazy complains that the country is in turmoil. He tells Serrette that he should take the army and take over the country. At the end of the song, Crazy pointed out to me, he used to say, "Don't worry, partner, I just finished smoking marijuana!"—as a means to protect himself from any legal pursuit or altercations with any of the patrons in the audience.

66. In Trinidad, the term "soucouyant" refers to the female folklore character that sucks the blood of her victims at night. One can prevent her from entering one's house by leaving a plate of rice or a bottle of salt, because she would have to count every grain before she comes in. An old woman living alone may be accused of being a soucouyant. I thank Rhoda Reddock for providing me with this information.

67. Please see and hear Crazy's "Nani Wine" (2004).

68. Khan (1993: 191).

69. Khan's reference to J. Alexander (1977) in Khan (1993: 189).

70. Crazy's parang soca in fact foresounds two musics that are constructed as part of Trinidad's national heritage: soca, because it is a musical offshoot of calypso, and parang, according to Khan summarizing Rohlehr, because "as a definitive representation of 'Spanish'... it has a priority of claim, a putatively extensive history of integration as part of the 'original' fabric of Trinidadian society" (1993: 195)—priority of claim, it should be remembered, by virtue of Trinidad's being initially a Spanish colony and authenticity through its temporal depth.

71. For further information on the calypsonian's role and reputation, see Rohlehr (2004c), in particular, his chapter "The Calypsonian as Artist: Freedom and Responsibility."

72. De Mighty Trini, interview with the author, Woodbrook, Trinidad, 17 January 2003.

73. Rummy (pronounced "romey" in Trinidad) is a card game.

74. Few calypsonians until the 1980s acknowledged the lyricists with whom they work. In this respect, Lord Relator was an exception when he released his LP in 1973 and acknowledged on the record jacket the name of another composer (Leighton James) for some of the songs he performed on that album. See Lord Relator, *White Heat* (West Indies Records, Pan 1249, 1973).

75. Please see and hear De Mighty Trini's "Sailing" (2004), a composition written by Winsford Devine.

Chapter 5: Independence, Innovation, and Authenticity

1. From James (1977: 199).

2. Several authors have closely examined the labeling of music under rubrics of genres and their "unstable" definitions. For a general discussion of the subject, see, for example, Frith (1996b), Negus (1999), Toynbee (2000), and Brackett (2002). For critical perspectives on the sociopolitical and economic implications of placing musical products under the name of a specific genre, see the informative example of Waxer (2002).

3. The few notable exceptions that focus on the sounds—as opposed to the lyrics—of calypso and its musical offshoots include Rohlehr's illuminating article "Calypso Reinvents Itself" (2004a), Balliger (2000), Dudley (1996), Manuel (2000a, 2000b), and Ranmarine (2001).

4. Other musicians became famous for their musical innovations during that period, notably Ras Shorty I (formerly known as Lord Shorty) in relation to soca. Such innovations related to calypso's musical offshoots will be discussed in part 2 of this book. In contrast, Shadow's musical innovations have been viewed in relation to a renewal within calypso itself.

5. Jazz studies differ from most other popular music studies in that they often address the work of arrangers.

6. Arrangers of chutney soca or ragga soca are mentioned less often for reasons that still need to be investigated.

7. Rohlehr (1990).

8. In local parlance, calypsonians and musicians are referred to as two separate entities, even though as composers and players of instruments (usually guitar or keyboard), calypsonians could also be called musicians. The term "musicians" here usually refers to band players or arrangers.

9. Because tents in Trinidad often featured, and continue to feature, renowned calypsonians from other islands, the influence of the tent's arranger could be said to have extended to these other islands when these performers returned home.

10. For this section, I draw on several hours of interviews with Frankie Francis (19 and 21 October 1999 and 28 February 2001) during which I respected his wish not to be recorded.

11. One notable exception in the mid-1940s was John Buddy Williams's orchestra.

12. Frankie Francis, interview with the author, Port of Spain, 19 October 1999.

13. Following *Grove Music Online,* by "head arrangement" I mean "an arrangement that is worked out in rehearsal and memorized by the musicians but generally not written down" (http://www.grovemusic.com).

14. I thank Lambert Philip for interviewing on my behalf the veteran and reputed lead trumpet player in the police band, Vialva Philip, whose knowledge of the musical scene during the 1940s has been invaluable for this study. For further information on arrangements, see Donald Hill's illuminating study of calypso arrangers in New York prior to the 1950s (1993).

15. Several authors have emphasized the importance of repetition in African diasporic musics "as practice" (Erlmann 1999: 250). In addition to Erlmann's insightful piece "Communities of Style" (1999), for an elaboration of the subject, see also Berliner (1994), Chernoff (1979), DeVeaux (1991), Floyd (1995), Jackson (2003), Monson (1996, 1999), Radano (2003), Ramsey (2003), Snead (1998), and Tomlinson (2002).

16. It is important to highlight that this notion of score, informed by classical musical traditions, contrasts markedly with other ways of conceiving scores. On this subject, see Mantle Hood's informative writing on distinct notational systems and their contrasting emphases (1971).

17. In the 1930s and 1940s, bands like the Roy Rollock Band usually included a clarinet, piano, bass, bongos, and maracas. In the 1940s, bands like that of John "Buddy" Williams started to include more instruments, including trumpets and trombones. In the first half of the 1940s, the saxophone replaced the clarinet.

18. The rhythm section could be supplemented at times by a triangle, a tambourine, a cowbell, and timbales. I thank Michael Germain for sharing this information with me.

19. Trombonist Lambert Philip mentioned Michelle Marfan and Juliette Robin as being among the first female instrumentalists to play in popular music bands.

20. In the Caribbean, each island can usually boast one police band. The musicians are full-time employees whose duties consist in playing for all the official functions throughout the year. For these musicians, the police band provides a training ground by reinforcing their reading and writing skills and enabling them to play a wide variety of musics from both classical and popular music repertoires.

21. From Trinidadian parentage but born and raised in England, Susan Quamie was the first woman hired full-time by the police band in 1993. After her father died, she and her mother settled in Trinidad. Before Roderick Urquhart hired her, the police band directors unanimously felt that women should not be part of the police band. According to Enrique Moore, the current police band director, "They believed that women would not adapt to the rigors of this job and that they would not be able to get maximum ouput from them—maybe because of biological things about the women" (Enrique Moore, interview with the author, Port of Spain, 11 January 2005). In addition, they feared that the presence of women in the band would only bring trouble—a fear that, in their view, was confirmed by the aborted attempts in England to do so at the time. Quamie dispelled these fears.

Formally trained in England, she appeared in several shows in Trinidad and became known in the artistic milieu. After indicating that she would like to be part of the police band, she was introduced to Urquhart, the group's director. Moving with the times and open to the idea of having a woman in the band, he set an audition and hired her. After her mother died, she left the police band to return to England in 2001. A saxophone and clarinet player, Quamie inspired other women to follow her example. In January 2005, the police band counted six full-time female players; before the end of the year, the current police band director planned to hire four more—bringing the total number of musicians in his band to eighty. In contrast to the police band, the number of women playing in steelbands has increased significantly since the 1970s. As steelbands have now become widely accepted as musical ensembles and have drawn musicians from all classes, they have become "safer" community activities for anyone to join in. In contrast to the historical rivalry among bands that often led to violent clashes, steelbands now focus on competing against each other in annual events such as Panorama. For an elaboration of the subject, see Dudley (1997) and Stuempfle (1995).

22. Pelham Goddard, one of the most renowned arrangers in Trinidad, provides a case in point. His mother, a piano teacher, gave him a few lessons before he began experimenting on his own with different types of music.

23. I am indebted to Richard Crawford for helping me to make these connections.

24. This appellation contrasts with the North American expression, which refers exclusively to instruments made of brass, such as trumpets, trombones, and French horns, to name only a few.

25. For further information on some of the characteristics of "traditional" calypso, see Dudley (1996).

26. Roy Cape, interview with the author, Port of Spain, 19 October 1999.

27. As Lambert Philip remarked, Francis could not often use a four-part harmony because many calypsonians feared that this would distract the listener from their singing. In addition, Philip added, many of them were musically "conservative" and heard chordal tensions as musically "wrong" instead of hearing them as part of an expanded harmonic vocabulary (Philip Lambert, interview with the author, Port of Spain, 9 January 2005).

28. Please see and hear Black Stalin's "Wait Dorothy Wait" (1991).

29. Daphne McIntosh, interview with the author, Port of Spain, 15 January 2003.

30. According to Enrique Moore, current director of the police band in Trinidad, Art de Coteau acquired his writing skills by working with Frankie Francis as a bass player in the early days of his musical career (Enrique Moore, interview with the author, Port of Spain, 11 January 2005).

31. It is important to stress that, even though de Coteau wrote the arrangements, the steelband players still learned their parts by rote. I thank Lambert Philip for sharing this information with me.

32. In 1970, with Shadow's first appearance onstage, the Victory tent had such a successful season that it presented three shows: 7:30 p.m., 9:30 p.m., and 11:30 p.m. (Daphne McIntosh, interview with the author, Port of Spain, 16 January 2003).

33. By the late 1970s, de Coteau had to compete with the growing popularity of soca and the new sounds it foresounded through its inclusion of synthesizers and use of a disco bass line and high-hat rhythmic patterns. Even though he adopted some of these new sounds in his own music, his prominence as an arranger then began to be challenged by musicians such as Ed Watson (whose arrangement of Lord Kitchener's soca song "Sugar Boum Boum" in 1978 became an instant success), Pelham Goddard (one of his former

band players, whom he helped train and who then became famous for his winning Road March arrangements), and, in the early 1980s, Leston Paul (a keyboard player who became one of the most renowned arrangers following his first breakthrough with the Mighty Duke's fifth album, *Harps of Gold*).

34. Nerville "Bonnie" Brown, interview with the author, Port of Spain, 3 January 1996.

35. Ottley (1998: 34).

36. See de Four (1993) for further information on the subject.

37. From Betaudier (n.d.).

38. Rohlehr (2004c).

39. Rohlehr (2004c: 407).

40. "Calypso Twist" was written in 1963, "Calypso Boogaloo" in 1968, and "Maria"— which Sparrow called a "Calypso cha cha cha"—in 1961. For further information on these songs, see de Four (1993).

41. Rohlehr (2004).

42. For an elaboration of this notion, see Jones (1967).

43. Quoted in Rohlehr (2004a: 219–20).

44. I am grateful to Clive Bradley (interview with the author, Port of Spain, 6 April 1997) and Ed Watson (interview with the author, Diego Martin, Trinidad, 4 March 2000) for sharing this information with me.

45. Please see and hear Shadow's "Bassman" (1995).

46. Nerville "Bonnie" Brown, interview with the author, Port of Spain, 3 January 1996.

47. I am grateful to Danny Bittkers for his extended loan of these LPs.

48. In addition to steelbands, brass bands also used to provide instrumental versions of the most popular tunes of the season on Carnival days.

49. The calypso arrangements written for Panorama are elaborate and can take as much as ten minutes to perform. For further information on this subject, see Dudley (2002).

50. Terry Joseph relates that in 1963 "the inaugural Best Road March Steelband Competition (Panorama) attracted two dozen bands." By 1978, he adds, the number of bands in one section of the country alone had doubled the 1963 national sum (Joseph 2006). Joseph's report does not include the dozens of school steelbands and the significant number of small bands that do not participate in Panorama but who would have also known Kitchener's compositions by either playing them through their own arrangements or listening to other bands. I thank Shannon Dudley for sharing with me this information.

51. The version of "Pan in Harmony" I listened to was rereleased in 1994 on a CD entitled *Lord Kitchener: Klassic Kitchener*, vol. 3, by Ice Records (941802). The name of the arranger in this compilation is not indicated. However, "Pan in Harmony" appeared on the LP entitled *Home for the Carnival* on the KH label (KDS 2006) in 1976. On this LP, the arrangement is credited to Pelham Goddard. On a 45 for the Kalinda label (KD-518) the arrangement of the tune is attributed to Clive Bradley. As I do not have these original recordings, I cannot tell which of these two versions is featured on the Ice Records compilation.

52. Dudley (2004: 44–45) describes lavways as "short refrains sung by a chorus and interspersed with the improvisation of a solo singer."

53. Please see and hear Lord Kitchener's "Tribute to Spree Simon" (1975, 1994).

54. Dudley (2004: 52).

55. Other calypsonians also helped to consolidate the partnership between pan and calypso, including the Mighty Terror, who wrote "Pan Talent" (1965), "Pan in Tune" (1972), and "Sugar for Pan" (1986)," to name only a few.

Chapter 6: Postindependence, Proliferation, and Permissible Traditions

1. Morais (1997; my emphasis).

2. Ramnarine (2001: 14). For an elaboration of the politics of labeling, see Guilbault (1997b).

3. According to David Harvey, neoliberalism is based on "the assumption that individual freedoms are guaranteed by freedom of the market and of trade." In this perspective, the state's fundamental mission is "to facilitate conditions for profitable accumulation on the part of both domestic and foreign capital" (2005: 7). Most scholars focusing on the United States link "embedded liberalism" to the historical period extending from after World War II into the 1970s, and neoliberalism to the period after 1980. Harvey contrasts the main constituents of "embedded liberalism" with those of neoliberalism as follows: "'Embedded liberalism' . . . signal[s] how market processes and entrepreneurial and corporate activities were surrounded by a web of social and political constraints and a regulatory environment that sometimes restrained but in other instances led the way in economic and industrial strategy." In this context, he adds, "State-led planning and in some instances state owner-ship of key sectors (coal, steel, automobiles) were not uncommon (for example in Britain, France, and Italy)." In his view, "The neoliberal project is to disembed capital from these constraints" (2005: 11). Hence, the freedoms that a neoliberal state enables "reflect the interests of private property owners, businesses, multinational corporations, and financial capital" (2005: 7).

4. Over the past two decades, several studies have emphasized how nationalism works through gender as much as it does through race and class. For further elaboration of the subject dealing with the Caribbean region, see M. J. Alexander (1994), Chin (1999), Niranjana (1999), Reddock (1998), and B. Williams (1996).

5. In order to avoid confusion with the letter "I" in the last name used by the artist, I use the abbreviated version "Ras Shorty" in the rest of the text.

6. Ras Shorty had already used East Indian elements in one of his first calypsos, "Long Mango," in 1958. However, he came up with the term "sokah" in 1973 when he decided to experiment with this musical fusion and make it the basis for his new compositions. It should be noted that the paternity of the musical style named "sokah"—renamed later "soca"—has been in dispute. Other artists also claim to have invented soca (including Hugh Quashie, known under the sobriquet King Wellington, and Eddy Grant), arguing that they were the ones who brought the changes of sound and rhythmic feel to traditional calypso. However, unlike Ras Shorty, these artists, along with many others experiment-ing with calypso in the first half of the 1970s, did not name the results of their experi-ments. Furthermore, it is not clear whether the changes they each made in their attempts to "renew" calypso were necessarily the same as Ras Shorty's. This controversy over the authorship of the music named "sokah" brings to the fore the sociopolitical importance of naming.

7. Quoted by Ahyoung (1981: 98).

8. The Indian and African diasporas constitute the two most important ethnic groups in Trinidad. Statistics on Trinidad and Tobago's demographics on 29 December 2004 give the following information: 39.6 percent African descent and 40.3 percent East Indian descent (http://en.wikipedia.org/wiki/Trinidad_and_Tobago#Demographics).

9. Ras Shorty, interview with the author, Piparo, Trinidad, 6 February 1997.

10. Mungal Patasar, interview with the author, Port of Spain, 6 February 1997.

11. Manuel (1998: 26).

12. Especially for the drummer, playing sokah as Ras Shorty wanted it played was revolutionary in at least two ways. To feature the rhythmic lines inspired by the East Indian

rhythms and to provide more color, the drummer had to use both an unfamiliar playing technique (crossing his hands) and a greater number of instruments in his drum set. In his change of instrumentation, Ras Shorty replaced the *dhantal* with the triangle, which after 1978 was eventually dropped in favor of the "iron" from the steel band. (The term "iron" refers to the brake drum from a car or truck, played with a metal bolt.)

13. It should be noted that Carnival songs are usually recorded before the calendar year ends and the Carnival season begins. In the case of "Sugar Bum Bum," for instance, the song was recorded in 1977 for the Carnival season in 1978.

14. Balliger (2000: xiii). For an elaboration of the cultural politics of "wining," see Miller (1991, [1994] 1997), Barnes (2000), and Dikobe (2003).

15. Cited in Kun (1997). As Kun mentioned to me in conversation, several decades before Canclini, Léopold Senghor, the Senegalese statesman and also one of the authors of Negritude, chose "not to be assimilated, but to assimilate" for a motto. Hence, both Canclini and Senghor position the subject as an active agent in history, not as a passive recipient.

16. For example, in Carnival 2002, a soca riddim called "Best Riddim" (riddims are often named) created by producer Sheldon "Shel Shok" Benjamin was used by Trinidadian artists Bunji Garlin ("We Doh Watch Face"), Denise Belfon ("De Jammet"), and Benjai ("Over and Over"). I thank Christopher Edmonds for this information.

17. Machel Montano, interview with the author, French's Camp, Piercy, California, 3 August 2003.

18. Rohlehr (2004c: 422).

19. Rohlehr (2004c: 422). For an elaboration of the musical style of dancehall, see Cooper (1993, 2004), and Stolzoff (2000).

20. Performing artists boycotted the Ragga Soca Monarch competition in 2003, because the winner of the previous year competition had allegedly not yet received his prize money. No such competition has subsequently occurred.

21. Canclini, cited in Kun (1997: 305).

22. Chutney soca combines the Indo-Trinidadian music called "chutney," developed from Bhojpuri folk songs and Hindu wedding music, and soca, as described above, derived from calypso and Indian rhythmic patterns. For further information on the subject, see Manuel (1998, 2000b) and Ranmarine (1996, 2001).

23. According to Manuel (1998: 42), it is not clear whether the term "chutney" derives from India. But, in his view, its occasional appearance on Bhojpuri folk music cassettes would suggest that it does. In this connection, Ramnarine raises the question, "With which place can a tradition like chutney be associated? India, the Caribbean, or the urban centres around the world which have become 'home' to Indian-Caribbean communities?" As she indicates, "Consideration of human mobility, and of migrants as carriers of traditions to different places, has expanded the commonly adopted ethnomusicological frame of reference of studying music in its cultural context in a specific geographic location" (Ramnarine 1996: 133–34).

24. Mungal Patasar, interview with the author, Port of Spain, 24 January 1997.

25. Dev (1995: 23).

26. The origin of the "chutney" tradition continues to arouse controversy. As Patasar explained, the music called "chutney" in Trinidad is also said to come from the tradition of the handicapped and the *hijra*—that is, the castrated male prostitutes who, in India, formed an "outcast" group. (The idea held by this outcast group was that their physical state or their sexual behavior would not be spread to the rest of the population.) Given these conditions, Patasar doubts that these people were ever taken to the Caribbean. In the absence

of this group, East Indian women in Trinidad—used to the musical tradition associated with childbirth—would have recreated it by singing the songs the outcast group used to sing. These songs, according to Patasar, are at the root of what are known today as "chutney" songs. Some of these chutney melodies would later have been used in the context of the wedding ceremony. Ethnomusicologist Selwyn Ellore Ahyoung confirms the connection of chutney songs with childbirth celebrations. But he makes the distinction between what he refers to as *sohar*, the songs based on themes appropriate to childbirth, and those called chutney, the "hot songs" performed after the *sohar* songs (1981: 158).

27. Ali, quoted in Ramnarine (2001: 144).

28. Manuel (1998: 21). The *manjira* (spelled "majeera" in Ahyoung 1981) is played by holding one cymbal in the left hand by the string and striking it with the rim of the other.

29. Manuel (1998: 22). For an elaboration of this argument, see Diethrich (2004: 207–30).

30. For Parmasad's historical analysis, see Diethrich (2004: 221).

31. This historical reconstitution of the 1960s and the 1970s is drawn from Manuel (2000b: 172–73).

32. Manuel (2000b: 172).

33. Diethrich (2004: 222).

34. Ramnarine (2001: 71).

35. Sundar Popo, interview with the author, Monkey Town, Barrackpore South, Trinidad, 2 March 1995. For further details on Sundar Popo's musical career, see Myers (1998).

36. Manuel (1998: 28).

37. Manuel (1998: 40).

38. Mungal Patasar, interview with the author, Port of Spain, 29 January 1997.

39. Manuel (2000b: 175).

40. For further information on chutney music, see Manuel with Bilby and Largey (1995) and Manuel (1998, 2000b).

41. It is noteworthy that the intertextuality that informs chutney soca draws on various media—not only musical recordings, but also films.

42. Rikki Jai, interview with the author, San Fernando, Trinidad, 15 January 2003. The relation between East Indian and India-born artists, however, is complicated by issues of authenticity. When Kanchan rereleased Sundar Popo's song "Kayse Banie" in 1982, as ethnomusicologist Helen Myers explained, "Sundar's 'local composed' took on a fresh sound and found a new validity, since Kanchan was herself authentic, that is India-born, 'from away.' For the Felicity villagers, she made the song truly Indian" (1998: 378). As Diethrich remarks, this example shows how the homeland in diaspora still "represents the bastion of 'authenticity'" (2004: 251). For further information on the interrelationships among the various Indian diasporic markets, see Manuel (2000a, 2000b) and Ramnarine (2001).

43. Diethrich (2004: 261). Ravi-ji de-emphasizes the influence of calypso and how it may have incited East Indian singers to perform from the East Indian musical repertoire songs that focused on social commentary. Rather, he emphasizes the Indian origin of pichakaaree and views its promotion and performance today as an attempt to recapture part of an Indian cultural heritage. Hence, for him, "Pichakaaree sinks its roots into the poetic tradition that has been escorted by the indentured people that connects it to an ancient civilization, and through that, intends to recover its poetic tradition" (1998: 83). According to Peter Manuel, pichakaaree refers to a "recently sponsored style of English-language song associated with Phagwa" performed by the descendants of indentured Indians from Trinidad and Tobago (2000b: 212). For further information on the subject, see Diethrich (2004).

44. Balliger (2000: 217).

45. Balliger (2000: 219).

46. Quoted from Fergusson (1994: 65). When Brother Resistance read the first version of this chapter, he corrected Fergusson's quote with the following: "We define Rapso as the power of the word *in the rhythm of the word*" (interview with the author, Berkeley, 9 September 1999; my emphasis).

47. Brother Resistance, interview with the author, Port of Spain, 16 August 1994.

48. These two characters portray the people traditionally associated with the lower class and the elite in Trinidad. As Brother Resistance explains, "The Midnight Robber speaks patois, dress in rags, and represent the poor. The Pierrot Grenade speaks English, dress with silk and expensive fabric, and represent the elite" (interview with the author, Berkeley, 9 September 1999). For more information on these characters, see John W. Nunley and Judith Bettelheim's *Caribbean Festival Arts: Each and Every Bit of Difference* (1988), a well-documented and beautifully illustrated study of the Carnival characters in Trinidad and other Caribbean countries; see also Crowley on the Midnight Robbers (1956) and Carr on Pierrot Grenade (1956).

49. Byron continued to perform as a rapso artist and as a member of theater companies in New York, where she also taught as an adjunct professor in the Mass Communication, Creative and Performing Arts and Speech Department at Medgar Evers College and in the English department at the College of New Rochelle. She died of cancer in 2003.

50. Brother Shortman left the group in 1984 to continue his career as a solo rapso artist in Sweden. Brother Moopsman died prematurely by drowning in 1977.

51. For further information, see Pollak-Eltz (1993).

52. According to Brother Resistance, the soca influence in rapso came most directly through Junior Wharwood, who introduced the electric guitar into the band and was best known for his contribution to soca music. He had then been playing in nearly every soca hit since soca's inception.

53. Balliger (2000: 111).

54. In 1988, Brother Resistance wrote "Tonight Is a Night for That" for the Carnival season, which was one of the first rapso songs performed by music bands in dancehalls and on the road on Carnival day.

55. S-O-B stands for Songs of Brazil, a famous nightclub in New York.

56. Fergusson (1994: 65).

57. The National Day of Rapso includes concerts and several hours of radio broadcast of rapso music during that day, but no competition—a conscious choice by its organizers to offer an alternative to the traditional format used in the calypso music scene to promote artists.

58. Balliger (2000: 109).

59. One of the most notable exceptions is Singing Sandra's 2005 song entitled "Clean Heart, Clear Conscience." According to Brother Resistance, the two female singers who have consistently performed and recorded in the rapso style over the past ten years are Sister Ama and Shakeela. In an effort to attract more women to sing in the rapso style, since 2000 the organizers of the rapso festival have included "Women of the Oral Tradition" as part of their shows (interview with the author, Port of Spain, 5 January 2005).

60. I owe this insight to Balliger (2000: 114). For more information on Kindred and Home Front and Kisskidee Records, the company that signed them, see Balliger (2000: 111–15).

61. Balliger (2000: 109).

62. Sankeralli (1997: 91).

63. Lyndersay (1998).

64. Rohlehr (1998: 87–88).

65. Rohlehr (1998: 91).

66. Lyndersay here constructs soca audiences as enacting the false consciousness that German philosopher and critical theorist Theodor Adorno decried in his writings on mass-mediated music in the 1940s. Like Adorno, he views soca audiences as people who are duped by the very products they profess to enjoy. For an elaboration of this issue, see Horkheimer and Adorno ([1944] 1999).

67. *Port of Spain Gazette,* 12 February 1907, cited in Rohlehr (1990: 49).

68. Indira Rampersad, quoted by Ryan (1998: 22). According to Ryan, "In her [Rampersad's] view, the efforts of the calypsonians to denigrate Indians had clearly backfired." As a demonstration of solidarity and consolidation of Indian nationalism, he adds that "she [Rampersad] observed that some 20,000 Indians . . . turned out to witness the chutney soca finals" (Ryan 1998: 22).

69. Rohlehr (1998: 91).

70. See Allahar (2000), Balliger (2000), Constance (1991), Manuel (1998, 2000b), Puri (1999), Ramnarine (2001), Reddock (2000), and Rohlehr (2004a).

71. Ramnarine (2001: 75).

72. Drupatee, interview with Danny (1998), quoted in Guilbault (2000: 442).

73. Quoted in Ramnarine (2001: 80).

74. Khan (1993: 190).

75. Khan (1993: 190).

76. Three comprehensive studies on creolization that appeared recently are Shepherd and Richards (2002), Puri (2004), and Khan (2004).

77. See Reddock (1996: 112–13). Percy Hintzen in his turn argues that from the mid-1940s to the 1980s, the term "Creole" was no longer defined in terms of racialized categories, but instead in relation to a particular socioeconomic and political space. This space included members of the black urban proletariat at the lower end of the Creole space, local whites, Christian and Muslim Indians, and middle-class Hindus. The term "Indian" during this historical period was used pejoratively to refer to unsophisticated, rural Hindus. In the mid-1990s, the Indian middle class began to seek out alliances with the lower-class Hindus. This shift has since entailed an increased racialized division, enacted most vividly in the formation of political parties. I thank Percy Hintzen for this information. For an elaboration of the subject, see Hintzen (1999, 2000, 2001, 2002), Puri (2004), and Khan (2004).

78. Vincent-Henry (1993: 28).

79. Manuel (2000b: 184).

80. Danny (1988: 10).

81. Manuel (2000b: 184–85).

82. Ramnarine (2001: 117).

83. See Ramnarine (2001), Manuel (2000b), and Ribeiro (1992).

84. Ramnarine (2001: 116).

85. Manuel (2000b: 188).

86. See Balliger (2000) for a detailed account of chutney soca's audiences at shows and concerts.

87. In an interview in the Trinidadian newspaper *Punch,* 17 December 1995, quoted in Balliger (2000: 221).

88. Balliger (2000: 221).

89. Reddock (1996: 139).

90. I intentionally did not refer to "participants *from* Barbados," and so on, but instead to "participants *living in* Barbados," and so on, to stress the mobility of the West Indian participants. For example, Gillo was born in St. Lucia but lives in Barbados. Roger George was born in Trinidad but now lives in Miami, and so on.

91. Henry and Nurse (1996: 41, 48, 55). In their report, Henry and Nurse speak about the need to develop a stronger tourist industry by attracting more visitors. In the minds of many, including the five-time Calypso Monarch Black Stalin, the members of the Caribbean diasporic populations constitute a high proportion of what are here called visitors. Black Stalin in fact refers to members of the Trinidadian diasporic population as "the local tourists." For further information, see also Nurse 1997.

92. By Caribbean diasporic aesthetics, I mean the musical values that have evolved from, and been nurtured by, the Afro- and Indo-Caribbean diasporas throughout their historical experiences in and outside the islands.

93. Gopinath (1995: 304, italics in the original). For further discussion of this argument, see how Edward Said addresses imaginary geographies of belonging in "Reflections on Exile" (2000: 173–86).

94. Gopinath (1995: 304).

95. Marcia Tucker, quoted by Nurse (2000b: 105).

96. Basch, Schiller, and Blanc (1994: 15).

97. Kasinitz (1992), Nurse (2000b: 96), Hintzen (2001: 42).

98. Nurse (2000b: 103), Ho (2001).

99. Gupta and Ferguson (1997: 10).

100. Hintzen (2001: 43).

101. Nurse (2000b: 103).

102. Quoted in Nurse (2000b: 105).

103. In festivals throughout Europe, where soca is also performed, large crowds of white people attend.

104. Nurse (2000b: 103).

105. Nurse (2000b: 109). For further information, see also Nurse 2000a.

106. Nurse (2000b: 107).

107. See Balliger (2000). As Denis-Constant Martin aptly writes, musical fusions do not necessarily signal that social antagonisms have disappeared (2002).

108. Stuart Hall (1986: 28–43).

109. The state altered its relation not only with the calypso competitions, but also with all the other nationally held competitions during Carnival.

110. Gray (2001: 88).

Chapter 7: Soca, Nation, and Discrepant Diasporas

1. Machel Montano has won many awards in the calypso music scene. In Trinidad, in addition to being the youngest artist to win the Road March competition (1997), Montano won awards in many categories, including Male Artist of the Year (1997) and Best Composer of the Year (1998). On the island and away from it (including in New York and Florida), the albums and songs he recorded with his group Xtatik won awards in categories ranging from Best-Engineered Record, Best Soca Album, and Best Record of the Year to Best Ragga Soca, Best Party Calypso, Best Soca Group, and Best-Playing Band on the Road. As a soloist, Rikki Jai has also won awards in several categories. He earned the title of Chut-

ney Soca Monarch four times in five years (1998, 1999, 2001, 2002) and the National Chutney Monarch title in 1999 and 2000. As indicated later in the chapter, Jai also tied for first place with Bunji Garlin in the Young King competition in 2001. In the same year, he was also crowned the South Calypso Monarch and the National Unattached Calypso Monarch.

2. This follows Hall's argument that "diaspora identities are those which are constantly producing and reproducing themselves anew, through transformation and difference" (1990: 235). For an elaboration of the notion of authenticity, see T. Taylor (1997).

3. Negus (1999: 17).

4. This critique is elaborated in Richard Peterson's work on music industries (1976). For further elaboration of the subject, see Negus (1999), Negus and Pickering (2002), Théberge (1997), and Toynbee (2000).

5. On the collaborative work involved in music making, see Hennion (1989), Negus (1999), and Toynbee (2000).

6. For an elaboration of subject positions, see Stuart Hall's critical discussion of Foucault on this issue (1997: 54–63).

7. "Reggae on the River" is a large festival that takes place yearly at French's Camp in Piercy, California, over a long weekend in early August. The festival celebrated its twentieth anniversary in 2003.

8. Machel Montano, interview with the author, French's Camp, Piercy, California, 3 August 2003.

9. Over the years, I, along with many other people, noticed indeed how, up to around 1997, the Soca Monarch competitions as well as fetes drew a wide range of people. Many calypso tent goers—who are usually over forty years old—would reserve Friday night before Dimanche Gras to attend the Soca Monarch competition. By 2000 or 2001, many of them no longer went to the competition, but instead watched it on television. As some of them explained to me, soca was now getting too fast, and lyrically too distant from calypso, which they like best. Hence, while soca has drawn an increasingly large audience, as Montano explained, it has attracted fans who cross over more in terms of class than— particularly over the past five years—in terms of age. As indicated in the preceding chapter, soca competitions continue to draw predominantly crowds of Afro-Trinidadians. In fetes, however, not only Afro-Trinidadians but also Indo-Trinidadians play soca extensively— albeit still for the most part in their own spaces.

10. The American rap artist and producer Sean Combs, known as Puff Daddy, later adopted another sobriquet, P. Diddy. I thank Val Morrison for bringing this information to my attention.

11. Montano's belief that acquiring new knowledge about sound technology and developing greater control over the band's own sounds would increase the band's chance to compete in global markets echoes Foucault's insistence on linking knowledge to power. See Foucault (1980).

12. Montano and his band members learned about sound technologies in recording studios in the United States in order to produce later in Trinidad "local sounds" that could allow them to be competitive in international markets. Such articulation draws together disparate places and people in ways that inform the band's identity, which extends beyond the nation-state, while embracing their sense of multiple belongings.

13. For example, Machel Montano and Xtatik recorded a song with Burning Flames entitled "Showdown (Band Meet Band)" on their 1999 CD *Any Minute Now* (VP1548). Xtatik band members also worked in collaboration with Branker and Coppin on their 2003 CD *The Xtatik Circus* (JW257). In addition, Montano composed and performed

several songs over riddims produced by Tony Kelly, among others, including "Powder Puff" over the "Warriors Riddim" and "Lock Smith" over the "Kiki Riddim" on vol. 3 of the CD *Triple Spin,* by VA-Triple Spin (Tony Kelley productions, 2000). I thank Christopher Edmunds for this information.

14. I am grateful to Percy Hintzen for reminding me to stress the importance Jamaican music holds for soca artists aiming to penetrate the global market.

15. In the calypso music scene, I interpret the term "authenticity" as referring to issues involving regimes of truth, and the term "originality" as being related to issues of musical creativity. Based on their most common usage, I emphasize how these terms in Trinidad are used in tandem with different modes of valorization. I am grateful to Horace Enriques and Tim Cooley for bringing to my attention several other usages of these terms in other spaces and places.

16. I understand Montano's reference to "minstrel" to allude to the transformation of a preexisting song into something different, mixing aspects of the former version with new musical elements. Rather than conceiving minstrelsy as a denigrating mimicry across race, Montano emphasizes creative dynamics of appropriation across generation: the appropriation of preexisting songs composed and performed by older calypsonians by young soca artists. In that sense, Montano evokes the musical practice of black minstrels who, according to Earl L. Stewart, "offered original and entertaining variations on formats invented decades earlier" (1998: 21).

17. Xtatik Ltd and Xtatik 5.0's CD entitled *The Collectors Riddim* is based on a riddim over which several Trinidad artists wrote their songs. These artists included Calypso Rose, the Mighty Sparrow, Bunji Garlin, Rikki Jai, Onika Bostic, and Scarface, to name only a few. Distinctive about *The Collectors Riddim* is the fact that it includes ska rhythms of the 1960s. For further information on riddims, see Stolzoff (2000); on ska, see White (1984, 1998) and King (2002).

18. Superblue (Austin Lyons, formely called Blue Boy) was known in the 1980s and the 1990s as one of the most important leaders of party songs in Trinidad. In 1980, two years after soca was firmly established with the enormous success of Lord Kitchener's song "Sugar Bum Bum," Superblue made his entry onto the Carnival scene with a series of soca hits by bringing what has been characterized by his biographers as "a new energy," "compelling rhythms," and an enticing focus on choreographed songs (Ottley 1995: 212). His electrifying performances punctuated with catchy chorus lines earned him the greatest number of Road March (songs that are played or heard the most on the road during masquerade on Carnival Tuesday) and Soca Monarch titles in the history of the Trinidadian Carnival music scene (he was Road March winner eight times and Soca Monarch six times). His success in winning competitions made him a trendsetter in the soca music scene, through not only his melodic lines, but also his tone of voice, rhythmic calls, and body movements. His performances linked identity and culture irrevocably with sexuality and spirituality, incorporating musical elements drawn from the Orisha yard and the Baptist Church and making dancing part of the songs.

19. For further elaboration of this subject, see Raymond Williams's discussion of "structures of feeling" (1977: 128–35).

20. In his glossary, Carol Martin defines extempo as "a competitive form of calypso in which opponents extemporaneously compose and sing clever and humorous repartee" (1998: 225).

21. I am grateful to Candace Hintzen for helping me to transcribe the lyrics of "You" and also to Liz Montano for sending me the official version of these lyrics. I thank both Joan and Candace Hintzen for helping me to transcribe the lyrics of "On the Road."

22. Here Montano refers to his song entitled "Luv 2U 2Nite" on *Machel Montano: 2000 Young to Soca* (JW198).

23. Here Montano's comments must be situated. Calypsonians, responding to severe censorship during the colonial regime, have usually referred to sex by using double entendre. As a result, in Montano's view, calypsonians would not likely be referring to sexual desires as directly as he does.

24. Double tracking is a recording technique in which, for example, one trumpet, one trombone, and one sax might be recorded and then rerecorded to increase the fullness of the sound, producing the same sonic effect with three players as with six. For more information on multitrack technology, see Théberge (1997: 214–41). See also Meintjes (2003) for a richly detailed ethnography of recording studio technologies.

25. Most soca bands have reduced their number of players, so that many brass and reed sections have shrunk to one trumpet and one trombone. In this regard, Roy Cape's All Stars band is a notable exception, carrying two saxophones (tenor and alto), two trumpets, and one trombone.

26. As discussed in chapter 6, the commercialism argument reduces the artists' orientations exclusively to the pursuit of economic goals, overlooking other factors that come into play in the production of musical practices. For an elaboration of the commercialism argument, see Max Horkheimer's and Theodor W. Adorno's classic article "The Culture Industry: Enlightenment as Mass Deception" ([1944] 1999). For a critical perspective on the subject, see Negus (1997, 1999), Théberge (1997), Toynbee (2000), and Shuker (2001).

27. Numerous publications focus on the socially gendered constructions in calypso. See, for example, Rohlehr (1988), Balliger (2000), Dikobe (2003), Rohlehr (2004b), and Reddock (2004).

28. On the construction of Indo-Trinidadian women, see Manuel (1998, 2000b), P. Mohammed (1998, 2002), Mehta (2004), Ramnarine (2001), and Reddock (1994a).

29. Rohlehr (2004c: 440–41).

30. Rohlehr (2004c: 440).

31. For Rohlehr (2004c), the song "Real Unity" was "not substantially different from Sparrow's 'Maharajin' (1982) and Iwer George's controversial 'Bottom in the Road' (1998)." The difference between these songs and "Real Unity," it could be suggested, is that in "Real Unity," the other (in this case, embodied by Drupatee) is involved in the performance of the song.

32. For a critical discussion of the notion of diaspora with an emphasis on the politics of exclusion, see Hintzen (2004). See also Hall (1990: 228), stressing how the difference and sameness—what he calls "doubleness"—among West Indians is most powerfully heard within the varieties of Caribbean musics, which, he adds, embody a cultural complexity "that exceeds this binary structure of representation." Depending on where, when, and for whom they are performed, these musics reconfigure distinct senses of belonging.

33. Montano described his listening to Fela Kuti's music as a transformative moment in his life that marked a deep affinity with Africa. The Nigerian artist Fela Kuti was known for his creative musical fusion and his primary role in the invention of Afro-beat as well as for his showmanship—artistic qualities that appeared to have inspired Montano. In addition, Fela's passionate advocacy of Pan-Africanism and call for a united, democratic African republic most likely resonated strongly with Montano's desire to promote Caribbean unity though his musical practice.

34. WITCO and WASA are companies whose staffs have got into the business of promoting Carnival fetes. WITCO is the acronym for the West Indian Tobacco Company and WASA for the local Water and Sewerage Authority. Soca Village (which no longer exits) was a venue opposite the Holiday Inn (now renamed the Crowne Plaza Hotel) that held many parties over the Carnival season. I am grateful to Michael Germain for providing me with this information.

35. Rikki Jai, interview with the author, Friendship Village, San Fernando, Trinidad, 15 January 2003.

36. For an elaboration on the cultural politics of permissible bodies in distinct musical practices, see Deborah Wong's illuminating intervention, "The Asian American Body in Performance" (2004).

37. It should be noted that as the female East Indian and Afro-Trinidadian dancers shift their body movements according to the musical traditions they want to evoke—chutney or soca—they transgress in that moment how these dancing styles have been historically mapped onto racialized bodies.

38. Rikki Jai initially worked as a store clerk and then held a post at the Ministry of Finance for twelve years before he returned to school in 1992. He then enrolled to study computer science at Queens College in New York. After his major hit "Wine On Ah Bum-see" in 1993, he quit his studies, as he found it too hard to combine his many performance engagements with the university schedule. He returned to Trinidad and resumed working during the day and performing at night. In 1996, Jai decided to devote himself to his musical career and quit his daytime job.

39. In an interview with me in Port of Spain on 29 January 1997, Mungal Patasar, then a chief adviser to the chutney soca judges, expressed his worry that many chutney soca songs presented in the preliminaries that year included hardly any elements from chutney. As he explained, to qualify as chutney soca a song "must carry the chutney melody or any of the related Indian melodies. And it must carry the soca beat. That's the two things." After the preliminaries, the judges agreed with him and thus selected from the semifinals only those whose songs corresponded to Patasar's definition.

40. This artist uses his first name only for the stage. His complete name is Rooplal Girdharrie.

41. At the time of my interview with him in 2003, Jai had also released a few CDs featuring exclusively calypso and soca. However, I chose to focus on *Chutney Vibrations* because this recording assembles many of Jai's musical tendencies and collaborations. When I met him in 2005, Jai was involved in still newer recording ventures. He had just finished recording a Hindi pop and chutney soca CD featuring two duets, one with Nadia Madoo and another one with Anil Bheem, two of the most acclaimed East Indian singers of Bollywood movie songs in Trinidad. He had also just produced a chutney soca riddim called "The Curry Riddim" and recorded that riddim with twelve artists. He was furthermore in the process of completing another CD based on a chutney riddim called "The Chutney Jump Around Riddim" for release after Carnival.

42. For an elaboration of this expression, see C. Martin (1998: 231).

43. The two spellings, *riddim* and *riddum,* are used interchangeably in many publications on the subject.

44. I thank Donald Moore, Christopher Edmunds, and Val Morrison for indicating the musical categories to which Sting's song is described as belonging.

45. Chuck Foster notes that, in dancehall culture, names of well-known stars often inspire others. For example, he writes, "Ninjaman inspired Ninja Kid, Ninja Force, Ninja Ford, and Ninja Turtle" (1999: 159).

Chapter 8: Cultural Entrepreneurship under Neoliberalism

1. These included not only TUCO, but also the steelband and mas band organizations.

2. The new style of governing in the 1990s could be seen as emerging in tandem with what Antonio Gramsci refers to as the "discipline of the conjuncture" (quoted in Hall 1988: 162).

3. Rose (1999: 3). Unlike Rose, who writes that governing refers to "*all* endeavors to shape, guide, direct the conduct of others," I stress that governing pertains to tactics of management to demarcate the field of its relevance. Not all activities can be looked at from a "governing" perspective. One child begging another to give her a toy, in my view, could not be described in terms of governing, even though one child tries to direct the conduct of the other. Unlike the tactics of management, this child's action is not part of a technology designed to discipline the other child's behavior. I thank Donald Moore for this insight.

4. See Constance (1996), L. Regis (1999), and Franco (2000), among others. I thank Rhoda Reddock for sharing these references with me.

5. Rose (1999: 5).

6. In any given historical moment, several political rationalities simultaneously exist and collide with each other in an attempt to launch projects and technologies along the lines of their own logic. In this chapter, I focus on the neoliberal political rationality that, I believe, has played a particularly strong role in shaping Carnival music activities.

7. As Wendy Brown (1998: 44–45) remarks in her study of Foucault's genealogical politics, the advantage of speaking of a political rationality is that, unlike the term "system," which suggests a coherent and closed ensemble of rules or principles, it reveals its historical contingency and the fact that it is an argument typically filled with contradictions, in collision with other discourses and forces, and thus perpetually in an embattled position.

8. By "political" objectives, I mean objectives that aim to effect changes; by personal conduct, I mean personal behavior. Linking political objectives to personal conduct implies that the goal is to change personal behavior.

9. Rose (1999: 139).

10. Bourne (1989: 276).

11. Bourne (1989: 278; my emphasis).

12. I borrow the terms "social state" and "enabling state" from Rose, whose description of Thatcher's governmental changes applies well here (1999: 142).

13. Rose (1999: 139).

14. Trinidad and Tobago Chamber of Industry and Commerce 2003.

15. Rose (1999: 150).

16. As Stuart Hall (1988: 163) would put it, in their "partial adaptation to the modern world," TUCO was "living through the neo-liberal and monetarist 'revolutions.'"

17. Brother Resistance, interview with the author, Woodbrook, Trinidad, 8 January 2003.

18. It should be noted that, since the 1970s, NJAC has been holding Queen Calypso competitions. According to Brother Resistance, the Carnival Queen competition was organized by TUCO at the request of several of its female members who were questioning the NJAC judging procedures (Brother Resistance, interview with the author, Port of Spain, 5 January 2005).

19. Rose (1999: 154).

20. This new emphasis has to some extent been offset by the desire to produce high-quality shows.

21. Winston Montano, a petroleum geologist, also helped Machel establish his musical career by playing an active role in the band's management. Over the past few years, he

has retired as a geologist and has used his business acumen to oversee Machel's real estate properties.

22. Full-time managers have been very few in number. The exceptions include Ellis Chow Lin On, who managed Charlie's Roots on a full-time basis for several years until he retired. In order to be able to work full-time in the music business, some managers have often combined several activities. This is the case, for example, of Cliff Harris, who works both as Atlantik's manager and as a promoter.

23. Liz Montano, interview with the author, Port of Spain, 14 January 2003; my emphasis.

24. At nine years old (in 1984), Machel already had recording equipment with which he could experiment. He also had already formed his own group, then called Pranasonic Express—"Prana," Liz Montano explained, meaning a breadth of life, and also the name of the housing development in Siparia where they lived at the time. The Ruf Rex recording studio was set up in the early 1990s, and was subsequently relocated in Port of Spain and renamed the EdGordon recording studio in June 2002.

25. From http://www.guardian.co.tt/featuresstory1.html.

26. For further information on the EdGordon studio and services, see http://www.machelmontano.com.

27. Rose (1999: 191).

28. Rose's reference to an ethical behavior that consumers "should" seek suggests not only that consumers have a choice—an assumption that brings to the fore the issue of class and privileges—but also that they live in conditions of their own choosing—a proposition that would be hard to sustain for the dispossessed. Furthermore, what constitutes "ethical behavior" in regard to judgments of good and bad, right and wrong, is a contested matter among people from diverse cultures, religions, and socioeconomic assets.

29. In January 2001, for example, one day after the demo copy of the newest compact disc by Roy Cape All Stars was distributed to the main radio stations, it also found its way onto the illegal market in the streets of Port of Spain before it was even released in record stores. For an elaboration on the shifting ethics of intellectual property, see Steven Feld's insightful article "A Sweet Lullaby for World Music" (2000).

30. Allison Demas, interview with the author, Port of Spain, 11 January 2005.

31. For further information on the subject, see Raymond Quevedo's pioneering study *Atilla's Kaiso* (1983), Gordon Rohlehr's colossal account of calypso's multifaceted practices in preindependence Trinidad (1990), Donald R. Hill's richly detailed information on the early Carnival music scene in *Calypso Calaloo* (1993), and Zeno Obi Constance's invaluable study (1991) of the East Indian contributions to calypso.

32. See Robin Balliger's pioneering study (2000) on the emergence of new cultural entrepreneurs and popular music consumption in Trinidad.

33. Alvin Daniell, interview with the author, Port of Spain, 8 January 2003.

34. Rose (1999: 149).

35. For an elaboration of the ethical responsibilities of the subject, see Foucault ([1984] 1986) and Rose (1999: 165–66).

36. Panorama tunes are the compositions played by steelbands in their yearly competitions held during Carnival.

37. The weekly broadcast of *Calypso Showcase* was designed to honor the lifetime achievements of some of the most prominent calypso and soca artists through interviews, videos, and film footage of their musical biographies.

38. George Singh, interview with the author, San Fernando, Trinidad, 10 January 2005.

39. The local and transnational corporations participating in the Chutney Soca Monarch competition include Carib, Angostura, Pepsi, Black and White scotch whiskey, Blue

Waters (a local water company), 103FM (one of the local radio stations), Citrus Growers Association of Trinidad and Tobago, TV6, Trinidad Express Newspapers, Guls City Shopping Complex, Motor and General Insurance Company, and Telecommunication Services of Trinidad and Tobago (TSTT).

Coda

1. Sugar Aloes, quoted by Hassanali (2005).

2. Excerpt from Joseph (2005: 14).

3. Advertisement in *Trinidad Express,* 10 January 2005, 10.

4. Here I rephrase Judith Butler's memorable expression appearing as the title of her article (1998) to emphasize the multifaceted aspects of musical practices.

5. For critical work on the notion of performativity, see J. L. Austin (1961), Butler (1993, 1997), Hirschkind (2001), Mahmood (2001), and Hollywood (2002).

6. Nettleford's introduction to his insightful book *Inward Stretch, Outward Reach* (1993: xiv).

7. Brown (2003: par. 280; emphasis in the original).

8. I use here the expression "neoliberal condition" following Akhil Gupta's description of the "postcolonial condition," in his words, "to draw attention to a specific conjuncture that has shaped the lives and experiences of people. . . . Thus, I am interested in the institutions and discourses which position subjects and which configure their experience in particular ways, and not just with a body of theory that may be labeled 'postcolonial' [read 'neoliberal']" (Gupta 1998: 10). In my case, I am also interested in examining what people are able to achieve within this condition.

9. For an elaboration of sentiments as forces of production, see Sylvia Junko Yanagisako's insightful book *Producing Culture and Capital* (2002: 7–12).

10. To view these technical services as commodities is not new in many countries, but they only recently have been in existence in Trinidad. Neoliberalism has unfolded neither in the same way nor at the same pace universally.

11. I am inspired here by Raymond Williams's useful terms, "the dominant, the residual, and the emergent" (1977: 121–27).

12. In June 2005, at the time of this writing, the East Indian former prime minister, Basteo Panday, was in jail for having allegedly mishandled public funds—an accusation that in the past has also often been made about some of the PNM representatives. He refused to pay the TT$500,000 bail—making the tensions between the Afro-Creole- and East Indian–led parties more intense than ever.

13. Paul Gilroy defines "conviviality" as "the processes of cohabitation and interaction that have made multiculture an ordinary feature of social life in Britain's urban areas and in postcolonial cities elsewhere" (2005: xv). In his view, a focus on the workings of conviviality might help us move beyond where so-called multiculturalism has failed. This focus underscores the salience of social interactions across and within difference in multicultural settings. As Gilroy aptly relates, "It [conviviality] does not describe the absence of racism or the triumph of tolerance. Instead, it suggests a different setting . . . in the absence of any strong belief in absolute or integral races. . . . It introduces a measure of distance from the pivotal term 'identity,' which has proved to be such an ambiguous resource in the analysis of race, ethnicity, and politics. The radical openness that brings conviviality alive makes a nonsense of closed, fixed, and reified identity and turns attention toward the always unpredictable mechanisms of identification" (2005: xv). For an elaboration of this notion, see Gilroy's last chapter, "The Negative Dialectics of Conviviality" (2005: 121–51).

REFERENCES

Adderley, Rosanne Marion. 2003. "'Africans,' 'Americans,' and 'Creole Negroes':
Black Migration and Colonial Interpretations of 'Negro' Diversity in
Nineteenth-Century Trinidad." In *Marginal Migrations: The Circulation of
Cultures within the Caribbean,* ed. Shalini Puri, 17–42. Oxford: Macmillan
Caribbean.

Ahyoung, Selwyn Ellore. 1981. "Soca Fever: Change in the Calypso Music
Tradition of Trinidad and Tobago, 1970–1980." M.A. thesis, Indiana
University.

Alexander, J. 1977. "The Culture of Race in Middle-Class Kingston, Jamaica."
American Ethnologist 4 (3): 413–35.

Alexander, M. Jacqui. 1994. "Not Just (Any) Body Can Be a Citizen: The Politics
of Law, Sexuality and Postcoloniality in Trinidad and Tobago and the Bahamas." *Feminist Review* 48:5–23.

Allahar, Anton L. 2000. "Popular Culture and Racialisation of Political Consciousness in Trinidad and Tobago." In *Identity, Ethnicity and Culture in the
Caribbean,* ed. Ralph R. Premdas, 246–81. St. Augustine, Trinidad: University
of the West Indies, School of Continuing Studies.

———. 2003. "'Racing' Caribbean Political Culture: Afrocentrism, Black
Nationalism and Fanonism." In *Modern Political Culture in the Caribbean,* ed.
Holger Henke and Fred Reno, 21–58. St. Augustine, Trinidad: University
of the West Indies.

Anthony, Michael. 1989. *Parade of the Carnivals of Trinidad, 1839–1989.* Port of
Spain: Circle Press.

Assang, Sharon Lee. 1998. "T&T's Mystic Monarch Reflects on His Victory."
Internet Express, 2 March.

Austerlitz, Paul. 1997. *Merengue: Dominican Music and Dominican Identity.* Philadelphia: Temple University Press.

Austin, J. L. 1961. *Philosophical Papers.* Oxford: Oxford University Press.

319

Austin, R. L. 1976. "Understanding Calypso Content: a Critique and an Alternative Explanation." *Caribbean Quarterly* 22 (2–3): 74–83.

Averill, Gage. 1997. *A Day for the Hunter, a Day for the Prey: Popular Music and Power in Haiti.* Chicago: University of Chicago Press.

Ballantyne, Gregory. 1998. "Jahaaji Blues." *Caribbean Dialogue: A Journal of Contemporary Caribbean Policy Issues* 3 (4): 113–15.

Balliger, Robin. 2000. "Noisy Spaces: Popular Music Consumption, Social Fragmentation, and the Cultural Politics of Globalization in Trinidad." Ph.D. diss., Stanford University.

Barnes, Natasha. 2000. "Body Talk: Notes on Women and Spectacle in Contemporary Trinidad Carnival." *Small Axe: A Journal of Criticism* 7:93–105.

Barriteau, Eudine, ed. 2003. *Confronting Power, Theorizing Gender: Interdisciplinary Perspectives in the Caribbean.* St. Augustine, Trinidad: University of the West Indies.

Basch, Linda, Nina Glick Schiller, and Cristina Szanton Blanc. 1994. *Nations Unbound: Transnational Projects, Postcolonial Predicaments and Deterritorialized Nation-States.* New York: Gordon and Breach Publishers.

Belasco, Lionel, and Leighla Whipper. 1944. *Calypso Rhythm Songs: Authentic Tropical Novelty Melodies Complete with Words and Music by Lionel Belasco and Leighla Whipper.* New York: Mills Music.

Bennett, Tony. 1998. *Culture: A Reformer's Science.* London: Sage.

Berland, Jody. 1992. "Angels Dancing: Cultural Technologies and the Production of Space." In *Cultural Studies,* ed. Lawrence Grossberg, Cary Nelson, and Paul Treichler, 38–50. New York: Routledge.

Berliner, Paul. 1994. *Thinking in Jazz: The Infinite Art of Improvisation.* Chicago: University of Chicago Press.

Best, Curwen. 1995. *Barbadian Popular Music and the Politics of Caribbean Culture.* New York: AC.

Betaudier, Holly. n.d. "The Story of Jean and Dinah." In *Sparrow: The Legend,* ed. Keith Smith. Port of Spain: Imprint Caribbean.

Bissoondialsingh, Tara. 1973. *Dhrupad Singing in Trinidad.* Trinidad: Bharatiya Vidya Sansthaan.

Blake, Dr. Felix I. R. 1995. *The Trinidad and Tobago Steel Pan: History and Evolution.* Trinidad: published by the author.

Blood, Peter Ray. 1998. "Where Are the Good Calypsos." *Trinidad Guardian,* 8 February.

Bourdieu, Pierre. 1986. *Distinction: A Social Critique of the Judgment of Taste.* New York: Routledge.

———. 1993. *The Field of Cultural Production.* Cambridge: Polity.

Bourne, Compton. 1989. "Imperatives of Caribbean Development for the 21st Century." In *CALACS/ACELAC Conference Proceedings: Prospects for Latin America and the Caribbean to the Year 2000,* ed. A. R. M. Ritter, 266–78. Ottawa: CALACS/ACELAC.

Boyce Davies, Carole. 1990. "Woman Is a Nation: Women in Caribbean Oral Literature." In *Out of the Kumbla: Caribbean Women and Literature,* ed. Carole Boyce Davies and E. Savory Fido, 165–93. Trenton, N.J.: Africa World Press.

Brackett, David. 2002. "(In Search of) Musical Meaning: Genres, Categories and Crossover." In *Popular Music Studies,* ed. David Hesmondhalgh and Keith Negus, 65–84. London: Arnold.

Brereton, Bridget. [1979] 2002. *Race Relations in Colonial Trinidad, 1879–1900.* Cambridge: Cambridge University Press.

———. 1981. *A History of Modern Trinidad, 1783–1962.* London: Heinemann.

Brown, Wendy. 1998. "Genealogical Politics." In *The Later Foucault: Politics and Philosophy,* ed. Jeremy Moss, 33–49. London Sage.

———. 2003. "Neo-liberalism and the End of Liberal Democracy." *Theory and Event,* vol. 7 (1).

Burton, Richard D. E. 1997. *Afro-Creole: Power, Opposition and Play in the Caribbean.* Ithaca, N.Y.: Cornell University Press.

Butler, Judith. 1993. *Bodies That Matter: On the Discursive Limits of "Sex."* New York: Routledge.

———. 1997. *Excitable Speech: A Politics of the Performative.* New York: Routledge.

———. 1998. "Merely Cultural." *New Left Review* 227:33–44.

———. 2000. "Agencies of Style for a Liminal Subject." In *Without Guarantees: In Honour of Stuart Hall,* ed. Paul Gilroy, Lawrence Grossberg, and Angela McRobbie, 30–37. London: Verso.

Cadogan, Glenda. n.d. "Calypso Rose." *EBM* [*Everybody's Magazine*], 8–12.

Calypso Talk '86: Antigua Carnival. 1986. St. John's, Antigua: Antigua Printing and Publishing.

Campbell, Horace G. 1987. *Rasta and Resistance: From Marcus Garvey to Walter Rodney.* Trenton, N.J.: Africa World Press.

Carr, Andrew T. 1956. "Pierrot Grenade." *Caribbean Quarterly* 4 (3–4): 281–314.

———. 1975. "The Calypso: A People's Poetic Platform." *West Indian World* 215:12–13.

Charles, Hubert (the Lion), and Atilla the Hun. 1943. *Victory Calypsoes 1943 Souvenir Collection.* Trinidad: Caribbee Printerie.

Chen, Willie. 1988. *King of the Carnival.* London: Hansib Publishing.

Chernoff, John 1979. *African Rhythm and African Sensibility: Aesthetics and Social Action in African Musical Idioms.* Chicago: University of Chicago Press.

Chin, Timothy S. 1999. "Jamaican Popular Culture, Caribbean Literature, and the Representation of Gay and Lesbian Sexuality in the Discourses of Race and Nation. *Small Axe: A Journal of Criticism* 5:14–33.

Chouthi, Sandra. 2000. "Ya Can't Shaddup dah Calypso Singers." *Dispatch Online,* 12 July, http://www.dispatch.co.za/2000/07/12/features/SINGERS.HTM.

"Chutney Flagship Star, Sundar Popo, Releases Spicy Ditty: Cool Yourself with Cold Water." 1995. *Sunday Punch,* 24 December.

Clifford, James. 1988. "Introduction." In *The Predicament of Culture: Twentieth-Century Ethnography, Literature, and Art.* Cambridge, Mass.: Harvard University Press.

———. 1994. "Diasporas." *Cultural Anthropology* 9 (3): 302–38.

"Colin Lucas Lashes Out at 'Fast Food Soca.'" 1998. *Newsday,* 19 February, 42.

Constance, Zeno Obi. 1991. *Tassa, Chutney and Soca: The East Indian Contribution to the Calypso.* Borde Narve Village, Trinidad: published by the author.

———. 1996. *De Roaring 70s: An Introduction to the Politics of the 1970s.* Borde Narve Village, Trinidad: published by the author.

Cooper, Carolyn. 1993. *Noises in the Blood: Orality, Gender and the "Vulgar" Body of Jamaican Popular Culture.* Durham, N.C.: Duke University Press.

———. 2004. *Sound Clash: Jamaican Dancehall Culture at Large.* New York: Palgrave Macmillan.

Corrigan, Philip, and Derek Sayer. 1985. *The Great Arch: English State Formation as Cultural Revolution.* Oxford: Basil Blackwell.

Cowley, John. 1996. *Carnival, Canboulay and Calypso: Traditions in the Making.* Cambridge: Cambridge University Press.

"Crazy: The Lovable Lunatic." 1988. In *The Official Calypso Revue '88,* ed. Kim Johnson. Port of Spain.

Crowley, Daniel J. 1956. "The Midnight Robbers." *Caribbean Quarterly* 4 (3–4): 263–74.

———. 1959. "Towards a Definition of Calypso." Pts. 1 and 2. *Ethnomusicology* 3 (2): 57–66; 3 (3): 117–24.

Daniell, Alvin. 1992. "De Judges Tief." In *Calypso '92: A Mirror, a Society Revealed through Its Songs,* ed. Michael Narine, 42–44. Port of Spain: ADEB Print and Computers.

Danny, Phoolo. 1988. "No Culture Barrier for Drupatee." *Sunday Express,* 7 February, 10.

De Cordova, Richard. 1990. *Picture Personalities: The Emergence of the Star System in America.* Chicago: University of Illinois Press.

DeCosmo, Janet L. 2000. "Crossing Gendered Space: An Analysis of Trinidad's Carnival from a Feminist and African-Centered Perspective." *Wadabagei: A Journal of the Caribbean and Its Diasporas* 3 (1): 1–48.

De Four, Linda Claudia. 1993. *Gimme Room to Sing: Calypsoes of the Mighty Sparrow, 1958–1993: A Discography.* Port of Spain: published by the author.

Desroches, Monique. 1996. *Tambours des Dieux: Musique et sacrifice d'origine Tamoule en Martinique.* Montreal: Harmattan.

Dev, Atul. 1995. "To Chutney . . . with Love and Devotion!" *Trinidad Guardian,* 30 May, 23.

DeVeaux, Scott. 1991. "Constructing the Jazz Tradition." *Black Music Research Journal* 25 (3): 525–60.

Diethrich, Gregory Michael. 2004. "'Living in Both Sides of the World': Music, Diaspora, and Nation in Trinidad." Ph.D. diss., University of Illinois, Urbana-Champaign.

Dikobe, Maude. 2003. "Doing She Own Thing: Gender, Performance and Subversion in Trinidad Calypso." Ph.D. diss., University of California, Berkeley.

Dudley, Shannon Kingdon. 1996. "Judging 'By the Beat': Calypso versus Soca." *Ethnomusicology* 40 (2): 269–98.

———. 1997. "Making Music for the Nation: Competing Identities and Esthetics in Trinidad and Tobago's Panorama Steelband Competition." Ph.D. diss., University of California, Berkeley.

———. 2002. "The Steelband 'Own Tune': Nationalism, Festivity and Musical Strategies in Trinidad's Panorama Competition." *Black Music Research Journal* 22 (1): 13–36.

———. 2003. "Creativity and Constraint in Trinidad Carnival Competitions." In "Contesting Tradition: Cross-Cultural Studies of Musical Competition," special issue, *World of Music* 45 (1): 11–34.

———. 2004. *Carnival Music in Trinidad: Experiencing Music, Expressing Culture.* New York: Oxford Press.

———. In press. *Music from behind the Bridge: Steelband Spirit and the Politics of Festivity in Trinidad and Tobago.* Berkeley: University of California Press.

Dunn, Christopher. 2001. *Brutality Garden: Tropicalia and the Emergence of a Brazilian Counterculture.* Chapel Hill: University of North Carolina Press.

Elder, Jacob. 1966a. "Evolution of the Traditional Calypso of Trinidad and Tobago: A Sociohistorical Analysis of Song-Change." Ph.D. diss., University of Pennsylvania.

———. 1966b. "Kalinda—Song of the Battling Troubadours of Trinidad." *Journal of the Folklore Institute* 3 (2): 193–203.

———. 1988. *African Survivals in Trinidad and Tobago.* London: Karia Press.

Erlmann, Veit. 1999. *Music, Modernity, and the Global Imagination: South Africa and the West.* New York: Oxford University Press.

Espinet, Charles, and Peter Pitts. 1944. *Land of Calypso: The Origin and Development of Trinidad's Folk Song.* Port of Spain: Trinidad Guardian Commercial Printing.

Feld, Steven. 2000. "A Sweet Lullaby for World Music." *Public Culture* 12 (1): 145–71.

Feld, Steven, and Keith H. Basso, eds. 1996. *Senses of Place.* Santa Fe, N.M.: University of Washington Press.

Fergusson, Isaac. 1994. "Brother Resistance and Karega Mandela: Rapso Kings." *Class (Arts and Entertainment),* February/March, 65.

Floyd, Samuel A. 1995. *The Power of Black Music: Interpreting Its History from Africa to the United States.* New York: Oxford University Press.

Forman, Murray. 2002. *The 'Hood Comes First: Race, Space, and Place in Rap and Hip-Hop.* Middletown, Conn.: Wesleyan University Press.

Foster, Chuck. 1999. *Roots, Rock, Reggae: An Oral History of Reggae Music from Ska to Dancehall.* New York: Billboard Books.

Foucault, Michel. [1971] 1977. "Nietzsche, Genealogy, History." In *Language, Countermemory, Practice: Selected Essays and Interviews by Michel Foucault,* ed. Donald F. Bouchard, 139–64. Ithaca, N.Y.: Cornell University Press.

———. 1980. *Power/Knowledge: Selected Interviews and Other Writings, 1972–1977.* Ed. Colin Gordon. New York: Pantheon Books.

———. [1978] 1990. *An Introduction.* Vol. 1 of *The History of Sexuality.* New York: Vintage Books.

———. [1984] 1986. *The Use of Pleasure.* Vol. 2 of *The History of Sexuality.* New York: Vintage Books.

———. [1984] 1986. *The Care of the Self.* Vol. 3 of *The History of Sexuality.* New York: Vintage Books.

———. 1988. "Technologies of the Self." In *Technologies of the Self: A Seminar with Michel Foucault,* ed. Luther H. Martin, Huck Gutman, and Patrick H. Hutton, 16–49. Amherst: University of Massachusetts Press.

Fox, Ted. 1986. *In the Groove: The People behind the Music.* New York: St. Martin's Press.

Franco, Pamela R. 2000. "The 'Unruly Woman' in Nineteenth-Century Trinidad Carnival." *Small Axe: A Journal of Criticism* 7:60–76.

Frith, Simon. 1996a. "Music and Identity." In *Questions of Cultural Identity,* ed. Stuart Hall and Paul du Gay, 108–27. London: Sage.

———. 1996b. *Performing Rites: On the Value of Popular Music.* Oxford: Oxford University Press.

Fulton, Carolyn J. 1993. "Trinidadian Parang: Caribbean Music for the Music Classroom." M.A. thesis, Pacific Lutheran University.

Gilroy, Paul. 1993a. *The Black Atlantic: Modernity and Double Consciousness.* Cambridge, Mass.: Harvard University Press.

———. 1993b. "It Ain't Where You're From, It's Where You're At: The Dialectics of Diaspora Identification." In *Small Acts: Thoughts on the Politics of Black Cultures,* 120–45. New York: Serpent's Tail.

———. 2000. *Against Race: Imagining Political Culture beyond the Color Line.* Cambridge, Mass.: Harvard University Press.

———. 2005. *Postcolonial Melancholia.* New York: Columbia University Press.

Gopinath, Gayatri. 1995. " 'Bombay, U.K., Yuba City': Bhangra Music and the Engendering of Diaspora." *Diaspora* 4 (3): 304.

Gordon, Colin. 1991. "Governmental Rationality: An Introduction." In *The Foucault Effect: Studies in Governmentality,* ed. Graham Burchell, Colin Gordon, and Peter Miller, 1–52. Chicago: University of Chicago Press.

Gorman, Patricia. 1945. "The Lion of Calypso." *P.M. Magazine* (New York), 16 September, 5–6.

Gray, Herman. 2001. "Prefiguring a Black Cultural Formation: The New Conditions of Black Cultural Production." In *Between Law and Culture,* ed. David Theo Goldberg, Michael Musheno, and Lisa C. Bower, 74–92. Minneapolis: University of Minnesota Press.

Grenier, Line. 2001. "Global Pop on the Move: The Fame of Superstar Céline Dion within, outside, and across Quebec." *Journal of Australian Canadian Studies* 19 (20): 31–48.

———. 2005. "Circolazione, valorizzazione e localizzazione della musica *global pop*: Il caso di Céline Dion." In *Enciclopedia della musica Einaudi,* ed. Jean-Jacques Nattiez, 5:199–224. Torino: Einaudi.

Guilbault, Jocelyne. 1997a. "Interpreting World Music: A Challenge in Theory and Practice." *Popular Music* 16 (1): 31–44.

———. 1997b. "The Politics of Labeling Popular Musics in English Caribbean." *Trans III,* ww2.uji.es/trans.

———. 2000. "Racial Projects and Musical Discourses in Trinidad, West Indies." In *Music and the Racial Imagination,* ed. Ronald Radano and Philip V. Bohlman, 435–58. Chicago: University of Chicago Press.

———. 2005. "Audible Entanglements: Nation and Diasporas in Trinidad's Calypso Music Scene." *Small Axe: A Journal of Criticism* 17:40–63.

Gupta, Akhil. 1998. *Postcolonial Developments: Agriculture in the Making of Modern India.* Durham, N.C.: Duke University Press.

Gupta, Akhil, and James Ferguson. 1992. "Beyond 'Culture': Space, Identity, and the Politics of Difference." *Cultural Anthropology* 7 (1): 6–23.

Gupta, Akhil, and James Ferguson, eds. 1997. *Culture, Power, Place: Explorations in Critical Anthropology.* Durham, N.C.: Duke University Press.

Hall, Stuart. [1986] 1996. "On Postmodernism and Articulation: An Interview with Stuart Hall." In *Stuart Hall: Critical Dialogues in Cultural Studies,* ed. David Morley and Kuan-Hsing Chen, 131–50. New York: Routledge.

———. 1986. "The Problem of Ideology: Marxism without Guarantees." *Journal of Communication Inquiry* 10 (2): 28–43.

———. 1988. "Gramsci and Us." In *The Hard Road to Renewal: Thatcherism and the Crisis of the Left,* 161–73. London: Verso.

———. 1990. "Cultural Identity and Diaspora." In *Identity: Community, Culture, Difference,* ed. Jonathan Rutherford, 222–37. London: Lawrence and Wishart.

———. 1997. "The Work of Representation." In *Representation: Cultural Representations and Signifying Practices,* ed. Stuart Hall, 13–74. London: Sage.

Harvey, David. 2005. *A Brief History of Neoliberalism.* Oxford: Oxford University Press.

Hassanali, Shaliza. 2005. "Aloes Bitter over Cro Cro Loss." *Trinidad Sunday Guardian,* 2 January.

Hennion, Antoine. 1989. "An Intermediary between Production and Consumption: The Producer of Popular Music." *Science, Technology and Human Values* 14 (4): 400–424.

Henry, Frances. 2003. *Reclaiming African Religions in Trinidad: The Socio-political Legitimation of the Orisha and Spiritual Baptist Faiths.* Mona, Jamaica: University of the West Indies Press.

Henry, Ralph, and Keith Nurse. 1996. "The Entertainment Sector of Trinidad and Tobago: Implementing an Export Strategy." Unpublished manuscript produced for the Industry and Trade Division, TIDCO, Port of Spain.

Herman, Andrew, Thomas Swiss, and John Sloop. 1998. "Mapping the Beat: Spaces of Noise and Places of Music." In *Mapping the Beat: Popular Music and Contemporary Theory,* ed. T. Swiss, J. Sloop, and A. Hermann, 3–29. Malden, Mass: Blackwell.

Hesse, Barnor. 2000. "Introduction: Un/Settled Multiculturalisms." In *Un/Settled Multiculturalisms: Diasporas, Entanglements, "Transruptions,"* ed. Barnor Hesse, 1–30. London: Zed Books.

Hicks, Albert C. 1940. "Calypso, Songs and Minstrels of Trinidad." *Travel* 76 (December): 16–19, 47, 48.

Hill, Donald. 1993. *Calypso Calaloo: Early Carnival Music in Trinidad.* Miami: University of Florida Press.

Hill, Errol. 1967. "On the Origin of the Term Calypso." *Ethnomusicology* 11:359–67.

———. 1976. "The Trinidad Carnival: Cultural Change and Synthesis." *Cultures* 3 (1): 54–86.

Hintzen, Percy. 1999. "The Caribbean: Race and Creole Ethnicity." In *The Blackwell Companion to Racial and Ethnic Studies,* ed. David Theo Goldberg and John Solomos, 475–94. Oxford: Blackwell.

———. 2000. "Afro-Creole Nationalism as Elite Domination: The English-Speaking West Indies." In *Foreign Policy and the Black International Interest,* ed. Charles P. Henry, 185–215. Albany: State University of New York Press.

———. 2001. *West Indian in the West: Self-Representations in an Immigrant Community.* New York: New York University Press.

———. 2002. "Race and Creole Ethnicity in the Caribbean." In *Questioning Creole: Creolisation Discourses in Caribbean Culture,* ed. Verene A. Shepherd and Glen L. Richards, 92–109. Kingston: Ian Randle Publishers.

———. 2004. "Diaspora, Globalization and the Politics of Identity." In *La Diaspora noire des Amériques: Expériences et théories à partir de la Caraïbe,* ed. Christine Chivallon. Paris: CNRS Editions.

Hirschkind, Charles. 2001. "The Ethics of Listening: Cassette-Sermon Audition in Contemporary Cairo." *American Ethnologist* 28 (3): 623–49.

Ho, Christine G. T. 2001. "Globalization and Diaspora-ization of Caribbean People and Popular Culture." *Wadabagei: A Journal of the Caribbean and Its Diaspora* 4 (1): 1–38.

Holder, Winthrop R. 2001. "'Nothin Eh Strange': Black Stalin Speaks." *Small Axe: A Journal of Criticism* 9:149–50.

Hollywood, Wendy. 2002. "Performativity, Citationality, Ritualization." *History of Religions* 42 (1): 93–115.

Hood, Mantle. 1971. *The Ethnomusicologist.* New York: McGraw-Hill Book Co.

Horkheimer, Max, and Theodor W. Adorno. [1944] 1999. "The Culture Industry: Enlightenment as Mass Deception." In *Dialectic of Enlightenment,* 120–68. New York: Continuum Publishing Company.

Ireland, Craig. 2002. "The Appeal to Experience and Its Consequences: Variations on a Persistent Thompsonian Theme." *Cultural Critique* 52:86–107.

Jackson, Travis. 2003. "Jazz as Musical Practice." In *The Cambridge Companion to Jazz,* ed. Mervyn Cooke and David Horn, 83–95. Cambridge: Cambridge University Press.

Jacob, Debbie. 1988. "Tight Race for BUCKS Title." *Trinidad Express,* 19 May, 27.

James, C. L. R. 1977. "The Mighty Sparrow." In *The Future and the Present: Selected Writings,* 191–201. London: Allison and Busby.

Jones, Charles (the Duke of Albany). 1947. *Calypso and Carnival of Long Ago and Today.* Port of Spain: Gazette Printer.

Jones, LeRoi. 1967. "The Changing Same (R&B and New Black Music)." In *Black Music*, 180–211. New York: William Morrow and Co.

Joseph, Miranda. 2002. "The Performance of Production and Consumption." In *Against the Romance of Community*, 30–68. Minneapolis: University of Minnesota Press.

Joseph, Terry. 1997. "Field Wide Open for '97 Monarchy: Chutney Soca the Perfect Mix." *Trinidad Express*, 11 January, 15.

———. 2002. "Homes of Kitchener, Lion to Be Museums. *Trinidad Express*, 11 February.

———. 2005. "Legerton: Tuco Pan-Kaiso $$ Not Diverted to Chutney." *Trinidad Express*, 10 January, 14.

———. 2006. "Panorama Pain." Terry-J Archives. http://www.trinicenter.com/Terryj/2006/Jan/27.htm.

Kasinitz, Philip. 1992. *Caribbean New York: Black Immigrants and the Politics of Race*. Ithaca, N.Y.: Cornell University Press.

Khan, Aisha. 1993. "What Is 'a Spanish'? Ambiguity and 'Mixed' Ethnicity in Trinidad." In *Trinidad Ethnicity*, ed. Kevin A. Yelvington, 180–207. Knoxville: University of Tennessee Press.

———. 2004. *Callaloo Nation: Metaphors of Race and Religious Identity among South Asians in Trinidad*. Durham, N.C.: Duke University Press.

King, Stephen A. 2002. *Reggae, Rastafari, and the Rhetoric of Social Control*. Jackson: University Press of Mississippi.

Koningsbruggen, Peter van. 1997. *Trinidad Carnival: A Quest for National Identity*. London: Macmillan.

Kun, Josh. 1997. "Against Easy Listening: Audiotopic Readings and Transnational Soundings." In *Everynight Life: Culture and Dance in Latin/o America*, ed. Celeste Fraser Delgado and José Esteban Muños, 288–309. Durham, N.C.: Duke University Press.

"Let Prisoners Take Part in Calypso Monarch." 1998. *Mirror* (Trinidad), 20 February.

Lewis, Rupert C. 1987. *Marcus Garvey: Anti-colonial Champion*. London: Karia Press.

Lipsitz, George. 1994. *Dangerous Crossroads: Popular Music, Postmodernism and the Poetics of Place*. New York: Verso.

Liverpool, Hollis Urban Lester. 1986. *Kaiso and Society*. Charlotte Amalie, St. Thomas: Virgin Islands Commission on Youth.

———. 1993. "Rituals of Power and Rebellion: The Carnival Tradition in Trinidad and Tobago." Ph.D. diss., University of Michigan.

Look Lai, Walton. 1998a. *The Chinese in the West Indies, 1806–1995: A Documentary History*. Cave Hill, Barbados: University of the West Indies Press.

———. 1998b. *Indentured Labor, Caribbean Sugar: Chinese and Indian Migrants to the British West Indies, 1838–1918*. Baltimore: Johns Hopkins University Press.

Lovelace, Earl. 1998. "The Emancipation-Jouvay Tradition and the Almost Loss of Pan." *Drama Review* 42 (3): 54–60.

Lowe, Lisa. 1996. *Immigrant Acts*. Durham, N.C.: Duke University Press.

Lucian Kaiso 1990. 1990. Castries, St. Lucia: Folk Research Centre.

Lyndersay, Mark. 1998. "Bring the Rhythm Down." *Trinidad Express*, 18 February, 9.

Maharaj, Shivannand. 1994. "The Development of Indian Classical Music in Trinidad and Tobago in the Twentieth Century." B.A. thesis, University of the West Indies, St. Augustine.

Mahmood, Saba. 2001. "Feminist Theory, Embodiment, and the Docile Agent: Some Reflections on the Egyptian Islamic Revival." *Cultural Anthropology* 16 (2): 202–36.

Malkki, Liisa. 1992. "National Geographic: The Rooting of Peoples and the Territorialization of National Identity among Scholars and Refugees." *Cultural Anthropology* 7 (1): 24–44.

Malm, Krister, and Roger Wallis. 1992. *Media Policy and Music Activity*. New York: Routledge.

Manuel, Peter. 1997–98. "Music, Identity, and Images of India in the Indo-Caribbean Diaspora." *Asian Music* 29 (1): 17–35.

———. 1998. "Chutney and Indo-Trinidadian Cultural Identity." *Popular Music* 17 (1): 21–44.

———. 2000a. "The Construction of a Diasporic Tradition: Indo-Caribbean 'Local Classical Music.'" *Ethnomusicology* 44 (1): 97–119.

———. 2000b. *East Indian Music in the West Indies: Tan-Singing, Chutney, and the Making of Indo-Caribbean Culture*. Philadelphia: Temple University Press.

Manuel, Peter, with Kenneth Bilby and Michael Largey. 1995. *Caribbean Currents*. Philadelphia: Temple University Press.

Martin, Carol. 1998. "Trinidad Carnival Glossary." *Drama Review* 42 (3): 220–35.

Martin, Denis-Constant. 2002. "No Pan-Dey in the Party: Fusions Musicales et Divisions Politiques à Trinidad et Tobago." In *Sur La Piste Des OPNI (Objets Politiques Non Identifiés)*, 365–95. Paris: Editions Karthala.

Marshall, Trevor G. 1986. *The History and Evolution of Calypso in Barbados*. Calypso Research Project, vol. 2. Port of Spain: Institute of Social and Economic Research, University of the West Indies.

McQuilkin, Elwyn (Black Wizard), and Lood (Mr. X) Panchoo. 1984. *Grenada's Calypso: The Growth of an Artform*. San Juan, Trinidad: Print-Rite.

Mehta, Brinda. 2004. *Diasporic Dis(Locations): Indo Caribbean Women Writers Negotiate the "Kala Pani."* Kingston: University of the West Indies Press.

Meintjes, Louise. 2003. *Sound of Africa: Making Music Zulu in a South African Studio*. Durham, N.C.: Duke University Press.

Miller, Daniel. 1991. "Absolute Freedom in Trinidad." *Man* 26:323–41.

———. [1994] 1997. *Modernity: An Ethnographic Approach: Dualism and Mass Consumption in Trinidad*. Oxford: Berg.

Mohammed, Patricia. 1998. "Ram and Sita: The Reconstruction of Gender Identities among Indians in Trinidad through Mythology." In *Caribbean Portraits: Gender Ideologies and Identities,* ed. Christine Barrow, 391–413. Kingston: CSDS and Ian Randle Publishers.

———. 2002. *Gendered Realities: Essays in Caribbean Feminist Thought*. Kingston: University of the West Indies Press.

Mohammed, Shamoon. 1982. *Mastana Bahar and Indian Culture in Trinidad and Tobago*. Port of Spain.

Monson, Ingrid. 1996. *Saying Something: Jazz Improvisation and Interaction*. Chicago: University of Chicago Press.

———. 1999. "Riffs, Repetition, and Theories of Globalization." *Ethnomusicology* 43 (1): 31–65.

Moore, Donald S. 2005. *Suffering for Territory: Race, Place, and Power in Zimbabwe*. Durham, N.C.: Duke University Press.

Moore, Donald S., Jake Kosek, and Anand Pandian, eds. 2003. *Race, Nature, and the Politics of Difference*. Durham, N.C.: Duke University Press.

Morais, Robin. 1997. "Ragga Soca Groove." *Sunday Punch,* 2 February.

Myers, Helen. 1993. " Indian, East Indian and West Indian Music in Felicity, Trinidad." In *Ethnomusicology and Modern Music History,* ed. Stephen Blum, Philip V. Bohlman, and Daniel M. Neuman, 231–41. Chicago: University of Illinois Press.

———. 1998. *Music of Hindu Trinidad: Songs from the India Diaspora.* Chicago: University of Chicago Press.

Negus, Keith. 1997. *Popular Music in Theory: An Introduction.* Hanover, N.H.: Wesleyan University Press.

———. 1999. *Music Genres and Corporate Cultures.* New York: Routledge.

Negus, Keith, and Michael Pickering. 2002. "Creativity and Musical Experience." In *Popular Music Studies,* ed. David Hesmondhalgh and Keith Negus, 178–90. London: Arnold.

Nettleford, Rex. 1993. *Inward Stretch, Outward Reach: A Voice from the Caribbean.* London: Macmillan Press.

Niranjana, Tejaswini. 1999. " 'Left to the Imagination': Indian Nationalisms and Female Sexuality in Trinidad." *Public Culture* 11 (1): 223–43.

Nunley, John W., and Judith Bettelheim. 1988. *Caribbean Festival Arts: Each and Every Bit of Difference.* Seattle: University of Washington Press.

Nurse, Keith. 1997. "The Trinidad and Tobago Entertainment Industry: Structure and Export Capabilities." *Caribbean Dialogue: A Journal of Contemporary Caribbean Policy Issues* 3 (3): 13–38.

———. 2000a. "Copyright and Music in the Digital Age: Prospects and Implications for the Caribbean." *Social and Economic Studies* 49 (1): 53–81.

———. 2000b. "Globalisation and Trinidad Carnival: Diaspora, Hybridity and Identity in Global Culture." In *Identity, Ethnicity and Culture in the Caribbean,* ed. Ralph R. Premdas, 80–114. St. Augustine, Trinidad: University of the West Indies, School of Continuing Studies.

Ottley, Rudolph. 1992. *Women in Calypso.* Arima, Trinidad: published by the author.

———. 1995. *Calypsonians from Then to Now.* Pt. 1. Arima, Trinidad: published by the author.

———. 1998. *Calypsonians from Then to Now.* Pt. 2. Arima, Trinidad: published by the author.

Pacini, Deborah Hernandez. 1995. *Bachata: A Social History of a Dominican Popular Music.* Philadelphia: Temple University Press.

Patasar, Mungal. 1995. "Modern Trends in Indo-Trinidad Music." In *In Celebration of 150 Years of the Indian Contribution to Trinidad and Tobago,* vol. 2, ed. Brinsley Samaroo et al., 75–85. Port of Spain: Historical Publications.

Patterson, Massie, and Lionel Belasco. 1943. *Calypso Songs of the West Indies.* New York: M. Baron Co.

Pearse, Andrew C. 1956. "Carnival in Nineteenth-Century Trinidad." *Caribbean Quarterly* 4:175–93.

Peterson, Richard. 1976. "The Production of Culture: A Prolegomenon." In *The Production of Culture,* ed. Richard Peterson, 7–22. London: Sage.

Pollak-Eltz, Angelina. 1993. "The Shango Cult and Other African Rituals in Trinidad, Grenada and Carriacou and Their Possible Influences on the Spiritual Baptist Faith." *Caribbean Quarterly* 39 (3–4): 12–26.

Pratt, Mary-Louise. 1992. "Introduction: Criticism in the Contact Zone." In *Imperial Eyes: Travel Writing and Transculturation,* 1–11. New York: Routledge.

Premdas, Ralph R., ed. 1993. *The Enigma of Ethnicity: An Analysis of Race in the Caribbean and the World.* St. Augustine, Trinidad: University of the West Indies, School of Continuing Studies.

————, ed. 2000. *Identity, Ethnicity and Culture in the Caribbean*. St. Augustine, Trinidad: University of the West Indies, School of Continuing Studies.

————. 2002. "Identity in an Ethnically Bifurcated State: Trinidad and Tobago." In *Ethnonational Identities*, ed. Steve Fenton and Stephen May, 176–98. New York: Palgrave Macmillan.

Prudent, Lambert Félix. 1989. "Ecrire le créole à la Martinique: Norme et conflit sociolinguistique." In *Les Créoles français entre l'oral et l'écrit*, ed. Ralph Ludwig, 65–80. Tübigen: Gunter Narr.

Puri, Shalini. 1999. "Canonized Hybridities, Resistant Hybridities: Chutney Soca, Carnival, and the Politics of Nationalism." In *Caribbean Romances: The Politics of Regional Representation*, ed. Belinda Edmondson, 12–38. Charlottesville: University Press of Virginia.

————. 2003a. *Marginal Migrations: The Circulation of Cultures within the Caribbean*. Oxford: Macmillan Caribbean.

————. 2003b. "'This Thing Called a Nation': An Interview with Gordon Rohlehr." In *Marginal Migrations: The Circulation of Cultures within the Caribbean*, ed. Shalini Puri, 240–69. Oxford: Macmillan Caribbean.

————. 2004. *The Caribbean Postcolonial: Social Equality, Post-nationalism, and Cultural Hybridity*. New York: Palgrave Macmillan.

Quevedo, Raymond (Atilla the Hun). 1983. *Atilla's Kaiso: A Short History of Trinidad Calypso*. St. Augustine, Trinidad: University of the West Indies Press, Department of Extra Mural Studies.

Radano, Ronald. 2003. *Lying Up a Nation: Race and Black Music*. Chicago: University of Chicago Press.

Ramaya, Narsaloo. 1990. "Chutney Singing: Its Origin and Development in Trinidad and Tobago." Manuscript. West Indies Collection, University of the West Indies Library, St. Augustine, Trinidad.

Ramdin, Ron. 2000. *Arising from Bondage: A History of the Indo-Caribbean People*. New York: New York University Press.

Ramsey, Guthrie P., Jr. 2003. *Race Music: Black Cultures from Bebop to Hip-Hop*. Berkeley: University of California Press

Ramnarine, Tina Karina. 1996. "'Indian' Music in the Diaspora: Case Studies of 'Chutney' in Trinidad and in London." *British Journal of Ethnomusicology* 5:133–53.

————. 2001. *Creating Their Own Space: The Development of an Indian-Caribbean Musical Tradition*. Mona, Jamaica: University of the West Indies Press.

Ravi-ji. 1998. "The Development of Indian Music in Trinidad and Tobago." *Caribbean Dialogue: A Journal of Contemporary Caribbean Policy Issues* 3 (4): 73–76.

Reddock, Rhoda. 1994a. "'Douglarisation' and the Politics of Gender Relations in Contemporary Trinidad and Tobago: A Preliminary Exploration." *Contemporary Sociology* 1 (1): 98–127.

————. 1994b. *Women, Labour and Politics in Trinidad and Tobago*. London: Zed Books.

————. 1996. "Contestations over National Culture in Trinidad and Tobago: Considerations of Ethnicity, Class, and Gender." *Contemporary Issues in Social Science: A Caribbean Perspective* 3:106–45.

————. 1998. "Contestations over National Culture in Trinidad and Tobago: Considerations of Ethnicity, Class, and Gender." In *Caribbean Portraits: Essays on Gender Ideologies and Identities*, ed. Christine Barrow, 414–35. Kingston: Ian Randle Publishers.

————. 2000. "Jahaji Bhai: the Emergence of a Dougla Poetics in Contemporary Trinidad and Tobago." In *Identity, Ethnicity and Culture in the Caribbean*, ed. Ralph R. Premdas,

185–210. St. Augustine, Trinidad: University of the West Indies, School of Continuing Studies.

———, ed. 2004. *Interrogating Caribbean Masculinities: Theoretical and Empirical Analyses.* St. Augustine, Trinidad: University of the West Indies Press.

Regis, Humphrey A. 1988. "Calypso, Reggae and Cultural Imperialism by Reexportation." *Popular Music and Society* 12:63–73.

Regis, Louis. 1986. *Black Stalin: The Caribbean Man.* Port of Spain: published by the author.

———. 1999. *The Political Calypso: True Opposition in Trinidad and Tobago, 1962–1987.* Mona, Jamaica: University of the West Indies Press.

Ribeiro, Indra. 1992. "The Phenomenon of Chutney Singing in Trinidad and Tobago: The Functional Value of a Social Phenomenon." B.A. thesis, University of the West Indies, St. Augustine.

Roach, Glen. 1972. "Calypso and Politics, 1956–72." Caribbean Studies thesis, University of the West Indies, St. Augustine.

Rohlehr, Gordon. 1970. "Sparrow and the Language of Calypso." *Savacou* 1 (2, September): 87–99.

———. 1972. "The Folk in Caribbean Literature." *Tapia* 2 (11–12). Reprinted as "Literature and the Folk," in *My Strangled City and Other Essays* (London: Karia Press, 1990).

———. 1975. "Sparrow as Poet." In *David Frost Introduces Trinidad and Tobago,* ed. Michael Anthony and Andrew Carr, 84–98. London: André Deutsch.

———. 1988. "Images of Men and Women in the 1930s Calypsoes: The Sociology of Food Acquisition in a Context of Survivalism." In *Gender in Caribbean Development,* ed. Patricia Mohammed and Catherine Shepherd, 232–306. St. Augustine, Trinidad: University of the West Indies Press.

———. 1990. *Calypso and Society in Pre-independence Trinidad.* Port of Spain: published by the author.

———. 1998. "'We Getting the Kaiso That We Deserve': Calypso and the World Music Market." *Drama Review* 42 (3): 82–95.

———. 2001. "The Calypsonian as Artist: Freedom and Responsibility." *Small Axe: A Journal of Criticism* 9:1–26.

———. 2004a. "Calypso Reinvents Itself." In *Carnival: Culture in Action—the Trinidad Experience,* ed. Milla Cozart Riggio, 213–27. New York: Routledge.

———. 2004b. "I Lawa: The Construction of Masculinity in Trinidad and Tobago Calypso." In *Interrogating Caribbean Masculinities: Theoretical and Empirical Analyses,* ed. Rhoda E. Reddock, 326–403. St. Augustine, Trinidad: University of the West Indies Press.

———. 2004c. *A Scuffling of Islands: Essays on Calypso.* San Juan, Trinidad: Lexicon Trinidad.

Rose, Nikolas. 1979. "The Psychological Complex: Mental Measurements and Social Administration." *Ideology and Consciousness* 5:5–68.

———. 1999. *Powers of Freedom: Reframing Political Thought.* Cambridge: Cambridge University Press.

Ryan, Selwyn. 1998. "Calypso and Politics in Trinidad and Tobago, 1996–1998." *Caribbean Dialogue: A Journal of Contemporary Caribbean Policy Issues* 3 (4): 5–30.

Said, Edward. 2000. "Reflections on Exile." In *Reflections on Exile and Other Essays,* 173–86. Cambridge, Mass.: Harvard University Press.

Sankeralli, Burton. 1997. "Creole and Post-Creole: The Music of Carnival." *Caribbean Dialogue: A Journal of Contemporary Caribbean Policy Issues* 3 (4): 89–92.

Savigliano, Marta. 1995. *Tango and the Political Economy of Passion.* Boulder, Colo.: Westview Press.

Scott, David. 1999. *Refashioning Futures: Criticism after Postcoloniality.* Princeton, N.J.: Princeton University Press.

Scott, Joan W. 1991. "The Evidence of Experience." *Critical Inquiry* 17:773–97.

Shepherd, Verene A., and Glen L. Richards, eds. 2002. *Questioning Creole: Creolisation Discourses in Caribbean Culture.* Kingston: Ian Randle Publishers.

Shuker, Roy. 2001. *Understanding Popular Music.* New York: Routledge.

Simpson, G. E. 1978. *Black Religion in the New Word.* New York: Columbia University Press.

Singh, Rickey. 2002. "Toilet Paper Caper on 'Gypsy.' " *Guyana Chronicle,* 12 February.

Skinner, Ewart C. 1990. "Mass Media in Trinidad and Tobago." In *Mass Media and the Caribbean,* ed. Stuart H. Surlin and Walter C. Soderlund, 29–54. New York: Gordon and Breach.

Smith, M. G. [1984] 1990. *Culture, Race, and Class in the Commonwealth Caribbean.* Mona, Jamaica: University of the West Indies, School of Continuing Studies.

Snead, James A. 1998. "Repetition as a Figure of Black Culture." In *The Jazz Cadence of American Culture,* ed. Robert G. O'Meally, 62–81. New York: Columbia University Press.

Steedman, Carolyn Kay. [1986] 1994. *Landscape for a Good Woman: A Story of Two Lives.* New Brunswick, N.J.: Rutgers University Press.

Stewart, Earl L. 1998. *African American Music: An Introduction.* New York: Schirmer Books.

Stokes, Martin, ed. 1994. *Ethnicity, Identity and Music: The Musical Construction of Place.* Oxford: Berg.

Stoler, Ann Laura. 2002. *Carnal Knowledge and Imperial Power: Race and the Intimate in Colonial Rule.* Berkeley: University of California Press.

Stolzoff, Norman C. 2000. *Wake the Town and Tell the People: Dancehall Culture in Jamaica.* Durham, N.C.: Duke University Press.

Straw, Will. 1991. "Systems of Articulation, Logics of Change: Communities and Scenes in Popular Music." *Cultural Studies* 5 (3): 368–88.

———. 2001. "Scenes and Sensibilities." *Public* 22–23:245–57.

Stuempfle, Stephen. 1995. *Steelband Movement: The Forging of a National Art in Trinidad and Tobago.* Mona, Jamaica: Press University of the West Indies.

Taylor, Julie. 1998. *Paper Tangos.* Durham, N.C.: Duke University Press.

Taylor, Timothy D. 1997. *World Music, World Markets.* New York: Routledge.

Théberge, Paul. 1997. *Any Sound You Can Imagine: Making Music/Consuming Technology.* Hanover, N.H.: Wesleyan University Press.

Thorpe, Marjorie. 1982. "Introduction." In *The Wine of Astonishment,* by Earl Lovelace, vii–xiv. Oxford: Heinemann.

Tomlinson, Gary. 2002. "Cultural Dialogics and Jazz: A White Historian Signifies." *Black Music Research Journal* 22, suppl.:71–105.

Toynbee, Jason. 2000. *Making Popular Music: Musicians, Creativity and Institutions.* London: Arnold.

Trinidad and Tobago Chamber of Industry and Commerce. 2003. "Carnival, the Industry." 27 February. http://www.chamber.org.tt.

Trotman, David Vincent. 1986. *Crime in Trinidad: Conflict and Control in a Plantation Society, 1838–1900.* Knoxville: University of Tennessee Press.

Turino, Thomas. 2000. *Nationalists, Cosmopolitans, and Popular Music in Zimbabwe.* Chicago: University of Chicago Press.

Varikas, Eleni. 1995. "Gender, Experience and Subjectivity: The Tilly-Scott Disagreee-
ment." *New Left Review* 211:89–101.

Vianna, Hermano. 1999. *The Mystery of Samba: Popular Music and National Identity in Brazil.*
Chapel Hill: University of North Carolina Press.

Vincent-Henry, André. 1993. "Talking Race in Trinidad and Tobago: A Practical Framework." *Caribbean Affairs* 6 (2): 23–38.

Walcott, Derek. 1993. *The Antilles: Fragments of Epic Memory.* New York: Farrar, Straus and
Giroux.

Wald, Gayle. 2002. "'I Want It That Way': Teenybopper Music and the Girling of Boy
Bands." *Genders,* vol. 35.

Wallis, Roger, and Krister Malm. 1984. *Big Sounds from Small Peoples.* London: Constable.

Ware, Opoku. 1997. *Calypso, Soca: 20th Century Musical Phenomenon.* San Fernando, Trinidad: published by the author.

Warner, Keith Q. 1982. *Kaiso / The Trinidad Calypso: A Study of the Calypso as Oral Literature.*
Washington, D.C.: Three Continents Press.

Warner-Lewis, Maureen. 1984. "Yoruba Songs from Trinidad." Unpublished manuscript.
University of the West Indies, Kingston.

———. 1986. "The Influence of Yoruba Music on the Minor Key Calypso." In *Papers:
Seminar on the Calypso.* St. Augustine, Trinidad: University of the West Indies, ISER.

———. [1996] 1997. *Trinidad Yoruba: From Mother Tongue to Memory.* Mona, Jamaica: University of the West Indies Press.

Waxer, Lisa, ed. 2002. *Situating Salsa: Global Markets and Local Meaning in Latin Popular
Music.* New York: Routledge.

White, Garth. 1984. "The Evolution of Jamaican Music." Pt. 1, "Urbanisation of the Folk:
The Merger of the Traditional and the Popular in Jamaican Music." *ACIJ (The African-
Caribbean Institute of Jamaica) Research Review* 1:47–80.

———. 1998. "The Evolution of Jamaican Music." Pt. 2, "'Proto-Ska' to Ska." *Social and
Economic Studies* 47 (1): 5–19.

Williams, Brackette, ed. 1996. *Women out of Place: The Gender of Agency and the Race of Nationality.* New York: Routledge.

Williams, Eric E. 1993. "Independence Day Address," 31 August 1962, and "The Chaguara-
mas Declaration: Perspectives for the New Society," 27–29 November 1970. In *Eric E.
Williams Speaks: Essays on Colonialism and Independence,* ed. Selwyn R. Cudjoe, 265–316.
Wellesley, Mass.: Calaloux Publications.

Williams, Raymond. 1977. *Marxism and Literature.* Oxford: Oxford University Press.

Wilson. Andrew, ed. 2004. *The Chinese in the Caribbean.* Princeton, N.J.: Markus Wiener
Publishers.

Wilson, Peter. 1973. *Crab Antics: The Social Anthropology of English-Speaking Negro Societies of
the Caribbean.* New Haven, Conn.: Yale University Press.

Wong, Deborah. 2004. "The Asian American Body in Performance." *Speak It Louder: Asian
Americans in Making Music,* 161–93. New York: Routledge.

Yanagisako, Sylvia Junko. 2002. *Producing Culture and Capital: Family Firms in Italy.* Princeton, N.J.: Princeton University Press.

Yelvington, Kevin A., ed. 1993. *Trinidad Ethnicity.* Knoxville: University of Tennessee Press.

Zuberi, Nabeel. 2001. *Sounds English: Transnational Popular Music.* Chicago: University of
Illinois Press.

SELECTED DISCOGRAPHY

Anon. 1956. "We Goin' to Cut the Wood." *Bamboo-Tamboo, Bongo and Belair.* Cook Records, COOK05017.

Black Stalin. 1991. "Caribbean Unity," "Black Man Music," "Burn Dem," "Wait Dorothy," and "We Can Make It." *Roots Rock Soca.* Rounder Records, 5038.

———. 1994. "All Saints Road," "Santi Manitay," and "Black Woman Ring Bang." *Rebellion.* Ice Records, 931302.

———. 1995. "Better Days," "Sundar," "In Times," "Iron Band Jam," and "Man Out for Change." *Message to Sundar.* Ice Records, 951402.

———. 2000. "Wine Boy Wine." *2000 New Times.* COTT 2000.

———. n.d. *Hard Wuk.* Electro Sounds Digital Publishers, ES0087.

Brother Resistance. 1996. "Cyar Take Dat," "Mother Earth," and "Ring de Bell." *De Power of Resistance: Rapso Anthology,* vol. 1. Rituals of Trinidad.

Calypso Rose. 1972. "Fire in Meh Wire." *Sexy Hot Pants.* Rose, SLP-002, Strakers, SR-7775.

———. 1977 (for Carnival 1978). "Come Leh We Jam." *Her Majesty: Calypso Rose.* C. L. O. Records and Charlie's Records, CLO-444.

———. 1979. "Ezekiel Coming." *Mass Fever.* C. L. O. Records and Charlie's Records, CLO-CR-666.

———. (in collaboration with Machel Montano). 2003. "What She Want." *The Collector's Riddim: Various Artists.* Mad Bull Music, JW 257.

Chalkdust. 1988. "Two Chords and Leston Paul." *The Master.* Strakers, GS2283.

Crazy. 1978 (for Carnival 1979). "Parang Soca," "Bachelors," and "Road March 79." *Crazy's Super Album.* CM Crazy Music, CM-001 LP.

———. 1979 (for Carnival 1980). "Muchacha." *Madness Is Gladness.* CM Crazy Music, CM003 LP.

———. 1997. "Mirror, Mirror." *Still Crazy after 25 Years.* JW Productions, JW 125 CD.

————. 2004. "Nani Wine." *Trinidad Crazy*. Hometown Music HTM Crazy, 001 CD.

De Mighty Trini. 2004. "Sailing" and "Curry Tabanca." *Classics Collection, 1987–1995*. JW Productions 014 CD.

Jai, Rikki. 2001. *Chutney Vibrations*. Rikki Jai Productions.

————. 2004. *Aashish: From Father to Son*. Samrai Jamungal Productions.

Lord Kitchener. 1975. "Tribute to Spree Simon." *Carnival Fever*. TRCS 4000. Rereleased in 1994 on *Klassic Kitchener*, vol. 3 (Ice Records, 941802).

————. 1994. "No More Calypsong" and "Margie." *Klassic Kitchener*, vol. 2. Ice Records, 941002.

————. 1994. "Pan in 'A' Minor," "Pan in Harmony," and "Sugar Bum Bum." *Klassic Kitchener*, vol. 3. Ice Records, 941802.

————. 2002. "London Is the Place for Me" and "Africa My Home." *London Is the Place for Me: Trinidadian Calypso in London, 1950–1956*. Honest Jons Records, HJRCD2.

Lord Relator. 1973. "None So Sweet." *White Heat*. West Indies Records (Barbados), Pan 1249.

Lord Shorty. 1973. "Indrani." 45 RPM recording. Shorty, S-002.

————. 1975. *Endless Vibrations*. LP. Shorty, SLP 1001.

Lord Superior. 1980. "Cultural Assassination." 45 RPM recording. Mabel 0002.

Manning, Sam. 1929. "Lieutenant Julian." *Calypso Pioneers, 1912–1937*. Rounder Records, 1039.

Maximus Dan (featuring Black Stalin). 2002. "Vampire." *The Stars of Soca Compilation: Soca Switch 8*. JW Productions, JWCL-238.

Montano, Machel. 2000. "Jab Jab," "Luv 2U 2Nite," and "Real Unity." *2000 Young to Soca*. Mad Bull Music, X24-11-74-25.

Montano, Machel, and Xtatik. 1997. "Big Truck," *Heavy Duty*. Rufnex Recording, X24-11-74-22.

————. 1998. "Daddy Axe." *Charge*. Mad Bull Music, X24-11-74-23; JW Productions, 145.

————. 1999. *Any Minute Now*. Mad Bull Music, VP1548.

————. 2003. "On the Road." *The Xtatik Circus*. Ruf Rex Productions, X24-11-74-28.

————. 2004. "Doh Tell Meh." *The Xtatik Parade*. Ruf Rex Productions, X24-11-74-29.

————. 2005. "You." *The Xtatik Experience*. Ruf Rex Productions, X24-11-74-30.

Plummer, Denyse. 1988. "Woman Is Boss" and "A Nation Forges On." *The Boss*. Weldon's Records, DP-00.

————. 1991. "La Trinity." *Carnival Killer*. Dynamic Sounds, DY3466.

————. 1994. "Your Woman." *Carnival 95*. Kisskidee Records, 1006.

————. 2001. "Nah Leaving." *Caribbean Party Rhythms Six (CPR6)*. Rituals Music of Trinidad, C08101.

Ramgoonai, Drupatee. [1988] n.d. "Mr. Bissessar." *Drupatee's Mr. Bissessar*. LP. ImPredisco, C.A.

Rudder, David. 1995. "Another Day in Paradise." *Lyrics Man*. Lypsoland, CR023.

————. 1996. "The Madman's Rant." *Tales from a Strange Land*. Lypsoland, CR 025.

Rudder, David. 2001. "Bigger Pimpin." *The Autobiography of the Now*. Lypsoland, CR 033.

Shadow. 1995. "Bassman." *Greatest Hits: Bassman, Ah Come Out to Play*, vol. 1. Strakers Records, GS2389.

————. [2000] n.d. "Yuh Lookin' for Horn," "HIV," and "Stranger." *Just for You*. Winston Bailey Productions, CRCD 008.

Superblue. 1994. "Jab Molassie." *Flag Party*. Ice Records, 931502.

The Atilla. 1938. "Fire Brigade." *Trinidad Loves to Play Carnival: Carnival, Calenda and Calypso from Trinidad, 1914–1939.* Matchbox Calypso Series, MBCD 302-2

The Mighty Sparrow. 1992. "Jean and Dinah" and "Mr. Walker." *Sparrow's Dance Party.* BLS Records, BLS 1015.

———. 1994. "Rose" and "Ten to One Is Murder." *Mighty Sparrow.* Ice Records, 941702.

The Mighty Terror. 1979. "Pan Talent" and "Chinese Children." *Calypso Hits.* MNE Productions, MNE-001.

Xtatik Ltd. 2003. *The Collectors Riddim.* Mad Bull Music, JW 257.